Reading Plotinus

A Practical Introduction to Neoplatonism

Kevin Corrigan

Purdue University Press
West Lafayette, Indiana

Printed in the United States of America

Library of Congress Cataloging-in-Publication Data
Corrigan, Kevin.
  Reading Plotinus : a practical introduction to neoplatonism / Kevin Corrigan.
     p. cm. -- (Purdue University Press series in the history of philosophy)
  Includes bibliographical references.
  ISBN 1-55753-233-8 (casebound) -- ISBN 1-55753-234-6 (pbk.) 1. Plotinus.
I. Plotinus. Enneads. English. Selections. II. Title. III. Series.

  B693.Z7C67 2004
  186'.4--dc22

                                                        2004006563

Contents

Chapter 3: The range of Plotinus' thought: From nature and contemplation to the One   86

Chapter 4: A world of beauty, from beautiful things to intelligible shapelessness

Chapter 5: Conclusion: Assessment and Afterlife

Abbreviations

AGPh	*Archiv für Geschichte*
ANRW:	*Aufstieg und Niedergang der römischen Welt*
CAG:	*Commentaria in Aristotelem Graeca*
CQ:	*Classical Quarterly*
DK:	Diels-Kranz (*Die Fragmente der Vorsokratiker*)
EN:	*Ethica Nicomachea* (Aristotle)
JHI:	*Journal of the History of Ideas*
JHP:	*Journal of Hellenic Philosophy*
IPQ:	*International Philosophical Quarterly*
LSJ:	*A Greek-English Lexicon,* H. G. Liddell and R. Scott, rev. and aug. H. S. Jones
LthPh:	*Laval Théologique et Philosophique*
PA:	*The Parts of Animals* (Aristotle)
RHR:	*Revue de l'Histoire des Religions*
Rmeta:	*Review of Metaphysics*
SVF:	*Stoicorum Veterum Fragmenta* (Fragments of the Ancient Stoics)

The Enneads

The following is a list of the treatises that make up the *Enneads* with their titles. The chronological order is indicated in brackets.

Acknowledgements

My very great thanks to my friends and colleagues, David Crossley, Graeme Nicholson, Adriaan Peperzak, Daniel Regnier, Frederic Schroeder and Carl Still who took the time to read a first draft of this manuscript and who made many invaluable suggestions. I am also grateful for the suggestions of the final anonymous reader for Purdue University Press as also for the support of Margaret Hunt at the Press throughout the project and for John Joerschke's editing of the manuscript. My thanks also to Patrick Atherton, of the Classics Department at Dalhousie University, who lent me his office where I wrote the first draft of the manuscript and especially to my mother-in-law, Marina Glazova, who not only fed and housed me during that period but, as always, provided inspiration and encouragement with her deep thirst for the beauty of intellectual and poetic things. Lynn Freistadt, my administrative assistant for many years and friend, has been, as always, of invaluable assistance throughout the project. I am grateful to the Social Sciences and Humanities Research Council of Canada and also to Emory University for their support. Finally, I want to express my gratitude to my friend and typist of many years, Jane Morris, as also to my family. The remaining mistakes are all mine, but the book would not have been written without the care and encouragement of these friends.

Introduction

Who was Plotinus? We know of Plotinus' life primarily because Porphyry, his pupil and colleague, wrote a *Life of Plotinus* and collected and edited his works, dividing some of the larger treatises to make a total of fifty-four, or six groups of nine ("Enneads," or "nines"). All of this material has been preserved, and so we have an unusually complete picture of Plotinus' life and of everything he wrote.[1]

We are, of course, quite right to be skeptical of Porphyry's account, which, like other *Lives* of the time, somewhat idealizes its subject. Nonetheless, we get a vivid picture of an accessible, gentle, and warm human being, loved by those who really knew him but also called a "big driveler" and plagiarist by those who did not (*Life,* 17). Plotinus was restless in youth, gentle and inspired as a teacher, a mystic in later life (on Porphyry's testimony, *Life,* 23) with a distinctive, critical philosophical mind but poor spelling and bad eyesight. At the same time, he was a practical person, ascetic but with a gift for friendship, whose house (not his own, by the way) was open to his many friends and "full of the young boys and girls" who had been entrusted to his care. He was, in short, a lover of wisdom who even took the time to listen to a boy in his care repeating the multiplication table.[2]

Plotinus was born in 204/205 in Egypt, probably in Lycopolis. We just do not know if he was of Egyptian origin or not—in later life he was reluctant to talk of his childhood. At any rate, he wrote in Greek and lived the last twenty-five years or so of his life in Rome. At the age of twenty-eight he went to study philosophy in Alexandria but was disappointed with the teachers he found until the advice of a friend sent him to a certain Ammonius, or Ammonius Saccas, about whom we know very little.[3] He stayed with Ammonius for eleven years, and his studies apparently awoke in him a desire to learn Persian and Indian philosophy. For just that purpose, he joined the army of the Emperor Gordian on a campaign against the Persians, but Gordian was murdered on the way and Plotinus escaped only with difficulty. He made his way to Rome, where at the age of forty he settled and established a school.

Plotinus must already have had connections, of course, in the first place to do this. Whatever the case, he showed a gift for attracting powerful supporters throughout his life (among them the emperor Gallienus and his wife). Many high-ranking people, on the approach of death, entrusted their children to him, and he looked after their property and fortunes in trust just as he did their welfare and

---

1. On the *Life,* see L. Brisson, 1982–1992.
2. *Life,* 9: or "revising the same lesson again and again" (Amstrong, Loeb, I, 30–1).
3. Cf. H. R. Schwyzer, 1983; F. M. Schroeder, 1987, 493–526.

education. He even tried to found a city based on Plato's "laws," Platonopolis, but political infighting at the emperor's court doomed the scheme. He had already written twenty-one treatises by the time he was fifty-nine when Porphyry came to Rome. Porphyry encouraged him to write more, and in the next few years the major works of Plotinus' most creative writing period emerged. Typically these treatises arose out of discussions in the school ("between friends," as we shall see below). Plotinus loved philosophical conversation. His earlier "seminars" apparently had been too full of students' chatter and so a bit chaotic. But Plotinus seems to have gone out of his way to make time for people, so much so that he spent three days discussing the soul-body relation with Porphyry; when a friend complained about Porphyry's questions and answers and wanted a set treatise, Plotinus replied, "But if when Porphyry asks questions we do not solve his difficulties, we shall not be able to say anything at all to put into the treatise" (*Life,* 13).

On another occasion, when Porphyry apparently was contemplating suicide, Plotinus unexpectedly visited him and told him his death wish had a physical, not a rational basis (i.e., "black bile"). Porphyry went off to Sicily for a rest cure and was therefore absent when Plotinus died, probably from a form of leprosy, under the care of Eustochius, a doctor-friend in Campania. Plotinus' last words, on Eustochius' testimony, are as enigmatic and as difficult to interpret as some of his writing: "Try to bring back the god in you to the divine in the all" (*Life,* 2). Perhaps they may be taken to sum up much of Porphyry's testimony in the *Life:* Plotinus' life was characterized by mindful attention to thought and to the self, by care for others, and by an essential connection between self, world, thought, reality, and divinity. Neoplatonism is sometimes thought to sublimate or bypass the individual or other person entirely. The evidence of Plotinus' life contradicts this. As Porphyry says, "he was present at once to himself and to others" (*Life,* 8).

In his writing, Porphyry tells us, Plotinus "took a distinctive personal line in his consideration, and brought the mind of Ammonius to bear on investigations in hand" (*Life,* 14, 14–16). Plato, Aristotle, and Pythagorean and Peripatetic commentaries were read in the school, but Plotinus characteristically would summarize the readings and then start critically and creatively to think through their inherent philosophical problems. The writings that emerged from these discussions Porphyry grouped into six *Enneads,* the first dealing with ethical matters; the second and third with the physical universe; the fourth with soul; the fifth generally with intellect and the three major realities, or hypostases (the One, intellect, and soul); and the sixth with being and the One (although Porphyry does not explicitly tell us its subject-matter). A list of all the *Enneads* with their chronological numbers indicated in parenthesis appears immediately before this introduction. Conventionally, we refer to the *Enneads* only in numerals: "III, 8 (30) 2, 1–6," for instance, means "third *Ennead*, eighth treatise (number thirty on Porphyry's chronological list), chapter 2, lines 1–6."

Plotinus' influence has been immense in the history of thought, from the development of later Neoplatonism in Christian, Jewish, and Arabic thought, up to Ficino in the Renaissance, and later to Coleridge, Emerson, Yeats, and others. In the twentieth century, and earlier too, philosophy was unsympathetic to Neoplatonism not only because of its difficulty but also because of its apparent mystical, religious, occultist, and metaphysical qualities. Our modern materialistic emphasis upon the facts and nothing but the facts does not exactly predispose us to alternative paradigms, to other more spiritual forms of thought, or even to deeper examination of the puzzling question of just what the nature of fact might be. This is unfortunate because Plotinus is the greatest philosopher after Plato and Aristotle until Augustine, and his influence in the West, though so often hidden or transformed by subsequent figures, has been immense. The only way really to decide these matters is to read Plotinus for ourselves, keeping an open mind, and being as well disposed to what we read and yet thoroughly critical of it at the same time, as he and Plato before him would have expected and, indeed, first insisted upon.

This book is intended for anyone who wants to read and understand Plotinus, first-time readers, nonspecialists, and specialists alike. It includes first a selection of passages to give an overview of Plotinus' thought and then three works on some of the most fascinating and influential topics in the *Enneads:*

I, 1 (53), On what is the living creature and what the human being
III, 8 (30), On nature, contemplation and the One
V, 8 (31), On intelligible beauty

Treatise I, 1 is a late work, chronologically the fifty-third of fifty-four treatises, written just before Plotinus' death in 270. Porphyry chose it to introduce the rest of Plotinus' writings, probably because its examination of who we ourselves are, like Plato's *Alcibiades* I, is a necessary propaedeutic to self-knowledge that marks the beginning of philosophy itself. Like Porphyry, I have put this work first even though its seeming simplicity is deceptive, and an intelligent reading presupposes much of what Plotinus had already written. So I have started at the end of Plotinus' writing, with his analysis of what it means to be human, and then turned to his middle writings with III, 8 and V, 8.

Treatises III, 8 and V, 8 are the first two of the "big work" (so called by German scholars: *die Großschrift*) divided by Porphyry into four individual treatises (to make up the number of six sets of "nines" [or *Enneads*]). They are among Plotinus' finest works, and they mark one of his most creative periods, chronologically being thirtieth and thirty-first respectively of the fifty-four treatises. They also present two of his most characteristic theories: creative or productive contemplation as the seminal power that brings all things to birth, from intellect and soul to the physical universe itself; and intelligible beauty in art, nature, soul, and intellect itself, a theory that had enormous influence in the Italian Renaissance and in so many ways helped to shape German Idealist thought as well as English and North American Romanticism. At the same time, these two works give us prolonged exposure to a mind capable of thinking its way with creative precision and flair through philosophical puzzles that had resisted resolution for centuries. Plotinus' theory of creation, in particular, was to be of enormous influence in all areas of Western philosophico-theological debate, Christian, Jewish, and Muslim. But for all their subsequent influence, they are worth reading simply for themselves.

Introductions to the *Enneads* often present fairly early treatises that are surprisingly interesting and useful—for example I, 6 (1), *On beauty*; VI, 9 (9), *On the good or the One*; IV, 8 (6), *On the descent of the soul*. My aim here is twofold: first, to give an overview of Plotinus' thought, together with selected passages from some of the above works and others, in order to awaken in the reader the need for the text as a whole; and second, to plunge the reader right into the middle of Plotinus' writing life and into some of his most revolutionary works. Every treatise is different. Plotinus never says exactly the same thing twice. Nonetheless, these treatises' range of thought presents most of the major issues of his thinking.

This book is designed so that each of chapters 1, 2, 3, and 4 has two parts, the first part being the text of the treatise and the second part being my commentary on it. The commentary in chapter 3 is somewhat more detailed because the rather difficult text of III, 8 seemed to require additional attention. I have, therefore, worked through III, 8 more or less line by line to give a sense of how someone who has read Plotinus for many years might set about making consecutive sense of the text. By and large, I have tried not to involve the reader in thorny philological issues in the Greek text, though I sometimes discuss the sense of a particular issue where I cannot altogether avoid it. Plotinus wrote nearly 600 years after the deaths of Plato and Aristotle. His very language is coloured everywhere not only by his vast knowledge and love for their works (Plato above all) and the whole subsequent tradition and more that he and Porphyry call "the ancient philosophy," but also by his interpretation of all those texts, which he rarely indicates explicitly. Those texts represented for him a living form of thought, meditation, and spiritual practice (by contrast with today's more "academic" disciplines). The early part of my commentary on III, 8 takes some time to get off the ground because so many issues and terms need explaining: for instance, power/potency, actuality/activity, matter, soul, and substance. On all of these issues, there is a vast scholarly literature, some of which I have indicated in Appendix B. I have tried to keep my presentation as forthright and free of unnecessary scholarly complications as possible.

In the cases of I, 1 and V, 8, I have taken a slightly different approach. Instead of writing detailed commentaries, I have asked and attempted to answer series of questions that, to my mind, any reader might reasonably pose. I hope these chapters will be useful guides. I have tried to indicate something of the breadth of Plotinus' influence directly and indirectly upon history and particularly upon literature and poetry. Lack of space, however, precludes more than a cursory nod to many different avenues of thought and practice that certainly require more thorough independent treatment.

Chapter 5 provides a brief conclusion assessing the importance of Plotinus in the history of thought and charting the considerable afterlife of Neoplatonism.

The first of the two appendixes comprises translations of passages from Plato's dialogues that were of special importance for Plotinus. The second offers suggestions for further study and reading.

Throughout the work I have avoided capitalization, as much as possible, to avoid making Plotinus' characteristic vocabulary into "things" or distinct entities. I believe that this is more in accordance with his open-ended way of thinking, with his emphasis upon activity or a simpler form of being than either activity or entity might suggest, and also with the ambiguities naturally pervading a text that is so often a living meditation rather than a didactic treatise.

In this book I have made my own translations of Plotinus (as of Plato and Aristotle) because it is important for the scholar to be appropriately immersed in the text. At every point, as will be evident, I have benefited from what is certainly the best translation available in English, namely, that of my friend and former teacher, A. H. Armstrong, to whom I dedicate this book, as also to my dearest wife, Elena.

Chapter 1

An Overview of Plotinus' Thought

Texts

1. The hypostases and our relation to them (V, 1 [10] 10–12)

10. It has been shown already[1] that we should consider this is the way things are, that there is first the One beyond being, of such a kind as our argument wished to show, insofar as it was possible to show proof in these matters, and then in turn being and intellect, and third comes the nature of the soul. [5]And just as in nature there are these three of which we have spoken, so we should consider them also to be in us. By "in us" I do not mean in perceptible things—for these three are separate—but in us as outside perceptible things, and outside is said in the same way as those realities are also said to be outside of the entire heaven. So also the realities of man [10]are said to be outside in the sense that Plato speaks of the "inner man".[2] Our soul, too, therefore is something divine and of a different nature like all the nature of soul; and the soul which has intellect is perfect; and intellect in two senses, the one that reasons and the one that provides the power to reason. Certainly, this reasoning power of soul [15] which needs no bodily organ but has its own activity in purity so that it may be able to engage in pure reasoning, one would not be mistaken if one placed it as separate and not mixed with body in the first intelligible sphere.[3] For we must not look for a place in which to seat it, but we must make it outside of all place. For in this sense [20]is it in itself, the outside and immaterial, whenever it is alone and has nothing from the nature of body. For this reason too again [Plato]says of the universe that the craftsman wrapped the soul around it from outside, pointing to the part of the soul that remains in the intelligible[4]; but in the case of our souls he concealed his meaning and said that the soul is on top of the head.[5] And the command [25]to separate [6] is not said in a spatial way—for this part of the soul is by nature separated—but in

---

1. I.e., in the previous nine chapters, which form an extended recollection of all that the souls of human beings have forgotten (cf. chapter 1) but remains implicit in the earlier history of thought (cf. 8–9). Chapter 10 is the most striking passage in the *Enneads* about the hypostases themselves.

2. Cf. Plato, *Republic* 587 a 7; I, 1 (53) 10, 15 (see chapter 2 below).

3. I.e., intellect.

4. Cf. *Timaeus* 36 e 3 (see Appendix A, 3).

5. Cf. *Timaeus* 90 a 5.

6. Cf. Plato, *Phaedo* 67 c 6. Plotinus means here (and in the following lines) not spatial separation but an inner orientation of detachment.

terms of her not inclining to the body and [not]having mental images and of alienation in relation to the body, if in some way one could lead the rest of the form of soul up and take together to what is above that part of the soul that is seated here, which alone is the craftsman [30]and fashioner of body and has its concern with the sphere of body.

11. Since then there exists a soul that reasons about what is just and noble and a reasoning that seeks to determine if this particular course of action is just and if this is noble, it is necessary that there be something permanently just from which reasoning also comes to be in the sphere of soul. Or how would it be able to reason? And if [5]soul sometimes reasons about these things and sometimes does not, there must exist in us an intellect that does [not]reason, but always has the just, and there must also exist the origin of intellect, the cause and god and he is not divided, but always remains, and since he does not remain in place, he is contemplated again in many things, in each of those who [10]are able to receive him as another self,[7] just as the centre of a circle too exists in itself, and each of the radii in the circle has its point in it, and the radii bring their individuality to it.[8] For by something like this in us we too touch upon him and are with him and depend upon him, and those who converge there are seated in him.

12. How then if we have such great possessions do we not consciously apprehend them, but fail to a large extent to activate them, and some never activate them at all? Those realities are always occupied with their own activities, intellect and that which is before intellect, always in itself, and soul as well [5]the ever-moving[9]in this sense. For not everything that is in soul is already perceptible, but it comes to us whenever it enters into perception; but when each individual active agent does not give a share in its activity to the perceiving subject, the activity has not yet gone through the whole soul. So we do not yet know it since we are together with the perceiving power and are not a part of a soul but the entire [10] soul. And further, each of the parts of soul, since it lives always, always activates in itself its own function, but there is recognition of this when sharing takes place and there is conscious apprehension. We must, then, if there is to be conscious apprehension of activities that are present like this, turn the power of apprehension inwards and make it pay close attention to what is there. Just as if someone [15]was waiting to hear the sound of a voice he wanted to hear and withdrew from the other sounds and woke up the ear to catch what is the best of sounds when it comes, in the same way consequently here too, letting perceptible sounds

---

7. Perhaps a passing reference to Aristotle's usage of the ancient Pythagorean saying: a friend is another self (*EN* 1166 a 31–2; 1169 b 6–7; 1170 b 6).

8. The metaphor of circle, centre, and radii is often used in the *Enneads* to illustrate the relationship between hypostases (as in VI, 8 [9] 18 of the relation of intellect to the One) or between immaterial indivisible being and divisible material being (as in IV, 2 [4] 1, 24–9 or IV, 1 [21] passage 4 below in this chapter).

9. Cf. Plato, *Phaedrus* 245 c 5.

go, except insofar as is necessary, we must keep the soul's power of apprehension pure and [20]ready to hear sounds that are from above.

2. Tracing degrees of unity back to the One. The nature of body, soul, and intellect, and the return to the One (VI, 9 [9] 1–3)

1.   All beings are beings by the one, both as many as are primarily beings and as many as are said to be included in any sense at all among beings. For what could anything be, if it were not one, given the fact that if deprived of the one which is said of them, they are not these things?[10] For neither does an army [5]exist, if it is not one, nor a chorus or a flock if they are not one. But not even do a house or a ship exist if they do not have the one, since the house at any rate is one and the ship, and if they cast it off, then neither is the house any longer a house nor the ship a ship. Continuous magnitudes, therefore, if the one were not present to them, would not exist; if they are cut up at any rate, to the degree [10]they de-stroy the one, they change their being. And the bodies of plants and animals too, though each of them is one, if they escape the one by being broken up into a mul-tiplicity of small pieces, they lose the substance they had, and are no longer what they were but have become those new entities to the degree that each of them is one.[11] And health exists too whenever the body is brought together into a one, [15]and beauty, when the nature of the one controls the parts [12]; and there is ex-cellence of a soul, too, whenever she is unified into one and into one agreement. Is it the case then that since soul brings all things to one by crafting and moulding and shaping and composing them we should say when we come to her that she [20]supplies the one and that it is she who is the one? Or just as with the other things she supplies to bodies it is not herself which she gives, for instance, shape and form, but they are other than she, so we should consider that even if she gives a one, she gives it as something other than herself and that in looking to the one she makes each thing one, just as by looking to man she makes [25]a man, taking along with the man the one in him. For of the things which are said to be one each is one in the way it also has what it is, so that things which are less beings have the one less and things which are more beings have the one more. And soul too since she is other than the one possesses in proportion to her more real being [30] the more one.[13] She is certainly not the One itself; for soul is one and the one is in a way incidental to her, and these, soul and one, are two, just like body and one. And what is separated, like a chorus, is furthest from being one, but the continu-

---

10.   Compare III, 8 (30) 10 and chapter 3 below.

11.   The scale of degrees of unity is Stoic. Cf. *SVF* II 366–8 and 1013.

12.   On beauty and unity (and health) see I, 6 (1) 2; V, 8, 5 and 11 (see chapter 4 be-low).

13.   I omit *mallon* (more) at line 29.

ous body is closer; and soul still more though she participates in it. But if because, without being one, β5]soul would not even exist, on this count someone brings soul and the one to the same, first of all each of the rest of things is what it is together with its being one; but still the one is different from themfor body and one are not the same, but body participates in the oneand then the soul is many, even the one soul and even if she is not composed ‡0]of parts; for there are a great many powers in her, the powers of reasoning, desiring, apprehending, which are held together by the one as by a bond. So the soul brings the one to things, being one herself also by virtue of another; and she also experiences this by the agency of another.

2. Is it the case then that for each of the things that are one as parts, its substance and the one are not the same, but for being as a whole and for substance, substance and being and the one are the same?[14] So that the person who has found out being has also found out the one, and substance itself β]is the one itself; as for example, if intellect is substance, intellect is also the one because it is primarily being and primarily one, and because it gives to other things a share in being, so too in proportion it also gives them a share in the one.[15] For what could anyone say it is apart from those? For either it is the same as beingfor "man" and "one man" ‖0]are the same [16]or it is a kind of number of each thing, just as if you said two things, so you say the one of something on its own. If number then belongs to real beings, it is clear that the one must too; and we must seek what it is. But if counting is an activity of soul going through things sequentially, the one would not be anything concretely real. But ‖5]th e argument said that if each loses the one, then it will not exist at all. We must see, then, if each one and each being are the same, and being as a whole and the one are the same. But if the being which belongs to each thing is a multiplicity, and the one cannot be a multiplicity, then each will be different. Man, at any rate, and animal and rational and ₂0]many parts and these many are bound together by a one; man and one are different, then, if one has parts and the other is without parts. And the whole being too which has all the real beings in it will be more many and other than the one, but it will have the one by sharing and participation. And being also has life; ₂0] for it is certainly not a corpse; being then is many. And if intellect is this, so also it must be many; and still more if it embraces the forms; for not even are the ideas

---

14. Cf. Aristotle, *Metaphysics* 1054 a 13.

15. As Armstrong observes (Loeb VII, 306–7), that intellect-being is the first principle was the view of most Platonists before Plotinus, including Plotinus' fellow pupil under their teacher Ammonius, Origen the Platonist (to be distinguished, probably, from Origen the Christian). See Origen (in Proclus, *Platonic Theology* II, 4, 31, 5–11, Saffrey-Westerink).

16. Aristotle, *Metaphysics* 1003 b 26–7. Throughout this chapter Plotinus has Aristotle's theory of intellect very much in mind, as well as the questions of unity and being associated with it.

one, but a number rather, both each and all together and so one as the cosmos is one. But altogether the one is the first, and intellect and the forms and being are not firsts. For each form is made out β0] of many and is composite and later; and the elements out of which each is composed are earlier than each. And that it is not possible for intellect to be the first will be clear from the following; it is necessary that intellect exists in thinking and that the best intellect at best, that is, the one which does not look outside itself, β5]thinks th at which is before it; for in turning back to itself it turns back to a beginning. And if it is what thinks and what is thought, it will be double and not simple and so not the one; but if it looks to another, this must be altogether to what is greater than, and before itself. But if it looks both to itself and to what is greater, even so it will be second. And we must suppose intellect to be of such a kind β0]as to be present to the good and the first and to look to him, but also as to be together with itself and to think itself and to think itself as being all things. It is far, then, from being the one since it is made of rich colours. So the one cannot be all things, for if so it would no longer be one; nor even can it be intellect, for β5] if so it would be all things because intellect is all things; nor even being, for being is all things.

3.   What then could the One be and what nature does it have? There is nothing remarkable in its not being easy to say, when it is not even easy to say what being or form is; but there is for us a knowing based upon forms. To the degree the soul goes toward the formless, being completely unable β]to comprehend it because it is not defined or stamped, so to speak, by a richly coloured stamp, she slides off and is frightened that she may have nothing. That is why she gets tired of such experiences and gladly goes down on many occasions falling away from all things until she comes to the perceptible and takes her rest, as it were, on something solid;[17] just as sight gets tired when it is occupied with β0]small objects and gladly embraces large ones. But when the soul wishes to see by herself, seeing only by being together with it and being one by being one with it, she does not think that she yet has what she seeks, because she is not different from what is being thought. Nonetheless, this is certainly what the person who is going to philosophize about the One must do. Since therefore, β5]what we seek is one, and we are looking out for the originary principle of all things, the Good and the First, we must not go far from the things around the firsts falling into the last of all things, but must hurry to the firsts, stir oneself up away from the objects of sense which are the last things, and become rid of all the evil, β0]since one is eagerly on one's way to the Good, and go up to the originary principle in oneself and become one from many if one is to be a person who sees the originary principle, the One. Therefore, one must become intellect and entrust one's soul to intellect and settle her under intellect so that what intellect sees she might be awake to receive and may by this means see β5]the On e without adding any perception or receiv-

---

17. Cf. Plato, *Phaedrus* 246 c 3 (see Appendix A, 2).

ing anything from perception into that intellect, but by pure intellect to see that which is purest and by the first of intellect. Whenever therefore he who has not set out toward the vision of this kind imagines either size or shape or mass in relation to this nature, it is not intellect in this which guides[18] [30]his vision, because it is not in the nature of intellect to see such things, but the activity belongs to perception and opinion following upon perception. But one must take from intellect the announcement of what it can do. And intellect can see either the things before it or its own things.[19] The things in it too are pure, [35]but still purer and simpler are the things before it, or rather that which is before it. Not even therefore is it intellect, but before intellect; for intellect is some one of the real beings, but that is not something, but before each, and nor is it being; for being also has a kind of shape of what really is, but that is without shape, without even intelligible shape. [40]For since the nature of the One is generative of all things, it is none of them. So it is neither something nor qualified or quantified or intellect or soul; it is not in movement or again at rest, not in place, not in time,[20] but itself by itself of single form,[21] and rather formless, being before all form, before movement, before rest; [45]for these belong to being and they make it many. Why then, if it is not moving is it not at rest? Because one or the other of these or both must belong to being, and what is at rest is so by virtue of rest and is not the same as rest; so that rest will be accidental to it and no longer will it remain simple. For to say that it is the cause is not to predicate [50]anythi ng accidental of it, but of us because we have something from it while that is in itself; but one who speaks accurately must not even say "that" or "is," but we run around outside it, as it were, in our wish to interpret our own experience of it, sometimes near it and sometimes falling away from it in our perplexities about it.

3. The derivation of everything (from intellect to matter)

a) IV, 8 (6) 6[22]:   If, then, it is necessary that there not be one alonefor all things would have been hidden having no shape in that one and not even would a single real being have existed if that one had stayed in itself, nor would there have

---

18. Cf. Plato, *Laws* 963 a 8.

19. I omit "or the things from it" (bracketed in Henry-Schwyzer, Opera Plotini 3). For the plural "the things before it," see also III, 8 (30) 9, 31 and 10, 7–10 and chapter 3 below.

20. Cf. Plato, Parmenides 139 b 3; 138 b 5–6; 141 a 5.

21. Plato, *Symposium* 211 b 1 (see Appendix A, 1).

22. In this work, *On the descent of the soul into bodies,* Plotinus is concerned (among other things) to reconcile the apparent contradiction in Plato between the notion of soul's fall and the notion that soul is sent into the world with divine purpose (see IV, 8, 5, passage 6 below). Though fall and descent are connected, it is necessary that the divine outgoing reach out as far as possible even down to the generation of matter. Soul, in fact, may not be harmed by her descent, and our highest part remains anyway in the intelligible world (IV, 8, 7–8). The first long sentence (which I have retained in translation) with its complex articulation of thought is characteristic of Plotinus.

been the multiplicity of these real beings which have been generated from the One [5]if the things after them had not taken their going forth, those things that have been allotted the rank of souls in the same way it was necessary too that there should be not just souls alone without the things becoming manifest that have been produced through souls, if at any rate this is in each nature, to make what comes after it and to unfold itself as from a seed[23] which proceeds from an origin without parts into a final goal that is perceptible [10] what is earlier always remaining in its own seat, but bringing to birth, as it were, what comes after it out of a power unspeakably immense as great as was in those earlier beings, which could not stand still as if it had drawn a line around itself out of selfish jealousy but had to go on always until all things have come to the farthest possible limit because of a boundless power that [15]extends to all from itself and that cannot allow anything to be without a portion of itself. For there was certainly nothing that prevented anything whatever from having a portion of the divine nature insofar as it was possible for each to participate. Either then the nature of matter existed always, and it was not possible for it, since it existed not to participate in that which provides the good to all [20]insofar as   each can or the generation of matter followed necessarily upon the causes before it, and not even so was it necessary for it to be separate because that which gave it being as a kind of gracious gift stopped out of powerlessness before coming to matter.[24] A manifestation of what is best in the intelligibles, therefore, is the fairest beauty of the perceptible world, a manifestation [25]of their power and goodness, and all things are held together forever, both those which exist intelligibly and those which exist perceptibly, the former existing from themselves, and the latter taking their being forever by participation in them, imitating the intelligible nature insofar as they can.

b) V, 2 (11) 1, 3–28[25]:   How then do all things come from a simple One with no rich diversity appearing in it, no doubleness of any kind? [5]It is because there was nothing in it that for this reason all things have come out of it, and so that being might exist, the One is not being, but the generator of being. This is the first act of generation, as it were: being perfect because it seeks nothing, has nothing, needs nothing, the One, so to speak, overflows and its overfullness has made another, and what has come to be turned back to it and was filled and in looking to it this came to be intellect. Its rest in relation to the One being, but its vision in relation to it (the One or itself?) made intellect. Since it stopped in relation to it (the One) so that it might see, it becomes at once intellect and being. This then being

---

23. Cf. III, 7 (45) 11, 23–7 (passage 10 below).

24. Typically, Plotinus appears to offer alternative views (an ungenerated and a generated matter) to show that his argument will apply to both. On the generation of matter see chapter 1, part II, 1.10. For different views see D. O'Brien, 1981, 108–23; K. Corrigan, 1996a, 263–6.

25. Cf. V, 4 (9) 1–2; V, 1 (10) 6–7; II, 4 (12) 5; and see chapter 3 below.

like that (One), makes similar things, pouring forth a multiple power [15]and this is also a form of it just as in turn that which was before it poured it forth. And this activity from the substance of intellect is the activity of soul which comes to be this while intellect remains (in itself); for intellect also came to be while that before it remained. But soul makes not by remaining, but having been moved she generated an image. Looking there, then, from where she came to be, [20]she is filled, and having gone fort h to another opposite movement she generates perception and the nature in plants as an image of herself. But nothing is separated or cut off from what is before it; that is why also the soul above seems to reach up to plants; for in a way she does reach that far, because the principle in plants belongs to her; certainly she is not entirely in [25]plants, but she has come to be in plants in the sense that she has gone forth so far toward the lower and has made another reality by her procession and by her desire for what is worse; and that which is before this which depends upon intellect lets intellect remain in itself.

4. The nature of intellect and soul, and soul's relation to bodies (IV, 1 [21])[26]

In the intelligible cosmos is true substance; intellect is the best of it, but souls are there too; for because they have come from there they are here too. And that cosmos has souls without bodies, but this one has the souls which come to be in bodies and that have been divided by bodies. [5]But there all intellect is together and not separated or divided, and all souls are together in the cosmos that is eternity, not in a separation that is spatial. Intellect, then, is always inseparable and not divided, and soul there is inseparable and indivisible, but she has a nature to be divided. For her division is to have stood off [10]and to have come to be in bodies. She is reasonably said, therefore, to be "divisible about bodies" because she stands off in this way and has been divided. How then is she also indivisible? Because the whole of her did not stand off, but there is something of her that did not come (down) which is not naturally divisible. The statement, therefore, "from the indivisible and that which is divisible about bodies"[27] [15]is the same as the statement that the soul is from that which exists above and that which is attached there but which has flowed right up to these things here, like a line from a centre (of the circle). But when she has come here to this part, see in what way she preserves the nature of the whole also in this very part. For not even here is she divisible only, but she is also indivisible; for what is divided [20]of her is indivisibly divided. For she gives herself to the whole body and is not divided in that she gives herself whole to a whole, but is divided in that she is present in every part.

---

26. Cf. IV, 2 (4); IV, 3–4 (27–28); VI, 4–5 (22–23). IV, 2 gives a much better account, but IV, 1 contains the essential details and is shorter. This chapter is the entire treatise.

27. Plato, *Timaeus* 35 a 1–3, Appendix A, 3.

5. World soul and individual souls (IV, 3 [27] 6)[28]

But why has the soul of the all, which is of the same form as the soul of the individual, made the cosmos, while the soul of each individual has not, though she
also has everything in her? For it has been explained[29] that soul can come to be
and exist in many things simultaneously. But now we must say for perhaps it
will also come to be known 5]how the sa me thing, now in one body and now in
another, does now this and now that or is affected in different ways, or both; this
at any rate is a question we must examine by itself how then and why has the
soul of all made a cosmos, while the particular souls look after a part of a cosmos? There is nothing remarkable, of course, that in the case of people who have
the same knowledge some have command of more and some 0]of less. But one
could ask why. But there is, one might reply, a difference among souls, all the
more so that the soul of the all has not separated herself from the whole soul, but
holds to the whole soul putting on body around her, while the individual souls,
since body already exists, have received their appointed portions when their sister
soul, so to speak, was already ruling as though she had prepared dwellings 0]
for them in advance.[30] There is also a difference in that she looks toward the
whole intellect, while they look more toward their own partial intellects. And perhaps these souls too might have been able to make a cosmos, but since she had already made one it was not possible for them because she started first. One could
have the same difficulty if any other soul had occupied the first place. 0]But it
is better to say (she made the cosmos) by being more attached to the things above;
for the power of beings who incline to those principles is greater, since they keep
themselves upon a secure foundation and therefore make with the greatest of ease;
for it is characteristic of greater power not to be affected in the things it makes;
and power comes from remaining above. Remaining in herself, therefore, she
makes and the things she makes come to her, 5]whereas the individual souls
went forth to the things. They have departed then into the depth or rather much of
them has been dragged down and has dropped them too along with it by their
thoughts to the lower existence. For we must understand the real meaning in the
statement that souls were called "seconds" and "thirds"[31] to the degree they are
nearer to the things above or farther from them, just as in us too not all souls are
similarly related to the realities there, but some human beings may unify themselves, while others come near 0]in   their longing and still others have it less insofar as they act by powers that are not the same, but some by the first power,

---

28. Plotinus has been arguing in the early chapters of this major work that our souls
are not parts of the World soul. For these chapters see W. Helleman-Elgersma, and for the
work as a whole, H. J. Blumenthal, 1971.

29. IV, 3, 3–5.

30. Cf. VI, 7 (38) 7, 8–16.

31. Plato, *Timaeus* 41 d 7.

others by that which comes after it, and others by the third, though all human beings have all the powers.

6. The descent and fall of soul (IV, 8 [5] 5)[32]

There is therefore no discordance between the sowing of the souls to birth and the
descent into the perfection of the all, and the judgement and the cave,[33] and necessity and free will, since necessity possesses free will, and the being in body as in
an evil; [5]nor Empedocles' flight from god [34] and wandering nor the fault for
which there is judgement nor Heraclitus' rest on the flight, nor generally the free
will of descent and the unwilled character of it again. For everything that goes to
what is worse does so unwillingly but, all the same, it goes by its own motion and
in experiencing worse things it is said [10]to pay the penalty for the things it has
done. But when it is eternally necessary by a law of nature to experience and to do
these things, and when what comes, as it descends from that which is above it, to
meet the need of something else in its approach to it, if someone should say that a
god sent it down, he would not be discordant either with the truth or with himself.
[15]For the last things are referred to   the originative principle from which each
thing comes, even if there are many stages in between. And since the fault of the
soul is double, and can refer either to the cause of soul's descent or to the doing of
evil things when she has come to be here, then punishment in the first case is just
this, what she has experienced in the descent, and in the second case the lesser
and quick entrance into other [20]bodies that results from the judgement of the
soul's desertsthe word   *judgement* indicates what happens by divine bondbut
the measureless form of wickedness is thought to be worthy of greater punishment
under the authority of chastising spirits. So although the soul is divine and comes
from the places that are [25]above, sh e comes to belong to body and, though a
god of the last order, she comes here by a free inclination and because of her
power and her setting in order that which comes after her. If she escapes quickly,
she is in no way harmed by acquiring a knowledge of evil and coming to know
the nature of wickedness and bringing her powers to the light of day and revealing

---

32. Cf. chapter 2, part II, 1.11. Compare V, 1 (10) chapter 1 on the fall of soul and
chapter 2 on the descent for the perfection of the universe. See also I, 1 (53) 12 (and chapter 2, part II below), and generally IV, 3 (27) 9; 12–16; III, 9 (13) 3. On IV, 8 see note 22
above. Although this is a difficult chapter, it provides a rather dramatic illustration of how
Plotinus can hold together viewpoints that are inevitably in tension with each other. Here
even soul's descent is a "fault" (*hamartia*) yet results in the realization of things that would
have been useless (or "in vain") had they remained in the intelligible realm!Plotinus, of
course, thinks both sides of this at once, both hidden power and hidden potentiality, i.e.,
both soul's power and potentiality in matter as the reflection of that power. For a development of this, see chapter 3.22 below.

33. For the judgement see the myth of Er in Plato's *Republic* X and for the cave the
beginning of *Republic* VII.

34. Empedocles, *DK* B fr. 115.

works and productions which, had they remained quiet in the incorporeal world, would have been of no use since they would not have come into actualization; and the soul herself would not have realized what she had if they had not been revealed or taken on their procession, since actuality everywhere has revealed completely hidden potentiality that is, so to speak, β5]hidde n from sight and non-existent because it does not yet really exist. For now everyone is in a state of wonder at what is within because of the rich variety of what is external and marvels at the nature of the doer because of these subtle things it does.

7. Matter[35] (II, 5 [25] 5)

How then do we speak about it? How is it the matter of real beings? Because it is they potentially. So then, because it is they potentially, is it already, therefore, as it is going to be? But being for it is only an announcing of what it is going to be, as if being for it is postponed β]to th at which it will be. Potential existence, therefore, is not being something, but being potentially everything; and since it is nothing in itself, but what it is, matter, nor is it in actuality. For if it will be something in actuality, it will be that which it is in actuality, and not matter; so it will not be completely matter, but matter in the way the bronze is.[36] This therefore would be non-being, not as other than being, like [10]movement; [37] for this also rides upon being, as if it has come from it and is in it, but matter is cast out, as it were, and completely separated and is not able to change itself, but what it was from the beginningand it was non-beingso it always is. And neither was it from the beginning anything in actuality, since it stood away from all real beings [15]nor did it come to be anything; for matter has been unable to take on any colour from the things that wanted to sink into it, but remaining in relation to something else it exists potentially in relation to what is next; and when those real beings had already stopped, matter appeared and having been caught by the things that came into being after it, matter took its place as the last even of these. [20] Having been caught by both, then, it could belong in actuality to neither, and it is left for it only to be potentially a weak and dim image unable to be shaped. Matter then is actually an image; so it is actually a falsehood; this is the same as "that which is truly a falsehood"; and this is "what is really not real."[38] If then it is non-

---

35. Compare II, 4 (12) 5 and chapter 3, part II, 3.

36. I.e., already a formed, actual thing, however indeterminate the bronze might be right now in relation to the statue, for example, that could be fashioned out of it.

37. Movement (kinêsis) is one of the "greatest kinds" (together with being, rest, sameness, difference) of the intelligible world, adapted by Plotinus from Plato's Sophist 254 d ff. On this see chapter 1, part II, 1.5.

38. The two quotations come from Plato, Republic 382 a 4 and Sophist 254 d 1, but from contexts which do not refer to matter (the word matter [hylê]is not used by Plato in this sense anyway; the concept is only developed by Aristotle, though in the Timaeus and elsewhere Plato has much to say about the material principle).

being in actuality [25] it is   more non-being, and so really not real. That which has its truth in non-being, therefore, is a long way from being in actuality any reality. So if it must exist, it must not exist in actuality, so that having gone out of true being, it may have its being in non-being, since with things that exist falsely, if you take away [30] their falsehood, you have taken away whatever substance they have, and if you introduce actuality to those things that have their being and substance potentially, you have destroyed the cause of their existence, because their being was in potentiality. If then, one must keep matter indestructible, one must keep it as matter. So one must [35] say, it would seem, only that it exists potentially, in order that it might be what it is, or one must refute these arguments.

8. Bodiliness[39] (II, 7 [37] 3)

But since we have made mention of bodiliness, we must examine whether bodiliness is that which is compounded of all a body's features or whether bodiliness is a form and an active forming principle that enters into the matter and makes body. If therefore this is the body, namely that which is composed of [5] all the qualities together with matter, then this is what bodiliness would be. And if bodiliness was an active forming principle that by coming to matter makes body, then clearly the forming principle embraces and contains all the qualities. But it is necessary this forming principle, if it is not to be like a definition that shows what the thing is, but a forming principle that makes [10] a thing, not to include the matter, but be a principle in relation to matter that enters into matter and perfects the body, and the body must be matter and indwelling forming principle, but the forming principle itself since it is a form must be contemplated bare, without matter, even if it is itself as inseparable as it can be from matter. For the separated form is different, the one in intellect; and it is in intellect, because it is also itself intellect. But this we take up elsewhere.[40]

---

39. Or corporeity, or what it means to be a body (*sômatotês*). This is the final chapter of a work directed to (and against) the Stoic materialist theory of complete transfusion, that is, that two material substances when they are mixed can completely interpenetrate each other.

40. Much of the fifth and sixth *Enneads* are devoted to the question of intellect.

Commentary

Plotinus' thought poses a special challenge for the contemporary reader. Not only is it among the most spiritual of all Western philosophies, but it also presupposes the whole of earlier thought from the Presocratics, Plato, and Aristotle, to the later Platonic Academy, the Peripatetic school of Aristotelian commentators, the Stoics, and the Skeptics. Consequently, individual treatises tend to be highly compressed explorations of philosophical puzzles and problems arising from the inevitably unfinished philosophies of those earlier thinkers. Plotinus depends upon what Porphyry calls the "ancient philosophy"; that is, a system of thought rooted in Plato and developed by later Platonists including Aristotle. But like any great thinker, Plotinus transforms everything he inherits by the very activity of thinking through that inheritance critically and creatively. In the *Enneads*, therefore, we have not so much a body of philosophical opinions as fifty-four philosophical meditations, many of which are quietly revolutionary in their scope and creativity. This book attempts to demonstrate something of that philosophical creativity, but first offers a general overview of Plotinus' thought as a map to unfamiliar territory.

1.1. The hypostases

At the root of Plotinus' philosophy are the three principles, beginnings (*archai*), or hypostases ("real existences") that underlie everything we experience:

1. The One (or the Good)
2. Intellect (or Being, together with all beings or intellects)
3. Soul (or all soul, from which at a lower level the World soul and individual souls derive)

As Plotinus puts this in an early work, "there is the One beyond being, . . . and next in order there is being and intellect, and the nature of soul is third. And just as in nature there are these three . . . so we should think that these are also present in us" (V, 1, 10, 1–6). The sensible, or physical, world is composed of form and matter and is a reflection, or image, of the content of soul, as is soul of intellect. Even the divine eternal intellect attempts to express in itself the immensity of a principle beyond thought and being, a pure unity or goodness greater than all other unities derived from it, the origin of all things. Intellect and soul in this sense are not our intellects and souls but the great principles from which our much weaker and more divided intellects and souls derive, as we shall see. The hypostases are "in" us not like different qualities "in" our bodies but in the sense that they are present to us without belonging to us.

Why should Plotinus think that these hypostases are the bases upon which sensible reality and our experience are founded? The search for a reality appearances is as old as Greek philosophy itself. Thales had thought "water" to be the origin of everything, Anaximander the "infinite" or "intraversible" (therefore, perhaps, another form of water, the ocean which is "intraversible" or infinite in Homer), Anaximenes "air," Xenophanes "fire," and so on. The search for unity Plotinus situates already in the *logos* of Heraclitus "who knew that the One is eternal and intelligible" and in Empedocles: "Strife divides, but Love is the One" (V, 1 [16] 9, 3–7). In the *Republic* Socrates supposed the Good to be beyond thought or intellect and the ultimate principle of the soul's quest for completion. Plato and the later Academy[1] posited the One (or Good) and the indefinite dyad (viz., a capacity for twoness or multiplicity) as the originary principles of everything, whereas Aristotle held intellect, or the Unmoved Mover, to be the ultimate principle of motion, even if the physical world itself did not come to be by the agency of any Divine Craftsman (as Plato had represented it mythologically in his *Timaeus*).[2]

Clearly then soul, intellect, and the One, or Good, are essential parts of Plotinus' heritage, though he understands them in rather new ways. He combines Plato's World of Forms with Aristotle's Intellect, but in such a way that no Form is merely a transcendent object. All Forms or intelligible objects are also subjects or intellects; and every intellect includes the whole of intelligible reality without losing its own distinctiveness. But intellect still is not ultimate for Plotinus because intellect involves the doubleness of subject thinking and object thought. Plotinus also adopts the Platonic division of reality into two worlds, intelligible and sensible. The soul is the amphibious traveller between these two worlds of eternity and time, inhabitant of both, so that sometimes the intelligible world refers strictly to intellect. Yet it also includes the whole range of soul; in some passages the intelligible world even seems to reach so deeply into the physical world that it is hard to see where the intelligible ends and the physical starts (e.g., VI, 2 [43] 20–1; V, 8 [31] 5). In other passages the division is made much more sharply: all of intelligible reality, intellect and soul, is being or substance, while physical reality is merely the qualitative, quantitative flux of reflected forms in matter (cf. VI, 3 [44] 8). We might then represent this larger view schematically:

---

1.   According to the "unwritten doctrines," on which see G. Reale, 1997.
2.   On causality generally in Plotinus and in earlier thought see below sections 1.3, 1.5, 2.5–2.6.1, 3.5–3.7, 3.31, 4.7–4.9.

The One, or Good

Intellect, or Being

Soul (which includes all souls)

Bodies (compounded of forms in matter)	Living bodies
	Nonliving bodies (e.g., the elements fire, air, water, earth)
Matter	As principle of spatial extension generated by soul
	As privation of form in its own nature.

Soul, intellect, and the One are therefore at the root of everything. But why should they form a hierarchy? Why do we need just these principles? And how are they related to one another?

The answer to the first two questions is that Plotinus thinks these hypostases are necessary to account for our ordinary experiences. His treatises typically start from everyday phenomena, such as our experience of beauty and art, and ascend to a deeper understanding of the principles involved, as in Plato's *Symposium* and *Republic*. Above all, the hypostases are necessary to account for our experience of degrees of unity and organization. Without unity no thing would be recognizable as such, neither the simplest elementary compound nor a loosely associated group such as a crowd nor a more highly organized compound such as a chorus, nor again at a different level, a complex living human body:

> All beings are beings by virtue of unity, both those that are primarily beings and those that are in any way said to be among beings. For what could anything be if it was not one? For neither does an army exist if it is not one, nor a chorus nor a flock if they are not one? (VI, 9 [9] 1, 1–6)

Things depend upon unity to be individual things rather than unity upon individual things. Thus, the organization, beauty, and order of both nonliving and living things cannot occur simply by themselves. Accounting for them requires a higher degree of unity—namely, soul. Moreover, soul is not a pure unity but a multiplicity of powers: thought, imagination, perception, among them:

> And the soul, too, which is different from the one has her being more one in proportion to her greater real being. Certainly, the soul is not the One itself, for the soul is one and the one is in a sense incidental to her, and these things, soul and one, are two, just like body and one. And what is discontinuous like a chorus, is furthest from being one, and the continuous body closer; but the soul is still closer even though she participates in it still? (VI, 9, 1, 30–14)

While soul and souls possess their own natural order (just as bodies do by virtue of soul), accounting for their unity also requires an organizing principle outside themselves.

Soul is a "one and many," says Plotinus; that is, an indivisible unity that comes to animate a world of many bodies.

> And then the soul is many and one, even if it is not composed of parts; for there are a great many powers in her, reasoning, desiring, apprehending, which are held together by the one as by a bond. The soul then brings the one to others being herself also one by virtue of something else. (VI, 9 [9] 1, 39–44)

Soul's organizing principle, in turn, Plotinus supposes, must be the more intensive unity of intellect, where unity and multiplicity are immediately reflected in each other. Intellect is a one-many (a one-in-many and a many-in-one), a world of intellects in each of which the whole of intellect is present. Each is a sort of holographic reality. Because intellect is a world despite its more intensive unity than soul, according to Plotinus it cannot be the first principle, "for not even is the idea one, but rather a number, both each and the totality . . ." (VI, 9, 2, 27–8). Or again: "intellect is of such a kind as to be present to the good and to look to him, but also such as to be present to itself and to think itself. . . . It is farther from being the one because it is richly various" (VI, 9, 2, 40–44). There must be a purer, simpler unity beyond intellect, namely the One, or the Good. Intellect, in fact, splits its vision of that pure simplicity into a world of beings: "Did intellect then when it looked toward the Good think that one as many and being one itself thought him as many, dividing him in itself by not being able to think the whole at once?" (VI, 7 [38] 16, 10–13). But the One itself (Plotinus tends to vary his use of the pronoun from "he" to "it") is beyond all intellectual determination, a simpler, formless, but more comprehensive presence than that of intellect. "But what does it make now?" Plotinus asks. "Now too it safeguards those things and makes the thinking things think and the living things live, breathing intellect, breathing life into them, and if anything cannot live, existence" (VI, 7 [38] 23).

1.2. Free spontaneous creativity: The One

How are the levels of reality related? To understand this more clearly, we must first see how Plotinus understands the One. The One is not like a monad or point; we must understand it "morely" (*pleonôs* VI, 9 [9] 6, 2): "when you think him as intellect or god, he is more" (6, 12). "When you see him, look at him whole" (V, 5 [32] 10, 10). The One then is infinite in the sense of unlimited unrestricted power (cf. V, 5, 10–11).

Of course, we cannot speak or understand the One because speaking and understanding involve multiplicity and the subject-predicate dualities of language. But we can "speak about it," Plotinus says, and we can "indicate" it from the experience of the One in ourselves, an experience that goes beyond our capacity to express fully (cf. V, 3 [49] 13–14). We also can say what it is not, but we must ensure that our affirmations and negations do not "add" anything to it (cf. V, 5 [49] 13). The One, or Good, is beyond everyone's grasp, and yet it is "gentle, kindly, and gracious, and present to anyone when anyone wishes" (V, 5 [32] 12). Though the One may be so utterly ineffable as to seem unrelated to ordinary experience, everything—ourselves included—has in fact come from the One.

Plotinus asks how this can be in many treatises, but his most compelling analysis is to be found in VI, 8 [39], *On the Free Will and the Will of the One*. The making, or creation, of all things is not some sort of reflex action of an insensible and unthinking principle; nor does it happen by simple necessity or in accordance with any determinate plan or choice between opposite courses of action, but instead it springs from the free spontaneous self-productive activity of a principle that makes freedom and will what they will be in its products: "being . . . is known from what comes after [the One]. And the question 'why?' seeks another principle (*archê*), but there is no principle of the all principle" (VI, 8, 11, 7–9):

> Certainly that which has made substance free, which clearly has a nature to make free and could be called a free-maker, to what could it be a slave? (12, 17–20)

Again:

> If willing comes from itself, it is necessary that its being is also from itself so that our reasoning has discovered that he has made himself. For if his will (*boulêsis*) is from himself and is, so to speak, his own work, and this will is the same as his existence (*hypostasis*), then he himself, in this way, will have caused himself to exist, so that he is not what he chanced to be, but what he himself willed to be. (13, 53–9)

Plotinus concludes that it is reasonable to think about the One as the preeminent source of all positive attributes, even if we cannot strictly predicate anything of him or even if we have to break the moulds of ordinary language in the attempt to indicate what we mean:

> If there is nothing random then or by chance and no "it just turned out like this" with the things which have their causes in themselves, and all things from him have their causes in themselves, for he is the father of reason, cause, and causative substance, which are indeed all far from chance, he would be the principle and, so to speak, the paradigm of the things which have no share in chance, . . . cause of himself and himself both from himself and through himself; for he is primarily himself and self in a way which is beyond being. And he, that same self, is lovable and love (*erôs*) and love of himself since he is beautiful only from himself and in himself. For surely his being together with himself could not be in any other way than if that which is together with and that with which it is together were one and the same. (VI, 8 [39] 14, 36–15, 5)

Thus, the One's unrestricted, infinite activity is creative, self-productive freedom that establishes everything else in being.

1.3. The derivation of all things: Procession and conversion

How, precisely, does everything come from the One? For Plotinus, there is an essential double movement in all being, a movement of procession outward (*prohodos*) or descent, and a movement of return or conversion (*epistrophê*) to the higher generative principle. He likens this movement, or activity, to light, smell, sound, perfume, the source from which tributary rivers will flow, or a circle unfolding itself into radii and circumference but still rooted in its centre, which is itself rooted in the centre of all centres beyond it (on this see 3.19.6 and 3.20.2 below); but unlike physical light and smells, which do not return to their sources, these movements are not spatial but rather denote the source and the goal of all real beings (intellects and souls)—that is, where they have come from and where they are going to. Since all being is timelessly dependent and derivative, that derivation has to be expressed in the time-bound language of movement out of, and movement back to, a principle. Since for Plotinus intellect is not just rest but also involves intellectual movement, this is not entirely inappropriate. In an important passage, V, 2 (11), *On the generation and order of those things after the First*, Plotinus first expresses this relation paradoxically (following Plato's *Parmenides* 160 b 2–3): "The One is all things and no one of them." He then goes on to describe the derivation, or emanation, as it is often called, but perhaps misleadingly since it is nonspatial:

> This is the first act of generation, as it were: being perfect because it seeks nothing, has nothing, needs nothing, the One, so to speak, overflows [*hypererruê*] and its overfullness [*to hyperplêres*] has made another; and what has come to be turned back to it and was filled and in looking to it this came to be intellect. Its rest in relation to the One made being [*to on*], but its vision in relation to it [either the One or itself: *auto* is ambiguous] made intellect. Since it stopped in relation to it [the One] so that it might see, it becomes at once intellect and being. This, then, being like that [One], makes similar things, pouring forth a multiple power. . . . This activity springing from the substance [*ek tês ousias*] of intellect is soul, which comes to be this while intellect remains in itself. (V, 2 [11] 1, 7–18)

We should note here, first, a principle that Plotinus emphasizes in many other places. All real beings are productive and give of themselves without being diminished. Physical things are not self-sustaining, but they act in a similar way:

> And all things as long as they remain in themselves, necessarily produce from their own substance out of the power which is present, a surrounding reality [*hypostasis*] directed to what is outside of them, a kind of image of the archetypes out of which they have grown; fire generates heat from it, and snow does not keep its cold only inside itself. . . . As long as they exist,

something goes forth from them around them, and what is near profits from their existence. And all things that are already complete generate: the One is always perfect and so complete eternally. (V, 1 [10] 6, 31–39)

This production, then, is a sort of double activity, an act *of* the substance that produces an act *from* or *out of* the substance of the thing.[3] What is produced is an image of the generator, and it acts by virtue of the power given to it. The power of the generator is nonetheless intimately present to it, since it exists by virtue of its immediate intimacy with the generator:

> [Intellect] sees him [the One] not as separated from him, but because it is after him and there is nothing in between, as there is nothing between soul and intellect; everything longs for its parent and loves this, and most of all when they are alone, parent and offspring; but when the parent is the best, the offspring is necessarily with him so as to be separated only by otherness. (V, 1 [10] 6, 50-3)

Second, if we return to V, 2 (11) 1, there is a moment of indeterminacy or hyperdeterminacy in the generation of Intellect: the "overfullness" or overflow of the One. In other passages, Plotinus represents this as the procession of a sort of unformed potentiality that must turn back to the One to be actualized as a distinct entity. In other words, the procession of pure power from the One is also the first moment of a new potentiality that must turn back to see the One and to see itself as other than the One and thus to "become" a self-thinker or distinct intellect. We might well suppose that since everything must be included in this procession (everything that will have any real being, that is, such as intellect, soul, and even their images in our historical existences, in bodies, and in matter), then all desires that in some way are based upon the Good must also in some sense be included. If so, then form and intellectual determination are not necessarily the most valuable signs of all manifestations of existence. A certain kind of unformedness like the One in us—in our desires, hopes, hunches—might be even more important in the meaning of human lives yet obviously will be easy to overlook since it is not a definite this or that. To an untutored eye it might look like nothing at all. Developing a thought in Plato (*Republic* 505 d: every soul pursues the real good and divines [*apomanteuomenê*] that it is something), Plotinus says we must consider

> that people have forgotten that which from the beginning till now they long for and desire. For all things reach out to that and desire it by necessity of nature, as if divining [*apomemanteumena*] that they cannot exist without it. And the apprehension of the beautiful and the astonishment and the waking up of love are for those who are already, as it were, knowing it and awake to it. But the Good, since it is long present to awake a desire natural to it, is pre-

---

3.   See also, e.g., II, 9 (38) 8, 22 ff.; IV, 3 (27) 10, 31 ff.; IV, 5 (29) 7, 17 ff.; V, 1 (10) 3, 6–12; V, 4 (7) 2, 27–30; VI, 2 (43) 22, 26 ff.

> sent even to those asleep and does not astonish those who at any time see it, because it is always there . . . (V, 5 [32] 12, 5–13)

For Plotinus, the quiet presence of the Good is at the root of all giving and receiving as well as at the root of the return of real beings (like soul and intellect) to self-knowing in the vision of the principles before them. This quiet presence is so familiar that we do not even notice it. Beauty, he says, astonishes and can be painful because one must have seen it to know passionate desire for it, whereas the desire for the Good is "more ancient and unperceived" (V, 5 [32] 12, 17–18).

A third important consequence of Plotinus' derivation theory is that reality is neither simply objective nor simply subjective but has to "bend back" or "return" through itself to its source. All being is, therefore, essentially self-reflexive. Following Plato's likening of the Good to the light of the Sun in the *Republic*, Plotinus emphasizes that the intelligibility of being depends not only upon the receptivity of being itself but, above all, upon the self-disclosing gift of the Good, which like the light of the Sun is the medium in which anything becomes visible. Consequently, in descriptive arguments about the derivation of intellect from the One and of soul from intellect, intellect is active in itself but passive to the productive power of the One:

> So then intellect came to be in being filled, and having been filled it was, and simultaneously it was perfected and saw. (VI, 7 [38] 16, 32–34)

In other words, none of the creative activities of life depend entirely on ourselves; rather, they require the awakening of a higher form of seeing and even the appropriate forms of invocation. In the approach to intelligible reality, for instance, Plotinus tells us to make a faithful picture of this world in our thought (*dianoia*) and "calling upon the god who made that of which you have the mental picture, pray him to come. And may he come, bringing his own universe with him. . . ." (V, 8 [31] 9). We can prepare for the vision but we cannot compel it. In this way philosophy and religion are not divorced from each other but are by necessity philosophically integrated with one another.

1.4. The return to union

The consequences of this for Plotinus' mystical thought in general are far-reaching. The ascetic, spiritual, and mystical[4] impulses are a natural response to

---

4.   By *ascetic* I mean simply the *practice* of a certain kind of life in order to discipline, organize, and direct our desires and thoughts. By *spiritual* I mean the proper attention to oneself that is necessary to develop an interior life and a deeper awareness of what the self—in a nontechnical sense—really involves. By *mystical* (a perhaps much overused term, but one that I will continue to use here for simplicity's sake) I mean simply intimate experience of the divine in whatever way. The term *mysticism* itself is much debated. Do we refer to "experience," and if so, how can we determine its coinage? Firsthand accounts of personal encounters do not necessarily describe genuine experience. And how can there

the eternal procession and conversion of reality. The articulation of ascent or return (by means of purgation, illumination, and unification, as later thinkers put it) involves active as well as passive moments because these moments can never be entirely in our own power. In one of the most striking expressions of his own experience in the *Enneads*, at the beginning of IV, 8 (8), *On the descent of the soul into bodies*, Plotinus writes a single long sentence, so characteristic of his tendency to articulate a complex thought in a unified and integrated way:

> Often have I woken up to myself out of the body and entered into myself, outside of other things, seeing a beauty of great wonder and trusting that then above all I belonged to the greater part, activating a best life and coming to identity with the divine, having been *seated* [*hidrytheis*] in it, coming to that actuality, *seating myself* [*hidrysas*] above every other intelligible object, after that rest in the divine when I come down to reasoning from Intellect, I am at a loss how I ever came down, and how my soul has come to be in the body when she is what she has shown herself to be in herself. (IV, 8 [6] 1, 1–11)

Porphyry tells us in his *Life of Plotinus* that Plotinus had genuine mystical experiences, and this passage seems to capture both the unity and perplexity of such experiences for Plotinus himself. Of course, "god" is not only, above all, the One, but also intellect and soul (see part I, passage 6 above); even our intellects Plotinus calls divine, or the "god" within. This passage, then, could describe union with intellect, but the phrase "above every other intelligible object" indicates that Plotinus probably is speaking of mystical union with the One. The active and the passive moments of such experience are evident in the active and passive participles of the verb "to seat" (*hidryein*), and there is a tension between entry into a deeper selfhood and yet the perplexity that one can find oneself back in ordinary, bodily consciousness. In other works, Plotinus links some of these elements to the experience of intellect itself, which must give up its intellectual nature, "walk backwards" (in III, 8; cf. VI, 9 [9] 11, 17–27), "veil itself from other things." In V, 5 (32) 7, for instance, on the basis of an analysis of light, which cannot be grasped as an object but is the medium and power in which every-

---

be experience without interpretation? There is, therefore, no simple dividing line between literature, experience, mystical theology, or philosophy, etc. On the other hand, what sort of experience does the mystic claim to recount? Is it just a deeper experience of nature, like some drug-induced experiences, or a pantheistic union (everything is god) or panenhenic (all in oneness), or in Plotinus' case, is it union with soul or intellect or the One? Does the self survive the deepest union (on which see below in this chapter)? For the purposes of this book I shall adopt the approach that Plotinus was a mystic in that he experienced the divine (soul, intellect, and the One) in intensely intimate, genuine unions in which his own perspective was fundamentally changed but which he necessarily expressed in his own ways in the languages available to him at the time. On these issues generally (and more) see B. McGinn, 1994.

thing else is seen, Plotinus argues that to see light as light would therefore be like seeing nothing:

> so intellect, veiling itself from other things, and drawing itself together inward in seeing nothing will look, not at one light in another, but at light alone and pure itself in itself suddenly appearing from itself, so that Intellect is at a loss how it appeared, from outside or within, and when it has gone away will say "it was within and yet it was not within." (V, 5 [32] 7, 31–35)

This need to move beyond one's own perspective to an entirely different vantage point, that of intellect or ultimately of the One, informs many of Plotinus' attempts to break the normal boundaries of language and to indicate the indescribable.

Why should there be this urge for the transcendent? Because, as Plotinus puts it, "the real desire of our soul is for what is greater than herself" (I, 4 [46] 6, 17), though he is also aware that all our experience is double-edged and that even our desire for the Good can sometimes get us into trouble ("for in fact the desire of good often involves the fall into evil," III, 5 [50] 1, 64–5). "The soul naturally then is in love with god and wants to be united with him; it is like the noble love of a noble daughter for her noble father" (VI, 9 [9] 33–4). This love transforms one's entire perspective:

> So then one does not see or distinguish or imagine two, but it is as if one had become someone else and is not oneself... but having come to belong to that is one having joined, as it were, centre to centre. For here too when the centres have come together they are one, but two, when they are separate. In this sense we also speak of "another" now. And that is why the vision is hard to put into words. (VI, 9 [8] 10, 14–20)

Human experience may be inadequate for understanding the intensity of union with the One, but love and friendship give us a sense of real perspectival change, of what it is like, for instance, to belong to another or to experience without self-deception the other's well-being as more important than one's own. Consequently, the approach to the One is not even really contemplation, but

> another kind of seeing, a being out of oneself, a simplifying and giving oneself over and desiring for touch and rest and a thought that seeks in every way to fit itself, if one will see what is in the sanctuary. (VI, 9 [9], 11, 23–25)

Finally, this natural desire of the soul is so real that in some passages it even appears to lift soul or you or me, the perceivers, not only up into intellect (so that she [the soul] becomes intellect) but through intellect to the One. In a striking passage from one of Plotinus' greatest works, VI, 7 [38], *How the multiplicity of Forms came into being, and on the Good*, the person who sees is "carried out of" the beauty of the intelligible world "by the surge of wave of intellect itself and lifted on high by the swell, as it were, one saw suddenly, not seeing how, but the vision fills his eyes with light and has not made him see something else through it, but the light itself was what one sees" (36, 16–21). What is this "swell" or "surge" of Intellect? In the previous chapter Plotinus likens it to a perspectival change:

> . . . it is as if someone entered into a richly decorated house and so beautiful, and inside it contemplated each of the decorations and was astounded before seeing the master of the house, but when he sees the master and takes delight in him not in accordance with the nature of the images, but as worthy of real vision, he lets these things go and looks at him alone from then on, and then, as he looks and does not take his eye away, he no longer sees a sight by the continuity of his vision, but mingles his seeing with what he contemplates, so that what was seen before has already become seeing in him, and he forgets all other objects of vision. (VI, 7 [38] 35, 7–16)

This simplest form of seeing, Plotinus insists, is one "by which intellect looks at what is beyond it by a simple sort of awareness and reception" (35, 21–22). Intellect is no longer "in its right mind," but has to be "drunk on nectar," a "loving intellect" (*nous eron*), and "out of its mind" (*aphrôn*) (35, 23–6): "it is better for it to be drunk with such drunkenness than to be more respectably sober" (35, 26–7). Again, the two moments of activity and passivity are unified in this experience: "then it loves [*eron*], simplified [*haplôtheis*] into enjoyment [*eupatheia*] of fullness" (35, 25–6). In mystical union, therefore, the simplicities of desire, simple touch, openness, even drunkenness, come into a radically new perspective.

This religious side of Plotinus' thought has attracted many readers and yet repelled others (for references for and against see A. H. Armstrong, 1947, repr. 1983, 183–4). A suitable principle for philosophical readers, one might suggest, is to combine charity of interpretation with critical spirit. We do our best to put the most worthy interpretation upon what Plotinus has to say in the context of all the evidence, and even try to understand him in ways that may not be our normal modes of understanding before examining more critically what we may all too easily have failed to understand. In this spirit and on the bases of Porphyry's somewhat hagiographical witness in the *Life* and of the *Enneads* themselves, it is reasonable to suppose that Plotinus did attain to genuine mystical experience and that this experience as presented and argued in the *Enneads* is not merely evidence of aberrant psychology or wish fulfillment.

The precise nature of this experience is another question. (1) Many readers in the first part of the twentieth century (and earlier) tended to see Plotinus' mystical expressions as the failure of reason and the renunciation of the true spirit of Classical Philosophy. (2) A typical interpretation even today is that Plotinus is a pantheist and antirationalist who thought the goal of spiritual life was the renunciation of clear distinctions, as well as of the beauties of this world that alone make us happy, in favour of our own extinction in the nothingness of pure Spirit. Others have seen union with the One in at least another three different ways: (3) either, in close relation to some forms of Hindu thought, as the realization of our preexisting identity with the One—we are the One in reality, the absolute self, and have only to reach this supreme self-realization; or, conversely, (4) as the extinction of soul and individual self in the Absolute; or (5) as a union of love with the transcendent Good in which the self is transformed and unified but not annihilated. Views 1 and 2, as we shall see for ourselves in this book (chapters 3.22 and 3.31), result from a combination of misreadings of the *Enneads*. Views 3, 4, and 5 are much more difficult to pinpoint precisely because of the misleading nature of much of the vocabulary we use; words like *individual* or *self*, for instance, whose status and meanings can be problematic also for Plotinus. Certainly, the reader familiar with the many forms of Hindu and Buddhist thought will find deep resonances in the *Enneads*. But so will the reader familiar with the various traditions of theistic mysticism in the West. Moreover, certain passages from the *Enneads* seem to favour views 3 and 4, while others favour view 5. I think view 5 is best, not least because Plotinus seems to insist that unities "in" the One, as it were, are not annihilated (see chapter 3.28 below) but, beyond this, because it is not at all clear how we are to understand something that is necessarily beyond understanding, that can only be pointed to at best or left to experience.

1.5. Intellect

Intellect (*nous*) and thought or understanding (*noêsis*) in ancient thought generally, and for Plotinus specifically, are not as we think of them in the modern world (i.e., rationality or thinking in a discursive, bit-by-bit way). For the ancients, intellect includes desire (*ordered* desire, as we shall see) and direct, immediate understanding, neither simply subjective nor simply objective, but both together in each other so that every object of understanding is also a subject understanding that object. This understanding is not the sort that has to work things out discursively bit by bit. Intellect's understanding is more like a complete grasp of the whole at one glance. Each part is not only in the whole but *is* the whole, so to speak, just by being itself.

In the hypostasis of intellect many influences coalesce: the Platonic Ideas (or what is truly real in itself), Aristotle's Unmoved Mover from *Metaphysics* XII (see Appendix A, 4); the demiurge, or craftsman, of Plato's *Timaeus* (Appendix A, 3), and Aristotle's active intellect from *De Anima* III, 4–6. What prompts these identifications? Evidently, if the Platonic Ideas are just what they are in virtue of themselves (and not by virtue of anything else), then they must constitute "real being," or "primary" substance, as Aristotle calls the Unmoved Mover (among other things, souls and compounds included). How could one have a "primary substance" that was not a real "subject" and individual in its own right? Intellect must be a subject thinking itself, active and productive in itself, and embracing a world of all intellectual subjects. Plotinus finds historical support for this development partly in Plato's *Sophist,* where being is said to have intelligence and life, and partly through a prolonged meditation upon the nature of intellectual substance, based not only upon Aristotle but upon later Aristotelian interpreters like Theophrastus and Alexander of Aphrodisias as well as upon the Middle Platonists. Above all, this meditation is in the context of Plato's *Timaeus.* In *Metaphysics* XII, 8, Aristotle suggests there may be as many as forty-seven or fifty-five Unmoved Movers to account for the movement of the heavenly spheres. This chapter appears to be a very late addition to his revision of the *Metaphysics* as a whole and its view of a primary Unmoved Mover apparently engaged solely in thinking itself (XII, 7 and 9). Also in XII, 8, Aristotle seems to favour what he calls the ancient view that the divine *embraces* the whole of nature. The most natural questions to ask therefore were these. First, how are all the celestial intelligences related and how do they form a world of primary substance ranged under the supreme intellect? Second, if intellect involves the identity of thinking subject and object thought while a conceptual distinction has to be made between subject and object, and there are many intellects, then surely thought cannot be pure rest but must also involve motion (i.e., spiritual, not spatial motion)? And third, how is this world of intellects related to the physical world?

In Plato's *Timaeus,* of course, Plotinus finds an initial answer to these weighty problems. For there Plato represents a divine craftsman looking to an "eternal paradigm" and then, through the instrumental causality of lesser deities, fashioning a physical universe of soul and body by imposing order upon primeval chaos. Just as this physical universe is a living creature, so too the intelligible world must be "an intelligible living creature" (*Timaeus* 30 c ff., Appendix A, 3).

Plotinus therefore naturally conceives of intellect in the following ways. First, intellect is an intelligible living organism that is a completely realized individual or primary substance organized, on Aristotelian lines, both by itself immanently and by the power of the One transcendentally. It is also the totality of all individual intellects:

> for since its life is intelligent and it is not an incomplete activity [*energeia ouk atelês*] it leaves out none of the things we now find to be a work of intelligence. . . . for the all there is complete or it would not be all—and since life runs over it, or rather is everywhere with it, all things necessarily become living beings . . . (VI, 2 [44] 21, 24–5, 50–2)

Second, as an organic world, intellect cannot be the primary principle of unity, yet it must be a self-thinker (otherwise it would be stupid) and must possess what it thinks from itself. At the same time, it thinks by virtue of the power given to it by the One. In the *Timaeus,* Plato represents the divine craftsman as looking to a paradigm in making the physical universe. Does this paradigm belong to the craftsman or is it beyond him? Plotinus argues in treatise V, 5 (32), *That the Ideas are not outside the intellect and on the One,* that intellect must possess its own intelligible objects, for otherwise they would have to be brought in from outside, and then intellect would not be a thinker in virtue of itself. So for Plotinus the "paradigm" becomes intellect's vision of the One as its own thought. We should remember that this thought (*noêsis*)—often translated as "intellection" or "understanding"—differs from ordinary thought, for it does not involve inferences or words but is immediately its own objects—that is, the causes or paradigms of everything else, whether ordinary human thought or natural objects:

> . . . [the One] will be an object of thought to intellect, but in itself neither thinker nor object of thought will it strictly be; for the object of thought is object for something else, and intellect has its intellectual effort of apprehension empty if it does not grasp and comprehend the object it thinks; for it does not have thinking without the object of thought. (V, 6 [24] 2, 8–12)

Intellect, therefore, is self-thinker, a productive demiurge, and yet because its vision comes to it from the One, its "search" for its own substance simultaneously expresses its dependence upon and derivation from the One:

> . . . the first is simple, and we give thinking to what comes from another and the search, as it were, for its own substance and its self and what made it . . . (VI, 7 [38] 37, 18–20)

Third, intellect is a whole of living intellects (its "parts"), while the whole not only contains the parts but is implicit in each (cf. VI, 2 [44] 20). If this were not so, then a part of substance would not be substance itself, and substance would be composed of nonsubstances, which would be a contradiction in terms. So Plotinus often describes the teeming life of intellect as one of pure transparent understanding in which individual identity is enhanced precisely because the individual also manifests the whole. In treatise V, 8 (32), *On the intelligible beauty* (included in this book) Plotinus writes:

> . . . all things are transparent, and there is nothing dark or resistant, but everything is transparent to everything right to the inmost and all things, for light is transparent to light. Indeed, everything has all things in itself and sees all things in turn in every other, so that all are everywhere and each and every one is all. . . . A different thing stands out in each, but in each all are manifest. (V, 8 [32] 4, 4–11)

In intellect, therefore, individual identity is increased to its intelligible maximum by being the medium of all other identities. One is most oneself by being or manifesting all others. As Plotinus says elsewhere, intellect is "an all-face thing shining with living faces" (VI, 7 [38] 15, 26). Or again, in a fascinating discussion whether or not souls will employ reasoning (*logimos*) in the intelligible world, Plotinus concludes that if reasoning is only a deficiency of understanding (i.e., trying to put things together bit by bit because we cannot grasp them whole), then souls will not use such reasoning. But if reasoning is a "steady disposition" and a "reflection" of intellect, it will be a part of intelligible life:

> For here too we can know many things just by the look of the eyes when people are silent; but there their whole body is clear ... and each is like an eye, and nothing is hidden or artificial, but before one speaks to another the other sees and known. (IV, 3 [27] 18, 19–22)

Implicit in the above, a fourth consequence of Plotinus' view of intellect is that he insists upon Forms of individuals. Socrates must be himself in the intelligible and not a universal or somebody else altogether (cf. V, 7 [18]; and 3.21 below). Nonetheless, while the divine intellect is infinite in power, the total number of Forms is finite (unlike Amelius, Plotinus' colleague, who supposed them to be infinite), presumably so that intellect's content is knowable. How metempsychosis is to be figured into this and what Plotinus means by individuality are more difficult questions still.

Finally, although intellect is a nonspatial and nontemporal unity, if thought necessarily involves both rest and motion, then intellect can be represented in its relation to the One or in itself as an unfolding activity of different moments, such as Being-Life-Intellect. It can be represented further in terms of the "five greatest kinds" or intelligible categories, which Plotinus takes from Plato's *Sophist:* being, rest, sameness, otherness, and motion. These are each distinct and yet interwoven with one another. Plotinus says that intellect's rest in relation to the One made being (*to on*), but its vision in relation to itself (or the One) made intellect (*nous*) (V, 2 [11] 1 [cited above]). Sometimes Plotinus represents being as the first moment of Intellect's own unfolding, a moment of remaining or abiding fixed in its source that then must be unpacked by the internal movement of Intellect's self-generative thought. Being, rest, sameness, motion, and otherness become integral features of such articulation, though Plotinus—like Plato—generally avoids rigid terminology. Hence:

> ... since being is the most firmly set of all things ... it has made rest exist. ... It is that in which thinking comes to a stop. ... And again the idea at rest is the limit of intellect, and Intellect is its movement. (VI, 2 [43] 8, 23–25)

Or again:

> Is not being, then, unified number, and beings number unfolded, and Intellect number moving in itself, and the living creature [of the *Timaeus*] number embracing everything? (VI, 6 [34] 4, 29–31)

Here Plotinus thinks of unified being as being unfolded into the multiple beings and then contained within Intellect's own internal motion and yet reaching down to embrace all life inclusively. The term *life* does not appear in the above passage, but it is prominent in others. For example, "for the activity of life ... pours itself forth as from a fountainhead" (III, 8 [30] 10). Life is the movement of Intellect:

> And he who takes a close look at this multiple power calls it "substance," according as it is a this, a kind of substrate, then calls it "movement," insofar as one sees it as life, then "rest" insofar as it is altogether unchangingly itself, "other" and "same" insofar as these are altogether one. (III, 7 [45] 3, 7–11)

Finally, then, the movement or life of intellect is what unites its doubleness (subject and object) and results in both unity and variety:

> But if something is not going to go forth to something else, it will be at rest; but when it is completely at rest, it will not think. That which thinks, therefore, when it thinks, must be in twos, and either one must be outside the other or both must be in the same, and thought must be always in otherness and necessarily too in sameness. . . . and yet again each of the things being thought brings out together with it this sameness and otherness; or what will one think that does not have one and the other? (V, 3 [49] 10, 21–9)

These passages together will provide a quick sketch of how Plotinus combines elements of his Platonic and Aristotelian heritage in new ways with his own ongoing philosophical meditations.

1.6. Soul and the sensible world

Soul is the great intermediary between the intelligible and sensible worlds, but she is also a hypostasis in her own right, part of the intelligible realm yet also a product, or "utterance" (*logos*), of Intellect, just as Intellect is an utterance of the One (cf. 3.7 below). Soul is not only the direct animator of the sensible world; she is a living organism in her own right. Less unified than intellect, she is an "all soul" from which come the World soul, responsible for the generation and maintenance of the whole physical world, and all the individual souls with their full range of individual faculties, from intellectual to reproductive and nutritive capacities. Everything below the level of soul is the product of soul and of her content, the *logoi* or forming principles that govern and are expressed in the development of all physical entities (on *logos* see especially 3.7 and 3.9 below). Namely these are matter itself (on matter see below in this chapter and also 3.8; 4.13), the living body of the sensible world, and all living and even nonliving things. In Plotinus' treatment of soul, Plato's influence is predominant, especially from the *Timaeus, Phaedo, Republic, Symposium,* and *Phaedrus.* But it includes many Aristotelian and Stoic elements too. In fact, Plotinus' treatment of the soul-body relation is so original that it overcomes the tension between the so-called "dualism" of some forms of Platonic thought and the "entelechism" of Aristotle in a way that deserves much better attention than it has ever received (see also chapters 1.8 and 2.6).

How is the hypostasis of soul to be understood? How is soul at once naturally spiritual and yet the animator of a physical universe? How are our souls related to the "all soul"? What is the difference between the World soul's relation to its body and that of individual souls? These are just some of the questions that immediately spring to mind. Against the Stoics, Plotinus argues that soul is not a body; rather, it is the animating form of a body (IV, 7 [2]); against the Aristotelians, he argues that soul cannot be simply the "entelechy" or active form of a body corrupted along with the body because this would force us to introduce a second entelechy, or form, to account for its intellectual nature (IV, 7 [2] 8[5]). For economy's sake and to avoid a plurality of animating forms, we should rather suppose that soul is the animating form of a body in the sense that she is a substance (not a quality or quantity) and immortal in her own right.

If soul is a substance, however, then Plotinus would seem to be committed to the rather strange view that all souls are one (a view rejected by Neoplatonists after Porphyry and one that seems contrary to common-sense experience). Nonetheless, Plotinus develops the idea of soul as substance in several works (IV, 9 [8]; VI, 4 [22] 4; IV, 3 [27] 1–8) and insists it does not commit him to an identity of experience in different souls. Our historical experience is different not only because our souls are different but also because we are different "composites" of soul and body. Differences between souls too, he argues, are perfectly compatible with soul's unity because soul is a "one and many" containing all differences within herself. After posing the problem of the absurdity of "my soul" and someone else's being one, Plotinus replies as follows:

> First, then, it is not the case that if my soul and that of another are one, my composite and the composite of another are just on that account the same. For when something is the same in one thing and in another it will not have the same experiences in each. . . . it is certainly not necessary that when I perceive another should have exactly the same experience. For not even in the one body does one hand perceive the experience of the other, but the soul in the whole body . . . and one should reflect also that there are many things the whole being does not notice, even of what happens in one and the same body. (IV, 9 [8] 2)

So there can be diversity of experience and yet a larger unity of which we are unconscious, just as on a lower level we are unconscious of most of what happens in our own bodies. In subsequent chapters Plotinus goes on to argue that this theory is compatible with the division of soul into rational and irrational parts as well as into different faculties. All souls are one in the sense that the many come from the one:

> How, then, is there one substance in many souls? Either the one is present as a whole in them all or the many come from that one soul which remains in herself. That soul, then, is one but the many are related to this as giving herself to multiplicity and not giving herself; for she is sufficient to provide herself to all and to remain one; for she can extend to all simultaneously and is

---

5. Cf. Syrianus, *In Met*, 147, 2–6.

> not at all cut off from each; the same therefore in many . . . for knowledge is a whole, and its parts are such that the whole remains and the parts come from it. And the soul is a whole, and the parts come from it, into which it naturally divides, and part is a whole and the whole remains an undiminished whole—but matter divided it—and all the parts are one. (IV, 9 [8] 5, 1–11)

Soul, therefore, is not divisible like a physical mass but is more like scientific knowledge or even biological development in the sense that a particular theorem implies potentially the whole body of knowledge of which it is a part (cf. IV, 9, 5, 12 ff.). In a similar way, biological development contains its own implicate order in which part and whole possess implicit mutual relations: bodies do not haphazardly spring up outside of determinate environments but unfold out of a pattern in the fertilized seed as whole organisms structured and organized by the design, the DNA, or soul-principle immanent therein. Just because the soul-principle is present to a particular part does not mean that she stops being soul. Further, just because our souls are ours, this does not mean they stop being soul as a whole—though clearly this presents major problems for the issue of individual identity.

How then is soul internally related? Plotinus adapts Plato's account of the making of soul in the *Timaeus* (see Appendix A, 3). Soul's substance has a nature to be both indivisible and yet divided about bodies. Soul herself does not get divided, but rather bodies and matter are responsible for the dividing in the sense that they receive what they can; different levels of organic and inorganic complexity relate to the whole soul in different ways. Plotinus often cites the famous saying from the *Timaeus* (36 a) that soul is not "in" body, but body rather "in" soul. Soul is the more comprehensive, indivisible presence, though experience and habit may suggest the reverse. He writes:

> Then "out of the indivisible and that which is divided about bodies" [Plato, *Timaeus* 35 a] is the same as saying that the soul is composed out of a part which is above and a part attached from there which has flowed up to these things here, like a line from a centre. But when she has come here in this part see how she keeps the nature of the whole in this same part. For not even here is she only divisible, but also indivisible; for what is divided of her is indivisibly divided. For she gives herself to the whole body and is not divided by giving herself to the whole and is divided by being present in every part. (IV, 1 [21] 14–22)

This "indivisible division" even in the sensible world means for Plotinus that "atomism" or "materialism" are false theories that cannot account for the organization of bodies. Only a holistic psychological paradigm can do this (an Aristotelian theory that Plotinus develops particularly in the early chapters of VI, 7 [38] in terms of the psychic power to animate bodies). In effect, soul is a different sort of energy or dimension than body. In *On the substance of the soul,* IV 2 (4), Plotinus puts this in the following way:

In the bodies in which she comes to be, then, even if she comes to be in the largest and that extended over all, by giving herself to the whole she does not abandon being one. She is not one in the sense in which body is one; for body is one by continuity, but each of its parts are different from one another and in different places. Nor is she one in the sense in which quality is. But the nature at once divisible and indivisible is not one as the continuous is one, but is divisible in that she is in all the parts in which she is, but indivisible in that she is present as a whole in all the parts and in any one part of it as a whole. And he who clearly sees this magnitude of the soul and sees her power will know what a divine and wondrous thing she is and that she belongs to those natures that are beyond things. (IV, 2 [4] 1, 57–69)

A consequence of this view is that soul is omnipresent (so too and even more so is being and, of course, the One). Plotinus pursues further the "presence of being, one and the same, everywhere as a whole" in very interesting ways in VI, 4–5 (22–23). Another consequence of his overall view is the theory that even our own souls have not entirely descended, but something of them remains even in the intelligible world (see IV, 8 [6] 8, 1 ff.; and among other passages on the descent of the soul, IV, 8, 6; IV, 3 [27] 13–15). Plotinus expressly realizes this is a controversial theory all of his own, and the later Neoplatonists, incidentally, rejected it.[6]

1.7. The World soul and individual souls

Granted that this is soul's nature, how does my soul differ from the World soul? Does Plotinus have a positive view of the soul-body relation and of the physical world in general? How does the soul fall, and is her fall different from her descent? Is the very fact of descending into the sensible world a fall, or does the fall of soul involve something more than descent? And, finally, how do bodies and matter fit into this picture?

The World soul, Plotinus says, is our elder "sister," with a different relation to body than our own:

> ... there is a difference between souls, and the more still in that the [world] soul has not separated herself from the whole soul, but remained there and put on the body about her, while the individual souls, since body already exists, received their portions under the rule of their sister soul, so to speak, as if she had already prepared dwellings for them. There is also a difference in that she looks to the whole of intellect, while the individual souls rather to their own partial intellects. (IV, 3 [27] 6, 11–17)

So there is a difference of focus and even of degree of power among souls (as also of character). Consequently, souls have different relations to their bodies. In

---

6.   See, for example, Proclus, *In Tim.* III, 333, 28 ff., *Elements of Theology,* 211. All Neoplatonists, except Theodorus of Asine, a pupil of Iamblichus. Cf. Wallis, 1972, 95 ff.

the heavenly bodies, or "gods," according to Plotinus, the matter is totally mastered by the form; there is no indefiniteness or indetermination about them (see V, 8 [31] 3 below), whereas in our case our much greater focus upon the body, and even our identification with the body, means that our focus is permeated by materiality—that is, a divided and ultimately corruptible existence. For Plotinus, "it is a function of greater power not to be affected in what it makes; and power comes from remaining above" (IV, 3 [27] 6, 22–4). Consequently, the World soul "makes by remaining in herself, and the things she makes come to her, while the particular souls themselves go to the things" (ibid., 24–5). Plotinus admits a variety of reasons for differences among individual souls:

> They become different either because of the variety of bodies into which they have entered or because of their fortunes or upbringing or they themselves bear the difference with them, or all of these or some of them. And some of them have become altogether subject to destiny here, but others are sometimes subject and sometimes they belong to themselves, while others accept all that it is necessary to bear but are able to belong to themselves in all that is their own work. (IV, 3 [27] 15, 7–14)

1.8. Soul-body

"To be unaffected," for Plotinus, does not mean "not to care for." Rightly or wrongly, Plotinus is of the view that souls care more for what is in their charge by remaining themselves than by identifying themselves wholly with material existence (on impassibility, see chapter 2.2). Porphyry's opening statement in the *Life* that Plotinus "seemed ashamed of being in the body" perhaps reflects Porphyry's own preoccupations rather than Plotinus'. Whatever the case, the wish to escape body represents only one aspect of what is a multidimensional view of body in Platonism generally. An integral soul-body relation for Plotinus is not one in which soul forfeits her own nature for the sake of body but one in which body attains to its own proper and most healthy functioning for the sake of the soul.[7] The healthy person, soul and body, is free and able to be freely at the service of his or her fellows. By contrast, "the sick person, concerned with the cares of the body, is at the service of the body and belongs to it" (IV, 3 [27] 4, 35–7). Plotinus uses the following analogy to describe the integral soul-body relation in the sensible world:

> Certainly there came into being a beautiful and richly varied house, as it were, not cut off from the maker; nor did she give it a share in her either; but the maker considered it all everywhere worthy of care that is useful to its

---

7.   Cf. *Republic* 519 6-e. For Porphyry, compare Augustine's critique (*City of God,* books 13 and 22) of the phrase *omne corpus fugiendum* (one must flee every body) and, for example, book 22, 26.

own being and beauty, insofar as it can participate in being but does him no harm in his presiding over it, for he rules over it by remaining above. It is ensouled in this way, having a soul that does not belong to it, but is present to it, ruled but not ruling, possessed but not possessing. For the world lies in soul that holds it up and nothing is without share of soul. (IV, 3 [27] 9, 29–38)

It is not possible, Plotinus argues, even to draw a simple hard and fast boundary between animate and inanimate things since "they do not show the soul they have" (VI, 7 [38] 11, 58–60) but bear a hidden, dynamic relation to soul since they can only be understood by virtue of the *logoi* or forming principles that are part of soul's content (cf. part I, passage 9).

In general, therefore, to determine where soul stops and body begins is no easy task in Plotinus, precisely because soul embraces the whole of body and because body reaches right into soul in the sense that since body also is a "form" it also finds its home in intellect. If we adopt too rigid a view of physical nature, we might read with surprise Plotinus' remarkable statement that the intelligible living creature had to be complete "and there are bodies there also since there is matter and quality" (VI, 2 [43] 21, 52–3). Or again, in a previously cited passage about what kind of reasoning we might expect in the intelligible world, Plotinus says that if reasoning means a "steady . . . reflection" of Intellect, then reasoning will be employed there. He adds that "there *all their body is clear* and pure and each is like an eye" (IV, 3 [27] 18, 20). This may look like a sudden lapse, the mistake of a scurrying calamos (pen), or seem as if we found ourselves in a Christian treatise on the nature of the glorified (i.e., resurrected) body. But in fact it is Plotinus we are reading and these remarks should also be taken into account.

1.9. Providence, freedom, and matter

As we shall see in the rest of this book (cf. 2.6), Plotinus has a positive view of the soul-body relation and of the goodness of the physical world. He certainly emphasized individual, free agency and the compatibility of providence with both freedom and fate. The work of the temperate person, for instance, is not "by providence," because it is done "by himself, but in accordance with providence" (III, 3 [48] 5, 48–50).[8] At the same time, Plotinus emphasizes that we are entirely unaware of most of who we are—not only of what goes on in our own bodies but of what our own lives really are, of past lives, and also of the teeming life of soul and intellect. After Plato, Plotinus is the rediscoverer of the unconscious and the preconscious. The world of intellect and soul, although a world of thought and understanding, precedes historical consciousness even if its presence makes our time-bound consciousness possible.

Given Plotinus' emphasis upon the active and passive aspects of procession

---

8.   On the question of providence, read III, 2–3 (47–48) and on fate III, 1 (3).

and conversion, clearly no single viewpoint is sufficient for authentic humanity or self-hood. The self, or *we* (*hêmeis*), one of Plotinus' favourite words for the self, is not only essentially dialogical and inclusive, it also manifests considerable range, as does Plotinus' notion of the human body (as we shall see in chapter 2). Plotinus has no difficulty seeing things multidimensionally precisely because he thinks in terms of varied multiplicity in unity and vice versa. Consequently, causality for him can be highly varied when we speak about all the different influences, for instance, on the makeup of character or events (cf. IV, 4 [28] 30–9; III, 1 [3]; V, 7 [18]; II, 1 [40]; IV, 3 [27] 15 1 ff.).

Nowhere is this multidimensional perspective more pronounced than in the problem of determining the good, the not-so-good, and the evil in the sensible world. Toward the end of the second of his major works on providence, Plotinus says:

> . . . since the universe is a living creature one who contemplates the things that come to be in it contemplates at the same time both its origins and the providence that watches over it; this indeed extends over all things including the things that come to be; and these are both living creatures and their actions and mixed dispositions "compounded of reason and necessity" [cf. Plato, *Timaeus* 47 e–48 a]; so he contemplates things that are mixed and continually go on being mixed; and he himself is not able to thoroughly distinguish providence and what is in accordance with providence on the one hand and again the substrate and all it gives to what comes from it. To do this is not the work of a man, except of some wise and divine man; or one might say that "a god would have this privilege." (III, 3 [48] 6, 8–17; the quotation at the end is from Simonides, as quoted in Plato, *Protagoras* 341 e 3)

First, Plotinus insists that providence extends to everything. This implicitly opposes the Epicurean denial of providence and Alexander of Aphrodisias' restriction of providence to the effects of the regular movements of the heavenly bodies; for Alexander providence does not extend to sublunary individuals (cf. R. Sharples, 1987). For Plotinus providence safeguards everything, no matter how humble, yet individuals and events can be free, depending upon circumstances, determining chains of causality, and so forth, and they are certainly complex (cf. III, 3 [48] 5). Second, from this complex nexus of causality (providence, what happens in accordance with providence, reason, fate or necessity, and the substrate) there emerges a sort of bipolar opposition: what comes from above (i.e., the form, providence, etc.) and what comes from the substrate (i.e., the matter, or "underlying thing"). The nature of matter is a problem in Plotinus' philosophy because of his identification of matter with evil, and I shall here take up the questions, first, of the generation of matter itself and, second, of the fall of soul and its consequences. The obvious questions in this context are how in a perfect intelligible world *could* soul fall, and if matter is generated by soul, then how is matter evil while soul is not?

1.10. The generation of matter

Matter is the lowest level in the Plotinian hierarchy. Sensible or lower matter is a reflection of the perfectly formed matter in the intelligible universe and of the matter in soul (Plotinus admits a distinction between intelligible form and matter; cf. II, 4 [12] 5). It is positively formed in bodies but in itself is absence, non-being, or privation (see part I, passage 8). Lowest matter, then, is a negative final shadow of being, formless, totally indeterminate, and neither space nor mass, but the principle of spatial extension in the sense that extension and dispersion in space are due to matter. So matter is positive in one way as formed, but negative in its own nature.[9]

This lower matter is generated by the partial soul or by the "soul in plants" (III, 4 [15] 1; this is the only relatively unambiguous account in the whole of the *Enneads* [see Part I, passage 3 a, above], namely, IV, 8 [6] 6). In III, 4 Plotinus tells us that when the soul that possesses the power of growth "comes to be" in plants it produces "no longer a form of soul . . . but absolute indefiniteness" (1, 1–12). There is indefiniteness before this, but it is always indefiniteness "in form" (13). He concludes the chapter with a rather strange statement: this absolute indefiniteness "is perfected and becomes a body taking a form appropriate to its potentiality, a receptacle for the principle that generated it and reared it up" (14–16). We might make three comments on this passage. First, "absolute indefiniteness" means lowest matter. Other passages are ambiguous on this question, but III, 4, 1 is not (cf. V, 1 [10] 7, 47–8; V, 2 [11] 1, 18–27; IV, 3 [27] 9, 20–6; II, 3 [52] 18, 10–13; II, 3 [52] 17, 21–5; III, 9 [13] 3; I, 8 [51] 14, 27–51). Second, there are other forms of indefiniteness, and they are important to keep in mind: forms of indefiniteness in soul and intellect (and from the One). Third, "absolute indefiniteness" nonetheless possesses a capacity for perfection to be in a certain way raised up into form; to this degree, matter's perfection is apparently compatible with its destitution in itself.

On the basis of this passage (and others), the generation of matter is clearly not evil in itself. To illuminate or to cast a shadow is not a fault. The fault rather lies with what is illuminated: "matter spreads itself out under soul and is illuminated and cannot take the source from which it is illuminated" (I, 8 [51] 14, 38–39).

---

9.   If you find this puzzling, please see my more detailed treatments of this question in chapters 3 and 4 and read what Plotinus says in II, 4 (12); II, 5 (25); III 6 (26); and I, 8 (15).

1.11. The descent and fall of soul

How then does soul fall if its descent is natural and in no sense evil?[10] Plotinus sometimes speaks of the "audacity" (*tolma*) that even intellect should separate itself from the One. But the derivation of intellect and soul and the descent of soul to make, organize, and care for the physical world are good and for the perfection of the whole, as we saw above (1.–1.8 and part I, passages 4–6). The audacity of souls, by content, is the forgetfulness of god, ignorance of themselves, the wish to belong to themselves and to be independent and as far from the intelligible as possible. Plotinus poses the question himself at the beginning of *On the three primary hypostases:*

> What is it then that has made the souls forget their father, god, and not to know both themselves and him though they are portions that come from there and altogether belong to him? The beginning of evil for them was audacity and coming to birth and the first otherness and the wishing to belong to themselves. Since they were clearly delighted in their independence and made much use of their self-motion, running the opposite direction and making as much distance as possible, they were ignorant that they themselves come from there, just as children torn at birth from their parents and long brought up far away know not who they or their parents are. (V, 1 [10] 1, 1–10)

Plotinus connects the fall of the soul with descent, therefore, but descent in an intensified form, namely the wish to belong only to oneself and to put as much distance as possible between the whole of being and what one takes oneself to be. Soul's fall is effectively the exclusion of being and the embrace of non-being in the sense that one wants to exclude intelligible being and cramp oneself into a kind of vanishing point. What we nowadays call the ego is for Plotinus a weakened form of being dangerously close to being nothing at all. The ego cannot belong only to itself, when the very nature of the self is to be a "we" in several dimensions simultaneously. In *On what are and whence come evils*, a late major work on the problem of evil, Plotinus puts this in the following ways:

> Matter darkened the illumination and the light from there by mixture and made it weak by providing generation and the cause of coming to it; for she would not have come to what is not present. And this is the fall of soul, to come in this way to matter and to become weak, because all her powers are not present since the matter prevents them from actualization by taking up the place that the soul holds and, so to speak, making her all cramped together. (I, 8 [51] 14, 40–48)

The ultimate cause of soul's fall, Plotinus concludes, is the constricting force

---

10. On these questions in the *Hermetica* and in Gnostic writings, see generally A. J. Festugière, vol. 3, 1953; D. O'Brien, 1993; J. Zandee, 1961.

of non-being on anything that enters into its negative field and comes to identify with it. Matter, in this sense, is a field of pure negativity that feeds off the power of the darkened soul and progressively restricts the soul's natural ability to turn back to her source so that she is even content to be in a prison of her own making. The source of evil is therefore non-being, but non-being in the sense that the absence of what might or should be present (limitation, ignorance, lack of thought or consideration, etc.) can have devastating consequences in ordinary experience.[11]

1.12. Nature, contemplation, eternity, and time

Of course, the fall of the soul is only one perspective, however significant, in Plotinus' much broader viewpoint. Bodies not only decay and die; individual souls do not always prefer blinkers. Bodies emerge as whole interrelated form-matter complexes capable, either more or less, of expressing understanding, thought, love, and the diversities of soul's nature. For Plotinus generally, if we take a material view of body, then bodies are qualities or accidents in matter (see, for example, VI, 3 [44] 8; II, 7 [37] 3); if we take a more formal view, then they are productive forms making the matter into definite things (e.g., II, 7 [37] 3; VI, 7 [38] 4–5). Plotinus' different viewpoints involve much from Aristotle, and we shall take a closer look at this in chapters 2 and 3 (on I, 1 and III, 8). The soul too is distinguished into higher and lower soul in rather different ways: the distinction is sometimes between soul as a hypostasis and partial souls; sometimes between the separate soul, present to the individual compound, and the soul in the compound (cf. chapter 2 below); and sometimes between soul as a hypostasis and nature as a lower soul-principle at work in the universe (as in III, 8, chapter 3 below).

In III, 8 Plotinus develops the view that generation, both intelligible and sensible, as well as action (*praxis*) and artistic production (*poiêsis*), are all forms or consequences of living contemplation (*theôria*). Here, as we shall see, he represents nature as a kind of vegetative contemplative activity that produces physical forms spontaneously from her contemplation. Nature is a formative principle (*logos*) and she collaborates with the individual "natures" or formative principles in living organisms to account for the development of bodies. Our individual souls, however, have a broader range than nature, for they also include the higher faculties. This results in a complex view of the nexus of formative principles at work in the individual organism. But it also results in a dynamic view of the relation between intelligible and sensible realities: action and production are the unfolding of intense contemplation. We make in order to see. Living insight, before we start to reason about things, is the spontaneous creative force that has made and is making everything around us entirely without discursive planning or deliberation. Our arts

---

11. For more on matter see 3.8 below, on evil 4.11.

or sciences are attempts to capture in various extended modes the intensive, non-extended unity of intelligible seeing or contemplation.

This way of thinking is very much connected with Plotinus' views of eternity and time, which he develops in relation to Plato's *Timaeus* (Appendix A, 3) as well as with reference to the theories of Aristotle, the Stoics, and the Epicureans in III, 7 (45), *On eternity and time* (see Part I, passage 10). Plotinus defines eternity as "the life that belongs to being (*to on*) and is in being (*en tôi einai*), all together and full, completely without extension" (III, 7, 3, 36–8). He defines time as "the life of soul in a movement of passage from one way of life to another" (III, 7, 11, 43–5). Eternity, of course, is a life also founded upon the One. Plotinus, as we shall see in III, 8 (30), conceives this dynamically to a point that scholars have thought to border upon the incoherent (e.g., III, 8, 11, 23–4: "and intellect is always desiring and always attaining what it desires") (on this see chapter 3). Time is the "image of eternity," and this means that in generating the sensible world soul unfolds in successive stages what is completely present without extension in the intelligible world. Soul's production of time is like unfolding a single strand of reality reflected from an immense totality and unfolding that trajectory into a sequence of tenses: a "this after this." As Plotinus puts it,

> all things therefore existed already and existed always and existed in such a way that one could say later "this after that"; for when it is drawn out and unfolded, as it were, it can display this after that, but when it is altogether it is all this. (VI, 7 [38] 1, 54–7)

1.13. Plotinus, the reader

Finally, in this introductory overview, I will say a few words about Plotinus, the reader, for in reading Plotinus we enter into his own reading—that is, his reflection upon all those earlier influences, which though long dead, continue to live in his words. What sort of reader was Plotinus? An answer to this question will help us to read him with greater care and attention.

In his *Life of Plotinus,* Porphyry says:

> In writing he is concise and full of thought. He puts things shortly and abounds more in ideas than in words; he generally expresses himself in a tone of rapt inspiration, and states what he himself really feels about the matter and not what has been handed down by tradition. His writings, however, are full of concealed Stoic and Peripatetic doctrines. Aristotle's *Metaphysics*, in particular, is concentrated in them. He had a complete knowledge of geometry, arithmetic, mechanics, optics and music, but was not disposed to apply himself to detailed research in these subjects. In the meetings of the school he used to have the commentaries read, perhaps of Severus, perhaps of Cronius or Numenius or Gaius or Atticus, and among the Peripatetics of Aspasius, Alexander, Adrastus, and others that were available. But he did not just speak

straight out of these books but took a distinctive personal line in his consideration [*idios . . . kai exêllagmenos en têi theoriai*] and brought the mind of Ammonius to bear on the investigations in hand. He quickly absorbed what was read, and would give the sense of some profound subject of study in a few words and pass on. (14, 1–18; trans. A. H. Armstrong)

This passage reveals, as Armstrong has observed, how scholarly and professional a philosopher Plotinus was and how he worked (Loeb I, 40–1). Severus, Gaius, and Atticus were Middle Platonist commentators on Plato of the second century A.D. Albinus, a pupil of Gaius, is the most important of the Middle Platonist philosophers. Atticus was the chief representative of the anti-Aristotelian Platonist group. Cronius and Numenius are usually classed as Neo-Pythagoreans, but here they are naturally included among the Platonists. What distinguishes Middle Platonists from Neo-Pythagoreans is more a matter of convention than substance. Numenius was of major importance, and Plotinus was even accused of plagiarizing him (*Life,* 17). Aspasius and Adrastus were second-century A.D. commentators upon Aristotle, and Alexander of Aphrodisias, head of the Peripatetic School of Athens at the beginning of the third century, was the most influential of all the Aristotelian commentators. The "mind of Ammonius" indicates the influence of Plotinus' teacher Ammonius Saccas, about whom we know little or nothing, but his mind must have been powerful, for Plotinus was clearly a profound, precise, but transformative reader and thinker. He quickly sums up his reading and moves on, taking a distinctive personal line. He is not a commentator but a philosopher. I suggest then that Plotinus is not the sort of thinker or reader in whose writings one can always discern simple one-on-one correspondences. His thought is many-layered in that his transformative readings form a varied and condensed background to the very way he thinks. They are full of Aristotelian, Stoic, and Peripatetic, as well as Platonic problems, puzzles, hints, and allusions but in such a way that you would not notice this at first if you were not aware of it.

This is a major part of the difficulty in reading Plotinus. Just like his intelligible world, the whole of his philosophy often seems implicit in each and every sentence. Or again, his use of words (*substance* [*ousia*], for instance) itself seems multilayered, as though all of the word's current and past meanings are in process of being transformed. Intellect can mean the divine intellect, the intellect of soul, or our individual intellects, and only the context discloses which meaning is appropriate. Reading and writing in the *Enneads*, therefore, are part of a richly varied but subtle and often hidden dialogue.

When one first reads Plotinus, his writings may look like straightforward treatises, even monologues. Before long, however, one becomes aware of an internal dialogue, questioning and answering itself. Other voices enter in major and minor keys, often subliminally, and only such indications as "and we shall reply to someone who held that view" reveal the presence of hidden interlocutors (e.g., II, 9 [33] 3). What sort of dialogue is this? Even contemporary scholars have disagreed. The great Italian translator of Plotinus, V. Cilento, thought that Plotinus' writings were like Cynic diatribes (i.e., one-half of a Platonic dialogue) (1967, 29–41), whereas the contemporary French scholar Marie-Odile Goulet-Cazé thinks their dialectical character reflects actual conversations in the school (*Porphyre: La vie de Plotin,* Paris, I, 1980, 231 ff.). I am decidedly in favour of the latter view, but you shall have to judge for yourself. By way of introduction I shall say only this: Plotinus' philosophy is inherently dialectical; it invariably involves a "we." That is to say, it is a conversation between friends. Other voices also intrude on that immediate conversation, and sometimes Plotinus adapts something of what they have to say as is own. Ways of speaking that may be "audacious," for instance, may nonetheless provide a means of getting at the truth (cf. VI, 8 [39] 7, 11 ff.; VI, 9 [9] 10, 13). The rather violent sophist, Thrasymachus, with Glaukon and Adeimantus, from Plato's *Republic,* makes no dramatic appearance. But Plato's view that discourse always has to be tested (as in the famous phrase of the *Seventh Letter,* "each of them being refuted in well-meaning refutations in a process of questioning and answering without envy" [344 b], or at each stage of Diotima's ladder of ascent in the *Symposium*; see Appendix A, 1 below) is fundamental to Plotinus' notion of philosophical conversation.

In the last of his works presented in this book, V, 8 (31), Plotinus emphasizes that the approach to union with intellect and the One involves thorough preparation, critical discernment, and transformation. To understand in this sense is not to look at an object from outside or to observe spectacular effects but to become completely different,

> and one must, in coming to learn about the god, remain within an imprint of him and exercise discrimination in seeking him [i.e., the god] to determine what he is entering into; and when he has learned in good faith that he is entering into the most blessed thing, he must already give himself to what is within and become, instead of one who sees, already an object of vision of another who contemplates him shining out with such thoughts as come from there. (V, 8 [31] 11, 13–19)

Chapter 2

Plotinus' Anthropology

Text: Ennead I, 1 (53): What Is the Living Creature and What Is the Human Being?

1. Pleasures and pains, fears and assurances, desires and aversions, and suffering—to what subject do they belong?[1] For they either belong to the soul or to soul using body or to some third thing made up from both. And this can also be taken in two ways, to mean either the mixture or another [5] different thing resulting from the mixture. And in fact the same is true of what comes to be as a result of these emotions, both actions or opinions. And so we must examine both discursive reason and opinion in order to determine whether they belong to the same subjects as the affections or whether some of them are like this and some of them different. We must also look at thoughts to determine how they operate and what they belong to and to decide, in particular, precisely what subject it is that [10] overlooks the activity and makes the enquiry and judgement about these matters. And, earlier, what does perception belong to? For it is appropriate to start from perception, since affections are a sort of perception or are not without perception.

2. First we must take soul in order to see whether soul is one thing and her essential being another. For if this is so, soul will be a compound thing, and there will be no absurdity already in her admitting affections of the kind mentioned above, if the argument turns out to favour this. [5] Or, if soul and her essential being are the same,[2] then soul will be a sort of form, which does not admit all these activities that it confers upon something else but has its own native activity in itself, whatever the argument reveals it to be. For if so, it is [10] true to say that the soul is immortal, if what is immortal and incorruptible must be impassible, giving of itself to another in some way but receiving nothing itself from another except all it has from the things before it, which are greater than it and from which it is not cut off. For what could such a thing fear if it receives nothing at all from outside? So let that thing [5] fear which can be affected. Nor then does it experience assurance; for how can there be assurance for those who are never in the presence of what is frightening? And how can there be desires, which are fulfilled by means of the body being emptied and filled, if what is filled or emptied is different from soul? And how could it be receptive of mixture? Substantial being is

---

1. Aristotle, *De Anima* 408 b 1 ff.; Plato, *Republic* 429 c–d; 430 a–b; *Phaedo* 83 b.
2. Aristotle, *Metaphysics* 1043 b 2.

unmixed. And how could substantial being receive any further addition? [20] For were it to do so, it would be hastening to the state of not being what it is. Suffering is also far from it. And how could it be in pain and with what? For what is simple in substance is self-sufficient, insofar as it remains in its own substance. And does it take delight if something is added to it, when nothing, not even a good, can make an addition to it? For what it is, [25] it is always. And besides, it will not even perceive, nor will reasoning or opinion belong to it; for perception is reception of a form or indeed of an affection of body,[3] and reasoning and opinion are founded upon perception. But we must examine how it is with thought, to see if we shall leave this to soul; and in the case of pure pleasure,[4] as well, to see if the soul experiences [30] this when she is alone.

3.   But we must in fact put soul in body, whether she is before body or in it, since it is from body and soul that "the complete living creature takes its name."[5] If soul uses body as a tool,[6] then she is not compelled to receive the impressions that come through the body, [5] just as craftsmen do not have to be affected by the properties of their tools[7]; perhaps she would necessarily have perception, if using a tool involves the soul knowing the impressions that come from outside as a result of perception, since using the eyes too is to see. But indeed there can be harmful results connected with seeing, so that pains, suffering, and [10] generally anything that may befall the whole body can follow; and so desires too may follow if the soul seeks the service of her tool. But how will the affections come from the body to her? For body will give a share of what belongs to it to another body, but how will body give to soul? For this is like saying that if one thing is affected so must another different thing [15] be affected. For as far as one is the user and the other what it uses, each of the two is separate. At any rate, before their separation by philosophy, how were they related? There was a mixture. But if there was a mixture, there was either a blending, or the soul was in some manner "woven through,"[8] or the soul was like a form [20] not separated from the matter, or a form touching upon the matter, as the steersman steers the ship, or one part was related in one way and another in another. And I mean that one part is separated, which is that which uses, and the other mingled in some way and on the same level with that which it uses, so that this lower part philosophy should turn toward the user and lead the user— [25] insofar as there is no absolute necessity for the relation, so that it may not always even have to use it—away from what it uses.

---

3.   Aristotle, *De Anima* 424 a 18.
4.   Cf. I, 1, 5, 26–8.
5.   Plato, *Phaedrus* 246 c 5.
6.   Plato, *Alcibiades* I 129 c–e.
7.   Aristotle, *Eudemian Ethics* 1241 b 18.
8.   Plato, *Timaeus* 36 c 2.

4. Let us suppose, then, that there is a mixture. But if there is a mixture, the worse will be better, that is, the body, and the better element worse, that is, the soul. And the body will be better by sharing life, and the soul worse by sharing in death and lack of reason. How in fact could that which has had its life diminished in some way [5] take on an additional power of perception? On the contrary, it is the body that, in taking life, shares in perception and the impressions resulting from perception. The body then will also desire—for it is the body that will profit from the objects of its desire—and will be afraid for itself; for this too will not find what is [10] agreeable to it and will be destroyed. And we must in fact investigate the manner of the mixture and see if it is not actually impossible, just as if someone were to talk about a line being mixed with white, one kind of nature with another.[9] The notion of "being interwoven" does not make the things interwoven similarly affected, but it is possible for that which is interwoven to be unaffected and for the soul [15] to permeate the body without experiencing the body's affections, just like light, and especially if she is so interwoven as to be interwoven through the whole. The soul will not experience the affections of the body if she is interwoven in this way.[10] But will the soul be in body as a form in matter? First, she will be like a separable form if, as is in fact the case, she is substance [20] and so will be more consistent with the notion of a using agent. But if we suppose the relation to be like the shape of an axe imposed upon the iron[11]—and then the compound, the axe, will do what it does, that is to say, the iron shaped in this way, though by virtue of the shape—then we shall rather grant all the common affections to the body, though to a specific kind of body "natural, [25] organic, potentially having life."[12] For he [Aristotle] also says it is absurd "to say the soul weaves,"[13] so that it is absurd as well to say she desires or is pained; we should attribute these affections rather to the living creature.

5. But we must say that the living creature is either the body of this specific kind or the conjoint of body and soul or some different third thing that has come to be from both.[14] However this may be, we must either truly keep the soul unaffected, as being herself the cause of such affections in something else, or have her also affected together with body, [5] and then either be affected by the same impression or a similar one, as for example, the living creature desires in one way, but the desiring faculty of soul acts or is affected in a different way. We should examine this specific kind of body later.[15] But how is the compound, for instance,

9. Aristotle, *De generatione et corruptione* 323 b 26.
10. Plato, *Timaeus* 36 e; cf. I, 1, 3, 19.
11. Aristotle, *De Anima* 412 b 12.
12. Aristotle, *De Anima* 412 a 27–8.
13. Aristotle, *De Anima* 408 b 12–13.
14. Aristotle, *De Anima* 408 b 29.
15. Cf. I, 1, 7.

capable of experiencing pain?[16] Is it that the body is disposed in this particular way [10] and the affection comes right through to perception and the perception ends in the soul? But it is not yet clear how perception takes place. Or is it that, when a feeling of pain takes its origin from an opinion and a judgement[17] that there is some evil present either for the person himself or for one of his household, there results from this a painful change for the body [15] and generally for the whole living creature? But in this case it is not yet clear to what subject the opinion belongs, the soul or the compound; besides, the opinion about an evil for someone does not include the experience of pain; for it is perfectly possible for an opinion to be present without one's being at all pained as a consequence, just as it is equally possible not to be angry [20] despite having the opinion that we have been slighted, and for our appetite again not to be moved when we have the opinion that there is a good present. How then are these affections common to body and soul? Is it because desire belongs to the desiring part and high spirit to the spirited part and movement outwards to anything generally belongs to the appetitive part? But in this case they will no longer be common affections, but they will belong to the soul alone; or do they also belong to the body, [25] because blood and bile must boil and the body be so disposed as to move our appetite, as in the case of sexual desire. Let us admit that the appetite for the good is not a common property but belongs to the soul, as is also the case with other affections; an argued account does not give all of them to the conjoint. But when a man has an appetite for sex, [30] it will be the man who desires, but in another way it will be the desiring part which desires. And how? Will the man start the desire, and the desiring part follow on? But how does the man desire at all if the desiring part was not moved? Granted, you will say, the desiring part will start. But if [35] the body is not earlier disposed in this particular way, where will it start from?

6.   But perhaps it is better to say that, on the whole, it is by virtue of the presence of the powers of soul that those subjects that have them are active in accordance with them, but that the powers themselves are unmoved, granting the power to act to the subjects that have that power. But if this is so, when the living creature is affected, the [5] cause of its life, which gave itself to the compound, can still be unaffected, and the affections and activities belong to the subject that has them. But if this is so, then life will belong not to the soul at all but to the compound. Or rather, the life of the compound will not be the life of the soul, and the power of perception [10] will not perceive, but rather the subject that has the power will perceive. But if perception as a movement through the body ends in the soul, how will the soul not perceive? It would seem that when the power of perception is present, then by virtue of this power's presence the compound will

---

16. Plato, *Alcibiades* I 130 a 9 (generally 130 a–c); also Aristotle, *Metaphysics* 1041 b 17, 19.

17. Cf. the Stoic notion of the emotions as judgements or opinions, *SVF* III 459.

perceive whatever it perceives. But if the power [15] is not going to be moved, how is it still the compound that perceives if neither soul nor even soul-power is counted in together with it?

7.   Let it be the compound then that perceives, and the soul by her presence does not give herself in this qualified way either to the compound or to the other element in the compound, but makes, out of the body qualified in this way and a kind of light that is given from herself, the nature of the [5] living creature, something different, to which perceiving and all the other affections of the living creature are said to belong. But how is it we who perceive? Presumably, because we are not released from the living creature of this particular kind, even if there are other things of more value than us that are present to the whole substance of a human being, which is made up of many things. And the soul's power of perception [10] need not be of sensible objects, but it must rather be able to apprehend the imprints from perception that come to be in the living creature, for these are already intelligible objects. So external perception is an image of this power of perception in soul, which is truer in substance and a contemplation of forms alone that remains unaffected. From just these [15] forms, from which the soul on her own already receives her leadership over the living creature, come discursive reasonings, in fact, and opinions, and thoughts; here precisely are "we" most of all. What is before these is ours, but we above all are what ranges from here upwards, since we are set over the living creature. And nothing will prevent us calling the entire thing "living creature," mixed as to the lower parts but, from this point on, the true man, we might say. And those are the [20] "lion-like" and generally the "multiform beast."[18] For since the human being is coextensive with the rational soul, whenever we reason it is we who reason, because reasonings are active operations of soul.

8.   But how are we related to the intellect? And by intellect I mean not that disposition of soul that she has as one of the things from intellect, but intellect itself. No doubt, we have this too as something above us. And we have it as either common or particular or both common and particular; common [5] because it is undivided, one, and everywhere the same, and particular because each one has it whole in the primary soul. So we also have the forms in soul in two ways, unrolled and separated, as it were, and in intellect all together. But how do we have god? No doubt, as riding upon intelligible reality and upon [10] substance in the real sense,[19] and we are third in rank from there, being formed, he [Plato] says, out of the undivided substance from above and the substance that is divided in bodies,[20] which we must effectively think of as being divided in bodies insofar as the soul gives herself to the magnitude of bodies in proportion to the size of each

---

18. Plato, *Republic* 590 a 9; 588 c 7.
19. Numenius, fr. 11, Leemans, ed.
20. Plato, *Timaeus* 35 a 1–3.

living creature, since she also gives herself to the whole universe, though [15] she is one; or in so far as the soul is imagined as present to bodies by shining upon them and making living creatures not out of herself and body, but by remaining herself and by giving images of herself, just as a face is seen in many mirrors. And the first image is perception in the conjoint; then, after this, comes everything else that is said to be a form [20] of soul, each different form coming always from another, terminating in the generative and growth powers and generally in the powers of making and perfection of things other than the making soul, while the making soul herself is turned toward the product.

9.   So the nature of that soul of ours, then, will be freed from responsibility for the evils a human being does and suffers; for these are related to the living creature, the common element, and common in the way we have explained.[21] But if opinion and discursive reasoning belong to the soul, how can she be faultless? [5] For opinion can be false and many evils are perpetrated under the guidance of false opinion. Or perhaps evil actions occur when we are overcome by the worse in us—for we are many—either by desire or passion or by an image of evil. And what is called thinking rationally of false things is a form of imagination that has not waited upon the judgement of the reasoning faculty, but [10] we have acted under the persuasion of our worse impulses, just as in the case of perception it happens that the common sense sees falsely before the reasoning faculty has passed judgement upon it. And intellect either laid hold of the true or not, so that it is faultless, or we should speak rather in the following way, that we either laid hold of the intelligible object in intellect or not; or of the intelligible object in us; [15] for it is possible to have the object and not to have it at hand.[22] So we have distinguished what is common to the soul-body conjoint and what is particular to the soul inasmuch as certain things are corporeal or not without body, while whatever does not need body for its operation, this is proper to soul, and when reasoning makes a judgement upon the imprints received from perception, it is already [20] contemplating forms and contemplating by a kind of intimate perception—at least in the case of the reasoning that belongs strictly to the true soul; for true reasoning is an activity of intelligible thoughts,[23] and frequently there is a likeness and community between the things outside and those within. So the soul will be no less calm in relation to and in herself. And the moods and [25] confused noise[24] in us arise from what is joined to us and from the impressions of the conjoint, as we have said,[25] whatever in fact this may be.

10.   But if we are the soul, and we experience these things, then the soul would be affected in this way and the soul again will do what we do, but we also

---

21. Cf. I, 1, 5–7.

22. Plato, *Theaetetus* 198 d 7.

23. For Plotinus' positive view of discursive reason see IV, 3 (27), 18, 1–4, 10–13.

24. Plato, *Phaedo* 66 d 6 and *Timaeus* 43 b 6.

25. Cf. I, 1, 7.

said that the joint entity is a part of us, and especially when we have not yet been separated from body; for what our body experiences [5] we say that we experience. So the "we" is taken in two senses, either with the beast included or with reference to that which is already above this; and the body given life is the beast. But the true human being is different, pure of these things, and possessing the excellences that pertain to thought and have their foundation, actually, in the separating soul herself; that is, a soul in fact separating and separable [10] even while she is still here; for even when the soul withdraws completely, the soul illumined by her also departs and follows along with her. But the excellences that do not pertain to thought but come about by habit and training,[26] belong to the conjoint; for the vices belong to this, since envy, jealousy, and excessive pity are found there. And to what do friendships belong? Some [15] to the joint entity, and some to the inner human being.[27]

11.   When we are children the faculties of the compound are active, and only a few glimmers of light reach the compound from the powers above. But when these are inactive in relation to us, they are directed above: but they act in relation to us whenever they reach up to the middle of our being. What then? Are "we" not also before this? [5] Yes, but there must be apprehension of it. For we do not always use everything we have, but only when we orient the middle of our being toward either what is above or its opposite, that is, in respect to everything we are involved in bringing from potency or state to activity. But how does the living creature include beasts? Perhaps if there are human souls in them, as is said to be the case,[28] [10] souls that have gone astray, then as much of the soul as is separable does not come to belong to the beasts but is present without being present to them; instead, their awareness includes the image of soul together with the body: a body then of a particular kind as to have been made by an image of soul; but if a human soul has not entered, it becomes a living being of this kind by an illumination from the whole soul.

12.   But if the soul is without fault, how are there judgements? But really this kind of argument is out of tune with all the arguments which hold that the soul is at fault and puts things right and undergoes punishment both in Hades and in passing on from body to body. Well, one should accept whichever [5] argument one wants, and perhaps one might discover a way in which they are not in conflict. For the argument that grants faultlessness to the soul supposes that the soul is one and completely simple and says that soul and soul's essential being are the same, while that which grants that soul can be at fault weaves together with her, and adds, another form of soul that experiences these terrible affections. [10] So the soul herself even becomes a compound, the product of all the things which go

26. Plato, *Republic* 518 e 1–2.
27. Plato, *Republic* 589 a 7.
28. Cf. Plato, *Phaedo* 82 1 a; *Phaedrus* 249 b 3–4; *Timaeus* 42 c 3.

to make her up and is subject to affection as a whole and the compound is at fault, and it is this for him [Plato] that undergoes punishment, not that simple soul. This is why he [Plato] says: "We have seen her, just like those who see the sea-creature Glaucus. But one must knock off the additions,"[29] [15] if one wants to see her nature, he says, and "look to her love of wisdom" to see "what things she lays hold of" and "by kinship with what things she is what she is."[30] So there is another life and other activities of soul, and what is punished is different. The withdrawal and separation are not only from this body but also from every addition. [20] For the addition occurs in coming into being; or rather, coming into being belongs altogether to the other form of soul. How coming into being occurs, has been explained,[31] namely that it occurs as the soul descends, when something else comes to be from her that descends in the inclination. Does she then let the image go? And how is the inclination not a fault? One may suppose that [25] if the inclination is an illumination directed to what is below, it is not a fault, just as it is not a fault to cast a shadow, but the responsible agent is that which is illuminated; for if it did not exist, the soul would have nowhere to illuminate. The soul is said therefore to descend and to incline in the sense that what has been illuminated from her lives together with her. She lets the image go, then, if there is nothing near to receive it, and she lets it go [30] not in the sense that it is severed from her but in that it no longer exists, and it no longer exists if the whole soul looks there (to the intelligible world). The poet seems to separate the image in the case of Heracles when he puts his shade in Hades but Heracles himself among the gods,[32] since he was bound to retain both stories, that he dwells among the gods and that he is in Hades; so he divided them. [35] But perhaps the story would be most plausibly explained in this way: because Heracles possessed a definite practical excellence and was counted worthy to be a god because of his nobility of character, but because he was active, and not contemplative, so as to have been wholly there (in the intelligible world), he is both above and yet there is also something of him below.

13.   What has performed the investigation of these matters, "we" or the soul? It is "we" but by the soul. And what does "by the soul" mean? Is it in fact by having soul that the investigation was performed? No, but insofar as we *are* soul.

---

29. Plato, *Republic* 611 b 5.
30. Plato, *Republic* 611 c–612 a.
31. Cf. IV, 8 (6).
32. Cf. *Odyssey* 11, 601–2 (and compare *Iliad* xviii, 117–19). The passage combines two traditions: Heracles, the mortal; and Heracles, who had become a god. On the difficulty of reconciling the presence of an *eidôlon* of Heracles in Hades with the continued existence of Heracles in heroic divinity on Olympus see *A Commentary on Homer's Odyssey* (A. Heubeck, S. West, J. B. Hainsworth), vol. 2, books 9–16, Oxford, 1959, 114 (on *Odyssey* 11, 601–27).

Will soul then be moved? It would seem that we must give a movement of this kind to soul, which is not the movement of bodies [5] but is soul's own life. And thinking is a greater form of life, both when soul thinks and when intellect is active in relation to us; for this too is a part of us and to this we go up.

Commentary

2.1. Introduction

Treatise I, 1 (53) is the last but one that Plotinus wrote before his death in 270, yet Porphyry made it the first treatise of the first *Ennead* (devoted largely to ethical questions) and an introduction, therefore, to the *Enneads* as a whole. Why? Treatise I,1, is a difficult work, presupposing much of what Plotinus has already written, but it attempts to answer the basic philosophical questions we might ask ourselves as complex, multiple, and not simple beings: what is the seat of the emotions we experience, and in what should we locate the physical and mental activities resulting from feeling?[1] Do opinions, reasoning, and thought all belong to us in the same way, and how could we tell? Or in other words, what in us judges such things? Who, for instance, is writing or reading the treatise? Plotinus therefore calls into question the basic elements of our being human that we take for granted, so that we can gather together or collect what makes us human and become aware of what we are.[2]

An earlier work, V, 3 (49), had examined the simple return of intellect or soul upon themselves in self-knowledge and had suggested the somewhat more laborious task that compound entities, like human beings, must undertake to know themselves.[3] Treatise I, 1 is effectively an analysis of that more laborious task (probably requested

---

1. The emotions Plotinus mentions are pleasures (*hêdonai*), pains (*lupai*), fears (*phoboi*), assurances (*tharrê*), desires (*epithymiai*), aversions (*apostrophai*). These are described in chapter 1 as emotions (*pathemata*) and affections (*pathê*), that is, feelings or emotions we experience rather than "passions," which can be a misleading translation of these terms. A stricter distinction between *pathemata* and *pathê* can be argued for elsewhere in the Enneads (see, e.g., B. Fleet, 1995 on III, 6 [26] 1, 1, where they mean "impressions" of sensible qualities and "affections" of the soul respectively), but the terms are used interchangeably in the context of this work and refer to the emotional experiences or feelings of the compound human being. In other works, pathos (and paschein) means "experience" in a wider sense, including the experience of the soul (as, e.g., in chapter 1, part I, passage 6).

2. On the question of human nature generally see also *Enneads* VI, 7 (38), 4–7; II, 3 (52), 9; on the range of the self III, 4 (15); VI, 7 (38) 6; and also A. H. Armstrong, 1967, 223–7; J. Igal, 1979, J. M. Rist, 1967, chapter 11; W. Beierwaltes, 1981; P. Hadot, 1973, chapter 2; G. J. P. O'Daly, (1973) *Plotinus' Philosophy of the Self,* Shannon, 1973.

3. Cf. V, 3, 17; and on the question of self-knowledge generally see E. Warren, (1964)" Consciousness in Plotinus," *Phronesis* 9, 83–97; G. J. P. O'Daly, 1971; W. Beierwaltes, 1991; K. Corrigan, 2000.

by the readers of V, 3), and so perhaps to Porphyry's mind, it served to introduce philosophical enquiry as a form of self-knowledge in which—in accord with the Delphic commandment, "know yourself"—the rest of philosophy and any authentically human, self-searching life have their birth. "I sought out myself," Heraclitus stated (*DK*, fr. 101). What apparently did he find? Among many other cryptic discoveries, he found that the landscape of the *psyche* was unlimited, capable of breaking down the barriers between otherwise divided lives: "For you would not find out the boundaries of *psyche*, even by traveling along every path: so deep a *logos* does it have" (fr. 45). This *logos* ("utterance," "proportion," "measure," "meaning," to mention but a few of the word's possible meanings in Heraclitus' day) is connected with shared intelligence and the divine *logos*, or fire, that guides everything. As Heraclitus again cryptically proclaimed, "one must follow what is with intelligence [*tôi xunôi*]; that is, what is common, for the common [*koinos*] is with intelligence [*xunôi*], but though the *logos* is common the many live as if they have private understanding" (fr. 2). The words *common* (*koinos*) and *with intelligence* (*xunos*) are interchangeable in meaning in Greek, and so Heraclitus' cryptic fragments suggest that to know oneself according to the *logos* is to go beyond a boundary into a shared and ultimately divine landscape.[4] Of course, for Socrates even in the face of death "the unexamined life is not worth living" (*Apology* 38a), by which he meant that his own practice of question and answer and the search to give a critical account, or *logos*, of himself in service of the prophetic god at Delphi, was his life's calling.

Plotinus starts here with a question from Aristotle's *De Anima*, whether soul is really moved by these affections or feelings,[5] and with Plato's *Alcibiades* I, which served throughout antiquity as an introduction to the Platonic dialogues and which asks how we can know which art makes human beings better and happier if we do not know what we are ourselves (128 e). Where, Plotinus asks in I, 1, is the seat of our feelings? He replies: either in "soul" or in "soul using a body" or in "some third thing made up from both." This last, in turn, can be either a "mixture" or some new form resulting from the mixture. In the *Alcibiades* I, Socrates also outlines three possibilities: the human being is "soul or body or the compound (of both)" (130 a); he then proceeds to eliminate body and the compound as adequate definitions of the human being, since they are not ruling principles. So "the soul is man" and (in relation to the body) "the soul which is man is a soul using the body as an instrument [*organon*]." Plotinus examines all three possibilities in rather different ways in I, 1 but he also holds a view very much related to the *Alcibiades'* enquiry, namely, that to know oneself involves knowing the best in oneself, the ruling principle that "looks over" what we do. In the *Alcibiades*, Socrates argues that the soul will know itself by knowing its highest aspect, namely wisdom, or *phronesis*, in which all the divine is reflected, just as someone may see himself reflected in the pupil of another's eye (133 c). Thus I, 1, serves Por-

---

4. On the meanings of *logos* see chapter 3.7, 3.9 below.

5. On Aristotle's conception of soul (and bibliography) see M. Nussbaum and A. Rorty (eds.), 1992, and within the broader context of ancient thought (from Heraclitus and Plato to Plotinus and medical paradigms) see generally S. Everson, ed., 1991.

phyry's intentions well by being a practical propaideutic to the question of self-knowledge and to the rest of Plotinus' philosophy, and chapter 1 indicates that the work as a whole will enquire freely into the full range of what it means to be human in the context of questions raised by Plato and Aristotle.[6]

I shall here take up a series of questions related to the text and intended to clarify issues in both this work and others:

1. What does Plotinus mean by the impassibility or unaffectedness of soul? Is this the view that the higher soul is entirely unaffected by the passions and perceptions of bodily life? Surely this would make little sense of what we actually experience.

2. What does Plotinus think perception is? Do "we" really perceive, or is it the soul that perceives through the medium of the compound or the body? Does Plotinus think perception is direct or mediate and representational?

3. How should we conceive the soul-body relation? This is a fundamental problem for readers of Plotinus or any later Neoplatonists. Are soul and body united in any genuine way or is there only an accidental connection? There is also a cognate problem: is Neoplatonism committed to the doctrine of a plurality of substantial forms, that is, to the thesis that there are many, not one substantial form in the human being, with the result that for Plotinus we are never truly "one." A corollary of this problem is the view of Bréhier (the great translator of the *Enneads* into French) that form and matter do not really combine in Plotinus' thought as they do in Aristotle's.[7] Is this true? Given the range of the higher soul and intellect (cf. I, 1, 8–12), it may seem to be an unavoidable conclusion.

4. Does the human being really disappear at the level of intellect, as Plotinus sometimes indicates, or does anything of what we consider genuinely human survive the separation of the immortal soul from the body? How does the treatment of self-knowledge in the case of simple substances, like soul and intellect, in V, 3 (49), relate to this more laborious task of working out our humanity in I, 1?[8]

2.2. What does Plotinus mean by the impassibility or unaffectedness of soul? (I, 1 [53] 2 and III, 6 [26])

A major problem for any reader of the *Enneads* (and particularly of III, 6 [26], *"On the impassibility of incorporeals"*) is that compound entities, human beings among them, seem to be sandwiched between two different kinds of impassibility, or incapacity to feel anything: an unfeeling matter and an unfeeling soul! The world may indeed

---

6. Cf. G. J. P. O'Daly, 1971, 7–19 on I, 1 and the Delphic commandment: know yourself.
7. E. Bréhier, 1928, 200.
8. For broader considerations of human-beingness, personhood, and identity in ancient thought generally, see C. Gill, 1990; 1991, 166–93; 1995.

be a cold place, but this looks too cold for comfort. How does Plotinus reach and state this position in I, 1, 2–3?

As so often throughout the *Enneads*, Plotinus' argument turns on the question of how we use language and what we mean by the terms we use. Aristotle too analyzes the claim of form to be substance (a "most puzzling" claim, he says) in *Metaphysics* VII (1029 a 33) in terms of what we could mean by it. Plotinus borrows some of this language, though to different effect. If soul and her essential being are different, soul will be a compound and there will be no problem in attributing all sorts of physical things and feelings to her. But if soul and her essential being are the same, then soul will be a form, and not a compound of form and matter, and it won't be correct to say that she feels, blushes, blanches, and so on, for what we mean will be, not that the soul is the subject of such things, but that the human being (that is, the individual compounds we are) has such experiences. Of course, on these terms the soul's immortality would seem to follow naturally, since she gives something but receives nothing (2, 9–12).

The problem lies with the assumption that there really is a sense in which one could say that "my" soul or "your" soul simply *is* essential being or substance. But can one? In fact, Plotinus gives a somewhat nuanced answer to this question, though you would not think so from just looking at chapter 2. His answer implicitly is that in our cases, soul is also an image in the compound (i.e., soul "gives something of herself to another"; for what this means see Plotinus' definition of the whole human perceiver at 7, 1 ff.), and a soul-image can feel all sorts of things, but just because it is an image, as we have seen above, it does not necessarily stop being soul. Many contingent, accidental things may in some sense rightly be attributed to the soul-image as a subject (though this would be a strange way of speaking, and we would more naturally attribute them just to the compound entity; that is, you, me, or the compound of soul/image-body). But the soul's problem is not simply solved there, for she must be a substance in some way too, particularly if she is an organizing principle or a form of the body (as Aristotle says she is in the *De Anima* (II, 1)—a complex view that Plotinus examines, below).

Aristotle asserts in the *Metaphysics* that each primary substance is identical with its essential being (VII, 6). He distinguishes between "things said in themselves," which are identical with their essential being (e.g., "to be a human being" denotes the essence of every individual human being), and "things said in the way of accident," which are not identical (e.g., to be a white human being is not identical with the essence of some human beings). When we come to questions such as "Is Socrates identical with his essence?" (cf. 1032 a 8; 1037 a 5–10), then the answer seems to be that it depends on what we mean in each case. If by Socrates we mean his soul, then this is the same as his essence; for soul is substance, Aristotle states, form and essence (for "essence" Aristotle uses that curious phrase, *to ti en einai*, or "the what it was to be"—on which see 3.7 below) of the qualified body (cf. 1035 b 14–22). If we mean the compound of soul and body, then Socrates is not identical with his essence (cf. 1043 b 1–4).

Plotinus is not simply making a plainly stupid assumption here or taking for granted what he is going to prove. If the soul is a real principle in any sense at all, we might say, then how we can speak about the soul in the language of essential predication will be a problem. Plotinus indicates several immediate pressing problems with such language at the end of chapter 2: the soul will not perceive, if perception is the reception of a form (2, 25 ff.). In Greek, *aesthesis*, like *perception* in English, can have both active and passive connotations. When it is passive, the translation "sensation" probably fits better, though I retain "perception" throughout (partly because even passive sensation depends upon active perception).[9] But the view Plotinus expresses here is intended to present a *problem* that he will take up in subsequent chapters. Nor will the soul in herself have reasoning and opinion, apparently, since they depend upon sense-data (2, 27). Then too, in the list of problematic consequences Plotinus draws the impassibility thesis, there is no way around the problem that the soul is in the body: "we must suppose soul in body" (3,1). In other words, we are going to have to think out how it is possible to put soul in body and yet make soul impassible. Thus, Plotinus is not simply assuming a naïve position that he will then defend at all costs. Instead, the assumption that "soul" or "soul-image" is a primary substance (though not absolutely incompatible with the other thesis that soul may in some sense be compound [cf. 7, 1 ff.]), while appearing to provide what he might anyway be committed to, leads to some strange modes of speaking about soul. These modes differ with other common modes of speaking that also require investigation.

To evaluate the impassibility thesis properly, we should have to examine it on its own terms in the whole course of Plotinus' argument. My intent here, however, is only to show that what looks naïve at first sight is upon closer scrutiny understandable as a genuine philosophical problem. The impassibility thesis is bound up with the problems of perception and of the soul-body relation. In examining these below we shall not be diverging from our consideration of impassibility.

Let us begin, then, by suggesting an answer to the puzzle that the human being is sandwiched between two kinds of "unfeelingness," soul and matter. We can then evaluate that answer in the context of perception and the soul-body relation.

When Plotinus says that the soul is impassible, he means that we cannot speak about the soul as if it were like an apple, a tree, or a human being. The attribution of physical changes to the soul is inappropriate, he argues on Aristotelian grounds in III, 6 (26), 2, 46–52, since the passage from potentiality to actuality in the case of immaterial things is not accompanied by qualitative change (cf. Aristotle, *De Anima* 417 b 5–16). Affections and changes should be attributed to the compound rather than to the soul, for otherwise "we run the risk . . . [of saying] that the soul blushes or turns pale" (III, 6 [26] 3, 7–11; cf. *De Anima* 408 b 11–15 and I, 1, 4, 25–7). Consequently, the part of soul that is affected is not the soul-power, which remains unmoved, but the form or soul in the compound.

> Certainly the desiring part is in matter and so, too, is the part that governs nutrition, growth, and generation, which is the root and principle of the desiring and affective

---

9.   For *aesthêsis* see particularly J. I. Beare, 1906; W. Beierwaltes, 1991, 193–4; E. K. Emilsson, 1988; H. Benz, 1990; K. Corrigan, 1996a, 135–145.

(*pathêtikon*) form. But it is not proper to any form to be . . . affected, but it remains at rest, and its matter enters into the state of being affected (*ten de hylên autou en tôi pathei gignesthai*) when it does so enter, and the form stirs up the affection by its presence. For, of course, the growth principle does not grow when it causes growth or increase when it causes increase. Nor in general when it causes motion is it moved by that particular kind of motion which it causes but either it is not moved at all, or it is a different kind of motion and activity. (III, 6 [26] 4, 32–41)

Note the nuances of the above passage that do seem to take account of our ordinary experience. Without soul we would not be able to feel anything because soul provides the power. But of the physical and even psycho-physical feelings we experience (if we make this distinction), we say that *we* experience; that is, we mean that the compound entity or embodied agent experiences them, not the organizing soul-power. "I" eat ice-cream, not my teeth, my mouth, my DNA, or my psychic capacity for enjoyment or the "nutritive power" of soul. We sometimes want to say something a little out of the ordinary (and the Greeks often did as an "ordinary" manner of speaking, e.g., as in Sappho, "my soul flew away with my wits,"[10] when she sees her beloved). For example, "hearing that violin changed *my life*" or "meeting that one person turned everything upside down." In such cases where what we *mean* is certainly an emotional experience but something more fundamental as well, then Plotinus says we are not speaking of qualitative change so much as of "a different kind of motion and activity" (cf. Aristotle, *De Anima* 417 b 5–16). Not only is the "impassible" soul the power *for* feeling in the compound, but here also is where more fundamental feelings that transform us (and perhaps leave the "compound" shaking with aftertremors, so to speak) are situated. This explains how Plotinus even can *ask* the question whether the soul experiences *pure pleasure* when she is alone (2, 29–30). The answer will be yes. "Let the appetite [*orexis*] for the good not be a common property but belong to the soul, as also with other affections," Plotinus states in the middle of a discussion about sexual desire (5, 24–6). Now of course we may want to plead in his defense: not sex too, Plotinus; you're supposed to be impassible—especially when the poor man writing this work probably was already in the terrible pain of his final illness. But the fact is that Plotinus treats sexual desire (which we might expect him to consign immediately to the compound) much more subtly as a genuine problem for philosophy since, as he argues in another late work, III, 5 (50), *On love*, such desire is incomprehensible without the Good (see especially 1, 26–8). Of course this may also be mingled with many other things and even distorted out of all recognition.[11]

The soul does have affections (*pathêmata*) or "feelings" (cf. III, 5, 1, 65), but they are her own feelings and not those of the compound or of the body. Plotinus' analysis of such different and complex feelings is subtle, clear-sighted, and at times downright prac-

10. Fr. 118 A. Edmonds, *Lyra Graeca,* J. M. Edmonds, London-New York, 1922–1927.
11. On the place of desire in Plotinus' work see R. Arnou, 1967; H. Blumenthal, 1971; K. Corrigan, 1996a, 273–83.

tical. The soul-impassibility thesis, then, is much more subtle than it first looks. For it tries to distinguish and to account for physical, psycho-physical, and psychological forms of experience in terms of an analysis of what we mean in ordinary speech.

Plotinus' analysis of matter is no less subtle. To say that matter is "impassible" is to acknowledge that when we speak of matter undergoing some affection, we do not mean that matter is some little agent experiencing x, y, or z or that the relationship between form and matter is one between two distinct physical things or "stuffs." Matter does not blanch or blush; *we* do. But matter, though "impassible" in this way, *is* passive in its own way to the operative power of intelligible form, as Plotinus makes clear in the later chapters of III, 6 (26). But this is a question of substantial transformation, not qualitative change: matter does not blanch or blush, but it is brought to perfection in compounds by the creative power of intelligible form (while as the matter *for every-thing* still retaining its own nature or no-thingness).[12]

So reading III, 6, 2 for the first time or in isolation from other treatises might give us the impression that soul is an unfeeling, abstract entity and that we are wedged uncomfortably between two undesiring undesirables (like "fire" and "ice" in Frost's poem or Dante's *Purgatorio* and *Inferno*).[13] But that impression is not only misleading; it is false. Plotinus' anthropology includes a much more subtle, multidimensional analysis of feelings, faculties, and their shades or nuances.

2.3. Do "we" really perceive and do we perceive directly or mediately? (I, 1 [53] 3–7 and other texts)

Hegel's whole *Phenomenology of Spirit* emerges out of what is implicit in, but cannot be contained by, the simplest perception or sensation of anything. There is much in perception that does not meet the eye, as it were. Nonetheless, it would be very hard to convince us that it is not "we" who are doing the perceiving or that we do not perceive real things directly, though we all perhaps experience disconnectedness from ourselves and from perceived objects, whether this be an experience of quasi-vampirish nausea, as in Jean-Paul Sartre's novel of the same name, or just the puzzle of our suddenly not knowing who "we" are. Simone Weil puts it this way: when a beautiful person looks in the mirror, she thinks, "That's me." When an ugly person looks in the mirror, "she knows she is not that."[14] So with the caution that what we might mean by "me" or "I"

---

12. On matter see chapters 1.10 and 3.8 and *Enneads* II, 4 (12); II, 5 (25); III, 6 (26); I, 8 (51).

13. Frost: "Some say the world will end in fire,/ Some say in ice./ From what I've tasted of desire/ I hold with those who favor fire." In Dante's *Inferno* Satan dwells not in fire but in a frozen pit. In the *Purgatorio* Dante emerges with relief from hell: "the heavens seemed to rejoice in their flames" (I, 25, tr. Charles S. Singleton, *Dante Aligheri. The Divine Comedy,* 3 vols., Princeton, 1970); but to climb the mount of purgatory is searing purgation. Compare T. S. Eliot's famous lines on "the torment" love: "We only live, only suspire consumed by either fire or fire" ("Little Gidding," in *Four Quartets*).

14. Simone Weil, *Gravity and Grace,* London, 1963 (Routledge and Kegan Paul), 29.

or "we" is not a simple matter, let us take up the question of who really does the perceiving and who perceives what and how in the *Enneads* first by looking at Plotinus' argument in I, 1, 3 ff., and then by situating it against the background of other treatises.

The question of perception, as we have seen, follows upon the dilemma between soul's impassibility/immortality and her position "in" body. If "soul uses body as an instrument" (according to the *Alcibiades'* definition above), then the soul might have some kind of derivative or vicarious experience, just as a craftsman may be said to experience things through his tools (3, 3–11). But how will affections (*pathê*) actually reach the soul (3, 12)? Are the soul and body mixed together so that sense-perception recognizes a bodily affection and perception ends up in the soul (3, 18–5, 9–11)? This does not begin to make clear how perception can take place, Plotinus states (5, 11–12). He is thinking here of perception of one's own physical or psycho-physical states. He goes on to suggest that we might look at the question from the reverse angle—that is, from soul to body—and see feeling (in this case *lupê,* or pain) as originating in a judgement, as the Stoics argue (5, 12–15). But to what does the opinion belong? Besides, one can have an opinion or make a judgement about something without any accompanying grief or feeling, just as one can be absolutely indifferent to present goods (5, 15–21). The question resolves itself, for Plotinus, into the problem of how the soul-powers as faculties of the *soul* are to be configured in relation to the compound (i.e., the embodied human being) and the objects perceived so that the whole organism is properly articulated and its powers and the subject that *has* those powers are distinguished (6, 1–7). Here Plotinus sees a threefold problem: 1) this seems to commit him to the view that only the compound, and not the soul, is alive (6, 7–10: "and the power of perception will not perceive, but the subject which has the power"); 2) if perception is a movement through the body that ends up in soul (i.e., in conscious awareness), how could we avoid saying that the soul perceives?; and 3) while we might get away with saying that "we" perceive by virtue of the presence of an unmoved soul-power, how can "we" perceive anything if we do not count that soul-power with the "we" or compound subject (6, 10–16)?

In I, 1, 7 consequently, Plotinus spells out his own peculiar idealist-realist, but definitely Platonist, version of perception, which he first couches in a complex view of the soul-body relation (7, 1–6) and which I take up directly in section 2.5 below. The upshot is that the compound being perceives not just by virtue of the presence of a soul-power but because the whole soul apparently is involved in what it means to be an embodied human being. Plotinus asks:

> But how is it we who perceive? Presumably, because we are not released from the living creature of this particular kind, even if there are other things of more value than us that are present to the whole substance of the human being, which is made up of many things. And the soul's power of perception need not be of sensible objects, but it must rather be able to apprehend the imprints [*typoi*] that come to be in the living creature because of perception; for these are already intelligible objects. So external perception is an image of this power of perception in soul, which is truer in substance and an impassible contemplation of forms alone. (7, 6–14)

Plotinus' view apparently is that perception is real and we do the perceiving. But the "we" referred to can mean different things, as he stipulates later (I, 1, 7, 14–24; 9, 15 ff.; chapters 10–11, *passim*). We might include the higher functions (like reasoning, opinion, and thought) or restrict the focus to the lower functions. In any case, the living creature who is the human being is also "we" in the broader sense, and more "we" if we include reasoning: "For since the human being is coextensive with the rational soul, whenever we reason, it is we who reason because reasonings are active operations of soul" (7, 21–3).

For Plotinus, then, what we might call passive perception is a human function we share with the rest of the animal and plant kingdom in different ways. But perception, in more meaningful ways, is cognitive and intellectual so that the same *power* of perception starts to flourish when we scrutinize or really pay attention to *what* we perceive. Perception thus becomes a genuinely creative part of a self-conscious, discriminating existence. Yes, it appears, *we* really perceive *things*, but "we are many" (9, 7), and so the cognitive, intellectual context of perception, which allows for the opening up of an authentic interior life (i.e., a life that is not just an illusion or a masked egotistical preference, but one that can be *tested)*,[15] is more the "inner human being" (cf. 10, 15)[16]: "here precisely are 'we' most of all" (7, 16–17).

Of course, when we look at the Platonism of this and the following chapters, we might find no realism at all in this view, but instead ghostly spiritual entities, or homunculi, squinting out at an equally insubstantial world of things. We might still see the spectre of early Stoicism's pitiless sage in a soul that remains unaffected by what "it" sees. Then again, what evidence is there in I, 1, that we actually perceive anything other than what our "souls" want us to see? In the context of the *Enneads* as a whole, two questions here are crucial to a balanced evaluation of Plotinus' theory: First, do we perceive things directly or only our affections about things? Second, how do the affections, or passivity, fit into this picture?

2.4. Do we perceive things or our impressions of things?

In the *Enneads* as a whole, on balance, Plotinus thinks we perceive things directly.[17] *Ennead* IV, 6 (41) 1, explicitly states: when we perceive anything, we look directly at it and perceive it there where it is (1, 11–18; 23–32), not in the sense that we get a physical sample of it or because we already have its form (1, 18–23). Perception is real, direct in its own right, and apparently takes place there where the object is (IV, 6 [41] 1, 14–18; VI, 4 [22] 12, 109–12). Since Plotinus rejects Aristotle's affected transparent medium as a sufficient condition for perception (cf. IV, 5 [29] 4, 1–7), it is difficult to

---

15. See Chapter 4 on V, 8 (31), 1, for the emphasis Plotinus puts upon the importance of testing one's opinions and conclusions. This is essentially Platonic.

16. Plotinus is deliberately citing Plato's *Republic* 589 a–b): "he who says that justice is advantageous would say that we should do and say these things from which the inner man (*ho entos anthrôpos*) of man will be strongest."

17. This section (2.4) is adapted from K. Corrigan, 1996a, 138 ff.

know what he means when he says perception takes place there where the object is. Aristotle supposes that subject percipient and object perceived are unified in the act of perceiving by a single activity, but Plotinus seems to go beyond this and to suggest that he thinks of the sensitive organ as extending right out to the object. This is perhaps by virtue of its being a sympathetic part of a larger organism, though as we shall see below, such sympathy does not dispense with the need for the power of perception to be actualized through the senses. However we are to interpret this, while the material impression is present as a transmission in the air (and is therefore divisible), the activity of sound or light as perception is to be understood as an indivisible discriminatory power of soul herself, on the part of both percipient and object perceived. We perceive an object that is genuinely external to us, but this requires interpretation and contextualization. So if the "we" who perceive are complex, the object perceived is similarly complex and requires an active discriminating perception to grasp its wholeness. Active perception in this sense, therefore, is the meeting of subject percipient and object perceived, and a real grasp of the object where and as it is. By contrast, passive perception, or perhaps a form of sensation that analyses without seeing the object whole, breaks up this wholeness into parts and into collections of discrete qualities, quantities, and relations and, to this degree, is more abstract.

In Plotinus' view, then, causality is not just a feature of *objects* acting upon us to produce ideas or sensations in the percipient subject; that is, "copies" or "resemblances" of patterns existing in material substances, as in John Locke's (1632–1704) theory of perception. In Locke's theory, our ideas are copies of primary qualities (extension, etc.) supposed to exist in the object, as opposed to secondary qualities (colours, sounds, tastes, etc.), which "are nothing in the objects themselves, but powers to produce various sensations in us . . . as colours, sounds, tastes." Nor in Plotinus' view is perception only a function of spiritual subjects, as might appear to be the case with George Berkeley's (1685–1753) alternative version of epistemological dualism.[18] Sense-objects must be grasped whole, and "what sees and what is seen must be two. What sees . . . must be another seeing the impression (*typos*) in another place, but not in that which sees it is" (IV, 6 [41] 1, 36–9). On balance, therefore, Plotinus' statements in IV, 6 (41) 1 and VI, 4 (22) 12, 10–12, support the view that his theory is realist, not conceptualist or representationalist.

On the other hand, two other passages, V, 3 (49) 3, 33, and V, 5 (32) 1, 15–19, suggest the opposite. Passage V, 3 (49) 3, says straightforwardly, "we perceive through perception and we are the perceivers" in the Henry-Schwyzer text; nearly every other editor (Theiler, Harder, Cilento, Armstrong, Beierwaltes) puts a negative into the line: "we are not the perceivers." Yet as Henry and Schwyzer point out, at lines 40–1 Plotinus says "for we always are perceiving," which renders the negative unlikely but perhaps does not clinch the issue. In the general comparative texture of the whole passage (perception, reasoning, and thought), however, even if Plotinus actually wrote a negative, he did not mean that we are not the perceivers but that perception is not as much "we" as is reason.

---

18. Though this will depend very much upon how one interprets Berkeley's theory. For one feature of this interpretation see K. Corrigan, 1994, 67–86.

This is also the point at issue, as I see it, in V, 5 (32) 1. Here Plotinus argues that sense-perception is an image (*eidôlon*) of the thing that "does not apprehend the thing itself: for that remains outside" (15–19). This passage is not fatal to the realist hypothesis either, for it makes a somewhat different point than might be supposed at first glance. Intellect knows its object as itself, for intellect knows the essence, or "what is," of the thing. Perception, however, is of the quality, not the essence (cf. V, 5 [32] 2, 1–9; II, 6 [17] 1, 42–9), and in perception the object *does* remain outside. When Plotinus asserts that *aesthêsis*, or perception, does not "take" (*lambanei*) the thing itself, he does not mean that perception is indirect but that unlike intellect, which "takes" and "has" its object directly as itself, perception cannot possess its object in just that way. Perception *is* less direct than thought. But this does not affect the direct vision hypothesis in its own context. Thus Plotinus holds that perception is active and direct, but less direct than thought.

2.5. How do the affections fit into the overall picture?

How do the affections fit into this picture?[19] In an earlier work, IV, 4 (28) 23, Plotinus makes clear that while perception may be direct, there can be no perception of sense-objects without the mediation of the compound and its affections. *Soul* does not perceive sense-objects directly; the compound is what perceives by virtue of soul's power.

> There cannot, then, be nothing but these two things, the external object and the soul: since then the soul would not be affected [*pathoi*]; but there must be a third thing that will be affected, and this is that which will receive the form [*to tên morphên dexomenon*]. This must be jointly subject to like affections [*sympathes . . . kai homoiopathes*] and of one matter with the sense-object [*hyles mias*], and it must be this that is affected and the other principle [soul] that knows; and its affection must be of such a kind that it retains something of that which produced [*to pathos*] it, but is not the same as it, but as it is between the producer of the affection and the soul, it must have an affection that lies between the sensible and the intelligible, a proportional mean somehow linking the extremes to each other [*meson analogon, synapton pôs ta akra allelois*], with the capacity both of receiving and of transmitting information [*dektikon hama kai apaggeltikon hyparchon*], suitable to be assimilated to each of the extremes [*epitêdeion homoiothenai hekaterô*]. (IV, 4 [28] 23, 18–28)

Plotinus is here adapting Aristotle's notion of the sense-organ as a proportional mean or balance between two extremes. The sense-organs do not receive sensible forms with matter; they take on those forms together with their material conditions but without the actual matter. What this means in Aristotle has been the subject of much debate, and Plotinus' view is arguably more obscure still. This much, however, seems likely. The sense-affection is not just a physical change (for example, a modification of the retina or the

---

19. For the difficulty of translating *pathê, pathêmata* ("passions," "affections," "impressions"), see note 1 above and D. B. Fleet, 1995, 72–3. On the affections see H. J. Blumenthal, 1971, 45 ff.; and K. Corrigan, 1996a, 269 (re: the "intelligible" affection of soul; cf. 1986a, 175 and n. 23).

eye becoming a certain colour in perceiving that colour) but a psycho-physical change in which the sense-organ receives an appearance of the thing (for example, the way a certain object is blue—whether this is conceived as the eye actually becoming blue or as the eye assuming the form of blue in the object), which is simultaneously an affection of the soul in the compound. What is passive from the viewpoint of the reception and transmission of the form is active from the viewpoint of the direct perception of the sense-object. The soul does judge and fit its perceptions to the higher standards of discursive reason and intellect (cf. I, 1 [53] 7; V, 3 [49] 3; VI, 7 [38] 5–6), but perception is not a process of soul judging its affections. The "soul," or "self," directly perceives sense-objects (already in an interpretive or cognitive way) by means of the affections of the compound or ensouled body. The affections, therefore, make a decisive contribution to the contents of sense-perception and surely also to the development of conceptual activities.

The point is this: while Plotinus' analyses of perception and sensation are sufficiently difficult and obscure to support significantly different interpretations, it would be mistaken to write off the impassible soul thesis as a form of preposterous dualism involving a ghostly Platonic soul intuiting things directly and somehow added to the compound entity of soul and body. Plotinus' position is more complex than this. The soul is not an added entity to the compound or ensouled body, but the unifying power that makes perception possible. The percipient subject is an organic unity by virtue of the presence of soul, so that one should not be able to say on this account "my hand or eye senses x and so do I" or "I perceive x and so does my soul." While some of Plotinus' treatments of perception and of soul, along with Augustine's early works against skepticism in search of indubitable principles, clearly foreshadow the Cartesian *cogito* and the modern mind-body problem (as E. K. Emilsson has suggested on the basis of a penetrating study of sense-perception in the *Enneads*), Plotinus' theory of the impassible soul should not be taken in any sense as an example or precursor of later introspective theory or of what Gilbert Ryle terms "Descartes' myth" in the *Concept of Mind*, for the soul in Plotinus is neither an addition to nor a part of nor even an additional level of explanation to the compound organism: the soul is about what the compound organism actually means. In other words, a guided tour of perception and of soul's place in perception in the *Enneads* would not enumerate all the parts and then look for the soul, for this would contradict what I take to be Plotinus' fundamental position that there are no parts in the first place without the principle that organizes and unifies them. Neither the soul perceives nor the organism, nor even "we" by "having" soul, but we "insofar as we are soul" (cf. I, 1 [53] 13). So the impassible soul thesis, at least on this account, is compatible with a realist view not only of perception but also of integral action in which the "we" who act are genuine agents and neither puppets nor additional spiritual entities nor indifferent superhuman sages.

2.6. Soul-body and beyond (I, 1, 4-7)

With the above in mind, we can look at the soul-body relation.[20] In I, 1, 7, Plotinus characterizes this relation in a single unifying sentence:

> Let it be the compound then that perceives, and the soul by her presence does not give herself in this qualified way either to the compound or to the other element in the compound but makes out of the body qualified in this way and a kind of light that is given from herself the nature of the living creature, something different, to which perceiving and all the other affections of the living creature are said to belong. (7, 1–6)

We cannot read the above sentence meaningfully without being aware of the tangled history of preceding thought on the question, particularly the following:

1. Plato's view of the soul as immortal, incorporeal, and incomposite (or noncomposite) in the *Phaedo* and yet composed in a different way, internally, in the *Republic, Phaedrus,* and *Timaeus.*[21]

2. Aristotle's view, in opposition to Plato, that soul as the organizing form of the living body is mortal, but that intellect perhaps, which does not seem to be the function of a particular bodily organ, may be immortal (*De Anima* II, 2; III, 4–5). The difficulty of accounting for these two views in Aristotle, however, is the subsequent history of interpretation of his *De Anima.*[22]

3. The Stoic materialistic view[23] that soul is a kind of body with, perhaps, a limited impersonal immortality and the Epicurean view that soul is a collection of fine (neuron-like) atoms, as opposed to the fatty atoms that make up our denser and slower parts.

In an early work, IV, 7 [2] (which is very worth consulting together with the major works on soul IV, 3–5 [27–29], and IV, 8 [6]), Plotinus argued that soul is not a body or something dependent upon the body or a harmony or epiphenomenon of bodily parts. His arguments are worth looking at, and for a quick sketch see O'Meara, 1993, 12–21).[24]

---

20. On the soul-body question in Plotinus see H. J. Blumenthal, 1971, chapter 2; A. N. M. Rich, 1963, 2–15; E. K. Emilsson, 1988, 145–8 compares Plotinus with Descartes; see also Emilsson, 1991 (in S. Everson, ed.), 148–65; D. J. O'Meara, 1985, 247–62; K. Corrigan, 1985; 1996a, 320–82.

21. On Plato's psychology see T. M. Robinson, 1970 *Plato's Psychology*, Toronto; W. K. C. Guthrie IV, 1975; S. Lovibund, 1991 (in S. Everson, ed.), 35–55.

22. See especially M. Nussbaum and A. Rorty, 1992.

23. On the Stoic notion of soul and body see A. Long, 1982, 34–57; on Plotinus' relation to Stoic thought see A. Graesar, *Plotinus and the Stoics,* Leiden, 1972, and in connection with his anti-Stoic polemic in IV, 7 (2), M. Van Straaten, 1975, 164–70.

24. See also Plato, *Phaedo* 42 a ff. (Socrates' refutation of Simmias' epiphenomenalist objection).

How does Plotinus approach the question in the earlier chapters of I, 1? He outlines a series of possibilities in chapter 3:

1. Soul and body are mixed, in the sense of a physical blending.[25]
2. The soul is "woven through" the body, as Plato describes the soul of the world as "woven through" its body at *Timaeus* 36 e 2 (see Appendix A, 3).
3. The soul is not separated from the matter (i.e., it is a form "in" matter).
4. The soul is a form touching upon matter, as the steersman steers the ship.
5. In one perspective, soul is separated ("that which uses" the body) and in another perspective, soul is mingled and aligned with the body.

Plotinus rejects number 1 on the grounds that a) rather than soul's being mingled with body the reverse should be true (body needs and desires soul), and b) the mixture is not possible anyway and is like talking about mixing chalk and cheese (4, 2–23). He is prepared to allow the Platonic form of number 2 on the grounds that "interweaving" could leave the soul unaffected like light in the world. But he seems determined not so much to reject number 3 as to turn it effectively into a species of numbers 4 and 5, which perhaps suits his argument but looks downright suspicious to the reader. There are good reasons why he should do this, but in order to see them we shall have to look briefly at how he treats number 3.

This is the non-separate form hypothesis, which Plotinus, following post-Aristotelian language, elsewhere calls an "enmattered" (*enylon eidos*) or immanent form of the body.[26] He goes on to cite Aristotle's most uncompromising analogy on this question: soul is the essence, or *logos*, of a physical body qualified in a certain way (i.e., not just any old body waiting around for a reincarnating soul), "just as if an instrument, axe, were a natural body; the substance of the axe would be what makes it an axe, and this would be its soul; for if this were separated, it would no longer be an axe" (*De Anima* 412 b 11–15). Aristotle's analogy seems clear: if the soul-body relation is like the shape of an axe to the iron of which it is made, then the soul cannot be its separable form. But strangely enough, Plotinus quotes Aristotle as if the analogy supported his own view, or at least did not oppose it:

> But if we suppose the relation to be like the shape of an axe imposed upon the iron, and then the compound, the axe, will do what it does, that is to say the iron shaped in this way, though by virtue of the shape, then we shall rather grant all the common affections to the body, though to a specific kind of body, "natural, organic, potentially having life." (4, 20–5)

---

25. For the Stoic theory of *krasis di' holou,* i.e., that one body can permeate another and yet remain unified, see *Ennead* II, 7 (37); Alexander of Aphrodisias, *De Mixtione.*

26. On immanent forms see A. C. Lloyd, 1981; R. W. Sharples, 1987. Cf. *Enneads* II, 6 (17); J. M. Rist, 1967, chapter 8; on the sensible object see K. Corrigan, 1981; E. K. Emilsson, 1988.

But how, we might ask, should we attribute "common" affections only to the "specific kind of body" if they are "common" to both soul and body? By "specific" or "qualified" body Plotinus means, like Aristotle, a natural organic body that has the potentiality for the specific form it takes in its development (e.g., cats' bodies are not potentially human). Plotinus' thought is far too compressed for ready comprehension here. He supposes for the sake of argument that since the specific body is itself a compound of form and matter then perhaps it could serve as the compound-subject we need. But by human being we do not mean "specific body," and Plotinus observes cryptically that Aristotle indicates this in the *De Anima:* "He also says it is absurd 'to say the soul weaves,' so that is absurd as well to say she desires or is pained; we should attribute these affections rather to the living creature" (4, 25–7). It is "better," Aristotle says in context, not to say that the soul does these things or that the soul thinks and learns but that the human being does these things by virtue of the soul (*De Anima* 408 b 11–15). On this understanding, Plotinus concludes, we should attribute these affections to the living creature, not just to the body, and this surely makes good sense.

This leads Plotinus to the central question of these early chapters, which is still situated in the context of number 3 above, the non-separate form hypothesis, or enmattered form. What is the living creature? That is, what is the organic human being as a whole whom we meet every day on the street? "But we must say that the living creature is either the body of this specific kind or the conjoint of body and soul or some different third thing that has come to be out of both" (5, 1–2). In other words, we have to decide from among the various options uncovered implicitly or explicitly thus far: qualified body, compound, or something else. Why this "something different"? Plotinus has not mentioned it explicitly yet because to him it is already obvious. Still we cannot help but think that he is slipping in a third option underhandedly so that he can develop his own spiritualist hypothesis. In fact, he is still thinking of the problems with the axe analogy in the context of Aristotle's thought as a whole and of how to get the most precise and reasonable view of the soul-body relation at the same time, though admittedly this is not apparent.

The trouble with the axe analogy is that while it expresses the concrete unity of the soul-body relation, it is still only an analogy drawn from an inanimate relation. This does not bother Plotinus so much as does its static character. (Aristotle probably did not intend this, since the form and matter of an artifact have to be conceived dynamically anyway to be comprehensible: an artist makes the form in the matter for a purpose). Are we to think of soul and body as: a) simply a shaped object; b) form *and* matter; or c) something new that emerges out of their causal interaction? Aristotle, in fact, insists that compounds cannot be properly understood simply as material aggregates (e.g., a line is not an assembling of points but a line, or a syllable is not just its elements [a and b] but, as he insists twice in the *Metaphysics,* a syllable or "something different" [*heteron ti*] [cf. 1041 b 16–19]); nor can it be understood without including the formal cause that makes them one. In looking for the cause of anything, we do not just want to know what it is made of (i.e., its constituents) but why x attaches to y (cf. *Metaphysics* 1041 a 11) or "why the matter is some definite thing" (cf. 1041 b 5–6). For Aristotle, we cannot express something's essential nature just by giving a constituent definition; we must give a causal definition of why the elements that make up the compound form a new organic unity.

This is precisely what Plotinus has in mind. The qualified body is not all that we mean by "living creature," nor do we mean soul *and* body, as a constituent definition or an aggregate of elements. Instead, a living creature is "something different" from its elements, and that difference has to be expressed as a causal interaction, not just as if we are talking of two objects or things (cf. II, 7 [37] 3). The definition has to take account of the whole range of the experience of the *human* living creature in physical, psychophysical, and psychological terms (partly, this is what Plotinus explores in I, 1, 5–6).

To summarize Plotinus' single sentence defining the human being in I, 1, 7, 1–6, cited above, the human being is the compound subject that perceives things directly but by virtue of soul (which is the cause of a thing's being human or being anything else). This organizing presence in the body is expressed not in terms of a quality being "in" matter, for soul is not "in" the body in that way (if soul is *substantially* present to the body), but as a causally creative, organic presence that does not lose her power as soul by being the organizing form of the body. How does Plotinus express this? First, "the soul by her presence does not give herself in this qualified way either to the compound or to the other element in the compound" (7, 1–3); that is, soul does not *stop* being the forming principle by her presence. Second, "she makes"; that is, she remains a causal power. And third, "she makes out of the body qualified in this way and a kind of light that is given from herself the nature of the living creature, something different" (7, 3–5); out of the body as potential in its own character and from what the soul, as the principle of life, motion, and cognition, gives to the compound, emerges a new concrete form: an ensouled or animate human being. Searching for an image to express the effect of soul on body in an earlier work, Plotinus preferred warmth to light (because light leaves body unaffected, whereas heat brings about change; IV, 4 [28] 18, 4 ff.; cf. IV, 3 [27] 22–3). But if light is the closest image to the incorporeal, as Plotinus often suggests,[27] then perhaps it remains the best means of suggesting the pervasive intimate presence of soul.

This view has two major consequences. First, the human being is a real agent and a concrete, unified being by virtue of the soul as the organizing principle of the whole body. "We" really perform our own actions, but we do so by the power of our souls, just as Aristotle says the human being weaves and thinks "by virtue of the soul" (408 b 14–15). Second, in us the soul is an immanent, indwelling form, but for Plotinus the soul is also a form that can be separated; she is not cut off from the rest of soul just because she makes us who we are. One of Plotinus' early criticisms of Aristotelianism is effectively that Aristotelianism itself gives rise to the problem of a plurality of substantial forms (IV, 7 [2]). Of course both Aristotle and Alexander of Aphrodisias later are concerned to avoid any such view. Aristotle argues, for example, that a substance cannot be composed of substances, and Alexander that the rational soul cannot exist on its own

---

27. On Plotinus' view of the incorporeality of light see I, 6 (1), 3; II, 1 (40), 7, 26–8; IV, 5 (29) 7; and W. Beierwaltes, 1961; R. Ferwerda, 1965; K. Corrigan, 1993a.

for this would mean that there would be many souls in the human being.[28] Not without good reason, however, Plotinus argues that if soul is the inseparable form, or "entelechy," of body, then one is compelled to introduce *another* entelechy, or substantial form, namely intellect, to account for soul. To avoid a plurality of such forms, Plotinus concludes, it is better to suppose that the soul is not an inseparable form but an immortal substance in its own right (cf. IV, 7 [2] 8 [5]). The range of soul and intellect in a single human being, and the many souls and intellects in the unity of soul and intellect, do not make for a quantitative plurality of substantial forms; rather, they denote directly what substance is.

In this light, the view that form and matter do not really "unite" in Plotinus as they do in Aristotle, or that "forms can be added to one another without the concrete being ever becoming one" (Bréhier, 1928, 20; tr. J. Thomas, 175), is simply false. It depends in each case what we are speaking about. The union of qualities and matter for Plotinus *is* an accidental, not a substantial union. There is, however, a more substantial unity of form and matter in the divine heavenly bodies (as we shall see in V, 8 [31] 3; chapter 4 below). At root, only in the light of the causal form, or *logos,* is the concrete being *one,* for the soul as an active principle in the organism is the true cause of its unity. Soul and intellect in their own natures are more intensive unities still, but it is by virtue of their presence everywhere that each thing becomes a concrete unity and that human beings as authentic agents of their own actions are individual beings.

Plotinus compels us to reverse our usual way of looking "out" at the world and seeing external things as thoroughly solid and ourselves as somewhat insubstantial. For Plotinus, as for Plato (Timaeus 36 d–e), soul is not "in" body; body is "in" soul (cf. IV, 3 [27] 22). There are good reasons for supposing this. Qualities need to be "in" things, because they do not just float around. They need subjects to qualify, just as verbs and adjectives need subjects in a sentence. Because of this need for subjects in ordinary experience and language, we say that souls and intellects are in bodies. In a simple way this is true since intellects do not just float around either. But if by bodies we mean organic assemblages of qualities, quantities, and the like, then we really mean that bodies are in souls in the sense that they depend upon agents, persons, or intellectual subjects for their meaning and articulation. Further, if the soul is the organizing principle, then what is organized must be "in" its organizing principle for its being, preservation, development, and intelligibility. Forms of address are similarly nuanced. Some people, it is true, just talk "at" you, as though "you" were an object to bear the torrent of their words, and we certainly can treat other people as though they were nothing but objects (i.e., objective qualities in a substrate); but most of the time, fortunately, we see people as agents or persons; that is, definitely not "souls" simply (though we sometimes can address the soul of another person directly, but we are aware that doing so is unusual). Nor do we see people as soul and body complexes (we could do so, but it would be terribly unwieldy) but as whole beings or structured and structuring agents. When we know people well and do not take them for granted, we meet them directly as whole persons with whom we can

---

28. Alexander, *De anima,* 6–11, Bruns.

share our thoughts and feelings immediately. Aristotle too holds the view that a proper form of self-relatedness is a precondition of what one gives to a friend, for in mutual friendship of the highest kind (beyond mere pleasure or usefulness, but inclusive of both) one is, and strives to be even more, a good for one's friend. In this sense, Aristotle argues, one should look to gratify and obey "what most rules in oneself" (EN IX, 8); instead of living the life of the compound (to syntheton, or what Aristotle calls the form "in" something else), he concludes, one should strive to live one's life "in" or according to a different principle, namely, the life of intellect, "which is man more than anything else" (EN X, 7, 1177 b, 25 ff.). The idea of turning the focus of one's being from things to soul and intellect, and in the most concrete, natural ways, is also fundamentally Aristotelian.

For Plotinus too the range of the human being is such that some of our friendships belong to the physical compound simply. Here Plotinus follows Plato in the *Republic* in talking about this compound form of existence as that of "the many headed beast" (*Republic* 590 a, 588 c), a life in which integrated human agency tends to be pulled apart in many different directions simultaneously. If we live only on the level of appearances, for example, our actions conflict with one another and contradict themselves, sometimes without our being aware of it. We are driven by circumstance and the gripping superficialities of passing desires or even of single-minded, steadfast, fully self-conscious drives for power or other goals, instead of being self-directed agents in a world which is not built up of our own preferences (cf. VI, 5 [23] 15). But not all of our actions need be like this. As in Aristotle, we can live the life of a higher compound existence which is more our own; so some of our friendships belong, Plotinus says, to "the inner human being" (I, 1, 10, 15; cf. *Republic* 589a).

Plotinus, of course, goes far beyond anything that Aristotle suggests. If substances are organizing principles, ultimately separable from the physical things they organize yet in a way containing within themselves the things organized, then what are we to suppose about such substances? Can it be that a) a world of such principles exists just by chance, or b) that all these principles (which already organize) are just waiting around to be organized themselves or c) that they are essentially unconnected with one another? They cannot come about by chance because chance, as Aristotle so powerfully argues in *Physics* II, is only meaningful in the context of the regular causality in the universe. We could not even recognize a "chance" or purely chaotic occurrence if the universe were not intelligible in the first place. They cannot be waiting around in a heap to be organized (as we shall see also in III, 8 [30] 8), since they are not unorganized heaps themselves to start with. Nor can they be essentially unconnected because if human beings and animals are connected at all they are more connected by shared experiences, lives, friendship, understanding, and love than by anything else. So connectedness seems preeminently to be a mark of soul, intellect, or the Good. Consequently, for Plotinus, souls and intellects must be organized from within already and must therefore be essentially connected so that the partial intellect and even the lowliest soul already bears an internal relation to the whole and the whole to the part. They must therefore constitute a many in one. This, at any rate, is part of Plotinus' thinking on the question, so it is natural for him to think of soul and intellect as the ultimate subject, that "in" which everything else is rooted and of which we are for the most part, if at all, only dimly conscious, just as we are unconscious of a good deal of what could be "ours" because we habitually define our normal frames of conscious reference so narrowly. "We do not always use everything we have" (I, 1, 11, 5–6).[29]

2.6.1. Problems in Plotinus' anthropology:
Intellect and the range of being human

There are many problems with the range of activities and beings Plotinus wants to include in the human being. Some of these are apparent in the later chapters of I, 1. First, the "we" seems to become so fluid that to pin it down precisely is very difficult (11, 1 ff.). Second, the language Plotinus uses seems to threaten any possible unity of the human being: "the human being within" (i.e., aligned with intellect), the human being as a concrete agent (7, 1 ff.), the living creature (i.e., the compound or ensouled body), the qualified body (which of course is ensouled, but the emphasis is rather upon body), and then "the beast." How can there be "human" oneness on these terms, especially when the rest of the animal kingdom seems quite intimately related to our lower humanity? My DNA structure may vary only slightly from that of chimpanzees, but from Plotinus one may get the impression that a chimpanzee or a lion threatens to leap out of my emotional experience, even my perceptual experience, if I am not careful. Plotinus is explicitly concerned with this problem since he mentions it directly (11, 8), but he does not give any real answer to it in this treatise. Third, I even seem in danger of being split up altogether, a little like the soul of Fra Alberigo in Dante's *Divine Comedy, Inferno* 33, 122–36, which is already in hell *before* his physical death. The case of Heracles is equally disquieting: part of him is here below, part above "because he was active and not contemplative" (I, 1, 12, 37). Finally, then, Plotinus' cavalier attitude to the problem of how we reconcile the true self's faultlessness with Plato's accounts of the soul's judgement and punishment after death ("Well, one should accept whichever argument one wants," 12, 4–5) may not exactly inspire confidence (cf. chapter 1, part I, passage 6).

I shall not take up all of these problems here. Instead I shall contrast several rather different views of the human being, all of which Plotinus tends to see at once, though they may seem mutually exclusive to us. Together, however, they shed light on the problems of how human beings are related to the animal and plant worlds as well as on how Plotinus views human substantiality and its limitations. My overall thesis could be summed up as follows: human beings, for Plotinus, are inherently multidimensional, and only as such are they definable. But they constitute one species only, and a narrow specific view is not enough for an authentic reflexive scientific model.

Instead of the two-man theory Plotinus proposes in I, 1 (53), 11, he sets out a three-man theory in VI, 7 [38] and thinks even "this man here" is definable in that context (as

---

29. See generally on this G. J. P. O'Daly, 1973.

well as the rest of the animal kingdom). There is (1) "man himself" in the intelligible, (2) "man" as the productive cause inherent in the thing, and (3) the "composite man" of process. This looks like Plotinus' solution to the "third man" argument: there is nothing to prevent there being a "Form" in intellect as well as the productive form in soul and the compound because we are not talking of a common abstract nature or concept in any of these cases.

The relationship among these three is complex but worth following through (see especially chapter 1, part II, passage 9). In each thought and activity of man, Plotinus says, "the whole man shone forth bringing himself along with the thought of him" (VI, 7, 2, 51–2). Now if we define the human being as only the casual association of rational soul and body (4, 12–18), we do not catch this wholeness of eternal existence but only "indicate" the "composite man" or "the man who will be" (Aristotle uses this phrase of the composite objects of physical science as opposed to the formal objects of theoretical science, *PA* 640 a 3–4). We do not even define what "enmattered" forms are (4, 16–20; these we met above in I, 1 [53] 3 ff.). But enmattered forms, as we have seen in I, 1, have to be defined in the light of the productive or causal form (4, 21) "that has made *this human being* [i.e., the composite man], that *exists in him* [*enhyparchon*], and is *not separate* [*ou choriston*]" 4, 28–30).

To summarize thus far, then, "intelligible man" is present in "man" as a productive cause, just as the whole is present to the part without destroying it or losing its own nature. "Composite man" cannot be defined unless he is brought into this perspective. This leads Plotinus to a very real difficulty, which we too have been feeling throughout our reading of I, 1. Yes, we might say to Plotinus, we are prepared to grant that the human being is a real agent (if you say so), but this business about "by virtue of the soul" (in I, 1), or by virtue of the "productive cause-man" and "man-himself" really makes soul or intellect the only proper subject, and the poor, composite third man a rag-and-bone affair to be manipulated by his two big brothers or sisters.

Plotinus actually formulates this problem and answers it in VI, 7, 4. Either "soul will provide the rational life," he says, "and the human being will be an act of soul and *not substance,* or the soul will be the human being" (4, 34–6). On the first horn of the dilemma, "soul" will be the form and the "human being" the matter; however, on these terms the human being will not be *substance*, that is, a proper subject in its own right, but a material puppet manipulated by soul. On the second horn of the dilemma, we should simply have to identify the human being and the soul (which is not possible because "this human being" necessarily includes "this body").

Plotinus rejects both alternatives. As to the first, he simply takes for granted in VI, 7, 4, that it is untenable. Throughout the *Enneads*, Plotinus insists on the substantial unity of the human being, which prevents manipulation simply by fate, for instance, as though the movement of my leg were determined entirely by cosmic influences (cf. III, 1 [3]), or my actions by providence. I am the agent of my own actions "with" or "against" the influence of providence (cf. III, 3 [48] 5, 48–50). The decision is mine. In I, 1, 13, Plotinus asks if it is "we" or "the soul" that has conducted the investigation.

It is definitely "we," he replies, "but by the soul." But what does "by the soul" mean? "By having soul"? No, Plotinus replies, we investigate insofar as we *are* soul (13, 1–3). In other words, the historical subject, or ego, is not a reflection or manipulation of a substantial principle but a subject in its own right to the degree that it *is* that principle. Plotinus does not mean that we simply are "soul" because "soul" possesses an extension that goes far beyond being only human.

As for the second horn of the dilemma, while the human being cannot be an act of soul, neither can he or she be soul simply, since if we define being human exclusively in terms of the rational soul, Plotinus asks, "whenever the soul goes into another living creature, how is the soul not man?" (4, 36–8). Just when we think we are getting to the heart of the matter, Plotinus introduces what to most of us looks like a dead-end: the transmigration of souls (although of course millions of people alive today believe in metempsychosis and, like Plotinus, could presumably offer a reasonable defence of their views). But Plotinus' point can surely be translated into terms that fit the present context and look much more reasonable. Why is the human being not soul simply? Because the term "soul" extends far beyond the species "human being." Human beings are only a part, and not the most important part (cf. I, 1, 7, 8), of the visible living creature, which is this world, and the intelligible living creature in which it has its meaning and being. So we cannot define "this human being" without all human beings concretely (for Plotinus) in the productive *logos* (through which the whole of intelligible "man" shines through), and we cannot define a single species as though it held supreme sway and bore no essential relation to everything else. There is no human being without all beings. At the same time, the human being can be defined, Plotinus concludes, not as an assemblage of contingent parts but as an active compound understood in terms of a causal relation among its elements: "what prevents man from being a compound, soul in a *logos* of a definite kind [i.e., a qualified body, as we saw in I, 1 above], the *logos* being an activity, so to speak, of a definite kind [i.e., the body understood as an active form, not just a potency], and the activity being unable to exist without the active subject [i.e., the body depends upon soul for its animation and organization]" (VI, 7, 5, 2–5).

The whole of this passage is intensely difficult and highly technical, and it is hard to see the significance of this final definition since it looks so abstract. But Plotinus' argument is rather revolutionary, for it brings together in a new way Aristotle's position that the soul is the nonseparate form of the body with Plato's position that the incorporeal soul is the true window upon the intelligible world. Only when the "three men" are brought together into a single view can the composite man of process become definable as an individual whole form. So Plotinus holds the following views. (1) Individuals are definable not because they share an abstract common nature, but because their whole beings can be seen in a causally active way when they are grasped in terms of the immanent productive soul that makes them. (2) Both matter *and* form enter into the substance of the human being. Neoplatonism is typically taken to task for its negative view of matter. But as we shall see (chapter 3.8), this depends upon what we *mean* in different cases. Here, if matter can be seen as an activity, then it becomes meaningful in principle. Thus, while soul is the productive principle, body and matter are transformed by soul into a specific *logos* (or as Aristotle calls it at *De Anima* 412 a 20-1, "a physical body potentially having life"). In the *Metaphysics*, Aristotle insists that the human being cannot be defined without bringing *human* matter into the form and that even bodily parts should properly be defined by reference to their *function* (1035 b 14–18; 1036 b 21–3). For Aristotle, this is a necessary consequence of stating "the substance according to the *logos*" or "the essence of a specific kind of body" (1035 b 15–16). In other words, the *Metaphysics* suggests that material potencies should be defined in terms of functions or activities.

This is precisely what Plotinus does in VI, 7, 4–5. The definition "soul in a specific kind of *logos*" brings form and matter together in the *substance* of the human being (cf. III, 3 [48] 4, 29–41). Soul also has other powers and a nature rather different from the way Aristotle conceives it. For Plotinus, then, the transmigration of souls is still possible (cf. III, 3 [48] 4, 40–4), but this does not affect the conclusion that the human being "here" (VI, 7, 4, 3), who is the object of Plotinus' enquiry, is the unity of both elements, soul and a specific human body, in the *logos*. The matter is "potential" in the sense that it cannot function without an active subject, but it appears in the definition as a developed activity. In other words, this developed matter, our living bodies, in the light of its cause, *is* form. This helps us to see much more clearly what Plotinus means when he says that matter itself is "an ultimate form" (V, 8 [31] 7, 18–23). Even the material cause is intelligible in the light of the active beauty of divine and human creativity. So for Plotinus an anthropology rooted in soul and intellect is one in which real human individuals and their determinate material structures emerge as intelligible.[30] Otherwise, the human being looks contingent and accidental, and matter becomes more or less only a vanishing point.[31] Somehow we find ourselves poised between these two anthropologies.

At the same time, perhaps this also will provide a framework for understanding the limitations of being human in intellect. To become a human being is in one sense to stop being everything: "And yet man also crafts a form other than himself since he has become other than what he is; for he has fallen away from being the all, now that he has become man; but when he stops being man he walks on high . . . for once he has come to belong to the whole he makes the whole" (V, 8 [31] 7, 31–5). Or again, when we become intellect, the human being "thinks himself again, not any longer as man but having become altogether other . . ." (V, 3 [49] 4, 10–12). The reason for this is that while intellect includes humanity in one sense (in many passages throughout the Enneads),[32] it is nonetheless a humanity transformed by the whole. As Aristotle says of theoretical wisdom or *sophia,* it would be absurd to identify a wisdom that contemplates the whole of being with the narrower interests of one species of being as though the human being

30. Though the negative perspective of "removal" is important. See V, 3 (49), 9, 1 ff.

31. To get a sense of the range of Plotinus' reflections upon matter, see chapter 1 and especially chapters 3.8 and 4.13.

32. E.g., VI, 7 (38), 4, 17; VI, 8 (39), 14, 1–4; and more generally VI, 7 (38), 4–7; II, 3 (52), 9.

were the best thing in the universe. One has to go beyond specific interests to see the intelligible wisdom of the universe in its own right (cf. *EN* VI, 6). Moreover, Plotinus never forgets that horses, plants, fangs, tusks, and teeth are not just lowlier forms that we can take or leave but safeguards that have appeared for preservation and protection in a deficient universe of which we are but partial guardians and whose "physical wisdom" we share with the rest of the animal and plant kingdoms.[33]

What precisely is involved in this broad extension of being human which ranges from intellect and the divine to human and animal consciousness?

First, how are we related to intellect (I, 1, 8, 1–8)? As we have seen, "we" are not simply intellect, though intellect is always present to us. Intellect is "ours" and "not ours" (cf. V, 3 [49] 3–4) in the sense that it transcends us and we have to put ourselves in touch with it and "use" it. In V, 3, 4, Plotinus distinguishes between being in touch with, or in accordance with, intellect and becoming identical with intellect. In an early work, these two phases are called "intellects" (V, 1 [10] 10, 12). One provides the power of reasoning to the soul (i.e., intellect proper), and one reasons (i.e., the intellect of soul). Sometimes, reasoning is a defect or weakness, but at other times, as both here in V, 1 (10) 10, and I, 1, 8, 2, it is in principle an intelligible reality. Since it needs no bodily organ for its operation, Plotinus argues in V, 1 (10) 10, one could place it as "separate and unmixed" (cf. Anaxagoras, fr. 12; Aristotle, *De Anima* III, 4–5) in "the primary intelligible realm" (see chapter 1, part I, passage 1). Here in I, 1, 8, 2, it is "that disposition of soul that she has as one of the things from intellect," and in 9, 23 ff., it is the "true discursive reason of soul" that "is an activity of intelligible thoughts and frequently there is a likeness and community between the things outside and these within." In fact, reasoning that has to adapt its vision of the good to the changing circumstances of life can provide "more beautiful" activities (*energeiae*) than the activities of the good person who does not have to make these adaptations (cf. I, 4 [46] 13, 1–4). Adaptive rational creativity can apparently manifest intelligible reality even more than where no adaptation is necessary (cf. IV, 4 [28] 2). The two aspects of reasoning, positive and negative, are treated together in IV, 3 (27) 18, 1–4, 10–13: the need for reasoning comes into the soul when she is in difficulty, full of care, and in a state of greater weakness; but if one understands reasoning "to be the state of mind [*diathesis*] that exists in souls always proceeding from intellect and that is standing activity and impression of intellect, they would employ reasoning in that other world, too." Reasoning in its positive aspect points the way to our identity with intellect, and the soul's manner of possessing forms "unrolled and separated, as it were," anticipates their all-togetherness in intellect (see chapter 3, sections 3.14; 3.19; 3.21).

Second, how are we related to god (I, 1, 8, 8–23)? "The god" is the One (or also, elsewhere, intellect) to which the higher soul naturally gravitates. Treatise II, 3 (52) 9, (written immediately before this work) is worth comparing generally: ". . . to the other soul, which is outside the body, belongs the ascent to the higher world, to the fair and divine that *no one masters,* but either *makes use* of it that he may be it and live by it,

---

33. Cf. VI, 7 (38), 8–10.

withdrawing himself; or else he is bereft of this soul, and lives under destiny" (24–28). (On the nature of soul and soul-powers see chapter 3.14, and cf. I, 4 [46] 3, 18–40). Third, compare I, 1, 12, and IV, 8 (6) 5–8.[34] Fourth, regarding the double "we" and the "middle" of our being (I, 1, 10, 1–10; 11), who are we? Either the beast is included in our nature (i.e., the ensouled body), or "we" are to be referred to the "true human being" whose excellences are rooted in the soul that separates herself (and is separable even here). I translate chôrizomenê (10, 9) as "separating" (cf. Phaedo 67 c 6 and II, 3 [52] 9, 20).[35] This (i.e., to retain her own nature) is the function of the pure soul even if she is immanent. Each is double; one human being is "the compound in a certain way," the other "himself" (II, 3 [52] 9, 30, 1–2); the higher man makes use of the higher soul "withdrawing himself" (like the soul above in I, 1, 10), while the common life belongs more to body (9, 19–27). Compare the three kinds of human being, and the double city in the best human being (one above and one composed of the lower elements ordered by the principles above) in IV, 4 (28) 17. I, 4 (46) 4, 6 and following indicates that one is not a human being at all if one does not have a complete life of perception, reasoning, and true intellect, but it is better to be (rather than have) this life. On the other hand, one does not have to be conscious of it, Plotinus argues later (I, 4 [46] 9); perhaps one has been drugged or overcome by magic, or one could simply be asleep. Wisdom does not stop existing in the sleeping person. So the activity is prior to our awareness of the activity (10, 1 ff.). Characteristic human life, it appears, begins with the integration of the human being (i.e., the self-organisation of perception and reasoning illuminated by intellect), but this does not depend on consciousness.

How then are we to take I, 1, 11? The subject of lines 2–4 is not expressed, but it could be either "the faculties of the compound" or "the powers above." I prefer the latter but have left it ambiguous in my translation (as Plotinus does). On this understanding, the powers above cannot illuminate us if we are not receptive, but in order to be receptive those illuminations have to reach the "middle of our being," and we have to become consciously self-receptive and reorient ourselves toward a particular focus (cf. chapter 1, part I, passage 1: V, 1 [10] 12). "We" therefore appear to be a kind of proportional mean between the higher and the lower faculties (as in so many other passages: III, 9 [13] 3; IV, 4 [28] 3; IV, 6 [41] 3, 10; I, 4 [46] 10, 1 ff.; V, 3 [49] 3, 38; 6, 23 ff.). The self is never static or a given but a complex spotlight always in actualization.[36] This does not mean that conscious awareness determines who we are (cf. I, 4 [46] 9–10). "Conscious awareness, in fact, is likely to enfeeble the very activities of which there is consciousness" (I, 4 [46] 10, 28–9). The range of the self does not depend upon consciousness, but

---

34. On the impeccability, or the culpability conversely, of soul see J. Trouillard, 1953; and cf. IV, 8 (6), generally on soul's descent (chapter 1, parts I and II).

35. Phaedo 67 c 5–7: "And purification . . . [is] the separating soul from body as much as possible and accustoming her to . . . live both now and in the future alone by herself." II, 3, (52) 9, 19–21: "So we must flee from here [cf. Theaetetus 176 a 8–b 1] and separate ourselves from what has been added to us."

36. Cf. generally G. J. P. O'Daly, 1971; K. Corrigan, 1996a, 223–30.

it has to be integrated by intellect for an authentic life, and yet far more abysmal potencies of that range (which we do share with the "beast") can be actualized if we wish. If
the human soul enters a different species,[37] then the separable soul simply is not capable
of being received by the animal (i.e., "it is present without being present"). If the animal
does not have a human soul, then the image of soul in it (cf. I, 1, 7, 4) is from the whole
soul (either soul-hypostasis or the soul of the world, unlike our souls that are ours).

On one reading of Plato's image of the sea-god Glaucus (*Republic* X, 611 c ff.),
when the image of soul becomes corrupted so that it comes to depend upon the external almost entirely, then the soul herself becomes a compound, the mechanical "product of all the things that go to make her up" (I, 1, 12, 8–12).[38] Here is the "ghost-in-
the-machine," a self to haunt itself, a multiphrenic self clinging with parasitic force to
the insubstantial things it believes alone define its being.

Finally (re: I, 1, 12, 30 ff.), the fate of Heracles is to be the ultimate schizophrenic,
part above and part below (Plotinus attempts to reconcile two traditions, Heracles the
mortal hero and Heracles the exceptional man who became a god; compare IV, 3 [27]
27; 32).[39] How we are to conceive this is problematic, to say the least, and much more
problematic than the case of Fra Alberigo in Dante's *Inferno,* whose soul is *already* in
the Inferno before his physical death (canto XXXIII, 122–36). In this case at least, the
continuity between the practical and the theoretical lives, which Aristotle attempted to
establish in the *Nichomachean Ethics* (and *Eudemian Ethics*) and which Plotinus, as
we shall see, transformed in a revolutionary way in III, 8 (30), is radically disrupted.
What seems to be at stake in the Heracles-image is the ontological and psychological
difficulty of freeing the "shade" or shadow-soul. No simple divine *fiat* or superficial
psychological scrutiny can make the shadow or image cast by any existing thing (no
matter how good) simply disappear. Even the "good" casts a shadow. There is no substitute for the return to being. In I, 1, 13, Plotinus asks who really oversees the writing
of the treatise. *We* do, but not inasmuch as we *have* soul but inasmuch as we *are* soul.
The return of soul to her true nature is the fulfillment of an outpouring of being that is
essentially self-reflexive from the beginning.[40]

The laborious route to self-knowledge that human beings have to take is to ensure
that their "return to themselves" is not superficial or empty of real content. For Plotinus,
as for Porphyry and Proclus, simple beings like soul and intellect "return" to themselves directly.[41] This direct form of self-knowledge is not solipsistic introspection,
which is why there is no shortcut for human beings except to come to know themselves
in and through the world. Plotinus, Porphyry, and Proclus call this laborious form of

---

37. On transmigration of the soul see III, 2 (47), 13, 11–15; III, 4 (15); and A. N. Rich,
1957, 232–8.

38. Cf. Plato, *Phaedo* 80 c–84 c; K. Corrigan, 1996 a, 223–30.

39. Cf. J. Pépin, *Idées grecques sur l'homme et sur Dieu,* Paris 1971, 167–99; H. J. Blumenthal, 1971, 86.

40. See especially J. Trouillard, 1955 a and b.

41. Plotinus, V, 3 (49); Porphyry, in Stobaeus 3, 579–83, Wachsmuth-Hense; *Proclus, Elements of Theology,* props. 31–35, 37–39, etc.

self-knowing a "complete" return to oneself, which reflects the perfect self-knowing of intellect. Aquinas, too, insists upon this *"reditio completa,"* and it is only God who knows all things, potencies, possibilities, even future contingencies, through and in his essence. Even angels have such knowledge only through God, not through themselves.[42] Plotinus is perhaps a *little* more optimistic because for him even the divine intellect "is a part of us and to this we go up" (13, 7–8). Even so, substantial self-knowledge is not directly in our power at all, though we are essentially reflexive beings; we can only prepare the organs of reception and the inclusive eye of the soul (as we shall see in V, 8 [31] 9) and address in practice and prayer the real source of reflexivity in us and the universe as a whole. Even then the very simplest things in this physical universe—bare possibilities, the vaguest of yearnings that we almost certainly should not notice at all, no matter how extensive the enquiry—can be knowable only from the simplest, most comprehensive self-reflexive power of all, that of the Good.

---

42. *De Veritate* X, 8; *Summa Contra Gentiles* III, 46; *Summa Theologiae,* I, Q.14, a 2.

Chapter 3

The Range of Plotinus' Thought:
From Nature and Contemplation to the One

Text: Ennead III, 8 (30): On Nature and
Contemplation and the One

4.   Just suppose we were to play at first, before undertaking to be serious, and say that everything desires contemplation and looks to this goal, not only rational but irrational living creatures,[1] as well as the nature in plants and the earth that generates them, [5] and that all things aim to attain to this insofar as they can and their nature permits, but that different creatures contemplate and attain to their goal in different ways, some truly, and some only by grasping an imitation and image of this—could anyone support the strangeness of the argument? Well, since this enquiry arises among ourselves there will be no risk in playing with our own concerns. [10] Are we also contemplating right now then as we play? Yes, no doubt we and all who play are doing this or, at any rate, this is what they long for in their play. And it is likely that whether a child or a man is playing or being serious, the one plays and the other is serious for the sake of contemplation, and [15] every action has contemplation as its serious objective, compulsory action dragging contemplation still more to what is external, and so called voluntary action less so, but even this comes to be from desire for contemplation. But this issue we will take up later;[2] but now let us speak about the earth herself, and the trees, and plants in general, [20] and ask what is their contemplation and how we are going to trace back what is made and generated from the earth to the activity of contemplation, and how nature, which they say is without imagination and irrational,[3] both has contemplation in her and makes what she makes through contemplation, which she does not have [and how].

5.   It is no doubt clear to everyone that there are in nature's case neither hands nor feet nor any instrument either brought in from outside or natural to her, but that there is need of matter upon which nature will make and which she brings under form. We must in fact exclude levering from natural production. [5] For what kind of thrusting or leverage can make so many different colours and shapes of every kind?[4] For not even the wax-modellers [or modellers of small figures]— to whom people actually looked and thought that the craftsmanship of nature was

---

1.   Aristotle, *Nicomachean Ethics* (*EN*) 1172 b 9–10.
2.   III, 8, 6, 1 ff.
3.   SV II 1016.
4.   Cf. Cicero, *De Natura Deorum* I, 8, 19.

in their work—have the power to make colours unless they introduce colours from elsewhere into the things they make. But, as a matter of fact, those who thought nature's production was like art [10] ought to have considered that even in the case of those who pursue arts of this kind there must be something in them that remains unmoved according to which they will make their works with their hands; they ought to have gone back to the same kind of principle in nature and understood that the power that does not make by means of hands had to remain unmoved here too—[15] indeed that all of it had to remain unmoved. For nature certainly does not need to have some parts remaining unmoved and others in motion—for matter is what is moved, and nothing of nature is in motion—or else that unmoving principle will not be the first mover, nor even will nature be this mover, but only what is unmoved in the whole. Someone might object that the forming principle, in fact, is unmoved, but nature is [20] different from the forming principle and is in motion. But if they are going to say that all of nature is unmoved, then the forming principle will also be unmoved. For nature must, in fact, be a form and not composed from matter and form; for what need does nature have of hot or cold matter? For the matter that underlies nature and is crafted by her comes to her bearing this [25] or becomes qualified in this way, although the matter in itself has no quality, in being shaped by a forming principle. For it is not fire that has to approach matter in order for the matter to become fire, but a forming principle; that is no additional small sign that in living creatures and plants forming principles are the makers and nature is a forming principle, which makes another forming principle as its product, [30] which gives something to the substrate, but remains unmoved itself. The forming principle that is operative in the visible shape then is already last and a corpse and no longer capable of making another, but the one that has life, since it is the brother of that forming principle that makes the shape, and since it has the same power itself, makes in that which has come into being.

6. How then does the forming principle make and, by making in this way, attain to a kind of contemplation? It would seem that if it makes by remaining unmoved and remains in itself and is a forming principle, then it would itself be contemplation. For action occurs in accordance with a forming principle though the action is evidently different from the forming principle. [5] However, the forming principle that both accompanies and overlooks the action could not itself be action. If it is not action, then, but forming principle, it is contemplation; and in the case of every forming principle its last form results from contemplation and is contemplation in the sense of having been contemplated, but the forming principle before this is everything, one aspect of it in a different way, which is not nature, but soul; and the other is the forming principle in nature and [10] is nature. Does the forming principle itself then also result from contemplation? Yes, altogether from contemplation. But is this because it has also contemplated itself? Or how? For it is a finished product of contemplation and of something that has been contemplating. But how does nature in this case have contemplation? Indeed, she

does not have it as a result of reasoning; and I mean by reasoning the process of looking at her own content. Why then does she not have it [15] if she is a life and a forming principle and a making power? Is it because the process of looking is not yet having? But she does have, and it is precisely because she has that she also makes. Her being what she is means precisely, in her case, making, and her making power is coextensive with what she is. She is contemplation and object of contemplation, for she is a forming principle. So it is by being contemplation, [20] object of contemplation, and forming principle that she makes insofar as she is these things. Making then has for us proved to be contemplation, for it is a finished product of contemplation when the contemplation remains unmoved and does nothing else but makes by being contemplation.

7.   And if someone were to ask her why she makes, if she were willing to listen and speak to the questioner, she might say: "You should not ask but understand, you too, in silence, as I am silent and not accustomed to speak. What then should you understand? [5] That what has come to be is the object of my vision, as I am silent and an object of contemplation that has come to be naturally, and that since I have come to be from this kind of contemplation I am possessed of a vision-loving nature. And my act of contemplating makes my object of contemplation, just as the geometers draw their figures as they contemplate; but I do not draw figures, but contemplate, and [10] the lines of bodies come to be as if falling out of my contemplation. And I have the same experience as my mother and the beings who generated me; for they also are the result of contemplation, and my birth is the result of no action on their part; instead they are greater forming principles and in their contemplating themselves I have come to be." [15] So what does this mean? That what is called nature is a soul, offspring of an earlier soul with a more powerful life, a soul that has contemplation silently in herself not directed to what is above or even again to what is below, but at rest in what she is, in her own stillness and [20] self-perception, so to speak, and in this understanding and intimate perception she saw what comes after her, insofar as she could and was no longer seeking but has perfected an object of contemplation that was splendid and full of grace. And if anyone wants to grant her a kind of understanding or perception, it is not the kind of perception or understanding to be found in other things but as if one were to liken the activity of someone fast asleep to that of someone awake. [25] For she is resting in contemplating the object of her contemplation, an object that has come to her because she remains unmoved in and with herself and is herself an object of contemplation; and her contemplation is noiseless, but less clear; for there is a different contemplation, clearer to see, and nature is the image of another contemplation. It is also for this reason in fact that what has been generated by nature [30] is altogether weak, because a weak contemplation makes a weak contemplative object; human beings, as well, when they become too weak for contemplating, make action a shadow of contemplation and reason. For since contemplation is not enough for them because of weakness of

soul, and they do not have the power to grasp the object of vision sufficiently and so [35] they are not filled yet still long to see it, they are carried into action in order to see what they cannot grasp by intellect. So whenever they make something, it is because they want to see it themselves and because they want everyone else to contemplate and perceive it, when their purpose is realized, as far as possible, in action. In every case actually we shall find that making [40] and doing are either a weakening or an accompaniment of contemplation, a weakening if one has nothing after what has been done, and an accompaniment if one has another object to contemplate before this greater than what has been made. For who, when he can contemplate what is primarily true, goes after the image of the true? [45] Less intelligent children also bear witness to this, who have no capacity for studies or contemplative pursuits and gravitate to arts and manual crafts.

8.   But since in the case of nature we have explained in what way coming into being is contemplation, let us now go on to the soul before nature and explain how the contemplation of this soul, her love of learning and enquiring spirit, the birth pains resulting from what she has come to know, and her fullness, [5] have made her, when she has become wholly an object of contemplation, produce another contemplative object; it is just as art produces; when each art is full, it makes another little art like it in a toy that has an image of everything in it; otherwise, however, these objects of vision and contemplation are unclear, as it were, and cannot help themselves.[5] [10] The first part [the rational part] of soul then, which is above and is always being filled and illuminated in her relation to that sphere above, remains there, but a subsequent part participating by the first participation of the participating subject goes forth, for life always goes forth from life; for actuality reaches everywhere and there is nowhere it fails. Yet, in going forth she lets her earlier part [15] (that which is before her) remain unmoved where she left it; for if she abandons what is before her, she will no longer be everywhere, but only in that in which she ends up. But what goes forth is not equal to what remains unmoved. If she must come to be everywhere then, and if there must be nowhere that the same activity is not present, and if the earlier must always be different from the later, and if activity [20] comes from contemplation or action, but action did not yet exist—for it is not possible for it to be before contemplation—then one contemplation of soul must be weaker than another, but all activity must be contemplation, so that what seems to be action in accordance with contemplation is the weaker kind of contemplation, for what is generated is always of the same kind as that which generates it, but weaker [25] because it loses its power as it descends. Everything, in fact, happens noiselessly because there is no need of any visible and external contemplation or action, and it is soul that in contemplating makes what comes after her, that which contemplates in this more external way and not like that which is before her. And contemplation makes

---

5.   *Phaedrus* 275 d ff.

contemplation. [30] For contemplation, no less than the object of contemplation, is without limit. And because of this contemplation is everywhere; for where is it not? For the same contemplative object is also in every soul since it is not bounded by spatial magnitude. To be sure, it is not present the same way in all, since it is not even in every part of soul in a similar way. That is why the charioteer gives a share of what he saw to the horses [35] and, in taking it, they would evidently have longed for what they saw, but they did not take it all.[6] And if in their longing they act, they act for the sake of what they long for; and that was object of contemplation and contemplation.

9.   Action, then, is for the sake of contemplation and object of contemplation, so that even for people of action contemplation is the goal, and what they cannot take from the straight path, this they seek to grasp by wandering around. For indeed when they attain what they wished for, what [5] they wanted to come into being, not so that they should not know it but in order to know it and see it present in the soul, evidently it lies there as an object to be beheld: for they also act for the sake of a goal, and this is not to have the good resulting from their action outside them or not to have it, but actually to have it. But where do they have it? In the soul. So action bends back again [10] to contemplation, for what one receives in the soul that is forming principle, what else could it be but a silent forming principle? And the more it is a forming principle, so much the more silent it will be; for then the soul keeps quiet and seeks nothing because it has been filled, and the contemplation, so disposed because soul trusts in her possession, lies within. And the clearer the trust, the quieter [15] too the contemplation in that it tends more to unity, and what knows, in proportion as it knows—for we must already be serious—comes to unity with what has been known. For if two, one will be one thing and the other different, so that they will, as it were, lie alongside each other and contemplation has not yet related this pair in kinship, as when forming principles dwelling in the soul do nothing. That is why [20] the forming principle must not be from outside, but must be unified with the soul of the learner until she finds it her own. When the soul, then, has been made kin and disposed according to the forming principle, she nonetheless utters it and holds it out in front of her—for she did not have it primarily—and she learns it completely, and by holding it before her she becomes different, as it were, from it, and by thinking about it discursively she looks at it like one thing looking at another; [25] and yet she too was a forming principle and a kind of intellect, but an intellect seeing something other than itself; for she is not full, but falls short of that which is before her; nonetheless, she herself too sees quietly what she utters; for what she has uttered well, she no longer continues to utter, but what she utters, she utters by deficiency in order to examine it and learn completely what she has. And in [30] matters of action she fits what she has to external things. And, insofar as soul possesses her content

---

6.   Plato, *Phaedrus* 247 e 5–6; 253 c 7 ff.; 254 b 4.6.

more completely, she is quieter than nature, and to the degree she has more content she is more contemplative, but because she does not possess it perfectly she longs to have a deeper learning of what has been contemplated and a fuller contemplation by examining it. And when she leaves herself and comes to be among other things, [35] then she goes back up again and contemplates by that part of her she left behind; but the soul that stays in herself does this less. That is why the serious person has already reasoned when he reveals to another what he has from himself; but in relation to himself he is sight. For already this person is directed to the one and to the quiet, not only of external things, [40] but also in relation to himself, and everything is within him.

10.   That all things then are the result of contemplation and are contemplation, both those that truly are and those that have come to be from them as they contemplate and are themselves objects of contemplation, some by perception, and some by knowledge or opinion, and that actions have their goal in knowledge [5] and the aim of their longing is for knowledge, and that the productions emerging from contemplation are directed to the perfection of another form and object of contemplation, and that generally all making things, in being imitations, make objects of contemplation and forms, and that the realities which have come to be and which imitate real beings show that their makers made them with the goal not of production [10] or even of action but to contemplate the perfected product, and that this too is what forms of discursive thinking want to see and, still earlier, perceptions whose goal is knowing, and that even before these, nature makes the object of contemplation that is in her and the forming principle by bringing to perfection another forming principle: all of these points are no doubt clear—some of them could be taken as evident in themselves, [15] and the argument reminded us of others. For this point too is clear, that it was necessary, since the first principles were engaged in contemplation, for all other things to long for this if, as must be the case, the originative principle for everything is the goal.[7] So too when living creatures give birth, the forming principles within them move them, and this is an activity of contemplation and a birth pain [20] of making many forms and many objects of contemplation and of filling everything with forming principles and a sort of eternal contemplating, for making is to make a form to be, and this is to fill everything with contemplation. And failures as well, both in the things that come to be and in what is done, are failures of contemplators that result from their swerving away from the object contemplated; [25] and the bad craftsman at any rate is the kind who makes ugly forms. And lovers, too, are among those who see and hurry on eagerly toward a form.

11.   This, then, is so. But as contemplation ascends from nature to soul and from soul to intellect and the contemplations become ever more akin and united with the contemplators, and in the serious soul [5] the things known are going to-

---

7.   Cf. Aristotle, *EN* 1143 b 9.

ward identity with the subject, since they are hurrying on eagerly to intellect, it is already clear in this case that both are one, not by a process of growing kinship, as in the best soul, but in substance and by virtue of the fact that "being and thinking are the same."[8] [10] For no longer is there one thing and another; for if so there will again in turn be another that is no longer one thing and another. So this must involve both really being one, and this is living contemplation, not an object of contemplation like one thing being in another. For what is in another is living through that, not self-living. If an object of contemplation and of thought then is to live, it must be self-life, not growth or perceptive life or the life that belongs to the rest of soul. [15] For the other lives are also thoughts in some way, but one is a growth thought, one a perceptual thought, and one a soul thought. How then could they be thoughts? Because they are forming principles. And every life is a thought, but one thought is dimmer than another, just like life. But this life is clearer and first life and first intellect as one. So the first life is a thought, and [20] second life a second thought, and the last life a last thought. All life then is of this kind and is thought. But human beings may possibly speak of different sorts of life, perhaps, yet they do not speak of different sorts of thought, but say instead that some are thoughts and some are not thoughts at all, because they do not search out at all what sort of thing life is. [25] But we must at any rate emphasize this point of ours that the argument shows yet again that all beings are a byproduct of contemplation. If therefore the truest life is life by thought, and this is the same as the truest thought, then the truest thought is living, and contemplation and the object of contemplation that is of this character are living and life and the two together are one. [30] If the two are one, then, how in turn is this one many? One may suppose it is because it contemplates it not as one; for even when it contemplates the one, it does not contemplate it as one; otherwise, it does not become intellect. But having begun as one it did not remain as it began, but without being aware of it, became many, as if weighed down,[9] and unrolled itself in its wish to have everything—[35] how much better it would have been for it not to have wanted this, for it became second—for it became like a circle unrolling itself, that is, into shape and surface and circumference and centre and radii, and some parts above and some below. Better is "from where" it came, and worse "to which" it goes, for the "to which" was not of the same kind as the "from which" and "to which," [40] nor again the "from which" and "to which" the same as the "from which" alone. And, to put this in a different way, intellect is not an intellect of some one particular, but it is also all; and being all it is the intellect of all. If it is all and of all, then, its part must also have everything and all things; otherwise, it will have a part that is not an intellect, and it will be put together out of nonintellects and will be a heap of things [45] that have just happened to be brought to-

---

8.   Parmenides, fr. B 3 (DK).

9.   Cf. Plato, *Symposium* 203 b 5–7.

gether, waiting around to become an intellect composed of all things. That is why it is infinite in this way too, and if something comes from it, it is not diminished, neither that which is from it because it too is everything, nor that from which it comes, because there was no composition out of pieces.

12. This intellect then is of such a kind; that is why it is not first, but there must exist that which is beyond it,[10] that for whose sake all the previous arguments have been undertaken, first because multiplicity is later than unity; and this intellect is a number, but the origin of number and of this kind of number is the really one; [5] and this is intellect and intelligible object simultaneously, so that it is simultaneously two. But if it is two, one must understand what is before the two. What is it, then? Intellect only? But the intelligible object is coupled closely with every intellect; so if the intelligible object must not be coupled closely with it, it will not even be intellect. If it is not intellect then, but is going to escape the two, that which is earlier than these two must be beyond [10] intellect. What then prevents it from being the intelligible object? No doubt, the reason is that the intelligible object is also coupled closely with intellect. If then it is neither intellect nor intelligible object, what could it be? We shall say that it is that from which intellect and the intelligible object with it have come. What is this then and what sort of thing shall we imagine it to be? For it will certainly be again either a thinking thing or something unthinking. [15] So if it is a thinking thing it will be intellect, but if unthinking it will be ignorant even of itself; so what will be exalted about it?[11] For even if we say it is the good and the simplest thing, we shall not be saying anything evident or clear, though we speak the truth, as long as we do not have any fixed point upon which to base our discursive reason [20] when we speak. For again if knowledge of other things comes through intellect, and by intellect we have the power to know intellect, by what simple instantaneous awareness could that which has passed beyond the nature of intellect be grasped? We shall say to the person to whom we must indicate how it is possible, that it is by virtue of what is similar in us. For there is something of it in us as well; or rather there is nowhere where it is not for the things that can participate in it. [25] For wherever you are, from just there you have that which is present everywhere, by setting to it what is able to have it: just as if a voice occupies an emptiness or even with the emptiness, there are human beings there too, and any point in the empty space you set your ears to listen, you will receive all the voice and yet again not all of it. What is it we will receive, then, if we set our intellect to it? [30] Rather, the intellect must retreat backward, as it were, and let itself go, so to speak, to those things that are behind it, since intellect is double-fronted, and in relation to those things behind it, if it wants to see that, it must not be altogether intellect. For it is itself a first life, since it is activity in the outward passage of all things, and an

---

10. Plato, *Republic* 509 b 9.
11. Cf. Plato, *Sophist* 249 a 1–2; Aristotle, *Metaphysics* 1074 b 17.

outward passage not in the sense that it is in process of finding its way out but rather in that it has already found its passage outward. [35] If then it is life and outward passage and has all things distinctly and not confusedly—for then it would have them imperfectly in a nonarticulate way—it must be from something else that is no longer in outward passage but is originative principle of outward passage and origin of life and origin of intellect and of all things. For all things are not an origin, [40] but all things spring out of an origin, but this origin is no longer all things or even some one of all things, so that it can generate all things, and not be a multiplicity, but an origin of multiplicity; for that which generates is everywhere simpler than what is generated. If this then generated intellect, it must be simpler than intellect. But if anyone should think [45] that the one itself is also all things, then either it will be each of the totality individually or all together. If it is all collected together, then, it will be later than all things; but if earlier than all things, all things will be other than it, and it will be other than all things; but if it and all things are simultaneous, it will not be an origin. [50] But it must be an origin and must exist before all things so that all things might also exist after it. And as for it being each of the totality individually, first any one of them will be the same as any other, and then all things will be together and one will distinguish nothing. And so it is not one of all things, but is before all things.

13.   What then is it? A power for all things; if it did not exist, neither would all things, and intellect would not even be the first life and all life. And what is beyond life is cause of life; for the activity of life, since it is all things is not first, but pours itself forth, as it were, as from a fountainhead. [5] For think of a fountainhead that does not have any other origin, but gives all of itself to rivers and is not consumed by the rivers yet remains quietly itself, and those that have gone forth from it, before each of them flows in their different directions, are still together with each other, but already each knows, as it were, where they will let their streams flow to; [10] or think of the life of a mighty plant going right through the whole of it, though its origin remains unmoved and has not been scattered over all of it, since it is, so to speak, seated in the root. This origin therefore provided all its multiple life to the plant but remained itself since it was not multiple, but an origin of the multiple. And it is no wonder. Or rather it is a wonder [15] how the multiplicity of life emerged from what is not multiplicity, and the multiplicity would not have existed unless what was not multiplicity had existed before multiplicity. For the origin is not divided into the all; for if it were divided, it would destroy the all too, and no longer could it still come into being if the origin did not remain by itself as different from the all. [20] That is also why the ascent is everywhere to a one. And in each case there is a one to which you will trace it back, and this universe to a one that is before it, which is not simply one, until one comes to the simply one. But this you can no longer trace back to something else. But if you take the one of the plant—and this is in fact its origin that remains unmoved—and the one of a living creature and the one of soul [25] and

the one of the universe, you take in each case what is most powerful and most worthy of honour; but if we take the one of the truly existing beings, the origin and fountainhead and power, shall we lose trust and suspect that it is the nothing? Certainly it is the nothing of those things of which it is the origin, yet it is of such a kind—though nothing [30] can be predicated of it, not being, not substance, not life—as to be that which is beyond all of them. But if you grasp it by removing being from it, you will be amazed. And throwing yourself upon it and attaining to it, take your rest within it and meditate more deeply in company with it, knowing it by a simple contact and by bringing together into one view its greatness from the things that exist after it but through it.

14.   And, yet again, look at it in this way; for since intellect is a kind of sight and a sight that is seeing, it will be a potency that has come into actuality. There will therefore be matter and form in it, but the matter will be that in intelligible objects, since actual seeing also has a doubleness to it; [5] before seeing at any rate it was one. So the one has become two and the two one. In seeing, then, fill-ing and a kind of perfection come from the sensible object, whereas for the sight of intellect the good is that which fills. For if intellect were itself the good, what need would it have to see or to act at all? For other things have their activity [10] around the good and because of the good, but the good is in need of nothing; that is why there is nothing to it except itself. So when you have said the good, do not think anything else in addition to it, for if you add something, you will make it in need of whatever you have added. That is why you must not even add thinking, so that you do not add something other than it and make it two, intellect and good. [15] For intellect needs the good, but the good does not need it. For this reason as intellect attains to the good it becomes good-formed and is perfected by the good, for the form that comes upon it from the good makes it good-formed.[12] A trace of the good upon it is seen in intellect, [20] and from the character of this trace it is appropriate to form a notion of its true archetype by recognizing it from the trace that runs over intellect. It has, therefore, given the trace of itself upon intellect to intellect to have in seeing, so that in intellect there is desire, and intellect is always desiring and always attaining what it desires, but the good is neither desiring—for what would its desire aim at—[25] nor attaining, for it did not desire? Not even, therefore, is it intellect, for there is desire in intellect and convergence upon its form. Indeed, intellect is beautiful and the most beautiful of all things, resting in pure light and pure radiance[13] and embracing the nature of real-beings; this beau-tiful universe is a shadow and [30] image of it; and it rests in pure radiance be-cause there is nothing unthinking or dark or unmeasured in it, and it lives a blessed life; so wonder would seize him[14] who saw this too and, as he ought, en-

---

12. Plato, *Republic* 509 a 3.
13. Plato, *Phaedrus* 250 c 4.
14. Homer, *Iliad* 3, 342.

tered into it and became one with it. As indeed a person who looks up to the heaven and sees the splendour of the stars [35] thinks about the one who made it and seeks him, so he who has contemplated the intelligible world and looked deeply into it and been amazed must also seek its maker and find out who it is who has brought such a world into being and how, he who has brought to birth such a child as intellect, a boy beautiful and filled full from himself.[15] He is certainly [40] neither intellect nor fullness at all, but before intellect and fullness. For after him came intellect and fullness, and they needed to have come into their fulfillment and to have thought. They are close to that which is without need and which has no need to think, but they have true filling and thought because they have them primarily. But what is before them neither needs nor has, or it would not be the good.

---

15. Plotinus plays here upon two of the meanings of *koros:* "boy" and "fullness."

Part II: Commentary

3.1. Introduction

If *Ennead* I, 1, provides an introduction to Plotinus' anthropology, then III, 8 shows us how the physical world, and both soul and intellect, are made and also introduces us to the full range of Plotinus' thought. In the *Timaeus*, Plato represented the world as brought into being by a divine deliberating craftsman. For Aristotle, nature, like art, needs no deliberation. If the world is eternal, then it has no need to be made. The Epicureans subsequently ridiculed the notion of a craftsman-god producing an inferior world full of imperfections, while the Stoics by contrast saw the divine fire literally permeating the whole world. Among the Middle Platonists there was major debate about what Plato actually meant in his *Timaeus* and whether or not the world must have a beginning.[1] In III, 8, 1–7, Plotinus thinks through this long-standing problem in an entirely novel way: There is no deliberation in the making of the world, for deliberation would indicate deficiency; and there are no mechanistic pulleys or levers. Instead, everything is timelessly and silently generated from within the creative contemplation of nature, the whole soul, and intellect, so that all forms of existence are actually living forms of contemplative thought, no matter how diminished some of them may be or how unaware of their own deeper significance they actually are. The world, therefore, is eternally created at each moment and, as we have seen in III, 7 (45) (*On eternity and time*), it is not generated *in* time so much as it springs out of soul together with time itself, which is "the life of soul in the movement of passage from one way of life to another" (III, 7, 11, 43–45). Since III, 8 is an important but difficult work, this chapter will provide a detailed commentary to follow Plotinus as closely as possible through what will be unfamiliar territory.

As its title indicates, treatise III, 8 deals with three principal subjects that divide—very roughly—into the following parts:

1. Nature, chapters 1–4

---

1. For the history see J. Dillon, 1977, 33, 45–9, 91–4, 108–110, 155 ff., 206–11, 242–6, 252–7, 285–7, 366–78.

2. Contemplation, soul, and intellect, chapters 5–9

3. The One, chapters 10–11.[2]

Ennead III, 8 is the first part of what German scholars have called the "big treatise" (*Großschrift*), that is, an extraordinarily long work, written against the Gnostics, or against "those who say that the universe and its maker are evil," and divided by Porphyry into four different treatises, which he then assigned to different *Enneads,* or "groups of nine," to increase their number to fifty-four (or six groups of nine).[3] Porphyry divided the "big work" into the following treatises: III, 8; V, 8, *On the intelligible beauty*; V, 5, *That the intelligible objects are not outside intellect*; and II, 9, specifically *Against the Gnostics*. The first two of these treatises are included in this book to give the reader a sense both of the extent of Plotinus' thought even in a single "big work" and of how he approaches in actual practice some of the well-known issues of Neoplatonic philosophy, from the origin and return of things to their principles, or hypostases: Soul, Intellect, and the One. Although a direct critique of Gnostic thinking occurs only in the last treatise (II, 9) of the big work, these first treatises set both the tone and the philosophical framework in which the critique is situated, thus giving us insight into the way Plotinus thinks.

Who were the Gnostics and why is III, 8 important? Gnosticism was at first a religious movement of considerable diversity, with Christian and Jewish roots, that spread throughout the Roman Empire in the first centuries A.D. promising salvation to those few who were in possession of a special revelation or knowledge (*gnôsis*). This knowledge declared the physical world to be fashioned by evil and ignorant forces; that is, by evil Archons, or Ruling principles, and an ignorant, fallen *Sophia*, or Wisdom. Fragments of a higher, good world are imprisoned in this world, like our own souls, and so we await liberation from the forces of

---

2.   The purpose of this apparently was to obtain a number that is the product of the perfect number *6* (*6* is both $1 + 2 + 3$ and $1 \times 2 \times 3$) and of the number *9* (*9* is the symbol of totality as the last of the "first" numbers [from 1 to 10]). Platonic-Pythagorean number symbolism looks just crazy to the modern eye, but it was an attempt to come to grips with the beauty and goodness of the universe in a mathematical and sacred way and to pay attention to the deeper harmonies of the interior life, or the life of soul. On its way through history it gave birth to many things, from enneagrams (via Sufi mysticism) to the great cathedrals of Europe (via the schools of St. Victor and others). I know of no work that traces all of these diverse influential themes, but for number symbolism in Plotinus and late antiquity see D. J. O'Meara, 1989; 1993, 9.

3.   For commentary in German on this treatise see Beutler-Theiler (1960–7) and Roloff; in Italian, V. Cilento, 1971; in French, E. Bréhier (Notice); Bouillet; in Spanish, J. Igal (complementary notes); in English there is a general commentary by J. N. Deck, 1967, and detailed commentary (on III, 8, 8, 26–11, 45). See also M. Santa Cruz de Prunes, 1979; and on the significance of Plotinus' thought about nature for modern philosophy of nature, see P. Hadot, 1968, M. F. Wagner (ed.), 2002.

darkness. Much of our information about the different forms of Gnostic thought (conveniently labelled under the names of some of its proponents [e.g., Valentinianism: Valentinus; Basilidianism: Basilides]) is tentative, to say the least, because it comes in the hostile accounts of Church writers. But a collection of Gnostic writings discovered in the 1940s near Nag Hammadi in Egypt and dated to the third or fourth century presents in part a more philosophical version of Gnosticism (sometimes called Sethian Gnosticism) that is plainly familiar with Plato's dialogues and some of the triads of so-called Middle Platonism (especially the famous triad "being-life-mind").[4] Modern scholarship has coined the term Middle Platonism to act as a catchall for everything from Plato and the later Academy up to Plotinus, by whom, it has commonly been thought, the new doctrines of Neoplatonism were developed. But these philosophical Gnostics regarded the ancient tradition of philosophy, based upon Plato and Aristotle, as part of their own heritage and must therefore have been an intellectual threat to non-Christian Platonist groups, such as the group of Plotinus and of his colleague, Amelius, at Rome. Christianity displayed a remarkable capacity to assimilate very diverse cultural, religious, and philosophical forms—not always to its credit in the critical eye of some of its opponents, among them Porphyry, who wrote a powerful work, *Against the Christians* (the remains of which are conveniently collected in R. Joseph Hoffmann, Oxford, 1994). At any rate, the Nag Hammadi collection contains versions of Gnostic texts actually named by Porphyry in the *Life of Plotinus* (chapter 16; e.g., *Allogenes, Zostrianus,* etc.). Plotinus was so concerned about the influence of these texts and their apparent distortion of Plato that he had his pupils write critiques of Gnosticism and took the trouble in the big work and in much of his later writing to answer the questions of pupils and colleagues and to try to meet the philosophical needs of those "friends" in his own circle who apparently had abandoned or were in danger of abandoning what Porphyry calls the "ancient philosophy" in favour of Gnosticism (cf. *Life* 16; II, 9, chapters 6 and 10).

In the context of Plotinus' works as a whole then, III, 8, and the rest of the big work, marks an important development. Plotinus by this time had already written some major works (for example, three works on matter (II, 4; II, 5; III, 6); two works on the "omnipresence of being" (VI, 4–5); and immediately before III, 8, a major examination of the problems concerning soul (IV, 3–5). But III, 8 gives us a rather different insight into the way Plotinus thought in the most creative writing period of his life and also shows how his thought was capable of significant development. We could think of Plotinus, for instance, like some Archbishop of Seville, in Dostoevsky's *Grand Inquisitor*, preserving orthodoxy at all costs, an orthodoxy

---

4.   On Gnosticism generally see H. Jonas, 1958; K. Rudolph, 1987; see also R. T. Wallis (ed.), 1992; J. D. Turner and R. Majercik (eds.), 2000; and on Sethian Gnosticism particularly see J. D. Turner, 1992; 2000.

already frozen immutably in a canon or, in this case, Plato's dialogues. Nothing could be further from the truth. Treatise III, 8 begins in "playful friendship," a marked characteristic of Platonic philosophy, and develops not dogmatic pronouncements or revelations from on high but a dialogue between ourselves that nonetheless includes many other implicit interlocutors, as we shall see below. Although Plotinus writes in treatise form, the character of all his writing is free, persuasive, creative dialogue in which the reader, together with the many other internal interlocutors, becomes involved as a participant subject, never as the object of an orthodox harangue. So we get to experience Plotinus' thinking in a very practical way, and this movement of thought itself is, above all, the heart of his originality. As Porphyry tells us in the *Life*, while the "ancient philosophy" is fundamentally Platonic, Plotinus' writings are also full of hidden Stoic and Peripatetic (i.e., the tradition based upon the philosophy of Aristotle) doctrines. In his wide reading, Plotinus "did not just speak straight out of these books but took a distinctive personal line in his examination [*theôria*]. He quickly absorbed what was read, and would give the sense of some profound subject of study in a few words and pass on" (*Life* 14, 14–17). So, internally persuasive dialogue marks Plotinus' thinking. But what about development of thought and what we sometimes perhaps mean by originality; that is, that a thinker comes up with a certain quantity of "new ideas"?

Plotinus started to write fairly late in life, and in all probability his mind already was fairly well made up on most of the major issues he treats. We experience no transformation of thought in Plotinus such as we seem to find in Wittgenstein, for instance. At the same time, each treatise adds a new dimension to what has gone before, and III, 8 is a particularly striking instance of this. After all, to the inexperienced reader, Gnosticism and Neoplatonism may look somewhat alike: both appear excessively mystical and mythical, and both seem ridiculously dualistic, contemptuous of body and the physical universe. Do not both then simply despair of the corruption and fatal ambiguities of our ordinary experience and, consequently, transfer all their hope to some static other world? For many readers of Plotinus, the physical world is *maya,* or mere illusion based upon nothingness. No true flesh-and-blood subjects (such as we find in Aristotle) actually live there, only the flickering appearances of their soul-ghosts as they take the elevator to the floor of the intelligible world. Even there, for some readers, these poor souls or intellects are no longer agents or selves in any recognizable fashion but instead cyphers for a pantheistic unity ("the One beyond being") that animates and moves them. How true are these impressions of an excessively spiritual, pantheistic Neoplatonism that apparently dispenses with material things and even with genuine, relatively independent selves, like some perverse form of Berkeley's subjective idealism?

One purpose of the present work is to allow you to make up your own minds on these issues *precisely as you read*. But two points are nonetheless worth making here. First, because of the attractiveness of Gnosticism for friends even of Plotinus' circle, the big work offers a remarkable opportunity to see just how positively a Platonist could view the physical world. Plotinus in fact develops an entirely new theory in III, 8, one that had never occurred explicitly in this form before, in order to explain how making, or creation, on any level (whether of actual substances or of things dependent on substance, such as properties or attributes) is possible without rational deliberation. Partly this problem comes to him from Plato's *Timaeus*, where the demiurge, or divine craftsman, is represented as deliberating about the physical universe he will make (in a later work, VI, 7 [38], this is in fact Plotinus' starting point for developing this theory in a different direction). But partly the problem also is to think through a viable model of positive creation by means of productive or creative contemplation that results in a good and, for the most part, rational physical world. This is in contrast to all the Gnostic revelations, with their divine actions that represent divinities deliberating mischief as well as good things. So III, 8 marks the beginning not only of one of Plotinus' biggest work but of some of his most creative thinking that would profoundly influence the subsequent history of Western thought (from Christians to Muslims and Jews) on the nature of creation, creativity, theology, and human life.

Second, what sort of originality is it reasonable to look for in Plotinus? Is there a certain quantity of new ideas by which we should judge him? The *Enneads* certainly set forth startlingly new ideas but the picture of Plotinus as the "father of Neoplatonism," a title to be weighed by the number of trail-blazing opinions attributed to him (e.g., the three hypostases—the One, Intellect, and Soul; emanation; etc.), is surely too simplistic if not completely false. According to the testimony of Simplicius (a Neoplatonist commentator after Plotinus), a certain Moderatus of Gades had already effectively worked out the system of hypostases approximately a century before Plotinus was born (*In Physica* 1, 230, 34–231, 27, Diels). Plotinus himself stresses in an early work (V, 1 [10]) that almost none of his apparently characteristic ideas are original with him. This may be taken as evidence of a welcome humility, but we have no reason to doubt its truth. Even Porphyry's relatively saintly *Life of Plotinus* paints a vivid picture of Plotinus as one writer among many others of his own time and one whose interpretations of Plato, for instance, were not accepted by Porphyry's former teacher in Athens, Longinus. Plotinus was in fact accused by some unnamed critics in Greece of plagiarizing the influential philosopher Numenius (*Life*, 17), whose voluminous works are extant now only in sparse fragments. In short, our evidence is very sketchy, but what evidence we have should make us extra cautious about assigning useful but misleading tags to individuals or periods (such even as Middle or Neo-Platonism). Plotinus' originality does not really lie in any potted version of opinions that can be attributed to him; it rather consists in the creative mind he tends to bring to a problem and the philosophical way in which he can think a problem through; perhaps in later times this came to embody the philosophical spirit of many opinions he did not originate. As we shall see, Plotinus is certainly spiritual and religious in the best sense of those terms, but he is a philosophical thinker of breadth, subtlety, and free innovation rather than a purveyor of original opinions if such a thing is even possible.

3.2. Play

Plotinus cites his ancient sources more or less directly (these references are indicated in the footnotes to the translation). But more often than not he refers to a text or texts or to a complete way of thinking in Plato, Aristotle, the Stoics, or others so indirectly that we have to find our way into his forms of thinking before we can hazard an intelligent guess at what he may be referring to. This manner of indirect quotation bespeaks a familiarity with Plato, Aristotle, and others that few, if any, of us today could ever hope to match.

The magnificent, lengthy question that opens III, 8 is a case in point. Here Plotinus weaves together two themes, one from Plato and one from Aristotle, that indicate how he will proceed. From Plato is the theme of "play," which frames the whole treatise. From Aristotle is a thematic problem or inner puzzle about contemplation, which provides the substance of the treatise. Let us take up the theme from Plato first, since its significance is easily overlooked.

The treatise opens in a spirit of play between friends who know each other but will be appropriately critical of a strange and novel thesis, namely that everything desires contemplation (*theôria*), even children playing or grownups doing philosophy. Plotinus catches with his opening words one of the most important features of Plato's dialogues ("Just suppose we were to play . . .": in Greek the participle *playing* [*paizontes*] is the first word of the treatise), namely that they are always playful and specifically with images and ideas. Plato is, of course, well known for his love of children's games, from lark-chasing to shell-tossing and twelve-sided ball games, which he builds right into his major dialogues.[5] Armstrong rightly emphasizes how Plotinus' tone of humorous half-apology when introducing something rather serious is entirely in the spirit of Plato (Loeb III, 360–61 n1). He suggests that in *paizontes* there is a reminiscence of Plato, *Laws* IV, 712 b 1–2 (where the old gentlemen imagining their city are called "old children") and VII, 803 c–d (where the human being is a plaything of god and one's highest and most serious activity is to play before him). Plotinus thinks directly of this last passage, for example, at *Ennead* III, 2 (47), 15. But here he is thinking even more directly of *Republic VII,* where Socrates has developed out of the divided line and cave similes a new notion of dialectic or philosophical conversation based upon turning the "eye of the soul" around from the flux of perceptual life to the "intelligible" realm illumined by the Good. "I forgot we were playing," Socrates says

---

5.   Cf. R. K. Sprague, 1984, 275–84; and see generally H.-G. Gadamer, *Wahrheit und Methode,* Tübingen, 1960.

after becoming a little hot-tempered at the thought of how much ridicule is brought upon philosophy by its sham students. How should we teach students then, he asks. Certainly not by compulsion, he replies, for "no free person should pursue any study like a slave" (*Republic* 536 c 1–2). Instead, children should be *nourished by play* (*paizontas trephe*) (537 a 1), and this free play can be given structure later by bringing all its unconscious pursuits together into the comprehensive, multidimensional view characteristic of the more serious dialectical thinker, who sees or attempts to see things as a whole: *synoptically*. Thus their kinship with one another and with reality can be seen (cf. III, 8, 10, 32–51).

I suggest that Plotinus has this passage in mind, at least partly. Philosophical conversation is a dialogue between friends that starts in the free play of ideas so that one can get an all-round view of what needs looking at and thus attempt to clarify what one wants to gain insight into. The free play necessary for the birth of new thought requires in such dialogue the sympathy of friends and an affinity with the subject: "there is no danger in playing with our own concerns," Plotinus says. At the same time, such enquiry is critical and situated in the open space of common scrutiny. It is not a diary or form of introspection but already includes others as fundamental participants in its questioning of a world generally taken for granted (see also chapter 1.13 above). Such dialectic then is provisional, recognizes and exposes its own limitations, and is always ready to begin its enquiry anew. In this sense, V, 8, is just such a new beginning, though it follows immediately upon III, 8, and Plotinus is always ready to point out, as is Plato, the inadequacy of his images and language. In the *Seventh Letter* attributed to Plato (which I shall assume in this book is either by Plato or by a mind comparable to that of Plato, and therefore by Plato), a passage describes dialectic in just this sense as the "rubbing together" of all the images and forms of language in conversation so that one can come to an understanding of what something *is* rather than what it *is like*:

> Only barely [*mogis*] when … names, propositions, as well as appearances and perceptions, are rubbed against each other, each of them being refuted through well-meaning [i.e., nonadversarial] refutations in a process of questioning and answering without envy, will wisdom [*phronêsis*] along with intelligence [*nous*] begin to cast its light in an effort at the very limits of human possibility. (344 b–c)

Though Plotinus writes treatises, he thinks dialectically. For Plato, dialectic begins in free play but looks toward the self-disclosure of the Good, whose light is the very means by which we see. Similarly, Plotinus in III, 8 indicates his aim to see things as a whole by starting with play for the sake of the more serious goal (*telos*) (cf. III, 8, 6, 16; 32–3; 7, 17–18), which will turn out ultimately to be the One, or the Good, reflected intimately even in every authentic *practical* good (such as ordinary moral action).

3.3. *Contemplation, action, and production: The problem*

The second theme, from Aristotle, poses the central problem of the first 8 chapters of the treatise and determines the course of the argument.[6] Aristotle's thought about contemplation, one could well argue, leads to a dilemma. On the one hand, he specifically states that contemplation is not productive; it "makes" nothing (*EN* X 8, 1178 b 20–21) Nor does it extend to brute animals (cf. Deck, 1967, 106–9). This seems to follow from the way Aristotle views the hierarchy of sciences: the theoretical or contemplative sciences (theology, metaphysics, physics) are clearly demarcated from the practical (politics, economics, ethics) and from the productive (the crafts and arts). The productive sciences examine the human being as a *maker* of objects outside of himself or herself (*poiêsis*). The practical sciences examine *action,* or what a person *does* (*praxis*) where the object of the action is more unified with the subject acting, as in all the cases of moral, economic, or political *self*-organization; in other words, there is a deeper or inner dimension to action insofar as action involves the development of character and of the self. Finally, the theoretical sciences see, or have insight into (*theôria*), the whole of reality, not just the human sphere of action or production, and no longer for the enquiring subjects' own sake but for the sake of things themselves. *Theôria,* the word for contemplation, signifies the capacity to look or to gaze at a spectacle. So far so good. The demarcations among the sciences seem to make good sense.

But in III, 8, Plotinus takes up a hidden problem. Is contemplation for Aristotle like looking at an object or spectacle? Because of one prevailing paradigm in modern science, we might agree that it is "objective" in the sense that it is a dispassionate scrutiny of the facts. But as Hegel long ago observed in his *Phenomenology of Spirit*, it is possible to do science in this way without ever being self-aware or having any minimal form of self-knowledge. One may be a brilliant "theoretical" technician, worthy of the Nobel prize, but at the same time a moral, intellectual, and spiritual child. Now, for Aristotle, theoretical science cannot be conceived in this way, for in contemplation, understanding of the world is raised into self-understanding so that self-understanding (i.e., the paradigm for all authentic understanding: God's life is an understanding of understanding or a thinking of thinking: *noêseôs noêsis, Metaphysics* XII 9, 1074 b 34) and understanding (*noêsis*) are one. This is conceived, of course, as an ideal to which a human being can only aspire at the limits of his or her being (*EN* X, 7). It is nonetheless essential for Aristotle (as also for Plato) that scientific thought break out of its own narrow individuality and, at its best, even out of its own specifically human focus, to see both the world and itself as permeated by a wisdom that is self-understanding. So, for contemplation, the world is not an object; rather, as Aristotle tends to say about even the smallest or apparently least divine things in the universe, the *parts*

---

6.   On Aristotle see espec. H. H. Joachim, 1951; J. Lear, 1988; T. H. Irwin, 1988; R. A. Gauthier-H. Y. Jolif, 1970.

of animals (cf. *PA* I 6), "there are gods even here" (citing Heraclitus with approval, see *DK*, Heraclitus A 9).

The juxtaposition of these two rather different perspectives—that is, contemplation as the highest human activity and contemplation as a divine activity already embracing and pervading everything—poses a major philosophical problem as well as a specific problem of interpretation in Plato and Aristotle. The Gnostics, on the good authority of the Bible as well as of Plato's *Timaeus*, represent divinities as doing and saying and working out many things. Their higher beings are visibly and audibly creative, an attractive feature for any human being who naturally prefers "sound and light" or special effects in Dolby stereo, and they are even more attractive in the absence of any powerful philosophical alternative. So the question for Plotinus is how we can think of the world by means of both perspectives simultaneously; that is, how can we see it as genuinely pervaded by contemplation and yet at the same time be able to trace back to an authentic paradigm the dim or more obscure sorts of contemplation we find embodied even in action and creative production in the physical universe. This is the question he attempts to answer in III, 8, 1–8.

However, this is not only a philosophical problem rooted in Plato and occasioned by the Gnostics. In this new conception of contemplation, Plotinus consciously develops a line of thought implicit and even important in Aristotle, but one that Aristotle did not develop himself. If the divine life of contemplation or self-understanding is what makes everything move (and "god moves," Aristotle says, "as being loved"; that is, god moves as the goal of all natural organisms), then how this goal-directedness actually operates in *all* of nature becomes a problem. If the divine life is the purest self-contemplation, then such goal-directness can operate only if contemplation has real creative effects in the world. Indeed, Aristotle appears to believe this—despite his claim at *EN* 1139 a 39 a 35–6 that "thinking [*dianoia*] moves nothing, but only thinking that is for the sake of something and practical"—since the productive intellect (*nous*) in *De Anima* III, 5, must be a contemplative power that *makes actual* the possibility and potentiality of the world. So too *sophia,* or wisdom, whose activity is essentially and comprehensively contemplative, is said to be not only the excellence (*aretê*) of art (*technê*) (*EN* VI 7, 1141 a 12; cf. V, 8 [31] 5, 4–5) but an internal productive power in its own way of happiness (*EN* VI 12, 1144 a 1–6) "as health makes health" (i.e., not as the doctor [efficient cause] but as the principle of health [formal cause] brings about a healthy condition). *Sophia*, or wisdom, then "makes" internally like a formal and final cause (just as any organism's own nature in its proper environment acts causally to bring it to maturity, etc.), *not* like an efficient cause (as *x* external to *y* moves *y* by pushing, kicking, etc.) (cf. Gauthier-Jolif II, 542–47). Although John Deck (1967, 107–9) proposes that Plotinus develops in III, 8 a curious kind of causality, not formal or final but a "real efficient causality," Plotinus is more concerned to show how the principles of things in their natural environment work from within (i.e., formally and teleologically), rather than from without by external agency.

Now for Aristotle it is no small statement to say that *sophia* makes well-being or happiness,[7] for this happiness is not just human (although *eudaimonia* appears as a specifically human goal in *EN* I) but coextensive with the well-being of all reality: "for if the state of mind concerned with a human being's own interests is to be called *sophia*, there will be many *sophiae*; there will not be one concerned with the good of all animals" (*EN* VI 7, 1141 a 29–32). *Sophia* is not limited to *specific* interests, but is "knowledge [*epistêmê*] and intellect (*nous*) of the things that are most held in honour by nature" (1141 b 2–3). *Sophia*, or *contemplative* wisdom, as opposed to *practical* wisdom, must therefore be internally productive of the well-being of all species and things if it is a contemplative activity rooted in the divine intellect and if that intellect not only moves the instincts, desires, and loves of all natural things by being loved but also makes, together with the immanent principles of organisms (i.e., their souls), the essential "health" of their being.

Aristotle, of course, never explicitly develops such a theory, but the theory Plotinus sketches of creative contemplation at work on all levels and in every thought, act, or making process in the physical universe is an innovative and highly accurate development of these genuine possibilities latent in Aristotle's teleology and theory of intellect. Contemplation does not do away with action or production but puts them in a new perspective: we make in order to be able to "see" what we cannot get at directly by any other means; we act or do things in order to unfold natural powers that are perfectly intelligible in themselves but remain too unified for us to approach directly through experience, perception, or reasoning. Actions and productions, therefore, unpack the unified content of contemplative reality into more discursive modes of apprehension (reasoning, imagination, etc.) so that we can "run through them" and come to see them for what they are.

In III, 8, 1–8 Plotinus implicitly brings together two powerfully different, but related ways of looking at things; the playful attempt of Plato's dialectic to see things whole in terms of their ultimate (serious) Good and, on the other hand, the contrasting attempt of Aristotle's contemplative wisdom to see things whole in

---

7.   The word *eudaimonia* is difficult to translate. The general sense is brought out by "living well," "doing well" (*to eu zein, to eu prattein*) (*EN* 1095 a 18). The English *happiness* is too narrow and suggests pleasure or the satisfaction of our sensual nature. The Greek conception involved the satisfaction of our active natures as well as the notion of prosperity (*euêmeria*) and even good luck (*eutuchia*) (cf. H. H. Joachim, repr. 1962, 28). Armstrong rightly translates "well-being." Some Aristotelian scholars insist on "human flourishing" (e.g., John M. Cooper, Indianapolis, 1986, 89–90). I prefer "happiness" here simply to avoid confusion. For the question of *eudaimonia* in Plotinus, see *Enneads* I, 4 (46) and I, 5 (36).

light of the entire universe's desire for the divine life, a wisdom reflected for Aristotle even in frog's legs or the baser parts of animals. For Plotinus, these two ways of looking at things, while different, are plainly not incompatible, and the attempt to think through the puzzles they present will have far-reaching consequences. The result is a new theory of nondeliberative but purposeful creation that will have immense influence in Christian, Arabic, and Jewish philosophical theology. God and creation do not operate in time, for there is no time before the beginning of time in which creation could occur. Instead, the physical world is timelessly unfolded from within the divine intellect. Thus, one can explain why things are like this (in many different ways, for example, by science or art), but one should not suppose that things are like this *because* of the reasons one gives. Intellect as a naturally creative force for Plotinus is like the conclusion *before* the syllogism (cf. V, 8 [31] 7, 36–41), *before* purposive thought (41–43). Our reasons for things, however accurate or not, are always after the fact since the fact and the cause are already one before we begin to think about them separately. The life of the divine intellect, therefore, is for Plotinus creatively *immediate:* directly and dynamically present *now,* neither distantly echoing some divine craftsmanship irretrievably past nor indefinitely postponed to some glorious, unattainable "future." This theory is also Plotinus' answer to the Gnostics: we do not need anthropomorphic audio-video revelations from other realms that we cannot test by philosophical thought or indeed even by more stable experience since we get swept away immediately by the apocalyptic glitz. Creative contemplation, by contrast, is silent and so intimately present everywhere for anybody and anything that we do not even notice it (cf. V, 5 [32] 12, 13–14: "but people do not see it because it is present to them as they sleep").

Presumably, the usual objections to Aristotle's teleology also will apply to Plotinus' theory of creative contemplation, namely (1) that it makes everything for the sake of the "whole" (universal teleology); or (2) that it is mere anthropomorphic mind-projection upon nature; or (3) that it involves vague spiritual "strivings" in nature.[8] Plotinus may well be open to these sort of objections, but in III, 8 and V, 8 (as well as later in VI, 7 [38] and VI, 8 [39]), he obviously does not *mean* such things. So it is important to give him the benefit of the doubt and to see if he can make a case for a contemplative teleology in ways in which other thinkers (from Aristotle to Leibniz and Kant) might not.

3.4.   An animated, freely dependent world (1, 11 ff.)

In chapter 1, 11 and forward, we see how Plotinus instinctively views such contemplation. Compulsory action depends not upon ourselves but upon some external agent or thing. Voluntary action springs from ourselves and is therefore less externally based. But to be an authentically "free" person is not what we normally

---

8.   Cf. M. Nussbaum, *De Motu Animalium*, intro., 1978.

mean by "voluntary action," for *voluntary* is a highly ambiguous term carrying a wide range of meaning. This is why Plotinus terms it "so-called voluntary action." Nonetheless, even in this preliminary stage, *free* action reveals its dependence upon a desire for contemplation.[9]

We should note too that the earth is animated. For Plotinus, there is a "soul of the earth" (IV, 3 [28] 30) as well as a "world soul" (IV, 3 [28] 1–9). Both are our "sisters," and the world soul is our "elder sister." In this perspective, there is nothing that is not pervaded by meaning or intelligibility. Even rocks cut off from the earth, Plotinus argues in VI, 7 (38), continue to grow. In other words, what is merely a stone for you or me could be a window upon a whole universe for a geologist. One has to be ready to "see" things as windows open to a universe of animate relations, or else one will see little or nothing.

This is particularly true of "nature." The Stoics used the terms "unimaginative nature" (*physis aphantastos*) and "intellectual nature" (*physis noera*) (*SVF* II 1016) to distinguish between irrational nature in growing things and the all-pervading divine reason, or *logos*. But on the Stoics' own terms, even so-called "irrational" nature has to admit to some sort of "rationality" or intelligibility if the divine *logos* pervades everything. So the question for Plotinus is how an irrational, unimaginative nature can be "traced back to" the activity of contemplation (for a rather different view of this question see IV, 4 [28] 13).

3.5.   Activity (energeia) and power (dynamis)

Already at 1, 21, the term *activity* (*energeia*) occurs, and any activity of contemplation naturally has to have something to work upon. So Plotinus thinks of matter (at 2, 1–3) or potency (*dynamis*), the correlative of activity, although he does not use the term *dynamis* until much later in the treatise. Without a proper study of Aristotle's thought, these terms, *dynamis* and *energeia*, so important for both Aristotle and Plotinus, are almost impossible to explain. For Aristotle, reality is made up not just of *actual things* (i.e., you, me, trees, or goats at various stages of development), but also of potentialities/potencies/powers and possibilities genuinely present in nature. How do we tell the difference between potentialities and possibilities? Often we cannot discern exactly, but we recognize from experience that a potentiality responds to something active that wakes it up and makes it develop. Other potentialities simply remain as possibilities but are activated only when the proper stimulus develops (e.g., the telegraph, telephone, electricity, space travel, fax machines, etc.). In each case, for a possibility to become a genuine potentiality, something active (i.e., an actual thing like you or me) is required to wake it up and develop it. The case of artifacts is analogous to, but different from, naturally occurring organisms. Like artifacts, we need to be awakened from

---

9.   On the relation between providence, fate, and free will see III, 2–3 (47–48); III, 1 (3); VI, 8 (39), 1–6. See also J. M. Rist, 1967, chapter 10; and G. Leroux, 1990.

our self-satisfied certainties into a *world* of joy and suffering, truth and beauty not determined solely by our own preferences, though more often than not we slumber uncritically most of our lives. The difference here is that we are not only a reservoir of potentialities, like the world, but also *self-actuating*; that is, we have an active principle in us that makes us who we are and what we become. This active principle in us is our "form," "energy," or intellectual soul. When united with matter, the "stuff" of which we are made, it results in the dynamic development and self-actualization of the potencies latent in that matter. The "form" comes to us from our parents with a host of environmental influences hidden within it and leads the development of our human nature in the natural direction of our fullest maturation (that is, the goal or final cause) if nothing gets in the way and if the matter is properly receptive and not defective. (For Aristotle, decay and death are not the fulfillment of any potencies but their *privation*).

So the terms *dynamis* and *energeia* are especially difficult to translate since they range considerably in meaning. *Dynamis* can mean "power," "potency," "possibility," "capacity," and *energeia* can mean "energy," "act," "activity," "actuality," "actualization," and "realization." For Aristotle, things are "actual" in a variety of ways: you and I are actual *things*, but our souls too, as the organizing forms of our bodies, are operating in us like (relatively) unmoved movers, or as several people have put it in the past twenty years, like the DNA design controlling and assisting all stages of our development. The fullest pure energy or activity is the life of God, which needs no developmental potency or matter because it expresses fully what it is. So even in "theology," *en-ergeia* expresses the *ergon*, the "work" or "function" of anything; for Aristotle, God is the purest expression of self-understanding, which apparently embraces everything in the universe. But in natural organisms *energeia* signifies *en-tel-echy* (literally, in-goal-having) insofar as the organism has its *telos* or goal in itself (as well as in God), which makes it an active, functioning, relatively developed instance of a particular species.[10]

For Plotinus, as for Aristotle (if in different ways), dormant or passive potentiality is a real feature of the world, but in every case such potentiality depends upon something outside of itself to effect its realization at a particular time and place (see chapter 1, part I, passage 6). The case of human beings is still more complex because we have the additional difficulty of having to develop integrated moral, cultural, intellectual, and spiritual lives. We therefore need the world, our families, teachers, and friends to wake us into our active selves, and we also need something more: an activity both within us and yet also in some measure beyond us and toward which we can grow as "intellectual" beings. This activity in soul and intellect is that to which Plotinus will attempt to trace back the so-called irrational functions of nature. This is no small matter: the term *intellectual* would on the face of it seem to exclude any person or thing without the necessary apparatus

---

10. Cf. Delbrück, 1971; also Corrigan 1996, 103 for *entelechy* and *energeia*.

for a certain level of thought. Plotinus' notion of intellectuality is not so exclusive, however. He calls even horses "intellects of a specific kind" in a later work, VI, 7 (38) 9. And in III, 8 he will argue for the somewhat novel philosophical view that all forms of life (even vegetative existence) are forms of thought. Thus, the terms *intellect* or *intellectual* go far beyond any modern notions of reason or rationality.

3.6. Nature (III, 8, 2)

Chapter 2 employs the notions of an unmoved activity, together with its "expression," or logos (which I translate as "forming principle" for reasons that will become apparent below), and matter, to express the precise sense of natural production that Plotinus has in mind (for nature generally see also IV, 3 [27] 1–10 and IV, 4 [28] 10–13). We tend to say, of course, that nature makes and forms things (or at least Aristotle, the Stoics, and Epicureans did), but we do not mean to anthropomorphize this, as if we were to imagine a little man, or *homunculus,* levering, pushing, or kicking reluctant potencies into realization. No, we *mean* that nature works on matter, but beyond that at this stage, we still are not really clear about what we *do* mean.

Natural production cannot be conceived even on the model of the most spectacularly successful art (e.g., wax-modelling), Plotinus argues, because nature makes entirely from herself, whereas the artist cannot do this. Technological art imitates nature but is too external to serve as a model for understanding natural production (Plotinus will take a rather different perspective in V, 8 (31) 1–2). But nature and the artist are analogous insofar as some unmoved organizing principle in both must be responsible for their respective products. We can see in 2, 9–15, how the "principle" of explanation and the real "principle" in nature apparently coincide. For Plotinus they seem to be merely two different ways of looking at the same thing. As later Medieval philosophers might have said, while the order of discovery (*ordo inveniendi*) and the order of being (*ordo essendi*) are different, they are rooted in the same principle.

The rest of the chapter is difficult, partly because of the internal dialogue (question-answer/objection-answer), and partly because Plotinus is quickly sketching a provisional conclusion that is all too obvious to him but not to us. If nature is a wholly active cause (which looks at first highly disputable), then the unmoved principle must be the whole of nature. Otherwise, we will have to divide nature into two: part unmoving and part moved, but this is unnecessary, Plotinus claims, since when we talk about a part of nature being moved, we actually mean matter, not nature. Alternatively, dividing nature in this way makes nature a sort of intermediate composite principle (i.e., compounded of both form and matter) so that we are forced (redundantly) to seek a primary natural mover elsewhere beyond this composition, which rather defeats our purpose in referring to nature as a principle at all. This second alternative makes sense, but the first looks suspicious:

if we define matter as what is moved and nature as what does the moving, we reach a trivial analytic conclusion: nature must be unmoved.

The objection that follows shows that Plotinus is reviewing different opinions or ways of talking about nature. We could say, for instance, that the forming principle, or *logos,* is unmoved, and not nature. Like the Stoics, we may well tend to look at nature as a passive stuff in motion to be distinguished from its active form, which is ultimately the *logos.* The problem with this position, for Plotinus, is that whether we regard the whole of nature as in motion or only a part of it as unmoved, we have to include its *logos,* or forming principle, with it, or else we are not referring to *nature* (which means for both Plato and Aristotle to have a definite "form"). This is why at line 22 Plotinus first introduces the word *eidos,* form. Nature must be a form and not a compound of matter and form, he concludes. This again hardly seems to follow logically from the argument or to be self-evident. Aristotle, for example, identifies nature with the "form" and the "compound," and the "matter" (in the sense of material definition or constituents) in *Physics* II. Why should Plotinus ignore these other obvious meanings of the word? Precisely, it would seem, for the reasons he has already rejected "nature" as a composite intermediate principle in favour of its primary meaning, form. Aristotle would agree: *form* is the primary meaning of nature.

In thinking of nature as form, we are not thinking of a principle that somehow requires hot or cold matter to give it flesh and blood. Matter is never without particular qualities or quantities, even though in itself it is "without quality," Plotinus states (2, 25). This is the most obscure statement so far. How can matter be without quality, and yet come to be with quality or become qualified in being shaped by a forming principle? What follows is even more obscure: a further supporting reason for this view of matter is that fire does not have to "approach" matter for matter to become fire, but a forming principle has to approach matter for combustion to occur.

Just what does Plotinus mean? Although the questions of matter and *logos* require separate treatment, perhaps we can look at the passage provisionally as follows. Matter, for Plotinus, is a "principle" of potentiality, that is capable of receiving forms only by not having a form itself. So matter has no quality or form and is therefore able to receive all the different forms from the active principle, that is, from form, *logos,* or nature. At the same time, what we actually *see* is never a quality-less matter (though it may be our hypothesis that space or matter or whatever we call it is infinitely plastic and devoid of qualities), but either proximate matter, as Aristotle calls it (i.e., matter already "worked up" and prepared for a new form), or more remote matter that still needs further organic development to receive an appropriate form. Now if we think only in terms of two "things" interacting when form and matter "come together" to form a new compound (as Gilbert Ryle [1973] conceives the mind-body dilemma in what he calls Descartes' myth), then we make a mental picture of a form "fire." But we cannot think of matter and form (or potency and actuality) in this way, Plotinus argues implicitly, for potencies can lie dormant for centuries if need be, and they need an active cause beyond themselves to wake them up. So, of course, it actually makes sense to say that it is not "fire" that needs to "approach," or wake up, matter, but form, or *logos*.

We now come to an even bigger difficulty: the last ten lines of chapter 2 are complicated. This is no small sign, Plotinus goes on to argue, that nature is a principle both external to things and yet also at work in things. Nature, he concludes, is (1) a forming principle that makes (2) another forming principle that gives (3) something (4) to the substrate (i.e., the underlying matter, proximate or more remote) but that—back to (2) again—remains unmoved itself. Plotinus specifies further that the forming principle operative in the visible shape (which is [3] above, the "something" given) is nongenerative, but the forming principle that has life (this must be [2] above), since it is the "brother" of the forming principle that makes the shape (which must be nature or [1] above), has the same power and makes in that which has come into being (i.e., [3] and [4]) a new compound entity). We should observe how Plotinus' articulation of the dynamic process as a whole (as of a conclusion to an argument rendered a little less obscure by the insertion of arabic numerals) actually captures something of the organic unfolding of the visible thing, starting from an unmoved nature and reaching full term in the emergence of a new compound. But what does Plotinus mean? Nature and the organizing principle in the thing (i.e., what later thinkers will call the substantial form, or principle responsible for the *substance*, are intimately linked but *different* (or else each of us would simply be the whole of nature, which we evidently are not). The third *logos* is the "last," and it is dead in the sense that it cannot make another *substance* whereas it can *qualify* or be further qualified since it is a principle operating in the visible shape: I can blush with love or blanch with fear, but I cannot (in this sense of *I*) make a plant or an animal or another *subject* of my affections. On the other hand, nature as an organizing principle actually in me, but not to be identified or ranked simply with the visible shape, is responsible for my being a distinct substance and, as a generative principle, is capable of helping to produce other substances.

3.7. Logos *and* logoi-*brothers (III, 8, 2, 27–35)*

The word *brother* looks too metaphorical to be truly informative, but it is in fact carefully chosen in view of the kinship metaphor that runs through these early chapters. We recall that Plotinus described the World soul as our "elder sister." Kinship or generative links, it would seem, aptly describe our genetic heritage as naturally functioning organisms. But Plotinus undoubtedly has in mind Plato's usage of such terms in, for example, the *Republic*, where all the different kinds of individuals (and constitutions) from the aristocratic to the tyrannic inherit the same genetic lines, however infinitesimally devolved or progressively watered down they may be, and actually live "in the same house." Here, however, there is more than a hint of the *Phaedrus*. *Logos*, of course, means—among many other things—speech or dialogue or account, a nuance simply untranslatable in the present passage. In the *Phaedrus*, in his radical critique of writing, Plato distinguishes between written speech, which looks as though it were alive but cannot answer questions and so is "dead speech" always requiring its "parent" to come to its rescue, and "living speech," which is called "brother" to written speech. Dead speech is externalized, cast into a supposedly fixed form but in fact subject to the constant flux of misinterpretation. Living speech, by contrast, is written in the soul of the learner and can defend itself. It is the original of which written speech is the image (*Phaedrus* 275 d–276 b).

In III, 8, Plotinus changes the Platonic context. The brother-*logoi* become nature herself and the substantial nature or *logos* in the thing, whereas "dead" speech becomes the expression of qualities and relations in the visible shape. This change is probably not accidental. Plotinus is thinking of the *Phaedrus* passage and its wider context. Dead, unproductive speech is of a lower order than living speech, whereas nature and nature at work in the thing are so genuinely akin that they speak to each other as family equals. Such free speech is the dialogue between souls, or what Socrates characterizes as the work of the dialectitian in the passage immediately following in the *Phaedrus*: namely, truly creative or generative discourse. The true dialectitian selects the right type of soul

> and in it he plants and sows his words founded on knowledge, words that can defend both themselves and him who planted them, words that instead of remaining barren contain a seed whence new words grow up in new characters, whereby the seed is vouchsafed immortality, and its possessor the fullest measure of blessedness that a human being can attain to. (276 c–277 a)

The generative power of the two forming principles exactly parallels the generative power of dialectic, which unites the living "speeches" of two different subjects in itself. Like chapter 1, chapter 2 is built on a problem in Aristotle, but it is delicately "framed" by Plato.

How does the word *logos* come to mean "forming principle," or as Armstrong often translates it, "rational forming principle" (Cilento: *"la forma rationale"*; Bréhier: *"la raison"*; Beutler-Theiler: *"die rationale Formkraft"*)? *Logos* can have a host of related but different meanings: "speech" (as above), "expression," "proportion," "word" (as in the opening to John's Gospel), "meaning," even "tale" or "story" (like *mythos*, as in Plato), "reason," "reasoning," "form," "definition," "intelligibility." How does the *logos* come to include intelligence, intelligibility, and formative activity that we find in Plotinus, for whom it is a living reality in soul and at work in the physical universe? Plato's influence is decisive: speech, or "word," is a double-edged medium. It can express a self-contained or self-satisfied private view that stultifies thought, like some of the early speeches in the

Symposium or Lysias' speech in the *Phaedrus*, or by being aware of its limitations, it can point beyond itself to a world that rouses up thought. The living word of dialectic, for example (as opposed even to the written word of Plato's own dialogues), is the closest a human being can come to genuine understanding (*noêsis, epistêmê, nous*) of real being or of the "what" something is (as opposed to what something is *like*). So it is by means of *logos* that we come to *see* for ourselves, but in the company of others, the nature of real things. In this sense, authentic dialogue is already a living reality of soul at work in the world.

The Stoics take this a little further in some ways. They adopt the distinction between an "inner" and an "outer" word (*logos endiathetikos* vs. *logos prophorikos*) and see this "word" in different forms operating at all levels in the universe from god to sperm (cf. Plotinus, I, 2 [19] 3, 27–30). They think of god as an immanent, organizing rational principle, of which we, as individual intelligences, are fragments. This divine *logos,* which pervades everything, also ensures that the world is open to understanding. As Heraclitus had already indicated in those gnomic fragments that we possess, it is by virtue of *logos* that we can share understanding rather than live hermetically sealed, private lives. The Stoics see this potentially shared understanding at work in different ways throughout the universe. Even in "sperm" there is an implicit rationality that we see unfolding as a newly fertilized organism starts to develop. So the Stoics talk of "spermatic *logoi.*" The whole universe is filled with divine rationality that may look like brute necessity in one place and good fortune in another but that in the divine perspective of the whole universe is the beauty of god's providence. The influence (at least in part) of the Heraclitean-Stoic tradition can be seen in the prologue to John's Gospel: "In the beginning was the word." So in Stoic thought the living "word" becomes an immanent organizing principle of rationality on every level of the universe. While Plotinus sees things rather differently (he uses the term *spermatikos logos,* for instance, but also distances himself from it [cf. IV, 4 (28) 39, 5–17]), Stoic thought is a factor in his use of the term.

Several other important factors of this polysemantic term can be grouped around one of its most important meanings: "definition." To define something, we have to employ a process of reasoning. In practice this means that if we claim to know something we can be asked to give an account (*didonai logon*) of our claim. This at least is what Socrates says the dialectitian can do in *Republic* VI–VII (and elsewhere). But as we see in a later dialogue, the *Theaitetus*, justified true belief (that is, correct opinion that such-and-such is the case, *plus* an account or *logos*) is not equivalent to knowledge, or *episteme*. Knowledge, it would seem, involves more than justified true belief; that is, it involves understanding or *noêsis*. An "account" is something we provide after the fact and so is more like an image of understanding rather than understanding itself. If knowledge is to go beyond justified true belief, it must again be knowledge of what x *is*, not of what x is *like*.

Here a consideration of *logos* as "definition" obtains. The word *logos* means both "definition" and "account," and from a philosophical rather than a historical point of view, the latter derives from the former. When we define something, we put together the elements of the definition (e.g., genus and specific difference, in Aristotle's case: "rational, human animal"), not to look at them separately or unpack their different meanings further but to see them conjointly as a single "expression" of what is real. This, at least, is the way Aristotle appears to view the "essence" in terms of that strange phrase he employs: the *ti ên einai*, or as it came to be translated into Latin: *quod quid erat esse*, "the what it was to be." The essence is the unified totality of all the elements in the definition (genus and difference) *seized in a single act of thought* (cf. Tricot I, 24; Ross I, 127). What is collected and presented discursively by a process of reasoning is united by thought and becomes one with the "real." A definition, therefore, represents discursively the world's intelligibility as understood by thought. So *logos* as definition is thought's encounter with *logos* as a principle really active in the world.

This approach to the polysemantic quality of *logos*, rooted in Plato and Aristotle, is more informative for our purposes than the admittedly important Stoic view, for it shows how the different meanings of *logos*, from the "intelligibility" or "inherent meaningfulness" of the world to the "reasoning" or "rationality" of someone who can "account" for a "claim," can be mediated by "definition." In turn, definition may "in principle" (*kata logon*) be an "expression" of soul's content, just as soul for Plotinus is an "expression" (*logos*) of intellect (and intellect of the One), as well as an "expression" of the nature of the real. Plotinus uses *logos* in all the above senses, and in this he is dependent also upon the earlier Peripatetic tradition (Alexander of Aphrodisias and others), which employs *logos* to mean "definition" as well as "forming principle" in or outside of matter. Forming principles in matter, Alexander calls *enula eidè* (enmattered forms), and forming principles without matter, *auloi logoi*.[11] Plotinus also uses these expressions (though not in the works we are considering here).

My reasons for translating *logos* as "forming principle" rather than "rational forming or formative principle" are, first, because such *logoi* are *actively* forming and, second, because *rational* can be misleading: *logoi* are active, unified expressions of pure intelligibility that we come to understand by rational, discursive means, but they are not rationally discursive in themselves.[12]

---

11. Cf. Alexander, *Questiones* 2, 10, 55, 9–10; cf. 1, 26, 43, 9; 1, 25, 39, 13–19; Sharples, 1992, 65 n. 192.

12. For the range of meanings in the *Enneads* see M. Atkinson, 1986, 51–54; and M. Fattal, 1998. *Logos* is the inner and outward "word" in both soul and intellect (I, 2 [19] 3, 27–30; II, 7 [37] 3, 14–15; IV, 3 [27] 5, 18; V, 8 [31] 2, 18–19; VI, 2 [43] 21, 29–30; V, 9 [5] 3, 30–6), and there are *logoi* in matter (II, 7 [37] 3, 12; VI, 1 [42] 29, 11; VI, 7 [38] 11, 10; II, 6 [17] 2, 15) and *logoi* that are active and productive (II, 8 [30] 2, 27–28; II, 3 [52] 16, 19–20; VI, 7 [38] 4, 25; cf. III, 3 [48] 4, 10).

In the *Enneads,* there are always many different perspectives. In III, 8, 2, we have three different *logoi,* one in matter and two without matter—that is, if the substantial form at work in the organism can be regarded as "without matter." Immaterial *logoi,* therefore, are distinct from matter; but elsewhere such *logoi* already *include* the matter in the sense that the qualities that this or that parcel of matter always possesses are really already a reflection of the *logos* in its pure intelligibility rather than of the matter in its tendency to indefiniteness.[13] Why this should be so, we must examine briefly before we come back to III, 8, chapter 3.

3.8. Matter: From Plato, Aristotle, and the Stoics to Plotinus

Plato does not use the term *matter* (*hylê*) as such.[14] Instead, in the *Timaeus* he speaks of the "receptacle" or "place" of coming-to-be in which the forms of things flicker in and out of existence so that we even have difficulty calling these particular things individual "thises" since they are always changing. So the "material principle," if we can call it this, has a kind of illusory or dream-like quality to it, and particular things find themselves poised uncomfortably between "being" and "non-being," as in the *Republic* (and the *Sophist*).

Aristotle discovers matter as such, we might say. He takes the word *hylê,* which means "wood" or "stuff," and makes it the underlying matter that, together with shape, form, and the definite natures we actually find in our experience, makes up individual compound things. Matter is a real underlying *subject* of change, for it acts as a subject in which change of form, or privation of that change (i.e., a blush or a blanch), can occur. These are the subjects we talk about and refer things to, the subjects of grammar and syntax that look so trivial and boring when we study them at school but that are in fact the "first substances" upon which our being able to talk intelligibly at all actually hinges. So much depends upon a red wheelbarrow, the poet William Carlos Williams writes; that is, upon an apparently insignificant but definite substance capable of moving the earth. So much also depends upon being able to distinguish subjects from adjectives, adverbs, verbs, prepositions, and other parts of speech and then to see the often overlooked significance of substances themselves.

But what happens when a new substance emerges or an old one disappears? In this case for Aristotle, given the absence of microscopes, we have to understand the form-matter relation analogously since we cannot determine exactly what the matter is at certain moments in the change. When we blush or blanch, these quali-

---

13. See II, 7 (37) 3; III, 3 (48) 29–34.

14. For "matter" in ancient thought generally and in Plotinus see H. Happ, 1971; F.-P. Hager, 1987; D. O'Brien, 1971, 1981, 1991; H. Benz, K. Corrigan, 1986a, 1992, 1993b, 1996a; H.-R. Schwyzer, 1973; J. M. Narbonne, 1993. On the question of the generation of matter in Plotinus (i.e., matter is not an independent principle but is generated from and by the One) see H.-R. Schwyzer, 1973; D. O'Brien, 1971, 1981, 1990, 1991, 1996; K. Corrigan, 1986, 1996a.

tative changes depend on us as already formed substances. But when we come-to-be or perish, a substantial change occurs, and the matter that is not a definite "this" (e.g., I can no longer say that it is you, me, frog's tails, or maggot soup) is in process of becoming a new substance. Even here, for Aristotle, the matter is not just nothingness but a sort of bare potential—with the emphasis on *potential*.

So matter is a positive notion in Aristotle's thought, as it is in a different way for the Stoics, since the divine *logos* and everything in the universe is actually material. Spirit and matter are not two separate realms but two different ways of looking at anything: plants, animals, human beings, demons, even god. I touch divinity even in the humblest righteous task. The great Benedictine motto, "to work is to pray," is not too far removed from this spirit.

What happens then with Plotinus to muddy this positive picture? It is a little like quantum physics or non-Euclidean geometry meeting a Newtonian or Euclidean view of the universe. Things appear to be so solid until we start to look at them and then, unfortunately, as Bertrand Russell observes in his little book *The Problems of Philosophy*, their solidity dissolves, and we seem to be left only with an enigma.

Before III, 8, Plotinus had already written three treatises on matter: II, 4 (12), entitled *On the two kinds of matter* (Plotinus assumes two matters: intelligible matter and the matter of the physical world); II, 5 (25), entitled *On what exists potentially and what actually*; and III, 6 (26), entitled *On the impassibility of beings without body*. Each work actually contributes a new perspective upon his overall theory, so we can only give a potted version of that theory here. Plotinus would later write one further work just before his death: I, 8 (51), *On the origin of evils*; we shall take up the question of matter-evil in V, 8. But the really significant point to be aware of is this: the question of matter troubled Plotinus in different ways throughout his writing career. So he evidently must have felt that he had not said the last word on this puzzling question.

The problem for Plotinus is what we mean and refer to when we speak, think about, and experience matter. The Aristotelian analysis is fine as far as a positive conception goes, but in Plotinus' view, philosophical analysis has to go a little further than Aristotle was prepared to take it. Yes, matter makes a positive contribution to the formation of bodies, but if we suppose that quality, quantity, and the like are forms and we therefore push further toward the indeterminacy of matter (an indeterminacy that Plotinus argues we experience even in ordinary life as absence, or non-being), we find a different picture. As contained by form, matter is positive, but as indeterminate, matter is "other" than everything else, bearing a kind of negative relation to form; nor even is it simply "other" if the word "other" implies a unitary, formal notion. Instead, Plotinus argues, at this level of analysis we should refer to it as "others"; that is, indeterminate *plurality* negatively characterized by *privation* or absence of form. Aristotle had made privation a formal concept (i.e., form and privation are contrasted with matter as their underlying "stuff"), but Plotinus insists that this is to leave indefiniteness unexamined; that is, to be satisfied with it as a purely formal concept and not to get at the negative, indeterminate plurality that for him is part of the analysis and experience of a non-formal matter (see II, 4 [12] 6–15). At the same time, matter's indeterminacy is such that it is *potentially everything*, while *actually* being no one thing (a formula employed in different ways by Plato, Aristotle, and the Peripatetics). So its *positive* quality (that it is potentially everything) is paradoxically a function of its very *negativity* (that it is actually *no thing*). The two, positive and negative, have to go together; but in terms of its negativity this means we cannot speak about truth or falsity in the same way that we can for a world of determinate, definite things (like you, me, or trees), for there are no things or distinct formal points of reference in an indeterminate landscape. Consequently, in II, 5 (25) and other works, Plotinus develops a kind of logic of the indeterminate in which the principle of non-contradiction no longer strictly applies because no principle of identity can be found in matter's indeterminacy as such. Instead of making true or false statements, we have to approach the puzzling character of indeterminacy by combining apparently opposite statements: x both is and is not. Plotinus does not, of course, anticipate quantum physics, but there is a certain similarity between the two insofar as contemporary physics has been compelled to think and speak of probabilities instead of precise scientific measurements and to recognize the indeterminacy of descriptions such as wave and particle, or again, velocity and position.

This is certainly more than we need for our purposes here in III, 8, or V, 8, but it provides additional background to help you make up your own mind on the issue.

How do we modern readers find our bearings in this strange world? Well, we could suppose that Plotinus is somehow committed to an actual "infinite-in-itself" or an essential indeterminacy in some way separate from things or that he simply wants to outdo Aristotle and get back to a Platonic "non-being" view of things. But in the first case, Plotinus argues precisely against an *essential* indeterminacy (II, 4 [12] 15), and in the second, he is much more interested in the philosophical problem than scoring sectarian points. We might then suppose that Plotinus' analysis anticipates the death-knell of such thinking in the British Empiricists. John Locke (1632–1704) supposes matter (and mind also) to be an "I know not what" indeterminate substratum. Bishop Berkeley (1685–1753) (a reader of Plotinus, by the way) consequently does away with the matter-hypothesis and puts everything into spirit as the true substratum or underlying "I know not what," on the (arguable) grounds that mind or spirit is knowable, whereas matter is not. Finally, David Hume (1711–1776) comes along and dispenses with *both* indeterminate substrata, mind and matter, in favour of "bundles," "constant contiguity," and "psychological association." Then Kant (1724–1804) tries to make the phoenix rise out of the ashes by arguing for the grounding of phenomena in the transcendental unity of apperception. Hegel more or less ignores (and yet incorporates) them all by unpacking the complete world of "spirit" out of the naïve immediacy of the sense-object.

This certainly might be one way of situating Plotinus' theory as one logically disastrous step toward the apparent absurdity of the problem in modern philosophy, but we should at the same time take account of some of the subtleties in his position. First, even the indeterminate substratum for Plotinus is not a quasi-independent "I know not what" principle. Plotinus argues, in fact, that we have a special form of "cognition" of such indefiniteness (II, 4 [12] 8–10), as Sartre (1905–1980) and Heidegger (1889–1976)[15] would also argue many centuries later. Second, the *meaning* of matter emerges in the light of form; matter is not done away with, as in Berkeley's imaginative universe, but rather comes into its own proper nature as fully expressive of form in the world of "intellect." By contrast, Plotinus' notion of matter, therefore, is multidimensional, ranging from pure indefinite multiplicity to formed physical things and ultimately to intellect (for evil see chapter 4.13 below).

Does Plotinus' theory of matter really do away with actual material subjects in the physical world, as is sometimes thought? Not according to III, 8, 2, at least, for matter comes in proximate (i.e., more developed or less developed forms, as we have seen [2, 23–25]). Matter could not, of course, be a genuine subject in the absence of form, but together with form it can assume all the different grades of subject-complexity that we find in Plotinus' thought, from elements or elementary compounds to human beings and their organizing principles, namely, souls and intellects. The matter of soul and intellect, however, is already a complete activity, or *energeia,* without physical potentiality, for it is identical with form and expresses perfectly the nature or substance of the thing. Plotinus calls this "intelligible" matter "whole illuminated substance" (II, 4 [12] 5, 22–23: "the subject there [i.e., in the intelligible world] is substance [*ousia*]"), and the only potentiality such substance has is in relation to its origin and return to the One. So for Plotinus matter is an authentic subject and substance only in the intelligible world; this does not mean, however, that the physical world is illusory but only that physical subjects are not capable of expressing completely what they are. What it means to call intellect a subject or substance we shall examine below.

---

15. See, for example, how absence foregrounds perception for Sartre: "The figure which slips [*qui se glisse*] constantly between my look and the solid, real objects of the café is precisely a perpetual disappearance; it is Pierre raising himself as nothingness on the ground of the nihilation of the café" (*L'Etre et le Néant,* 1943, 15th ed., Paris, 47–52; *Being and Nothingness,* tr. Hazel E. Barnes, Philosophical Library, New York, 1956. For Heidegger in his early lecture *What is Metaphysics?* the "Nothing" is essentially repulsion that does not annihilate or spring from a negation but rather nihilates: *Das Nichts selbst nichtet* ("The Nothing itself nihilates") (*Wegmarken* II, Klosterman, Frankfurt, 1967). For further comment in context see K. Corrigan, 1996, 169–75.

3.9.   Logos *and action, a way of understanding* Neoplatonic contemplative production *(III, 8, 3)*

In chapter 2, Plotinus reaches the conclusion that nature as a whole and the individual natures in things are forming principles, and he sketches the relation of these forming principles to their natural products. Such forming principles act as unmoved movers in moving physical things (a view Aristotle had originally suggested in *Physics VIII* 6, 258 b 12–13). In chapter 3, he now explores what it means to say that forming principles make. We could suppose that in their making they grasp or attain to some form of contemplation (3, 1–2). The verb Plotinus uses here is *ephaptesthai* ("to attain to"), a common enough verb in the *Enneads* with a range of different applications. Here it appears to have the sense of the *logos* reaching beyond itself, as in the ascent to the "beautiful itself" at the end of Diotima-Socrates' speech in the *Symposium*, where the lover finally "attains to" truth, no longer an image (212 a 4–5). Plotinus immediately excludes this sense of the *logos* rising beyond itself to attain to contemplation since if the *logos* remains unmoved in itself (a most important Neoplatonic principle, as we shall see), which is to say that its making is not like physical action always being concerned with something outside itself, then it must already *be* contemplation. Plotinus then illustrates what he means by drawing an example from concrete human action.

According to Aristotle, when we act in a successful moral way, we actually hit a proportional mean between excess and deficiency (too much or too little). This proportional mean (again, *logos*) is not a fixed arithmetical mean (as if we simply applied a preestablished blueprint) but is based upon sufficient information, good judgement, deliberation, and our experience of life so that we can get it "right" in varying particular circumstances. We have to "find" this proper mean and fit it to our action. Moral action then is not a question of absolutes, nor is it purely relative. Each moral action is different but must be informed by a *logos*; that is, an intelligent proportion between extremes, a proportion sensitive to one's own developing nature, to other people, and to circumstances. This *logos* is the sort of thing of which we can in principle give an "account" afterward, but in the habitually good moral person (the *spoudaios;* cf. III, 8, 6, 16, 37), it is intelligent self-awareness in action, just as a brilliant goal scored from any angle under any circumstances is not simply chance but the product of years of training and practical insight. The goal is "perfect." So too with other forms of action. Right action embodies a kind of discovery of the real, for each *logos* or proportional mean shows us the world in a new way.

Something of this Plotinus argues here, though in shorthand. Action is different from its forming principle and is guided by it, but if the forming principle cannot be reduced simply to action, then it must be contemplation or, as Lonergan rightly puts it, a form of insight. In this context, *insight* is a better translation of *theôria*, for insight is clearly not action; yet, if genuine, it is *real*, not just my own wistful rationality. Insight, however, does not fit *theôria* in other contexts, so I have preferred the traditional *contemplation*. Nor does insight fit all action, since Plotinus is not just talking about right action.

So how does contemplation fit all action? Plotinus' notion of action is not without significant problems for the modern reader. We tend to think of action as having little to do with reality; though we know theoretically from electron microscopes that the observer influences the field of observation, we see no dialectical interaction on the macro-level between our actions and so-called reality beyond our impression that both are "constructs" (in a sort of muddled Hume-Kantian way). Plotinus would not deny that some actions are thoughtless, purposeless, or badly executed or that even right action may happen by accident. But he would claim that right action, insofar as it is cognitive, voluntary, and embodies the right ordering of one's emotions, is not just my construct of the real, but the real actually shaping me. By the very token that we can call actions thoughtless or accidental, we place all action implicitly in the context of intelligibility so that all action has some sort of "purpose," even if we are unconscious of it or want to do away with purposes altogether. So all action, and not just right action, is stuck with the intelligibility of reality, whether it embodies this intelligibility in new or ordinary or unconscious ways or whether it attempts even to destroy intelligibility or to reduce meaningfulness to subjective constructs.

Plotinus goes on to apply the specific case of action more broadly. If physical states, things, and events in the sphere of action are the final results of forming principles and forming principles are contemplation (as we have already agreed), then the final physical instance resulting from any forming principle must be the result of a contemplation that has already been contemplated. The perfect tense in *tetheôrêmenos* (3, 8) has a sense of the present. From the perspective of the physical thing, the act of contemplation *already has* been there from the beginning of its existence. But for the forming principle it is present now and not as a mere spectacle or object but as an active contemplation that also is being contemplated. A dialectical "twoness" of subject and object within it already exists. To understand is also to be understood. To act is to express however imperfectly an intelligibility, and intelligibility is not an object or blueprint but essentially a dialogue. This living contemplation is actually operative in things, though we are unconscious of its activity.

Here already we have an unfamiliar way of understanding the Neoplatonic theory of production, or emanation. All substances when they are complete give of themselves to their products while remaining undiminished in their own natures, just as the Good in Plato's *Republic* makes things "good-formed" by its light. This principle often is encapsulated in the later Latin phrase: *bonum diffusivum sui* (the good is diffusive of itself). Or as Plotinus says later in the big work, the good "is gentle, kindly, and gracious, and present to anyone when one wishes" (V, 5 [32] 12, 33–34). To describe this undiminished self-giving Plotinus uses images of light, smell, sound. Sometimes he uses the language of two acts, one of which *belongs* to the substance and the other of which springs *from* the substance and serves to generate something new. In this context, A. C. Lloyd has shown how Plotinus adapts Aristotle's psychological and physical models of causation from the *De Anima* and *Physics* respectively for his own Platonic purpose (1987, 155–86). The maker and the thing made form a *single* activity in the making, though they are, of course, distinguishable. The same is true, though even more intimately, of the relation between each activity and action of ours and the whole soul that makes them possible. Such production is unconsciously part and parcel of every action or production. Making is coextensive with being. So the Neoplatonic theory of the generation of spiritual principles (intellect and soul) is apparently a concrete feature reflected even in the most ordinary experiences.

Treatise III, 8, 3, 8–10 is puzzling. We act according to a *logos* whether consciously or unconsciously. But the *logos* before this, Plotinus goes on to say, is *everything* and under two aspects: nature and soul. What does Plotinus mean? The claim looks absurd: I am aware of myself, yes, and I can make some sensible differentiation, perhaps, between my "ego" and a "self." I may even recognize a "transcendental ego" insofar as I cannot seem to catch the "ego" that organizes my field of consciousness actually in that field. But I could nowhere claim access to *everything*. Plotinus' argument, however, is not introspective in this way. My individual nature is a brother-*logos* that comes from nature as a whole, and this whole nature is the lowest manifestation of soul. But if soul animates the whole universe—that is, if it contains all the forming principles and is therefore everything—then nature and soul are in different ways the whole of what is. For Plotinus, the distinction between the animate and the inanimate makes sense from a particular viewpoint, but it is ultimately artificial since everything (even the apparently inanimate elements) is pervaded and formed by soul's intelligibility (cf. VI, 7 [38] 10–11), as it is for Plato in the *Timaeus* (36 e ff.).

So the forming principle is the result of another (bigger) contemplation, and again this is not an object only, but the result of a subject contemplating (line 12). Nature, therefore, is contemplative, not because of reasoning (3, 13 is a good example of how *logos* retains the meaning "reasoning") or by examining her content item by item. To be in the process of looking is not yet to have, just as Socrates stands in porches or in fields *looking*. *Skopein* is the verb Plato uses in the *Symposium* of Socrates: he is always in search.[16] Nature's contemplation is not like this: she makes simply by *being* what she is, and as the maker of everything, she is not dead or a plastic blueprint but a living contemplation contemplating herself, needing no feet, hands, or action to give life to the universe.

---

16. On his way to Agathon's house Socrates stops off in a neighbour's porch wrapped up in reflection "paying attention to himself" (174 d 5–8). This is not a fit of some sort for he is aware of what is happening and tells Aristodemus to go on without him. Alcibiades later describes how he became engrossed in a problem while on a military campaign and "stood looking" (220 c 4–5) to the great amusement of his fellow soldiers.

3.10.   The silent speech of nature (III, 8, 4)

Why should Plotinus make nature herself speak in chapter 4 after he already has gone to the trouble of deanthropomorphizing her? As Plato provides myths, examples, playful interludes, dramatic enactments, as well as different sorts of arguments, so Plotinus provides a dramatic enactment for us to see through it to the sort of living contemplation in nature for which he has been arguing. He has another reason too. Gnostic "principles" have very dramatic roles and do a lot of apocalyptic talking. Plotinus makes nature's speech dramatically attractive but emphasizes her *silence*. He gently reprimands her curious questioner—"you should be silent like me"—and then describes what she sees in her *silence*.[17] In a later treatise on providence, Plotinus has the universe reply (3, 19–20: "if you contemplate this") to someone who blames the whole because of its parts (in this case a Gnostic) in terms reminiscent of St. Paul's words on the body of Christ, or at least of a Gnostic version of St. Paul: it is not the function of the finger to see, but the eye in the context of the whole body (III, 2 [47] 3, 21–42). Here too in III, 8, he has the Gnostics in mind, or at least those friends in his own circle who had been attracted by Gnosticism.

The central image of nature's speech is that of natural geometry. In Plato's *Republic* VI (510 d–e), geometers use visible forms to think through them to their intelligible paradigms. Here in III, 8, they likewise draw figures "as they contemplate," whereas the source, nature, contemplates and the figures fall out into the lines of bodies. Plato represents this activity mythically in the *Timaeus* as the intelligible ordering of primordial chaos with geometrical forms by the divine demiurge or craftsman.[18]

---

17. Cf. Rilke, *Ich bin, du Ängstlicher*: "... Siehst du nicht meine Seele, wie sie dicht/vor dir in einem Kleid aus Stille steht?/ ... Wenn du der Träumer bist, bin ich dein Traum./Doch wenn du wachen willst, bin ich dein Wille/und werde mächtig aller Herrlichkeit/und ründe mich wie eine Sternenstille/über der wunderlichen Stadt der Zeit" ("My soul, dressed in silence, rises up/and stands alone before you: can't you see?/If you are the dreamer, I am what you dream./But when you want to wake, I am your wish,/and I grow strong with all magnificence/and turn myself into a star's vast silence/above the strange and distant city, Time"). *The Selected Poetry of Rainer Maria Rilke*, ed. and trans. Stephen Mitchell, Vintage, New York, 1982, 2–3. Compare the Russian poet F. I. Tyutchev (1803–1873), *Silentium* (trans. Yuri Corrigan): "Be silent, cover yourself, and hide/Your feeling and your dreams/Let them into the soul's depths/Let them rise and stay/Silently, like stars in the night/Delight in them–and be silent/—How can the heart articulate itself?/ How can another understand you?/Will he grasp how you live?/A thought, once spoken, is a lie/Erupting, you cloud the springs/Drink from them—and be silent/—Learn only to live within yourself/There is a whole world in your soul/Of mysterious—magical contemplation/That is drowned out by external noise/The day's light disperses the rays/Attend to their song—and be silent."

18. Compare Coleridge's view of this passage in his *Biographia Literaria*, chapter 12. The reality of the "far higher and far inward sources" can be adequately gauged only by

3.11. Synaesthêsis (III, 4, 15 ff.)

What is the character of nature's contemplation? Nature's contemplation is a re-flexive self-presence, a sort of trance-like contemplation asleep with itself, by contrast with the "clearer" contemplation of the higher soul, which like Aristotle's divine thought in the *Metaphysics* is like self-reflexive thought waking up (cf. VI, 9 [9] 3, 24). Yet even in this dim contemplation everything is included and there is "with-knowing" (*synesis*, translated here as "understanding") and "with-per-ception"[19] (*synaesthêsis*, translated here as "intimate perception"). This with-perception involves a kind of awareness of what flows from nature (just as the World soul has such an awareness in III, 4 [15] 4, 10–11 and just as discursive reason is said to be aware of sense-impressions in I, 1 [53] 9, 20). Treatise IV, 4 (28) 13, represents nature as below reason and imagination and specifically denies understanding (*synesis*) to her. This *synaesthêsis* (a kind of "common sense" that is aware of the many individual sense-data), includes a sense of the relatedness of a whole to itself: the world is said to have such a *synaesthêsis* (cf. IV, 4 [28] 24; 45, 8). Two passages even appear to attribute *synaesthêsis* to the One (V, 4 [7] 2, 18 and V, 1 [10] 7, 11–13), but in each case the context requires that the unspeci-

---

experience and represented best by silence. Coleridge links this passage to V, 5 (32), 8: "one must not seek whence it comes" and comments as follows: only those who prepare themselves in silence to see "can acquire the philosophic imagination, the sacred power of self-intuition, who within themselves can interpret and understand the symbol, that the wings of the air-sylph are forming within the skin of the caterpillar; those only, who feel in their own spirits the same instinct, which impels the chrysalis of the horned fly to leave room in its involucrum for antennae yet to come. They know and feel that the *potential* works *in* them, even as the *actual* works on them! In short, all the organs of sense are framed for a corresponding world of sense; and we have it. All the organs of spirit are framed for a correspondent world of spirit: though the latter organs are not developed in all alike. But they exist in all, and their first appearance discloses itself in the *moral* being. How else could it be, that even worldlings, not wholly debased, will contemplate the man of simple and disinterested goodness with contradictory feelings of pity and respect? "Poor man! He is not made for *this* world" Oh! Herein they utter a prophecy of universal fulfil-ment; for man *must* either rise or sink." Compare Rilke (re: his poem "Gravity" on "taking life heavily") in a letter to Franz Xavier Kappus, July 16, 1903: "He who is solitary . . . can remember that all beauty in animals and plants is a silent, enduring form of love and yearn-ing, and he can see animals, as he sees plants, patiently and willingly uniting and increas-ing and growing, not out of physical pleasure . . . but bowing to necessities that are greater than pleasure and pain, and more powerful than will and withstanding. If only human be-ings could more humbly receive this mystery—which the world is filled with, even in its smallest Things—, could bear it . . . more solemnly, feel how terribly heavy it is, instead of taking it lightly. If only they could be more reverent toward their own fruitfulness, which is essentially *one*, whether it is manifested as mental or physical . . ." (*Selected Poetry*, Mitchell, 342).

19. For *synaesthêsis* see F. M. Schroeder, 1992; A. Graeser, 1972.

fied subject is intellect as it comes to be from the One and has a sort of preintelligible awareness of its multiple power.[20] At any rate, Plotinus defines *synaesthêsis* in V, 3 (49) 13, 21–22 as "a perception of something that is many" and excludes it from the One at V, 7 (24) 1–5, and VI, 7 (38) 41, 25–8; if anything belongs to the One, it is far beyond *gnôsis* and awareness of itself (*synaesthêsis heautou*). So this intimate perception, or "withness," of nature's dim contemplation looks forward to the *synesis* and *synaesthêsis* of true self-thinking, which Plotinus tells us takes care not to stand off by itself from union with its object in wanting to perceive too much (V, 8 [31] 11, 23). Aristotle uses *synaesthêsis* to describe the shared consciousness of thought and existence between friends (*EN* 1170 b 10). There is a similar, less explicit delicacy in nature's vision-loving character here, even in Plotinus' representation of her including the questioner in her otherwise silent contemplation.

3.12.   The nature of images and productive art: Plato and Plotinus (III, 4, 39 ff.)

Nature, however, is an image (*eidôlon,* III, 8, 4, 44) because the truth of her vision is not in herself but comes from soul and intellect. So the apparently solid products of her vision are in fact images of images (as Socrates had argued in *Republic* X). Much of Plotinus' language in these chapters bears an extra resonance from Platonic usage in the *Symposium, Republic,* and *Phaedrus,* and some of his casual remarks nonetheless capture the essence of the way Plato uses images, particularly the notion of "filling and being filled" that runs right through Plato's middle dialogues. In Plotinus' view, the soul turns to action and production, for instance, because she wants to see the object of vision but is too weak to contemplate it directly and be filled with it (4, 34–6). Because of this, Plotinus goes on to argue, making and doing are either a "weakening" or an "accompaniment" (*parakolouthêma*) of contemplation. They are a weakening simply if action and production, as it were, exhaust the vision and leave the agent with nothing beyond the artifact, and they are an accompaniment if the artifact or action somehow opens a path to something greater than itself (4, 41–3).

Contemporary scholarship sometimes uncritically assumes that Plato's critique of mimetic art in *Republic* II, III, and X is his last word on the subject and that it is left to Aristotle to point out a higher function of art (e.g., in the *Physics,* II 199 a 15–17: "and generally art partly brings to completion what nature cannot accomplish, and partly imitates"). This is too simplistic an approach to a multifaceted thinker like Plato. The *Republic,* it is true, criticizes mimetic art because it takes to be the truth images that come to assume such a hold over us that the focus

---

20. Cf. K. Corrigan, 1984; F. M. Schroeder, 1986a; J. Bussanich, 1988.

of our world narrows to the private pursuit of shadow-images, as in the cave-analogy. But this is not only true for images of physical things. *Any* image, for Plato, can become an idolatrous cul-de-sac for thought. Even the images and examples of science, for example, or of scientific hypothesis can obscure and limit what they purport to represent if they do not open new pathways for thought and understanding. So art and its images are *always* double-edged. Plato never changes his view of the fatal limitations of mimetic art (even the late *Laws* [816 d ff.] disapproves of imitative comedy and tragedy). Yet at the same time even in the *Republic* a more positive view of a nonimitative art (in this sense) is suggested, if the images and hypotheses can be "destroyed" in order to free art to see through those images to the vaster "sea of beauty" or being that they imperfectly represent (533 c; 501 a–c). Consequently, Socrates speaks of the "philosophical Muse" (499 c–d), because only dialectic, or the critical but well-meaning conversation between friends that leads to the "study" (*mathêma*) of the good and beautiful, frees and reorients the soul to enter into a world of shared realities rather than private semblances (*Republic* VII 522 b ff.). In Diotima's ladder of ascent in the *Symposium* (cf. Appendix A, 1), it is the vision of the truly beautiful, a vision freely bestowed, uncompelled, and only prepared for by the ascent, that gives lover and beloved together the possibility of giving birth to "true things" (*talêthê*), not "images" (*eidôla*) (212 a). In the *Symposium* too Socrates broaches the further possibility (rejected in *Republic* III) of a more authentic notion of art, one that can comprise both tragedy and comedy (223 d). This is surely the unique sort of philosophical art reflected in the *Symposium* itself, which dramatizes the "comitragedy" of life (cf. *Philebus* 51 b) in a way that permits the reader to see beyond the dramatic images to the dialectical invitation of the work as a whole.

However this may be, in III, 8 (30) 4, as later in V, 8 (31) 1–2, Plotinus is well aware of this double function of the image. On the one hand, the weakness of soul leads to the privation or extinction of insight.[21] Some artworks, we might say, leave nothing beyond themselves. They function like matt surfaces or even black holes. Other images bend back, in, round, and through themselves to open pathways for living thought. For one who can see, even a stone reflects the whole universe and more, but from its own point of view. But for Plotinus the crucial feature of the successful image is that it frees vision from the straitjacket of *only* its own point of view: action or production is an accompaniment if one has another object of contemplation before this (4, 42–3); that is, if the product opens up the essential connectedness of living thought. This is the point at which the notion of "filling and being filled" comes into play.

---

21. On Plotinus' approach to art see A. N. M. Rich, 1960; J. Anton, 1964–5, 1967–8; E. de Keyser, 1955; R. Ferwerda, 1965; A. H. Armstrong, 1975; K. Corrigan, 1993a.

3.13.   The problem of degrees of reality:
Filling and being filled (III, 8, 4–5)

In chapter 4, Plotinus sees action and production as consequences of the soul's failure to be filled by what is primarily true (*proêgoumenôs*, 4, 44; cf. 33–44). Then in chapter 5 he speaks of soul's "fullness" and her "birth pains" (5, 4; cf. 6, 12–13) and applies the metaphor to art: "when each art is full, it makes another little art like it in a toy that has an image of everything in it" (5, 6–8). What Plotinus could mean by this last image is extremely difficult to understand. Moreover, the metaphor of filling arguably masks a central problem, one that is felt somewhat more forcefully when Plotinus applies these metaphors elsewhere to the creative production of the hypostases themselves. In being filled by its vision of the One, intellect itself comes to be, Plotinus argues (VI, 7 [38] 16, 31–17, 6), and this fullness in intellect is ultimately the cause of intellect's giving birth to soul. For generations of more practically minded souls this sort of metaphoric language has simply given Neoplatonism a bad name. But the problem is evident already in Plato; it may be termed the "degrees of reality" problem, a way of thinking defended by scholars like Maritain but criticized heavily by others (e.g., Vlastos, 1965).

In the closing sections of the first nine books of the *Republic* (585 c–586 e), Socrates argues for the superiority of the philosophical life over the honour-loving and money-making lives on the grounds that the former is in fact the more inclusive and pleasurable since it involves being filled by real and true things rather than by empty images of the truth. Socrates' view is not unlike that of Plotinus in III, 8. We look to the "truth" in order to be filled with real things, but when we focus the whole soul upon things that are less real, like honour or money, we are not really filled at all but get carried away into various forms of isolated action that try to substitute for the real thing. On the account of the *Republic*, the tyrant is the ultimate form of such perverted emptiness, for in the figure of the tyrant everything is parasitic appearance rather than substance: the appearance of strength, but the reality of slavish dependence on the mob. In his master-slave dialectic, Hegel later charts this contradiction between appearance and reality as the apparent master whose word is law for the slave gradually becomes enslaved himself to the slave's services, while the slave conversely becomes an emancipated self-consciousness through his fear of the master and his work. This dialectic was of great importance throughout the nineteenth century in the thought of Marx, Kierkegaard, Nietzsche, and others. But the notion of "more or less" reality, so fundamental to the Platonic tradition from Plato to Augustine, and which Hegel may appear to avoid by charting the phenomenological stages of the movement of one state into its opposite, has proved problematic for recent scholars.[22] How can

---

22. For Hegel, see *The Phenomenology of Spirit*, section on self-consciousness, "The Truth of Self-Certainty."

one speak of "degrees of reality" or of being filled by "wisdom" more truly than by "bread"? How can one exist or be a human being more or less? Existence and humanity do not admit of degrees in this way. Either we exist or we do not; there is no in-between. Plato and Plotinus, however, envisage life as somehow suspended by degrees between being and non-being and appear to be of the view that what one knows, thinks, imagines, or sees has a fundamental effect upon the character of one's life. Dover, for example, finds it absurd that Plato should assume a correlation "contrary to ordinary experience . . . between the truth of a belief and its effect upon the conduct of the believer" (Dover, 1980, 159). Since this problem threatens to undermine the coherence of Platonism, we need to tackle it directly here.

Let us grant with Vlastos this oddity to modern ears of Plato's and Plotinus' manner of speaking. In fact, Plotinus, like Porphyry and Augustine after him, says that the closer we are to the One "the more we are" (*mallon esmen*).[23] But the real question is what do Plato and Plotinus mean? By more being, or more truly being, Plato means, almost quite literally, *fuller* being; that is, not just to activate one *dynamis*, power, or part of the soul and live exclusively within the confines of that part, but rather to live according to the integrated powers of the whole soul. For Plato, only in the context of "the whole soul" recovering "its best nature" is the proper care of the body established: the harmony of the body for the sake of the harmonies of the soul (*Republic* IX 591 b–d). But it is not enough for the soul to puff itself up like a frog in order to attain a whole existence. The soul has to be transformed by its experience of a reality outside itself, so that she does not become the sole criterion of what is real. Pausanias in the *Symposium*, for instance, exposes a Platonic-sounding distinction between soul and body, and he pushes all the right-sounding buttons when he talks about excellence and wisdom as the true criteria for right action. Yet these terms are empty of content and so perhaps unwittingly may mask only his own preferences (namely, that the beloved have sexual intercourse with the lover, in this case a teacher like Pausanias, for the sake of virtue or excellence). Socrates, by contrast, establishes the problem of "filling" in his opening words to Agathon: if only wisdom could flow from the wise to the unwise by physical proximity, he ironically states, what a bargain that would be (175 d–e). The problem—in the context of *Symposium*—is that such material transfer involves only the repletion and evacuation of fleeting bodily, psychic, and even epistemic identities: we have to learn new things just to stem the drain of all the bits of knowledge we are constantly losing (cf. 207 d–208 a). If "filling" in a more authentic, vertical sense means anything, then, it involves being transformed by a divine principle, namely, the beautiful itself. In Socrates' case, this results in

---

23. See, e.g., Porphyry, *Maxims* 40, 48, 5–51, 2 (Lamberz); and Augustine, *De Vera Religione* XI, 22, Bibliothèque augustinienne, 8, 54; *Contra Secundinum*, Bibliothèque augustinienne, 17, 574–5; 10; 15.

his utter uniqueness, his superiority to the constant succession of opposites, and the image Alcibiades uses of those dolls in the marketplace that, when opened, possess little divine images inside that "alone have intelligence within them" and "extend to everything" (*Symposium* 222 a, 2–5). The "divine" for Plato is not closed off from human experience; it is rather the practical basis, or "good," of all experience, discovered in the dialectical quest for what is best in self and other, capable of being *tested* at every level of ascent (as in the *Symposium*),[24] and with very *practical* consequences for the self-organization of individual and political life.[25] So for Plato fullness of being involves *wholeness* of soul, *dialectical transformation* of the self by the world and by the divine, *practical*, *testable* consequences or *offspring* in every perspective of existence, and if it is genuine fullness, a *uniqueness* and *comprehensiveness* manifest even to the naked eye, like perfect little works of art sold in the marketplace. Modern thought tends to function in a planisphere or on a single level in which truth is a question of correspondence, consistency, or preferred representation. But for Plato human life is empty and truth merely a boring convention without the search for the good and the beautiful, which belong exclusively to nobody.

Something of Plato's vision is basic for Plotinus, but especially the character of *search*. The dialectical movement toward being, or the good, especially for discursive thought, is never simply accomplished. Even intellect, Plotinus argues later in this treatise, is "always desiring and always attaining" (11, 23–4). Elsewhere, as we shall see, he strikingly uses discursive language of intellect's being or becoming "most what it is" to emphasize not only the limitations of language but the eternal trajectory of desire, which starts in fullness and ends in fullness but without satiety (cf. III, 8, 11, 35–44).

3.14. The landscape of soul (III, 8, 5)

The concept of filling and being filled is specifically important for understanding how in III, 8, 5, Plotinus weaves two different ways of looking at the soul: the vulnerable, discursive soul of our present experience and the fullness of soul as a whole (i.e., what we might call soul-hypostasis). Soul produces a world of learning and a physical world (together with nature) not unlike the way "each art" produces an image of the universe, some arts more completely than others. Each artist has to soak up and be transformed by the world just as the soul has to be filled in order to give birth. But the products of art—like the dead speech-*logos* in the

---

24. *Symposium* 210 a.

25. In the *Symposium*, Alcibiades witnesses to these consequences in Socrates' own life. Because of the character of his pursuit of the Beautiful, he is "unlike" any other human being (221 c 4–5), and he and his words, when opened, are the only ones that "have intelligence within them," that "extend to everything that is suitable for the person of real quality to consider [*skopein*]" (221 a 1–6).

visible shape (2, 30–3)—are no longer living speech: they cannot help themselves (i.e., respond to their own defence). This is part of Plato's critique of writing at the end of the *Phaedrus*. The written word, like the painting, looks as if it were alive, but if you question it, it cannot reply because it is dead and frozen at a moment in time, unlike living speech in the soul, which is reflexive, dialogical (i.e., it knows to whom it speaks, can ask and respond) (*Phaedrus* 274 c–278 b). The written word is an image (*eidôlon*) of the living, ensouled word (*logos*) (*Phaedrus* 276 a). In III, 8, 5, Plotinus brings this understanding implicitly to bear on the "toy that has an image of everything within it" (an image coloured by Alcibiades' likening Socrates in the *Symposium* to a doll one can open to reveal the beauties inside) but "cannot help" itself (5, 6–9). This is a good example of how Plotinus' images themselves can be densely layered. At this point—that is, at the disappearance of dialogical life in the "objective" fixed form—Plotinus naturally returns to the question of soul's fullness.

Previous readers and editors evidently felt this transition too violent, and so the gloss, *to logistikon*, the rational part, (deleted by Kirchoff, but bracketed here) crept into the text to link the sequence of thought with the soul's "love of learning and enquiring spirit" earlier (5, 3). But the phrase *to prôton autês*, "the first of her," naturally signifies the whole of soul hypostasis in her fullness, even if the concept and the subsequent language seem a little abstract at this point. The "first" of soul is not the rational part that belongs to us in the sense that, for the most part, it is in our power to reason whenever we wish and in the sense that the ability to reason defines us as beings who have to work things out laboriously bit by bit. By contrast, the whole soul, perfectly conformed to intellect, is not in our power in the same way, for we have to look up to her, as it were, rather than simply being capable of "downloading" her at will. In other words, we have to prepare ourselves to receive the fullness of her pure intellectual activity, even though we too are "parts" of her whole nature. Plotinus does say in a later work that it is the rational part that first receives intellect (V, 3 [49] 3, 31–32), but he appears to mean even here that it receives the intellectual activity of soul conformed to intellect or that it is "our intellect" (3, 24). Whatever the difficulties of terminology here— "intellect of soul," "our intellect"—Plotinus argues that it is "both ours and not ours": "it is ours when we use it, but not ours when we do not use it" (3, 28–29).

The whole nature of soul is similar for Plotinus.[26] It is not simply "ours," because the focus of our psychic awareness is normally so narrow (and we even connive to reduce it further) that we are unconscious of most of what we are or could

---

26. On soul see H. Blumenthal, 1971; W. Helleman-Elgersma, 1980; D. J. O'Meara, 1993. On the question of omnipresence see D. J. O'Meara, 1980; F. M. Schroeder, 1980, 1992; and *Enneads* VI, 4–5 (22–23). On the unity of all souls see IV, 8 (8) and on the differences between soul, world-soul, and individual souls see IV, 3 (27) 1–8; IV, 4 (28) 13– 14; II, 1 (40) 5.

be. So the fullness of soul, as a living reality in which everything in the universe has its birth and being, is foreign to our normal historical mentality, which becomes content to take only the external signs of things for the whole of the real. Treatise III, 8, 5, 10 ff., then, comes with a bit of a shock: "The first [of soul] then that is above and is always being filled and illuminated in her relation to that sphere above remains there, but a subsequent [part] participating by the first participation of the participating subject goes forth, for life always goes forth from life; for actuality reaches everywhere and there is nowhere it fails." What does Plotinus mean?

3.14.1. The nature of soul as a one-many: Procession and omnipresence (III, 8, 5)

We must look at three ideas in this difficult sentence: first, the nature of soul herself; second, the notion of participation and procession; and third, the omnipresence of soul (as of all real being). All of these ideas are interconnected, but let us start with the soul herself. The soul, for Plotinus, is both one and many, indivisible and yet also divisible about bodies (as Plato describes the making of the World Soul in the *Timaeus*, 35 a). Divisibility as such is not a characteristic of soul but of body; and so when Plato or Plotinus says that soul has a nature to be divided about bodies, he does not mean, according to Plotinus, that soul becomes physically divided but rather that soul is able to animate physical multiplicity without losing her own nature. What is that nature, then? Soul's nature is a simple activity with many different powers, among them the powers of life, locomotion, reproduction, perception, and thought. Is there then just one soul for everybody and everything? Yes and no. Yes, there is a single all-soul, but no, soul is not like a physical unit or point (compare IV, 9 [8] generally; VI, 9 [9] 1). So there are no ghostly homunculi lurking behind each physical instance of a rational animal on a quantitative, one-on-one basis, yet our individual lives and experiences (despite what Plotinus says about the loss of memory in the intelligible world—because we do not need memory when everything is eternally present anyway) are not illusory. To be me or you is inherently meaningful for Plotinus (cf. IV, 3 [27] 15, 9–10), but to be only me to the virtual exclusion of everything else *is* illusory. So "greatsouledness," an important virtue for Aristotle, takes on a new meaning in Plotinus. "We" are much larger than we take ourselves to be, but so too are horses and the rest of the animal and even elemental dimensions.

Plotinus has this to say in one of his early works on the substance of soul, (IV, 2 [4] 1, 66–76):

> And he who sees clearly *this* magnitude of soul and sees her power clearly will know how divine and wonderful a thing she is and that she is one of the *natures* beyond *things*. Having no magnitude she is together with every magnitude . . . not with a different part of herself, but with the same . . . for she

remains whole with herself, but she is divided in relation to bodies by virtue of the special divisibility of bodies, which are unable to receive her indivisibly, so that the division is an affection of bodies, not of her.

Soul then is a single activity, but one and multiple, and not like one and many individual physical units since, as Plotinus argues, "by giving herself to the whole she does not abandon being one" (IV, 2 [4] 1, 59). He describes this undiminished self-givingness of soul, therefore, as a timeless procession or giving of herself to the many souls and to the physically many compounds she animates *and* a timeless return to her own whole undiminished nature. Later Neoplatonists came to describe this as a triad: abiding unity-procession-return (*monê-prohodos-epistrophê*),[27] but that triad is implicit in Plotinus, who like Plato frequently avoids overschematizing things. The first two moments of this triad we can see clearly in another passage from the same work on the substance of the soul, which is worth citing because it provides a parallel with III, 8, 5, 10 ff. Plotinus argues that the first timeless "moment"[28] of soul is her indivisible nature or substance (*ousia*):

> But again, next to that altogether indivisible nature there is another reality [*ousia*] following upon it and deriving from it, having indivisibility from that other nature, which hastening in its procession (*prohodos*) from the one to the other nature, established itself in the middle between the two. . . . (IV, 2 [4])

So procession involves a kind of articulation and transformation of indivisibility into a kind of proportional mean between soul's pure unity, on the one hand, and body's dividedness, on the other. Again, Plotinus is thinking of the making of the World soul in Plato's *Timaeus* (34 b–37 c), but the more limited point we should notice is that this articulation of soul's internal nature matches what we find in III, 8, 5, 10 ff. As a pure indivisible unity, soul is filled and illuminated by intellect, whereas in her procession she unfolds into a form of participation, whereby different forms or powers of life (i.e., presumably the various powers of soul Plotinus talks about later in III, 8, 8, 14–16: growth-soul, perceptive-soul, etc.) become unfolded or actualized (cf. IV, 8 [6] 8, 11–16). Plotinus tells us in an earlier work (V, 1 [10]) that perhaps his only original contribution to ancient philosophy was the theory of the "undescended soul"; that is, the view that the soul remains as a unity in the intelligible world despite its "descent" into this world (or as Andrew Marvell [1621–1678] puts it in his poem "The Definition of Love," "where my extended soul *is fixed*"). However this may be, Plotinus' phrase "par-

---

27. In Proclus, for example, *Elements of Theology* 35; for Iamblichus, *In Tim.* III, 45, 5 ff.; cf. Wallis, 1972, 132–3.

28. We shall examine problems with this sort of language later when we come to discuss intellect.

ticipating by the first participation of the participating subject" (3, 11–12) has an uncharacteristic formulaic ring, as though by employing a kind of philosophical jingoism he signals *en passant* the technical context to which he refers, a context that both he and the often philosophically formulaic Sethian Gnostic texts have inherited from earlier Platonists.

"Participation," of course, does not mean that such a theory is only "Platonic" since Aristotle conspicuously uses the word in relation to his own theories of categories and of intellect (probably the human, rather than the divine intellect) participating in the intelligible object.[29] But implicit here is that soul's procession is the articulation of a single *subject* that reaches *everywhere* in the physical universe despite the unfolding of different kinds of life and the emergence of many different soul-subjects. Soul is not split up, as it were, into a higher soul that then becomes simply an object for a very different lower soul. There is a continuity of subject that paradoxically provides both for soul's omnipresence and yet for her multiplicity. Since this is also a feature of Plotinus' treatment of "being" as a whole, and since this continuity of subject in intellect is given striking treatment by Plotinus' colleague and friend, Amelius, in his theory of three intellectual *subjects* (the one who is, the one who has, and the one who sees),[30] it must have been of particular importance to Plotinus and his school. Yet, for many modern readers, the Plotinian view of the omnipresence of all being simultaneously (on which Plotinus had previously written two works (VI, 4 and 5 [22–23]) looks so strange it helps to mark the parting of the ways between hard philosophy and religious fancy. Yet this certainly is not the truth of the matter—at least not for Plotinus.

3.14.2. Soul-substance: With-ness and in-ness (III, 8,5, 14 ff.)

The nature of soul, where substance really starts for Plotinus, involves with-ness and co-presence, whereas the nature of bodies, where appearances and the flux of qualities, quantities, and relations lead the eye away from substance, involves dividedness and yet dependence.[31] This is the point of the difficult lines beginning at 5, 14: "for actuality reaches everywhere. . . . Yet in going forth she lets her earlier part . . . remain unmoved where she left it; for if she abandons what is before her, she will no longer be everywhere but only in that in which she ends up." Physical dividedness results in one's living the life only of an external part and clinging to that, but soul's omnipresence means we have to change our external point of view and recognize that, though soul may appear to be "in" body, it is rather the case that, as Plato argues in the *Timaeus* (36 d–e), body is "in" soul and that, since no bit of soul is cut off from any other, the whole of soul is present everywhere. Now, this seems to run counter to our normal experience in which—

---

29. Cf. Aristotle, *Metaphysics* 1030a 11–14; 1037b 14–21; 1072b 19–20.
30. See Proclus, *In Timaeum* I 306, 2–3.
31. Cf. F. M. Schroeder, 1992.

for better or for worse—our thoughts and feelings are for the most part irreducibly ours. I cannot experience directly your joy or pain, although I may very well have some idea what it is like to be you even if I do not know you well.

How can the soul be everywhere and yet my experience be mine and not yours? These and related problems Plotinus tackles in the works on omnipresence (VI, 4–5 [22–23]) and on the soul (IV, 3–5 [27–29]; see especially here IV, 3 [27] 2–8), but he gives an implicit answer too in III, 8, 5. My soul and your soul are not simply the whole soul, but images of that soul, and images that have come to be conditioned by the capacities and viewpoints of the particular spatio-temporal coordinates we inhabit. The whole soul remains present to us, but we are unaware of her true extent, and so we do not "use" her. Instead, since it is the nature of an image to be "in" something else (for images are not free-floating phantoms but manifestations of energy or actuality that need some support or foundation), then the image comes to identify itself with what appears to be its foundation: "that in which" it ends up, namely, its particular body and environment. But this sense of being "in" something is ill-founded. As Plotinus argues elsewhere, the exclusive focus on the body is a vanishing-point where the jumble of qualities, quantities, relations, and the like not only proves ephemeral but also tends to the disappearance into non-being of the organizing principle, which is soul. But soul is already present "before" bodily organization takes place (i.e., not temporally but in the sense that there could not be an organic body without the organizing principle that makes it be). Or as Plotinus puts it here: "if the earlier must always be different from the later, and if activity comes from contemplation or action, but *action did not yet exist*—for it is not possible for it to be *before* contemplation—then one contemplation of soul must be weaker than another, but all activity must be contemplation." So it is not the case that the organizing principle disappears into non-being. The problem rather is that we look at the soul-body question the wrong way round. Yes, the body and matter too are subjects, but only insofar as they are *forms* or are maintained by soul's energy. So the soul must be the real subject. But while "my" soul may be an image limited by its viewpoint, she must also be the organizing principle, in the broader psychic environment that makes up the world (since "I" am only part of one species), that articulates the whole of my biological, moral, cultural, and intellectual development. So the soul in this immediate but broader sense must contain all *logoi,* or forming principles, and be the proper foundation for body. And all the different images of soul, powerful or weaker, must be rooted in this broader unified totality of soul.

Aristotle and his later commentators (notably Alexander of Aphrodisias in the third century A.D.)[32] have a rather different way of tackling this problem, and Plotinus likes to use their language. The nature of an image is to be dependent on

---

32. Alexander, *De Anima* 13–17; *Quaestiones* 1, 8; 2, 17; 2, 26 (Bruns). Compare Plotinus IV, 3 (27) 20–22.

something else (it is "in another," as Plato states in the *Symposium* and *Timaeus*). Derivative categories, like quality, quantity, and so on, are dependent on something else for their existence, body or matter, since they are not in body as "in a substrate," for soul is substance in the primary sense (as Aristotle argues in the *Metaphysics*),[33] and substance is not predicated of a subject; it *is* the subject (cf. IV, 3 [27] 20 ff.). When we refer to substance then, we are not predicating one thing (i.e., a quality) of another (a subject) but pointing directly to what the thing already is. The definition of the substance of something, therefore, is different from the external predication of a quality of a particular substance; what we refer to in the former case is a unified grasp of what the thing is. It is here that Plotinus goes beyond Aristotle and Alexander. Though my argument here does not appear in III, 8, 5–7, it is certainly implicit in these chapters, and it becomes explicit in the treatment of intellect later in chapter 8, 40–8. If soul is substance in the "primary" sense (though soul is "primary" for neither Plotinus nor Aristotle; in the *Metaphysics* the divine intellect is the first substance or *ti ên einai*, the "what it was to be" [see 3.7 above]), and if souls are many and possess diverse activities, then soul too has to be organized by something, for otherwise soul-substance would be a chance event just "waiting around to be put together" in an organized way, as Plotinus puts it in III, 8, 8, 45. But even chance and spontaneity (what we might call "randomness" today) are meaningful only in the context of regular causality (as Aristotle argues in *Physics* II). So the principle of intelligibility in the universe is not solved by an uncritical appeal to chance or pure randomness.

What then organizes soul? It cannot be body, for soul is "prior" to body, and it cannot be chance because intelligibility is what gives meaning even to chance events. Soul therefore must be organized from within by the unified whole that is what soul really is, and it must be organized from even more deeply within by intellect. So even if soul is finally an image in any sense, as it is an "image"—though a substantial, not a qualitative image—or "expression" of intellect, then the subject or substrate (i.e., underlying subject or organizing principle) of soul is not body but intellect. So if body is really "in" soul, soul too is really "in" intellect. Consequently, souls can be one and many, but in the many activities (even if some are psychic images of a higher reality) the same single unbounded activity is glimpsed: "For contemplation is . . . without limit. And because of this contemplation is everywhere; for where is it not? For the same contemplative object is also in every soul since it is not bounded by spatial magnitude" (5, 30–33). So contemplation weakens as it descends precisely because it gets divided by its more particular focus. But the hierarchy of the spiritual world is radically democratic, for it is present to everyone and limited only by the capacity and function of the recipient. Thus, the phrase "according to the capacity of the recipient" (*kathoson dynatai*) becomes characteristic of all later Neoplatonism.

---

33. E.g., *Metaphysics* 1035 b 14–16; 1043 a 35–36.

What precisely is involved in this same activity being present everywhere (5, 18), or in "the same thing" (*to auto*) being in every soul (5, 32)? At this point in the argument we cannot tell, except that it is the whole soul and the totality of intelligible being reflected in soul. Does this "sameness" result in universality or bland conformity, or does its active presence make us individually what we are? The last of these alternatives would seem to be the case, but as yet we have no means of determining precisely why this should be so.

3.15. Love and beauty (III, 8, 5, 34 ff.)

Plotinus draws out the consequences of this radical view in III, 8, 5–7, first, on the terms of the *Phaedrus'* analogy of the tripartite soul, charioteer and horses (see Appendix A). Bridled and even unbridled erotic passion, that of one of the horses or of the lover who leaps upon the beloved, is a kind of imperfect, partialized longing for the vision of the good or beautiful: "the horses would evidently have longed for what they saw, but they did not take it all" (5, 35–6). In a later work, "On Love," III, 5 (50) 1, Plotinus meditates upon the ambiguous quality of beauty —how, for instance, some people even worship earthly beauties and this is enough for them, while others come to recognize their intelligible archetype (60–2); or again how even "desire of the good" often involves "the fall into evil" (64–5). Nonetheless, Plotinus argues, sexual intercourse and its overwhelming emotions become explicable only if the good and the beautiful are the source of nature (23–9; cf. VI, 7 [38] 31, 11 ff.; 34, 8–27). Similarly for Socrates in the *Republic,* the soul "divines" obscurely even in its least important experiences that the good is there; or in the voice of Aristophanes in the *Symposium,* lovers locked in each other's arms "divine" that what they want is something that their souls cannot fully express.[34] Plotinus states his view succinctly at the end of III, 8, 7: "And lovers, too, are among those who see and hurry on eagerly toward a form" (26–7).

3.16. Walk-about, bending back, and trust (III, 8, 6)

Since it is the whole vision of soul that people really want, and since they cannot grasp this directly, they come to it, so to speak, by going "walk-about" (III, 8, 6, 3: *periplanômenoi*): that is, indirectly. We act not simply for the action's sake but for the good from action (6, 8–9), In this we are already implicitly on the path of soul's return to her source, for we want this good not to be external to us but a part of what we really are, namely, our soul: "and this is not to have the good resulting from their action outside them . . . but . . . to have it . . . [in] the soul. So action bends back again [*anekampsen oun palin*] to contemplation" (6, 7–10). Aristotle uses the verb *anakamptein,* "to bend back," in the context of circular and rectilinear motion returning upon itself, and Alexander uses it in the context of the

---

34. Cf. *Republic* 505 e; *Symposium* 192 c–d.

reverberation of an echo.[35] Plotinus uses it to describe the doubling of self-consciousness in its return upon itself (I, 4 [46] 10). Such "bending back," therefore, is akin to the natural *epistrophê*, or return of the soul within itself.[36] Plotinus emphasizes the internal, *silent* nature of this activity, presumably against the Gnostics, and the sort of silent conviction, or *faith* (*pistis*, 6, 15–16)[37] that accompanies it: "for what one receives in the soul that is forming principle, what else could it be but a silent forming principle? And the more it is a forming principle, so much the more silent will it be; for then the soul keeps quiet and seeks nothing because it has been filled, and the contemplation, so disposed because soul trusts in her possession, lies within. And the clearer the trust, the quieter too the contemplation in that it tends more to unity" (6, 10–15). Elsewhere in the *Enneads* Plotinus contrasts the epistemic necessity (*anangkê*) proper to intellect with the need for persuasion (*peithô*), conviction, or faith proper to soul (cf. V, 3 [49]).[38] Here the inwardness of this silent speech and the quiet faith of the soul's more unified contemplation contrast strongly with the apocalyptic audio and video appearances of divine or semidivine figures who are invariably represented externally even in the more sophisticated philosophical Gnostic texts that we possess under the names of *Allogenes, Zostrianus, Marsanes, Tripartite Tractate, Three Steles of Seth*, and others.[39] Plotinus is not dismissive of the Gnostics, at least in the ancient mode of direct and mordant invective, for his line of thought is not *ad hominem* but bears always upon the subject matter at hand.

3.17.   The dialectic of play and seriousness: From the inertia of indifference to kinship of soul (III, 8, 6, 15 ff.)

Thus with the strongest contrast between the inward silent *logos*-vision and its implicit counterpart, the external spectacle, Plotinus comes at last to the other side of Platonic dialectic; that is, he comes from playfulness to earnestness. In both the *Republic* and the *Phaedrus*, dialectic and discourse in general are playful, but their underlying purpose is serious: to lead us to the Good.[40] Here in the deepening unity of the soul with what is known, "we must already be serious" (III, 8, 6, 16).

This unity which requires us to be serious is not just an automatic psychic event that comes to the soul from on high but rather a challenge to it from within, for "kinship" between *logoi* does not come already packaged and labeled with the right directions for address and approach. Every movement of the soul, in terms

---

35. Aristotle, *Physics* 261 b 27 ff.; Alexander, *De Anima* 48, 9 (Bruns).
36. On *epistrophê* see W. Beierwaltes, 1991, 192; M. Atkinson, 1983.
37. On the later Neoplatonic triad, "faith-truth-love," see Wallis, 1972, 154.
38. See also on V, 8 (31) 11 below.
39. Cf. J. D. Turner, 1992, 425–60.
40. *Republic* VII 536 d–537 c; *Phaedrus* 277 e–278 b.

of both action and production, has external and internal dimensions. When we pursue the external dimension, we are in one way or another bent back into the internal dimension, so that something that seems purely random and unconnected in the external sphere of action displays sense and meaning in the internal dimension. On the other hand, *logoi*—definitions, speeches, accounts, tales—can appear indifferent to each other and to us. We can be bored by even the most significant of events. In the language of W. H. Auden's *Musée des Beaux Arts,* suffering is always depicted in the Old Masters of painting while some other perfectly ordinary event is happening, its subjects totally unaware of the suffering nearby: "the torturer's horse scratches its innocent behind," and in Breughel's painting of Icarus' fall, the farmer ploughing his field does not even notice a boy falling into the sea.[41] There is then a terrifying unconnectedness in life that makes us despair of the world and ourselves "as when forming principles dwelling in the soul do nothing" (6, 19). So convinced is Plotinus of this existential brown-study in human experience that in a later work he says that even the beauty of the divine ideas themselves in intellect is boring or idle for us (*argon*, as in inert argon gas) without the light of the Good to enliven them (VI, 7 [38] 22, 10–17). There, as here, he uses the word *parakeisthai* "to lie beside." In VI, 7, 22, the soul becomes winged with passion for what lies beside it, yet it rises higher to something greater that somehow prompts its memory. The image is taken from Plato's *Phaedrus* and the erotic story of the soul's wings (Appendix A, 2). Here in III, 8, 6, there is a highly compressed but exceptionally clever implicit reference to the *Symposium.* These *logoi* in the soul "will, as it were, lie alongside each other," just like the *logoi*—that is, the speeches or the participants—in Plato's *Symposium,* who literally lie alongside one another on their banquet couches. Contemplation, Plotinus continues, has to relate the *logoi* in kinship not from outside but from within. For Plato in the *Republic,* the natural kinship between studies and pursuits has to be united by dialectic into a single synoptic view so that one can see at a glance the interrelations between things. "Only the synoptic view is that of dialectic" (*Republic* VII 537 c). Similarly in the *Symposium,* the speeches lie alongside one another, and their kinship has to become a living reality in the contemplating soul. If Plotinus has this in mind, it is a far more profound insight into the *Symposium* and the *Republic* than much in modern scholarship and should at least be noted alongside Plotinus' interpretation of the birth of Eros (in III, 5 [50]), which is all that Plato scholars tend to notice (and invariably negatively).

---

41. "About suffering they were never wrong,/The Old Masters: how well they understood/Its human position; how it takes place/While someone else is eating or opening a window or just walking dully along;/ . . . In Breughel's *Icarus*, for instance: how everything turns away/Quite leisurely from the disaster; the ploughman may/Have heard the splash, the forsaken cry,/But for him it was not an important failure . . ."

3.17.1. To make something one's own: Oikeios (III, 8, 6, 19 ff.)

The challenge for the soul is to break free from "alongsidedness" and the inertia of "doing nothing" to make this kinship *her own*. Again, the word *oikeios*, important enough as it is in Stoic thought, is crucial to Plato's *Republic,* where part of Socrates' challenge to Glaukon, Adeimantus, Thrasymachus, and the others is first to recognize just how many individuals and types live with us in the same "house" (*oikos*)—from the best to the worst—but also in a self-organized way to discover the complexity of what is involved in what is our own. It is no simple matter to reach Socrates' conclusion in *Republic* IX that what is best for each most belongs to each (*eiper to beltiston hekastô oikeiotaton* [*Republic* 586 e]), for this involves seeing justice in a wider context than Cephalus and Polemarchus had done in *Republic* I (i.e., giving back what one owes or helping one's friends and harming one's enemies), that is, in the broad context of the many dimensions of human individual and social life so that doing the proper task of each part (*Republic* II: *prattein to heautou*)[42] can be integrated in the light of a more comprehensive synoptic vision. For Plotinus, speech and discursive reasoning help us to examine things from their many different angles and "to learn them thoroughly," but this we still undertake as a kind of scrutinizing intellect "seeing something other than itself" (6, 21–6). But seeing or seeking in this way is the result precisely of not being "full": we want to learn something more deeply, and so we talk about it or externalize it; or in acting we fit the content of soul (i.e., our experience) to external circumstances (6, 29–30). Plotinus' language here of soul's being disposed (*diatethei*) according to the forming principle but nonetheless uttering it (*propherei*) and holding it out in front of her to see it, is reminiscent of the Stoic distinction between two forms of speech, the inner word, or conception (*logos endiathetikos*), and the outer word, or expression (*logos prophorikos*).[43] So the "two-act" theory (the act of substance and the act from substance that makes another reality), so fundamental to the Neoplatonic production of realities—often termed emanation theory—is part of all immediate reality, the conception-expression of speech as well as the double-sided character of ordinary action (*logos—praxis*). Plotinus here speaks of fitting the inner to the outer circumstances (*epharmottei*) (6, 30; cf. VI, 7 [38] 29, 19; VI, 8 [39] 7, 23), an expression used particularly by the Stoic Epictetus (e.g., 2, 11, 4), of adapting our thoughts or preconceptions (*prolêpseis*) to individual things (*tais epi merous ousiais*).

---

42. E.g., *Republic* 369 e ff.

43. The *Corpus Hermeticum* (13, 7) also uses the expression "inner man" (*endiathetos anthrôpos*). For variants on these forms of "speech" in relation to soul elsewhere in Plotinus, see V, 1 (10), 3, 7–10: as expressive speech is an image of speech in soul, so is soul the expressive speech of intellect and both its whole activity and the life it sends forth to establish another being (cf. V, 1 [10] 6, 44–5; IV, 3 [27] 5, 10; I, 2 [19] 3, 27).

For Plotinus, then, the soul is even quieter than nature. This inherent stable quietness is what most characterizes the Platonic or Stoic sage, or even more so the Aristotelian person of practical wisdom (the *spoudaios* in the *Nicomachean* and *Eudemian Ethics*) who serves as the practical model for right action[44]—that is, someone who can hit upon the right *logos* between excess and defect in ordinary moral conduct that sets up a new transformative resonance between the self, the real, and the divine. For Aristotle, habitually good moral action opens the human agent to self-understanding, to other agents as friends and fellow-citizens, and thereby (especially through "true" friendship based upon the good) to the need to share in a divine self-understanding that goes beyond both self and others. This is the practical teleological ideal that Aristotle outlines in his *Ethics* and with which Plotinus concludes the first part of his argument about contemplation in this treatise.[45] The person of practical wisdom is already contemplative vision in relation to himself and self-manifestation for his friend, not because he is self-absorbed but because there is a transformative world alive in and through him:

> That is why the serious person has already reasoned when he reveals to another what he has from himself; but in relation to himself he is sight. For already this person is directed to the one and to the quiet, not only of external things, but also in relation to himself, and everything is within him. (6, 37–40)

3.18. Plotinus' theory of creation in context (III, 8, 7, 1–15)

The first long sentence of III, 8, 7, 1–15 summarizes the results of the argument thus far. What is striking in this conclusion is how Plotinus thinks his way so simply and freely through a problem that had troubled the whole course of earlier philosophy but in ways that suggest solutions at once unfamiliar yet illuminating of puzzles in Platonic, Aristotelian, Stoic, Epicurean, and Middle Platonic thought. Plato had represented the world as being made in time by a deliberating, although divine, craftsman (in the *Timaeus*). Yet as Diotima tells Socrates in the *Symposium,* and elsewhere in the dialogues, it is clear that if the gods are wise, they do not need to deliberate in this way.[46] Aristotle rejected Plato's model of a labouring craftsman. Nature has no need either of deliberation or of birth-pangs to produce. Moreover, if the world has no beginning but is eternal, then it cannot be "made." At the same time, however, as we indicated above, the divine intellect not only

---

44. Cf. *EN* II, 6, 1106 b 36–1107 a 2: "Virtue then is a state of character concerned with choice, lying in a mean in relation to us, defined by a rational principle [*logos*], and by that principle by which the person of practical wisdom [*ho phronimos*] would define it."

45. This covers the span of Aristotle's analysis in *EN* II–X. On the role of the person of practical wisdom, the *phronimos* or *spoudaios,* see H. H. Joachim, 1951, 104.

46. *Symposium* 204 a 1–2: "No god philosophizes or desires to become wise, for gods are wise."

moves things "by being loved," but some form of intellect, divine or human (and at least coextensive with *sophia*, or contemplative wisdom), is said to "make" everything, including health, and the unmoved mover apparently embraces the whole cosmos. But how? Again, for the Stoics, the divine productive *logos* works from within matter and not upon matter, but how an articulated intelligible order arises out of matter is unclear. On the other side are the Epicureans who poke fun at the idea of a manual labouring god producing a botched world full of imperfections and evil. One has only to think of Voltaire's antiteleological remark to catch the force of Epicurean criticism: how clever of God to put holes just where the cat's eyes would be! Finally, among the Middle Platonists, we encounter a complex debate about the making of the world, some holding that it must have a beginning on Plato's account and others holding that the world is eternally coming to be as the result of a combination of independent, unmade causes (e.g., the world-soul, matter, god).

For Plotinus, the world is made neither in time nor by deliberation, toil, tools, anthropomorphic divine figures or with apocalyptic sound effects. Everything (including even matter) timelessly and silently comes to be out of the omnipresent creative contemplation of nature, the whole soul, and intellect, and we can see in ordinary action and speech, as well as in all forms of generation, the sort of longing for fullness, vision, birth, and care for offspring characteristic of the generation of soul from intellect and of intellect from the One.[47] The Platonic epistemological and existential model of (a) procreation upon the beautiful,[48] (b) the pain of giving birth (with the help of a midwife in the *Theaetetus* or of a guide in the *Symposium*),[49] and (c) caring for and educating or testing the offspring can be retained and developed within this nondeliberative model of causality (cf. 7, 18–21), for everything is creatively contemplative in its own way from successful forms of artistic and natural generation to their failures and perversions (4, 7, 21–7). In successful forms "making . . . is to fill everything with contemplation" (21–2). To make something new involves not just bringing a form into being, as Plotinus says, but to bring a new contemplative orientation to the world: that is, in being filled, to fill everything with contemplation. This is a remarkable statement. In terms of a modern subjective-objective epistemological dichotomy, what Plotinus appears to suggest here is simply absurd. Creativity not only changes the way

---

47. For the generation of matter, see III, 4 (15) 1. For other related passages see chapter 1.10.

48. Cf. *Symposium* 206 c: "All human beings . . . are pregnant in body and soul, and when they come to the right age, our nature desires to give birth. But it cannot give birth in the ugly, but it can in the beautiful."

49. *Theaetetus* 150 b–c: "My art of midwifery . . . differs . . . in that its concern is with men's souls giving birth. And this is the greatest feature of my art, that it can test by every means whether the thinking of a young man gives birth to an image that is false or one that is fertile and true"; *Symposium* 210 a 6: "if the one leading him leads correctly."

we look at the universe; it intensively fills the universe in a new way. Heidegger speaks in his little essay "On the Origin of the Artwork" about the world emerging dynamically as if for the first time with the appearance of the artwork. When the temple is built at Delphi, for instance, the strife and dynamic interaction between earth and sky so created call out the essential activity of the world in a new way; or in Heidegger's always curious language "die Welt weltet" ("the world worlds"). If Heidegger's language looks absurd, Plotinus seems to go even further. Since the world is timelessly, silently, and eternally being made by living, self-giving vision, any form of genuine creativity actually makes the whole of things *more* what they are. Conversely, failures or evil emerge as a swerving-away from (*paraphora*) or deformation of what is contemplated. To use an image that Plotinus elsewhere borrows from Plato's *Seventh Letter*,[50] the soul's eye, slips away from the substantial reality it wants to see and turns only to the flux of qualities and quantities, thereby making something less than what it really is or could be. Or again, if ugliness is a deprivation of form, as Plotinus argues elsewhere, the soul not only makes a category-mistake or fails to capture the fuller vision but in fact misforms its products so that instead of opening pathways for thought it extinguishes being in non-being. Ugliness and evil, for Plotinus, are not just absence of form but a negativity that tends to annihilate form (on evil see 4.13 below). The Epicureans had supposed a random swerve of atoms falling through the void that led to the formation of an imperfect universe. The physical universe for Plotinus is imperfect, but it is not the botched product of some inferior divinity or inexplicable randomness, for regular whole-formation is a product of intelligible contemplation, while failure and ugliness are deviations from, or simple absence of capacity for, the complex and dynamic world of contemplative form.

3.18.1. Creative contemplation and finality

At the same time as Plotinus develops the Platonic side of this question, his theory of productive contemplation is also a radical development of Aristotle's theory of finality. For Aristotle, nature works from within to produce the regular whole-formation of organisms, and just as "art does not deliberate," neither does nature (cf. *Physics* II, 8, 199 b 28; *Ennead* IV, 8 [6] 8, 13–16). The various forms of movement, instinct, and desire in the universe, on Aristotle's account, are expressions of this finality and ultimately of the causality of substance as the purest form of self-reflexive energy. In III, 8, Plotinus produces a new philosophical way of thinking through this problem in Aristotle. This is not an attempt to reconcile the thought of Plato and Aristotle (at least on the evidence of III, 8, 7). Porphyry is reported to have written two treatises on this problem of reconciliation, and it is true that reconciling Plato and Aristotle was a favourite Neoplatonic preoccupa-

---

50. See II 6 (17) 1, 42–44; *Seventh Letter* 343 c 1: "the soul seeks to know . . . not the quality but the what . . ."

tion.[51] But Plotinus does not even begin to make such an attempt: he is more interested in following out a train of thought that seems simply evident to him, as 7, 14–15 indicates. So a puzzle in Plato and Aristotle leads here to a rethinking of Aristotle's notions of contemplation, activity, and finality. Plotinus does not abolish Aristotle's distinction between the theoretical, practical, and productive sciences but shows how the practical and productive are grounded in, and flow as consequences from, the theoretical. Nor does Plotinus develop a sort of "real efficient causality" or only an archetypal formal causality.[52] Creative contemplation works and unfolds from within the natural forms of things as their constitutive outpouring and immanent finality. Plotinus suggests the inner link with Aristotelian philosophy as a living, open-ended form of on-going thought by emphasizing the word *telos*, goal, three times in this chapter and by further drawing our attention to the question of finality with the classic-sounding Aristotelian teleological formula (at which he, of course, looks differently than Aristotle, as we shall see) about the epistemic necessity proper to intellect: "it was necessary, since the first principles were engaged in contemplation, for all other things to long for this if, as must be the case, the originative principle for everything is the goal" (7, 16–18).[53]

3.19. The problem of intellect (III, 8, 8)

For Plotinus, intellect is "separate" in the sense that it is not "in" anything except the One, and it constitutes an intelligible world where the Platonic Forms and Aristotle's Intellect, through the medium of the intervening Platonist tradition, seem to coalesce.[54] It also can be seen properly only by virtue of itself, so all of our images, drawn as they are from elsewhere, are plainly inadequate. So why should Plotinus suppose there to be such a principle in the first place? On Aristotle's authority alone? And then why should this intellect be two rather than one and many rather than two? And why should there be something beyond it? Furthermore, how can we speak about it if this intelligible world is nondiscursive; that is, spiritual, nonspatial, and not "one thing after another" but "everything together," in the phrase Plotinus likes to quote from Anaxagoras (*DK* fr. 1)? Does Plotinus have any good arguments to prevent us from thinking that this is just concept-projection or a deeply religious nostalgia for what should have been but is hardly ever going to be the case? Even if we think finally that he does not, is there anything useful in the enterprise, or to be fair, since usefulness should not be our un-

---

51. Cf. Armstrong, 1967, 275, 302.

52. As, e.g., J. Deck, 1967, suggests.

53. Cf. Plato, *Republic* 509; Proclus, *Elements of Theology*, propositions 12 and 33.

54. On intellect generally see further A. H. Armstrong, 1967, 1971; J. Bussanich, 1988; P. Hadot, 1961 in *Les Sources de Plotin,* "Etre, vie, pensée chez et avant Plotin", 107–41"; D. J. O'Meara, 1975, 1993; T. A. Szlezák, 1979.

wieldy criterion, especially in this case, does Plotinus manage to chart a path of enquiry that helps us to think philosophically in new directions? Above all, if we find ourselves daunted by the abstract quality of this "idealism," let us just try to follow a human being thinking through a problem that for him is very real, since intellect for Plotinus is not at all abstract as are perception and discursive reasoning in some ways. Intellect is actually closer to what the world means, for it (intellect) is immediately and directly what things *are* rather than what they are *like* (for discursive reason) or what they *appear like* (for perception). In fact, in Plotinus' view, intellect is not a type or a universal nature (if a universal nature is like a grab bag of types or instances) but a completely individual reality that contains everything, not as objects but as *subjects*. Intellect is truly "primary substance," and Plotinus applies to it Aristotle's term for a primary substance: intellect is a *tode ti*, a "this individual"; that is, it is not an instance or a type but a distinct, individual, and unified totality, as subject in object. Every bit of intellect is simultaneously intellect and subject. Nothing in intellect is merely object. There are no objects that are not simultaneously subjects. Here then, paradoxically enough, before the discovery of holograms (in every bit of which everything is virtually present) and before the discovery of the behaviour of subatomic particles (we could say that there is no particle without all particles) there is already a sort of prescientific intelligible model for understanding such things. Here too, before Descartes' realization of the priority of the infinite over the finite in *Meditation* III, is the organic articulation of that infinity as the ground of all reality—inwardness and outwardness. By a similar token, however, this ground is already what a later "Neoplatonist," Kant, would call "the transcendental unity of apperception," yet these ancient *noumena*, or objects of thought, break modern thought's mould of subjectivity and objectivity, and so in Plotinus' perhaps overly optimistic vision they already constitute a kind of super-kingdom of ends-in-themselves, to borrow Kant's term from the *Metaphysic of Morals*—that is, subjects that never should be treated only as means. Indeed, in Plotinus' own words elsewhere, intellect is like "a wholly-face thing shining with living faces" (VI, 7 [38] 15, 26). We need only to look at contemporary Continental philosophy, for example Levinas' powerful phenomenological analyses of the irreducible character of the "face of the other," to recognize an affinity with what Plotinus is trying to express in his own way.[55] So let us put aside our preconceptions as much as we can and our instinctive prejudices about archaic, religious-looking forms, and try to see if we can follow on his own terms this thinker who makes us see the world inside out and impregnated at every point by the desire for an unseizable transcendent.

---

55. See, for example, E. Levinas, *Autrement qu'être ou au-delà de l'Essence,* Dordrecht-Boston-London, 1991.

3.19.1. Self-living vs. image-living (III, 8, 1–17)

How do we approach intellect and what is its nature? We approach intellect through the "serious" or "best" soul (as well as from anywhere, since living contemplation is everywhere), because here we begin to see that unity is a gradational term and we experience identity in a new way.

In earlier stages of ascent we have to look through images, to see one thing "in" another (8, 11), in order to experience the kinship of *logoi* in the soul. While this is a form of unity, it is not the identity of two-in-one that is characteristic of intellect thinking itself. According to Plotinus, the characteristic of the serious soul is an eagerness for this identity of intellect, which is not just to know things but to know them as oneself, so that one experiences both the world and oneself as self-living (8, 12).

Here again is that "self"/"same" word (*auto* in Greek, in which two senses coalesce: the pronominal and the intensive) so important for speaking about identity: "sameness." We explored the phrase *to auto* earlier: "the same in every soul" or "the same activity" everywhere (5, 18, 32). Plato often refers to the "form" as *auto kath' auto* (itself in itself). In the *Alcibiades* I, Socrates and Alcibiades search for the *autotauto*, the same itself, the ultimate identity of human self-knowing.[56] Scholars have found this "impersonal" (e.g., Annas, 1985), which in a way it is because it seems to go beyond individual or personal identity. Yet the image Socrates uses is very intimate, the eye of the soul finding itself and the divine reflected in the eye of one's friend with practical consequences for both and for society.[57] In the *Symposium,* too, the vision of the beautiful is a vision of "itself always being in itself with itself of single form" (*auto kath' hauto meth' autou monoeides* [211 b 2]),a passage Plotinus loves to cite. Again, if this is the goal of "Platonic love," scholars perhaps understandably have considered such love to be "impersonal" (e.g., Vlastos, 1973, 3–42; Nussbaum, 1986, 178 ff., etc.). But Plato knows very well the kind of love we normally accept as personal, for he portrays it vividly—both in Aristophanes' speech, the desire for our other half, and in Alcibiades' eulogy of his beloved Socrates, so he plainly must have thought that these forms of love, while common, are not what most deeply characterize individuals as such. This may sound strange, but truly *individual* love in Plato's terms, as for Plotinus, has to have a *vertical* axis,[58] and so it is Socrates, on

---

56. *Alcibiades* I, 129 b: "Come then, in what way may the 'same itself' be found? For in this way we might find what we ourselves are . . . "

57. *Alcibiades* I, 133 b: "If an eye is going to see itself, it must look to an eye, and to that place of the eye in which the excellence of an eye is situated; and this presumably is sight. Then, my dear Alcibiades, if the soul is going to know herself, she must look to a soul, and above all to this place of the soul in which the excellence of soul is situated, that is, wisdom, and to any other part of a soul which is like this?"

58. On this see chapter 4.6 and following.

Alcibiades' testimony, who, transformed by his life-long pursuit of the "single-form beautiful" is not merely a "character" or generic type, but *unique* (i.e., unlike everyone else). If Socrates is unlike others, then the Platonic "form" itself is surely the source of such uniqueness. Or as Plotinus puts it here in a variant of the "third man" argument, if there is not an identity of subject and object, but only one thing and another (that we can compare and over which we can predicate a further abstract unity), then we still have to stop somewhere to prevent the regress and suppose a genuine subject-object identity where each reflects the other as self that we experience in thought and that Hegel calls the beginning of "Spirit."[59]

Such a self-living then (8, 12) is different from everything else, but because it is the identity of thought and being, we can also see in its light that all forms of life are in fact forms of thought, more clearly in the intellectual soul and less clearly in the apparently autonomous lower psychic powers (8, 14 ff.). As Plotinus says in VI, 7 (38), 7, "these perceptions here are dim thoughts, but the thoughts there are clear perceptions" (29–31).

3.19.2. Intellect and all things

Not only forms of apparently thoughtless life but all *beings* (*panta ta onta*; in this case, not just real beings, but anything that *is*), Plotinus says, are byproducts of contemplation (8, 25–26). This fits Plotinus' later major analyses of what intellect must include. For example, brute animals should be included in intellect (VI, 7 [38] 7–10), to which animals Plotinus—just like Sextus Empiricus, and therefore radical skepticism—seems prepared to allow even "many works of discursive reason" (*polla dianoias erga*, VI, 7 [38] 9, 13–14). Even particular forms of apparently thoughtless life (e.g., horses) are in reality "a particular kind of intellect; for it is a particular kind of life" (VI, 7 [38] 9, 28–29): "For just as any particular life does not cease to be life, so neither does an intellect of a particular kind cease to be intellect" (9, 29–31). If even in apparently inanimate things (i.e., the elements) one can still "deduce the life in them" (VI, 7 [38] 11, 51–53) so that they can be linked with *logos* and soul, and if even "bodies and matter" are said to be part of the content of the divine intellect (VI, 2 [43] 21, 52–53), then this holographic view not just of the direct content of intellect but of every particular form of existence that springs from it would have had little difficulty assimilating and surpassing some of the more weird aspects of modern science (including our revised notions of the extension of life into supposedly inanimate matter or, again, of artificial intelligence). Plotinus like some modern physicists, for example, believes that rocks "grow" if they are attached to the earth.[60]

---

59. This is already implicit in Hegel's treatment of "Stoicism, Skepticism, and the Unhappy Consciousness" in the *Phenomenology of Spirit*.

60. Cf. VI, 7 (38) 11, 24–32: "the growth and formation of stones, then, and the inner formation of mountains in their growth one must suppose . . . takes place because an en-

3.19.3. Life and intelligible biology

The notion of life (*zôê*) plays a crucial role in Plotinus' thought (and particularly his later writings) not only in soul and her animation of the physical world but also within intellect, as in variants upon the famous triad, being-life-intellect, which attempts to chart the moments of intellect's emergence from an original unity with the One (on which see III, 8, 9 below). This triad is familiar in the Sethian Gnostic texts of the Nag Hammadi corpus[61] as well as in the *Anonymous Commentary on Plato's Parmenides*,[62] attributed by Hadot to Porphyry, but possibly earlier than Plotinus.[63] It derives from Plato's "intelligible living creature" in the *Timaeus* (30 c ff.) and from his decisive move to attribute motion, life, and intelligence to intelligible being in the *Sophist* (248 c–249 d), as well as from Aristotle's ascription of life (*zôê*) and even "way of life" (*diagôgê*) to the divine self-thinking intellect (see Appendix A, 4).[64] In fact, in Middle Platonism (particularly Alkinous and the Neopythagorean Numenius)[65] and in Plotinus we have the development of what is effectively an intelligible biology or zoology (both terms, *bios* and *zôê,* mean life, but it is the latter that is applied to intellect), an inclusive prefiguration in the life of the divine mind of the teeming variety of species and even *sensual* characteristics in the physical world. In a famous passage, Plotinus says that in the complete intellect there is no poverty or lack of resource[66]:

> but all things are filled full of life and, so to speak, boiling with life. They all flow, as it were, from one fountain-head, not like one particular breath [*pneuma*] or heat, but as if there were one quality that possessed and kept in itself all the qualities of sweetness with fragrance and was at once a quality

souled forming principle is working from within them . . . and when the stone is cut out it is in the same state as if something is chopped from the tree . . ."

61. For what is included under the rubric "Sethian" see J. D. Turner, 1992, 425 ff.; for an example of the triad see *Allogenes* 49, 28–36: "For then that-which-is constantly possesses its vitality and mentality, and vitality possesses being (*ousia*) and mentality; mentality (*noêtês*) possesses life and that-which-is" (trans. J. D. Turner, 437).

62. See the *Anonymous Commentary* (text in Hadot II, 1968b) XIV, 10 ff.: "With respect to [existence (*hyparxis*) alone] it is one and simple . . . with respect to existence [*hyparxis*], life [*zôê*] and thought [*noêsis*] it is neither one nor simple."

63. See G. Bechtle, *The Anonymous Commentary on Plato's "Parmenides,"* Bern, Stuttgart, Vienna, 1999; and K. Corrigan, 2000b, 141–78.

64. Cf. P. Hadot, 1961, 1968.

65. In Alkinous and Numenius there appears to be a growing interest in the problem of how being, life, and thought come to be prefiguratively articulated in an eternally actual intellect so that the natural compounds of our experience (architects and artisans) bear that intelligible imprint at the root of their own creativity. For Alkinous, see the tripartite prefiguration of the tripartite embodied soul (*Didaskalikos* 178, 40–5, Hermann), and for Numenius see frs. 12, 13, 14, 15, Des Places.

66. Cf. the S*ymposium* myth of the birth of Eros.

of wine and the powers of all tastes, sights of colours and all the cognition of touch; and all that hearings hear, all songs and every rhythm. (VI, 7 [38] 12, 21–30)

As part of Plotinus' inclusive view of intellect, as well as of his development of an intelligible biology prefiguring natural biology (somewhat like a scientific model), there is also frequently a more intensive sensuality of description, as if the irresistible *reality* of all scents, feelings, and perceptions, is experienced in a deeper, noetic way only at the level of intellect or on one's approach to it or, again, as if *body* only comes into its full meaning in intellect (which it must do, if body is a form). Plato speaks in a similar way in the myth at the end of the *Phaedo*,[67] a myth Plotinus loves to cite (as, for example, in V, 8 [31] 4 below).

3.19.4. The structure of intellect (III, 8, 8, 18 ff.)

But what is the *structure* of intellect in III, 8, 8, and following? Plotinus gives us a rapid series of sketches that prove rather difficult to interpret, even by comparison with similar texts elsewhere. If the truest life and the truest thought are the same, then intellect must be both: a self-living thinking (see also Aristotle, Appendix A, 4). But if these two are one, how can they be many? Aristotle, we recall, asked a variant of this question in *Metaphysics* XII, 9, but left the matter unresolved because, of all the things that intellect might think about, it was inconceivable that it should think unworthy things. Yet, on Aristotle's terms we might further suppose it is inconceivable that intellect should think only one object, for if intellect thinks itself, then it must be two, and if the self it thinks is not going to be a mere unit or a solitary abstract thought, then it must be the nature of such an intellect to think *everything*. For Aristotle in the *De Anima* (III, 4), the human intellect has two aspects: as passive (corresponding to the matter in it), it "becomes everything"; as active, it "makes everything." Now, in the divine intellect there can be no such passivity, for the divine intellect must be purely active. So if the divine intellect can be said in any sense to "make everything" (as Alexander of Aphrodisias supposes to be true of his own "first intellect"),[68] then everything must be part of the divine self-thinking. Neither Aristotle nor Alexander takes this particular view, but Plotinus certainly does as a way of coming to grips with the problem not just of how all fifty-five or forty-eight "unmoved movers" of Aristotle's *Metaphysics*

---

67. E.g., *Phaedo* 110 d–111 c: "and in this richly varied earth the things that grow, the trees and blossoms and fruits are proportionately beautiful; and so too the mountains and the stones are smoother, more transparent, and more lovely in colour than our earth . . . and there are groves and temples of the gods in which the gods really dwell, and speech, prophecies, and *perceptions* and such gatherings with the gods occur there face to face."

68. Cf. generally F. M. Schroeder, 1981, 1982 "The potential or material intellect and the authorship of the *De Intellectu:* A reply to B.C. Bazàn", *Symbolae Osloenses,* 57, 115–25, 1984, and with R. B. Todd, 1990.

XII, 8, or the unmoved "souls" of *Physics* VIII (chapter 6) actually move things, but rather of how such intellects and souls are related *internally* to each other and to things. Leibniz's *Monadology* and *New Science* are a modern attempt to grapple with this problem.[69] Plotinus' project, however, is to think through a problem left largely unexplored by Aristotle's *Metaphysics* and Plato's *Sophist, Parmenides*, and *Timaeus* but rendered more urgent by Alexander's treatments of intellect and Middle Platonist attempts to think out the internal relations of intellect or intellects.

3.19.5. Why is intellect many?

If intellect is self-thinking, why can it not be just "two" and not many? If reading this treatise is one's first exposure to the *Enneads*, the answer is puzzling. Even if intellect sees itself as one, it does not contemplate itself as one but makes itself into many, for according to Plotinus this is precisely what it does when it contemplates the One (8, 30–2). There is a unity even beyond that of intellect that Plotinus calls the One and, even in seeing this inexpressible unity, intellect is essentially a pluralizing vision. That unity is so rich, or overfull (V, 2 [11] 1, 8–9), that intellect needs to break it up into a world just so that it can see it as itself. Plotinus also argues in VI, 7 (38) 8, 22–32, that intellect cannot be two simply, because even in its dyadic character (i.e., its twoness in one), each unity in this twoness cannot itself be purely one (like Plotinus' first principle, the One, for otherwise it would simply *be* the One). Instead it must involve at least a further twoness, and so on with each unity in each new appearing twoness.

3.19.6. The origin and return of intellect

If intellect is a pluralizing vision, we seem to be committed to the view that it must be everything, not one thing after another in serial succession but everything together. So intellect's totality must involve not quantitative infinity but a different sort of infinity bounded only by its original vision of the One, which is its origin, goal, and horizon. If so, then the structure of intellect must depend on the One and its own self-articulation in relation to the One. Thus in Plotinus' "normal" accounts of the origin of intellect, intellect emerges in a sort of preintellectual stage from the One, establishes or defines itself as fully constituted intellect by virtue of the power of the One, and timelessly returns to the One in its dependence, passionate love, and desire to be united with it.

Plotinus describes this originative activity in many different ways:

---

69. See, for example, *Monadology*, prop. 56: "Now this connexion or adaptation of all created things to each and of each to all, means that each simple substance has relations which express all the others, and, consequently, that it is a perpetual living mirror of the universe" (tr. and ed. by R. Latta, Oxford, 1898, repr. 1948).

a) In the case of living things (e.g., in Plato's *Symposium* or Aristotle's biology), when they reach maturity, they normally procreate; so intellect and soul in their fullness give birth to new realities (e.g., V, 4 [7] 1, 25–30).

b) There is also a more general pattern in all things: a radiation of light from its source or an overflow from the One that makes something "different," which then turns back and is filled by the One to become intellect; fire gives off heat (V, 4 [7] 2, 27–33), the sun gives light, snow gives off cold, and roses fragrance (V, 1 [10] 6, 28–35). Things give of themselves (and thereby are diminished), but divine principles (and sometimes we, too) can give without being diminished. The divine is ungrudging, Plato says at *Timaeus* 29 c. For Plotinus, this becomes undiminished, self-giving generosity.

c) Within activities and their developments, this can also be described as an unformed potentiality, or "a sight not yet seeing," an "indefinite desire" with a "phantasm" of the One that comes out into intelligible multiplicity (e.g., V, 3 [49] 11).

d) Or even within speech, as a kind of argument articulating itself and including every logical possibility, intellect does not remain at rest in pure self-sameness but also moves into otherness and so possesses in its own being motion and rest, sameness and otherness (as Plato calls sameness, otherness, motion, rest, and being "very important kinds" that can pervade each other in the *Sophist* 254 d) (cf. VI 7 [38] 13; V, 3 [49] 10, 18ff.).

e) Or again this can be described as internal to Intellect (like the simple activities of being-having-seeing or the unfolding of an Aristotelian [*dynamis/hexis/energeia*] or Stoic potency into act) as a three-part or even four-part structure (i.e., being-life-mind or abiding-procession-return or again being as unified number— multiple beings as number unfolded—intellect as number moving in itself—living being as number embracing everything; this last four-part structure is from Plotinus' difficult work on numbers, VI, 6 [34] 9, 29–31).

Sometimes in these argument-descriptions, "being" (*to on*) is the first "moment" in intellect's derivation from the One (VI, 6 [34] 9, 29–10, 4; sometimes it is activity like pure thought (*noêsis*) (VI, 7 [38] 40); sometimes, an unformed potentiality (II, 4 [12] 5, 32–35); sometimes, life (as in III, 8); sometimes, the return of intellect to a state of indefiniteness (V, 3 [49] 11). Plotinus, like Plato, seems to avoid a set terminology. Typically, his descriptions comprise a single sentence with many subordinate clauses in which a single subject, activity, or vision articulates itself and is also articulated by the power of the One in it. The first sentence of IV, 8 (6) eleven lines long, is a striking example of the unified articulation of Plotinus' own experience, as we saw in chapter 1. Treatise VI, 7 (38) 16, 16–22 is a classic passage with a remarkable but precise use of tense, voice, and mood. It was not yet intellect when it looked to the Good, Plotinus states, but it looked unintellectually. He then goes on to make the following precision:

> Or we should say that it did not ever see the Good but lived toward it and depended on it and turned to it, and its movement *having been filled* by its moving there and round that Good *filled* it and no longer was it movement alone, but movement thoroughly replete and full; and in turn it became all things and knew this in intimate perception of itself and was already intellect, *having been filled* in order that *it might have* what *it will see* but *looking at them* with light from that which gives those things and *receiving* this with welcome. (emphasis added)

By means of passive and active moments that remain a persistent feature even of the completely articulated intellect, preintellect moves from the past tenses of simple concentrated life, through the subjunctive (so that "it might have") and future ("what it will see"), which emerge from the passive participle, "having been filled" (signifying the One's power), into the present active participles "looking" and "receiving," punctuated by the gift of the giver, the medium of light.[70]

Typically, too, in certain passages we can never be entirely sure what Plotinus' pronouns (e.g., "this," "that," "it" [*auto*]) refer to: the One, intellect, or some stage in between the two? However, if ambiguity is a sort of heuristic part of intellect's waking to itself from the One, then the ambiguity certainly should be retained.[71]

3.20.   Four puzzles: From the drunken circle to haphazard heap (III, 8, 8, 30–48)

Treatise III, 8, chapter 8, provides four compressed "sketches" of multiplicity in relation to unity that are significantly puzzling and lead to new accounts of this relation in later chapters. First, Plotinus implicitly likens intellect's generation from the One to Plenty, or Resource, in Plato's *Symposium* weighed down with a belly full of nectar and unrolling itself (dare one say) into one of Aristophanes' monstrous globular forms. No wonder Plotinus seems reminded of the Gnostic *tolma,* or audacity, and adds that it would have been better for it not to have done this. My love is my weight, Augustine would say, but weight elsewhere in Plotinus is associated with soul's forgetfulness in descent, and so "they drag with them much that weighs upon them" (IV, 3 [27] 15, 4–7; VI, 9 [9] 9, 59). Plotinus does say

---

70. See also V, 2 (11) 1; V, 4 (7) 2; V, 1 (10) 5–7; VI, 8 (6) 6; VI, 7 (38) 17, 14–19; 35–36.

71. See further K. Corrigan, 1987a, 1987b, 1996a; J. Bussanich, 1988.

elsewhere that intellect "somehow dared to stand away from the One [*apostênai de pôs . . . tolmêsas*]," but after all how could the generation of intellect involve a fault (cf. V, 1 [10] 1, 1–5) when the ultimate responsibility must lie, as Armstrong observes "with the One or Good itself. And if it originates in the Good, it cannot be bad" (1978, 117). But Plotinus' description is worse still, for how can a divine intellect get a skinful of nectar, become many without noticing it, and roll itself into a circular glob just because it wants to have everything? In V, 1 (10) 1, Plotinus tells us that "the beginning of evil for souls was audacity and birth . . . and wishing to belong to themselves." Self-willed audacity we can understand, but divine drunken and very childish roly-polies are not so easy to explain.

The next three sketches are obviously related in Plotinus' mind, but less obviously by his calamos, or pen. First, when a circle unrolls itself, why is the centre so far down the list (after shape, surface, and circumference)? And second, why do we need directions at this point: the "from where" and the "to which"? What is the "from where" if not from the centre? And how does the "from which" on its own differ from the "from which" and "to which" together? To make matters worse, the manuscripts have a different reading at line 39, which could well make perfect sense on its own. Dodds inserted the first "to which" for "from which" in the following sentence to avoid what he considered otherwise a monstrous tautology:

> "To which" was not of the same kind as the "from which" and "to which," nor again the "from which" and "to which" the same as the "from which" alone.[72]

But even to point out Dodds' insertion just compounds the absurdity if one does not have a clue what Plotinus is talking about in the first place. Finally, how is the third sketch about intellect's not being a haphazard heap but a totality related to circles and centres and then to these rather strange directions?

3.20.1. Roly-poly intellect (III, 8,8, 30–36)

First, let us take up the puzzle about the roly-poly intellect. Armstrong was of the view that this passage "represents a passing emotional intensification of the mystic's sense of the worthlessness of all things in comparison with the absolute Good, which leads him for a moment to say that it would have been better if they had never been" (1978, 118). Armstrong is surely right, and it is probably not coincidental that this is one point the Gnostics and Plotinus can agree on: it would have been better to stay with the One. But note the difference between this passage and soul's *tolma* and descent in V, 1 (10) 1. There is no hint of evil here, and intellect, unlike soul, does not wish to belong to itself but to possess its own total-

---

72. E. R. Dodds, 1956, "Notes on Plotinus, Ennead III, 8," *Studi italiana di filologia classica*, 27–28, 108–13.

ity. Indeed, while it is certainly a good for intellect to come into being, since the Good itself is "responsible" for this, as Armstrong puts it, nonetheless a product is always "responsible" for itself too. Thus, it is possible to think that intellect's causality is not so good as that of the One.

Beyond this, however, Plotinus gets a little carried away with his image. To be fair, drunkenness is not part of the scenario of this procession, but the word *bebarêmenos* "weighed down" means here that Plotinus thinks of *Poros* (Plenty, or Resource) who, in the *Symposium* 203 b 5–7, "drunk on nectar (for wine didn't exist yet) had gone into the garden of Zeus and weighed down with drink [*bebarêmenos*] was sleeping." This image, which Plotinus actually forces us to consider, is curious indeed. Quite apart from sexual relations with Poverty, surely festive drunkenness in a divine being is precisely what Socrates found objectionable in his critique of the poets in the *Republic*. Even if the *Symposium* were an early dialogue, as some scholars have wrongly supposed, it is not plausible to think that Plato had different views on this matter apart from those he expressed in the *Republic*. So why should Plotinus think of this image when he has all the dialogues from which to choose?

The answer is (relatively) clear. To be weighed down with nectar is not to be a drunken lout but to be filled with divine content. And to go into the garden of Zeus where Poverty will be impregnated is to be capable of embracing and reaching down to everything (even things of a lower order; e.g., in the circle, some parts are above, and others below [8, 38]) without departing from one's own proper nature. For Plotinus, to begin as one but not stay as one is to be capable of procession while abiding in unity. To become many without noticing it is to be asleep in the divine content; there is no deliberation in this case (unlike the case of Zeus in the speech of Aristophanes, who takes an awfully long time to decide to bisect the monstrous globs with a hair or knife like eggs or apples). But for Diotima (or Plotinus) this nondeliberative sleep or unconsciousness is *not* drunken stupor or adolescent stupidity but a form of divine wisdom since Diotima also makes clear in context that the gods do not need to seek out things and that they are not wise at some times and foolish at others. They are always wise (*Symposium* 204 a). So Poros is plainly a mythical but philosophically conscious paradigm of divine generosity or abundance. It is true that Plato does not approve of *hyponoia,* or allegory, in certain circumstances, but he actually invites *hyponoia* in the case of his own myths. Indeed, Plotinus just gets carried away for a moment with a favourite image and even thinks of Aristophanes' monstrous globular creatures. But he thinks of them in their intelligible Platonic form, for the geometrical entities in this passage must be taken as intelligible realities, even shape and surface (which are included in the intelligible world as unextended figures in VI, 6 [34] 17, 21–29; cf. VI, 2 [43] 21, 44–50).

3.20.2.   Circles, centres, and logocentrism: Platonic and Aristotelian Pythagoreanism (III, 8, 8, 36–38)

Is there any method in Plotinus' circle analogy here? The metaphor of the circle and its centre is perhaps *the* most recognizable emblem of a logocentrism or of a typical Western myopia that builds its ontologies upon a rational centre and fails in a centreless world to include the marginalized for what it really is. But is this entirely fair? The metaphor and its cognates are certainly very old. The movement from point to solid was a commonplace of ancient Pythagoreanism, Plato's Academy, and later Neopythagoreanism. Ancient Pythagoreanism, for instance, seems to have included a form of mathematical atomism that, in Aristotle's view, mistook the nature of numbers for the nature of things: the "one" symbolized the point, the "two" the line, the "three" the triangle, and the "four" the solid. A cosmos or world (i.e., the solid), then, can be "generated" out of unity (i.e., the point), and the sum of the first four numbers $(1 + 2 + 3 + 4)$ is the total of the first numbers, or the perfect number, 10, which the Pythagoreans called the *tetraktys*. On Aristotle's report, Plato came to hold the view that the Forms, which he identified as numbers, are derived from two prior principles, the "one," a principle of limitation, and the "indefinite dyad," a material principle that is limited by the one.[73] What Plato might have meant by this is entirely unclear, but according to Alexander of Aphrodisias, Plato and the Pythagoreans viewed the production of reality as a kind of mathematical progression:

> For they took the first and non-composite as cause, surfaces being first in relation to bodies, being more simple and independent in their being of body, lines being first in relation to surfaces, and points are first in relation to lines, being totally non-composite and having nothing prior to them.[74]

Modern scholars are divided about these reports of Plato's later views. Some hold that Aristotle simply misunderstands Plato, a rather dubious hypothesis when we recall that Aristotle's intellectual life was shaped almost entirely by Plato's Academy since he came as an orphan to Plato when he was only seventeen years old. Others suppose that his reports reflect an esoteric "oral teaching" given by Plato that we can reconstruct in part by a careful rereading of the dialogues in the light of what we do know (see, for example, Krämer, Reale, and others). Plotinus at any rate accepts these reports and argues for the derivation of intellect from the One by using such terms as the *"indefinite dyad."* For example, "out of the indefinite dyad and the one derive the forms and numbers; for this is intellect" (V, 4 [7] 2, 8–9; cf. V, 1 [10] 5, 6–17). By numbers, however, Plotinus does not mean

---

73. Cf. J. Dillon, 1977; D. J. O'Meara, 1993; G. Reale, 1997.

74. Alexander, *On Aristotle's Metaphysics,* ed. M. Hayduck (Berlin, 1891), 55, 20–6, trans. W. Dooley, London, 1989, 84.

quantitative number but its intelligible paradigm, which he calls "substantial number"; that is, the unified infinity of number within substance, a very mysterious notion that we shall examine below (section 3.21.1–4).

Plotinus' sketch here is so compressed partly because it reflects for him an ancient and well known tradition. But it is important to realize that by Plotinus' time this was already more than just a Platonic-Pythagorean tradition. Elements of Aristotle's *dynamis-energeia* theory (power/potency-actualization) already appear as commonplace in the "Neopythagorean" Nicomachus of Gerasa. And Alexander of Aphrodisias, in particular, already applies the circle-centre analogy to explicate the sort of unfolding and yet unity at work when we say that we are aware of being aware, as in the case of the "common sense" being aware of the data of the individual senses.[75] These data, like the radii on the circumference of the circle, have to be synthesized by the centre, and so self-consciousness (*synaesthêsis*) unfolds itself and the world out of its own centering unity. Already by Plotinus' time, then, the circle analogy expressed not only derivation from a prior principle but the structure of any activity that doubles itself while remaining unified; that is, elementary self-consciousness or the "common sense" (cf. Plato, *Timaeus* 34 a ff.; Appendix A, 3).[76] This makes it ideal for Plotinus' purposes in this treatise (cf. his analysis of *praxis,* action, earlier), and it accounts for the versatility of its use throughout the *Enneads.*

To get the sense of the differences between Plotinus' use of the image here in III, 8, 8, and elsewhere, let us compare perhaps its most important appearance in the *Enneads.* In a later work, Plotinus argues the One is the "outside" of everything or, rather, the "within in depth," and everything else is "outside," touching it and dependent on it:

> Just as a circle, therefore, which touches the centre all round in a circle, would be agreed to have its power from the centre and to have in a way the centre's form [*kentroeidês*], in that the radii in the circle coming together to one centre make their terminal point at the centre like that to which they are carried and from which they, so to speak, grow out, though the centre is greater than is proportionate to these lines and their terminal points, the points of the lines themselves—and the terminal points are like that centre, but only a dim image of that which has power to produce them in having power also to produce the lines; and what that centre is like is revealed through the lines; it is as if it was unrolled without having been unrolled [*hoion exelichthen ouk exelêligmenon*]—it is like this that we must appre-

---

75. Nicomachus, *Eisagôgê* II, 8, p. 88, 9–10, Hoche; cf. Iamblichus, *Theol. Arith.* 16, 4–6, de Falco; Theon of Smyrna, *Expositio* 37, 15–18, E. Hiller, *Theonis Smyrnaei philosophi Platonici Expositio rerum mathematicarum ad legendum Platonem utilium,* New York, 1987. Alexander of Aphrodisias, *De Anima,* 61, Bruns.

76. Cf. also Aristotle, *De Anima* III, 2; also Emilsson, 1988, 94 ff.

hend that intellect and being, having come to be from that Good and as if poured out, unrolled, and hanging out from it, give evidence from their own intellectual nature of something like intellect in one that is not intellect [*ton hoion en heni noun ou noun onta*]; for it is one. (VI, 8 [39] 18, 7–22)

It is noteworthy here that Plotinus situates the metaphor within the placeless-ness, or centrelessness, of the One, just as Nicholas of Cusa will later argue that the universe can have no proper centre (neither earth nor sun nor anything else) but the divine, and since the divine is everywhere but nowhere, maximum and minimum, there is no centre in the sense that a centre could be located at some point when the centre is anywhere, everywhere, and nowhere (*De Docta Ignoran-tia*). In this sense the One's power cannot even be localized *intelligibly:* "it is as if unrolled without having been unrolled"; it simultaneously embraces being from within and without, but also being unfolds out of it, hangs from it, and yet mani-fests, in its very structure as an unfolding unity a different unity, that goes beyond it. Three notions of "centre," therefore, converge: the One as a centreless centre, the centre as internal unity of intellect, and the centre as internal unity of the many intellects within intellect.

3.20.3. From circle to termini (III, 8, 8, 39–40)

How does this compare with the image in III, 8, 8? Perhaps the complexity of centres is implicit in the passage, but the overall force is rather different. The cir-cle does not need to emerge out of a localized centre since intellect's prior unity has already been emphasized. Instead, the circle articulates itself out of placeless-ness, first by *proceeding outward* to what we might call the more "material" as-pects of a circle (shape, surface, circumference) and then implicitly by *turning back* upon itself to recognize its centre from which the radii and the inner dimen-sions are constituted. *Procession*, then *conversion*, and then *autoconstitution* are the essential characteristics of this image; we have, therefore, a precise use of an image. But it is still a *visual* image, and so in the next compressed sketch the vis-ual image is taken away and we are plunged, as it were, into a complex thought that we could visualize, perhaps, but that actually forces us to fill it with thought if we hope to understand it.

From our reading of other treatises we might understand this in the following way. In the timeless generation of intellect, the procession and return of an indefi-nite product upon the One to be actualized are clearly part of what it means to be an intelligible *substance*, for if we wanted to know what a substance was we should want to determine not only its constituent elements but also how those ele-ments (i.e., the substance's form and matter) are related in its present nature. We can only know this if we can see where the substance has "come from" (i.e., its ef-ficient and material causes) and where it is "going to" (i.e., its final cause). For Aristotle, every motion possesses two termini, a source (*ek tinos*, from something) and a goal *(eis ti,* to something) (cf. *Physics* 224 b 1–2). For Plotinus, the source and the goal of intellect (that is, the "from which" and the "to which") (cf. III, 8, 8, 39–41; V, 3 [49] 11, 15–20) define intellect as a substance because without these termini nothing substantial would ever occur. Intellect would see nothing and would not be intellect. Plotinus admits in several places that a purely self-directed activity of extreme simplicity is possible and in a way thinkable. In VI, 8 (39) he argues that purely unified, unrestricted activity characterizes, however inadequately, the infinite nature of the One (a pure "power for all things," for example, or *dynamis pantôn,* as in III, 8, 10, 1 ff.). Elsewhere he also holds that such an activity, which strictly transcends any intelligible, or sensible, compound subject, also belongs to the highest moment of intellect's being (VI, 9 [9] 6, 50–55; 10, 9–17; 11, 4–16; 38–42; V, 1 [10] 7, 11–17, VI, 2 [43] 8, 18). However, intellect's vision needs something to "lean upon" (cf. VI, 8 [39] 8, 13: *hoion epereideto;* and see III, 8, 19, 16–19) we cannot say anything clear about the Good without discursive thought's having something to "lean upon," if it is to see anything at all:

> For self-directed activity is not substance, but being is that to which the activity is directed and from which it comes [*eis ho kai aph' hou to on*]; for what is looked at is being, not the looking; but the look too possesses being, because it comes from and is directed to being [*hoti aph' hou kai eis hon on*].
> (VI, 8 [39] 8, 13–16)

These two movements, therefore, procession away from the One and conversion back, are both real and interdependent. Intellect's indefinite potentiality is not just an indeterminate desire or an unshaped capacity to see (cf. III, 8, 11)—as would be the case in the sensible world if the right conditions for its actualization never materialized—but a potentiality that is an integral part of the unfolding of a *single* intelligible activity. So intellect cannot be just "source" (the "from which" only), for even an intelligible multiplicity is not *thinkable* unless the termini of its being go together ("from which" *and* "to which"). So Plotinus' compressed sketch removes the visual image and forces us to think about intelligible substance as *thought.*

3.20.4.   *The removal of the linear image: Totality (III, 8, 8, 40–48)*

Such termini, though placeless, are still one-dimensional and implicitly linear, while intelligible substance is neither. In the final compressed sketch of the chapter, Plotinus also removes the linear, particularized image. If intellect is everything, then its part also must be everything (cf. V, 8 [31] 4 below). Otherwise substance will be composed of nonsubstances and will be a "heap" *(sôros).* This puzzle had exercised Aristotle considerably in the *Metaphysics* (VII–VIII). A constituent definition of substance will enumerate only its parts or elements, but substance cannot be simply its elements or a bundle of qualities, quantities, relations, and the like. Rather, in substance, the matter is transformed so that potency and actuality become one in the emergence of something "different" from either potency or actuality considered separately (cf. *Metaphysics* VIII, 1045 b 20–3; and see chapter 2.6).

3.21.   The problem of substance in the Enneads

Does Plotinus then simply project Aristotle's view of physical substance onto the intelligible plane and thus create an abstract, universal intellect while rejecting particularity?[77] "And, to put this in a different way, intellect is not an intellect of some one particular, but it is also all" (8, 40–41). The answer clearly is no: intellect is both individual and all. Plotinus emphasizes this in many places. For instance:

> For just as any particular life does not cease to be life, so neither does an intellect of a particular kind cease to be intellect: since the intellect appropriate to any particular living being does not on the other hand cease to be the intellect of all, of man also, for instance, granted that each, whichever one you take, is all things, but perhaps in different ways. For it is actually one thing, but has the power to be all. (VI, 7 [38] 9, 29–35)

On the understanding of this passage, even things in this world (like human beings and horses, as we saw above) do not stop being everything just because they have determinate specific characteristics that look at first sight incompatible with intelligent life.

But this problem of intellect's substance is one of the most important in the *Enneads,* and despite the compression of Plotinus' sketch here, we cannot skip over it as quickly as he does because we really do not know what he is talking about at this stage. How can we even begin to conceive the necessity of such "with-ness" and "everything-ness"? We can employ such formulaic phrases as "there is no human being without all human beings," and we can undoubtedly mean them (even from a genetic point of view), but it is still difficult to see what we really do mean. We might even say with Plotinus that there is no one thing without all things, but a logical atomist might well disagree, and we have anyway lost the comforting certitude in an exponentially expanding information world that any so-called synoptic view of a totality is anything more than self-deception. But the problem is also reflected in elements of Plotinus' own thought. He himself seems to have a double-sided view of what we might call "Forms of individuals"; that is, of what Forms precisely intellect holds: you, me, dogs, cats, identical twins, clones?[78] Some passages seem in favour of such Forms (e.g., V, 7 [18]; IV,

---

77. For very different views of this whole question see K. Wurm, 1973; T. A. Szlezák, 1979; A. C. Lloyd, 1990; K. Corrigan, 1996a, 298–395.

78. On forms of individuals see J. M. Rist, 1963; H. J. Blumenthal, 1966; A. H. Armstrong, 1977.

3 [27] 5; 12, 1–5), but others against (e.g., V, 9 [5] 12; VI, 5 [23] 8), though in the wake of emendations of some of the texts recent consensus is in their favour. The problem at root for Plotinus is that determining what makes for authentic individuality is no simple task. Much of what we do is determined by appearance, convention, even self-deception. Consequently, Plotinus' notion of the self is enormously complex and subtle, so subtle in fact that even whether he has a genuine notion of the self at all has been questioned. Perhaps, it has been suggested, the only "self" is the One.[79] But this is surely unwarranted by the text.

What prompts Plotinus to think of substance as holistic in this way? And how does intelligible substance include individuals? As we have seen above in the case of soul, so also with intellect here. If substance is a one-many and every part of its content directly characterizes its substantial nature (e.g., even our intellects in a way), then we appear to be committed to a very different way of speaking about substances than we use to speak of apparently solid things in the physical world. For unlike the quantitative unities of the physical world, each substance bears a perhaps implicit but necessary internal relation to every other substance. This for Plotinus is what calling substance "one in number" really means (VI, 5 [23] 1, 1–4; cf. *Categories* 3 b 12; 4a 10–11). Of all things that have real existence, he says, "since they are not produced by composition [*ek syntheseôs*], the existence of each is in that which it is, numerically one, which is there from the beginning" (IV, 3 [27] 8, 25–30). The intelligible unity of all substances is guaranteed from the beginning, therefore, but this does not obliterate the individual: "the intellects are not dissolved into unity because they are not corporeally divided, but each remains distinct in otherness, having the same essential being" (IV, 3 [27] 5, 2–9). Whether this is true or not, it could be argued that it makes sense, for if substance is a one-many and one in number and if each of the many in substance directly characterizes this nature, then the many substantial individuals cannot be obliterated, for otherwise they could not be features of *substance*. On the other hand, this way of thinking has some rather strange consequences. I cannot simply abstract a particular feature of substance (rationality, for example, or a definition of "you" said according to your soul) and say without falsifying the reality of the situation that this is substance, because this is to exclude it from the rest of substance by turning it into a particular set of qualities. In other words, to say that substance is an individual form is a profoundly misleading way of putting it, for as soon as I think I understand what intellect or the soul as a one-many means, I appear to be committed to an *organized* one-many, from which I cannot separate out the one without losing the many.

---

79. Compare G. J. P. O'Daly, 1973, and for a strong monistic view of Plotinus L. Sweeney, 1983, 190; 1992b, 381–424; cf. E. Bréhier, 1958, 173–79.

3.21.1. Intelligible substance and III, 8, 8, 40 ff.

This is the root of Plotinus' final sketch in III, 8, 8. If substance in the strict sense is an organizing principle and an organized one-many, then it cannot without absurdity be said to occur by chance; nor can it be composed from all its content (*syntheton ek pantôn*) because then either the whole will be substance and not the parts (which is logically impossible since each feature of substance is by definition the whole but without obliteration of its own identity) or the whole will be "a heap of things that have just happened to be brought together, waiting around to become an intellect composed of all things," which would contradict its very nature. Consequently, intellect, the organizing principle, must be an organic whole before we even think, name, or abstract pieces out of it. But, in fact, we cannot even abstract pieces out of it (except the images we make of it) because, as Plotinus concludes the chapter, "there was no composition out of pieces."

3.21.2. The problem of substance and individual form

Three corollaries of this are important for our understanding of the *Enneads* as a whole. First, in the light of this analysis, it becomes clearer why Plotinus should sometimes indicate that the "species," or "individual form," views of substance, which are favourite candidates for substance in modern Aristotelian scholarship, are not adequate representations of its meaning. To say that the "last difference" or the "individual form" is substance comes perilously close to contradicting oneself, *if* one understands that each and every part is substance and yet one refers *only* to a particular form or specific difference. Individual forms only make sense in the context of all forms, for substance must by definition be the interconnectedness of a totality organized by a unifying principle. To limit this to one individual form is absurd, and to suppose an abstract universal nature unifying all forms is to contradict the direct concreteness of what is meant by substance. If we simply back off from the issue, then the principles will perhaps be indifferent for us or admit of randomness (cf. II, 4 [12] 2, 9–10), which would seem to contradict the whole enterprise anyway.

This, at any rate, is why Plotinus can sometimes deny the substantiality of particular things or assert that *ousia* (substance) cannot simply be taken as an individual (*atomon*) (VI, 2 [43] 22, 11–13) or as a particular form (VI, 3 [44] 2, 9–19). It is also why in VI, 4–5 [22–23] being appears as a single comprehensive subject unified implicitly by the presence of the One (cf. VI, 5 [23] 1, 14–21) and present simultaneously everywhere. This does not mean that substance is a universal, common nature or a single undifferentiated unity, for it is present everywhere "as a whole." Substance is a single subject in the sense that it includes all subjects in their own way as itself. So when Plotinus says that form and substance cannot be "of" something, if they are to be substance, he does not mean to do away with individual forms as some scholars have supposed (e.g., Lloyd, 1990,

103; 86 ff.), but rather to save those forms by providing an intelligible foundation even for a logic that may appear to dehydrate them utterly of their living colour (the great logical treatises, VI, 1–3 [42–44], should be read with this in mind).

3.21.3. Intelligible substance: Plotinus and Aristotle

The second corollary is that Plotinus' notion of substance in III, 8 and elsewhere is not driven by an urge to extirpate the Aristotelian view but rather to think through the problem of substance somewhat further than Aristotle managed to but with some agreement on fundamental Aristotelian principles. In this process, of course, Plotinus turns out to have a very different view of the question. If contemplative vision is the real ground of the practical and productive sciences, so much so that it is alive even in our actions, however dimly, as a form of finality, then there is no need to suppose external principles at work such as the Gnostic fallen *Sophia* or evil Archons (Ruling principles) dominating an evil world. Instead, as Plotinus will make explicit in V, 8, 5, "a wisdom [*sophia*] everywhere guides making"; "a physical wisdom" (i.e., of nature), he calls it, "no longer composed of theorems" (i.e., discursive objects of contemplation abstracted from their full intelligible context), "but a single whole not compounded from many into one" (cf. III, 8, 8, 41, 45, 48), "but rather loosened up [i.e., analyzed] from one into multiplicity." If this is so, then the intelligible characteristics of substance must be capable of applying both to separate substance in intellect proper *and* to the separable, but presently nonseparate, form (i.e., soul and her content—the *logoi*) present to the physical compound as its substance.[80] Yes, perceptible substance for Plotinus is, strictly speaking, a "shadow of being" in that, as Plato puts it in the *Seventh Letter* and as Aristotle further develops it in the early chapters of *Metaphysics* VII, one moves from the "what" of the thing to its quality or likeness alone. Such substance appears to be only qualities in matter, from this perspective, or composed out of "non-substances" (cf. VI, 3 [44] 8).[81] But this is to look at "substance" from a constituent, material viewpoint (i.e., what it is composed *out of*) and not to see it from the perspective of the contemplative *logos* that already makes it a whole. If we can see such a view of substance implicitly developed in III, 8, and following, it is not because Plotinus' Platonism prompts him "in mysterious ways" but rather because he believes that the logic of the problem and the logic of Aristotle's own position on contemplation, theoretical wisdom, and substance require this critical development in order to show the primary intelligible application to the sphere of being of what are derivative usages, for Plotinus, in Aristotle's natural philosophy, biology, psychology, and even metaphysics. This

---

80. Cf. III, 8, 8, 46: "and if something comes from it, it is not diminished, neither that which is from it because it too is everything . . . ")

81. Cf. *Seventh Letter* 343 c and *Metaphysics* VII, 3.

innovative thinking is not a trivialization of Aristotelian philosophy but a genuine critical development.

3.21.4. The need for an organizing principle (III, 8, 9–11)

The third corollary of Plotinus' view of substance is the need for a transcendent organizing principle for the immanent unity and multiplicity of such an organic life, a need that concerns Plotinus from here forward in chapters 9–11. Of course, intellect is capable of organizing itself, but such multiplicity, no matter how unified, could never account entirely for its own unity. For Aristotle, every organism has two sources of organization: its own form, within its local and broader environments, and the unmoved mover. But if the unmoved mover is an organism, the same logic should apply to it. For Plotinus, while intellect in one way is complete in itself, it is never complete in relation to the One. Even the ground of its own substance is something of which it stands in need. Intellect in a sense has to go in search of its own substance (at least when we come to speak about intellect's relation to the One).

Because intellect is of this kind, we need something "beyond it" (9, 1–2). It is typical of Plotinus to cite Plato's *Republic* in this way, where Socrates puzzles Glaukon with the statement that the idea of the Good is beyond being (and intellect). However, even modern scholars are by no means in agreement on what Plato means in this passage. Being is what is knowable, yet it would seem that if the Good is a form, it must in some sense be knowable. Plotinus' indirect quotation here tends to provoke thought rather than settle a complex issue. Perhaps we could look to other passages in Plato for help in interpreting what it means to be "beyond" intellect. In the *Timaeus,* the demiurge is said to be difficult to discover and impossible to communicate to everybody (28 c). The *Parmenides* states that there is no name for the "one" (142 c). And the *Seventh Letter* (of particular importance for Plotinus, and rightly accepted at the time as genuine) is clear that there can be no written work on the subject of dialectical enquiry since it "cannot be expressed in words as other studies can, but instead from a lot of get-together around the subject itself and living with it [*ek pollês synousias gignomenês peri to pragma auto kai to syzên*], suddenly as a light struck from a leaping fire, [it(?)— there is no expressed subject] comes to be in the soul and already itself nourishes itself" (341 c 5–d 2).

This passage is very close to the spirit of Plotinus, and it shows vividly something that Plotinus himself must have known very well: there is *no* easy way to read Plato. At this point several crucial questions emerge. (1) Does Plotinus cite Plato simply to back up his argument (from authority) or to point out the path of his thinking to his colleagues and students or even to offer a kind of in-depth meditation upon the meaning and difficulty of other texts as he follows out his own train of thought? Probably a little of all three, but if this is so it does not make our task easier because we should simultaneously have to make intelligent decisions about many other extremely difficult texts in order to read Plotinus intelligently. Yet none are more vexed or more crucial than *Republic* VI–VII. (2) If the One is unspeakable, how can we speak about it? Plotinus spends a good deal of time in the *Enneads* talking about the unspeakable, so it is important to determine how he understands this to be possible. (3) A version of the same question applies to intellect. If intellect is timeless and nondurational, how can Plotinus introduce durational language into his descriptions of it? Is intellectual thinking (*noêsis*) propositional, or should propositions only be the province of discursive reasoning (*dianoia*)? This is a pressing problem for any reader of III, 8, 9–11, for nowhere else in the *Enneads* do we have quite such strange statements as "intellect is always desiring and always attaining" (11, 23–24), or in the image of the fountainhead, each of the rivers in unity with its origin (i.e., the One) "already . . . knows, as it were, where they will let their streams flow to" (10, 9–10). If the idea is strange that intellect, a nontemporal being, has a history "endlessly exploring the rich and varied life that is itself" (Armstrong 1971, 73), then the idea that something in intellect knows how it *will* develop into an actualized intellect is even weirder.

The most important of these three interrelated questions is the second; that is, how are we to speak about the unspeakable One? I shall take up this question first and summarize how I situate it in relation to the *Enneads* in general. This will provide some reference points on a difficult but crucial matter that has been almost entirely misunderstood in modern times until very recently. I shall then take up the question of propositional language and intellect as part of the broader question of the One before going on to apply this to chapters 9–11. This will help us to get a clearer idea of how Plotinus implicitly reads such vexed passages as Plato's *Republic* VI–VII and to determine whether his approach to Plato makes sense even in the context of modern thinking.

3.22. Speaking about the One: The character of a simplicity beyond intellect

Plotinus' negative theology is not a tidy business.[82] He seems to come at the problem from a jumble of different angles simultaneously rather than from any orderly procedure of kataphatic or aphophatic theology according to which one may first examine what affirmations one may make or are made about the One, then negate them, and finally negate the negations to ensure not only the unsaying of what has been said but equally the unsaying of what has been unsaid. This quite reasonably is to ensure that we do not covertly make a transcendent god in our own image or

---

82. On negative theology and Plotinus' mysticism in general, R. Arnou, 1950, 1967; see A. H. Armstrong, 1977, 1979, 1990; W. Beierwaltes, 1985, 1987; P. Hadot, 1981b; J. M. Rist, 1967, 1973; G. J. P. O'Daly, 1971 (chapter 4), 1974; R. Mortley, 1975, 1986. On language and related issues see J. Pépin, 1982; D. J. O'Meara, 1990; M. Fattal, 1998.

likeness or according to our own preferences. Nonetheless, we might come at the problem in the following way.

3.22.1. Self-referential language

The language of substances, or things, cannot apply to the One, for the One is not a "something." The *auto* is before the *ti*, Plotinus says at V, 3 (49) 12, 51–2, by which he appears to mean that the "itself," or pure unrestricted self-identity, is prior to the "something"—that is, determinate being. Consequently, (a) while we cannot say what the One is, we can say what it is not, so negation can perhaps tell us something negative or indirect about it; and (b) while we cannot say *it*, we can speak "about it," by virtue of the fact that we are "about" or "around" it, and there is something of it in us too. Such statements, of course, will be self-referential in that they indicate our own experiences of the One in us rather than speaking directly of the One. However, if Plotinus can show good reason to suppose that these statements are not simply about ourselves but indicate beyond themselves to a hermeneutical meeting of horizons that preserves the ineffability of the One, then such language is meaningful, not irrational. We find this sort of approach to the question in many passages: "we can say nothing of it; we can only try, as far as possible, to make signs [*sêmainein*] to ourselves about it" (V, 3 [49] 13, 5–6).[83] "How then do we speak about it? We do indeed say something about it, but we certainly do not say it, nor do we have knowledge or thought of it. How then do we speak about it if we do not have it? But if we do not have it in knowing, do we not have it at all? But we do have it in such a way as to speak about it but not to say it. For we say what it is not" (14, 1–6). Or, to say that the One "is" or "is one" or "is good" is actually to speak of a deficiency in us rather than of any positive attribute in the One, "for to say that it is the cause is not to predicate something incidental of it but of us, because we have something from it while that One is in itself, but one who speaks precisely should not say 'it' or 'is,' but we run around it outside, in a way, and want to explain our own experiences of it [*ta autôn hermêneuein ethelein pathê*], sometimes near it and sometimes falling away in our perplexities about it" (VI, 9 [9] 3, 49–54).

To sum up then, (a) negation may tell us something indirectly of the One, and (b) if speaking about its presence in our experience is to say something more than that experience, then such language is not irrational.

3.22.2. Affirmation and negation

Though at first sight it may seem paradoxical, affirmation and negation together might suggest a reasonable way of speaking about the One. If, for example, our radical dependence on the One is actually the presence of the One in us, then on

---

83. Compare Heraclitus, *DK* fr. 93: "The Lord whose oracle is at Delphi neither speaks nor hides but makes signs [*sêmainei*]."

the one hand we can reasonably speak of this presence as that *of the One* as long as on the other hand we make sure to negate the multiplicity of the language itself. The experience of divine rapture or madness in poetry, divination, prophecy, and the like (of which Plato speaks in the *Ion, Phaedrus,* etc.) is an experience of something beyond us yet in us, so it is our experience of a genuine "other." This is the sort of line Plotinus takes in V, 3 [49] 14, 8 ff., and it is a crucial element in Platonic thinking:

> just as those who have a god within them and are in the grip of divine posses-
> sion may know this much, that they have something greater within them,
> even if they do not know what, and *from the ways in which they are moved*
> and *from the things they say* get a certain *perception* of the god who moves
> them, though these are not the same as the mover; so we seem to be disposed
> toward the One, divining [*chrômenoi*] when we have our intellect pure, that
> this is the inner intellect, which gives substance and everything else . . . but
> that he is . . . higher than speech and thought and perception, giving us these,
> but he is not these himself. (14, 8–19)

This remarkable passage provides a double key to Plotinus' language about the unspeakable One. First, affirmation and negation clearly work together here: we can learn something genuine about the One from the ways we are moved and what we say; at the same time "he is not these," or as Plotinus concludes this treatise, how can we see the One? "Take away everything" (*aphele panta* [17, 37–38]). A radical experience also entails a radical negativity, an emptying or stripping away of everything. Second, we should note Plotinus' language here. *Perception, divi-nation, imagination, indefinite desire* are, from one perspective, more abstract than *thought* (cf. VI, 7 [38] 35–36; V, 3 [49] 11, 1–8; 14, 8–19). Thought knows directly the "what" something is, perception only the likeness (V, 5 [32] 2, 1–9; 1, 15–19; II, 6 [17] 1, 42–49). From another perspective, however, perception and desire are simpler, more immediate terms open to everyone, however profession-ally unqualified they may be. So divine madness and the simplest of experiences, like *perception* when we do not expect such a word, can capture the affective character of our experience of simplicity better than philosophical or intellectual terms.

At the same time, however, Plotinus rather daringly brings such a simple ex-perience back into the context of intellect in the above passage, even going so far as to refer to it as "the inner intellect." This is because there is something even in intellect that is hyper-noetic or hyper-ontic—beyond being or determination; this is the self-reflexive light of the Good, which is the gift and activity *of the Good* but *in and for intellect*.[84] If the Good is not an object but can only be experienced

---

84. Cf. V, 5 (32) 7: the medium "is seen together in and with the form; this is the rea-son why it affords no clear perception of itself, since the eye is directed to the illuminated object. . . . Just so intellect, veiling itself from other things and drawing itself inward, when

as the medium in which "objects" come to assume their forms and as the purely self-reflexive giving that is present in every activity, then the experience of the radical simplicity of ordinary activities is a perfectly reasonable ground for developing a language that is compelled to use affirmation and negation simultaneously about the One. Or, to put this another way, (a) a language of apparent contradiction is the only *reasonable* form of speaking in this case; (b) such language is rooted in intellect's origin and very being; yet (c), since it goes beyond intellect's structure into the simplest origin of everything, the simpler, least intellectual, most elemental experience or image might be more appropriate than accepted or acceptable intellectual categories.

3.22.3. The breaking of images and determinate linguistic forms

Plotinus' language about the One is inherently disruptive in that it consciously but rationally approaches such unrestricted meaning from every angle and seeks to undermine its own saying or unsaying within the thinkable possibilities of the sayable. This involves the constant breaking of images in several different ways: (a) by the contradiction of epistemic thinking through the introduction of the simplest, but apparently inappropriate, *physical* things: for instance, origins, seeds, rivers; in a similar iconoclastic fashion, Plato pricks the mystical revelation of the "beautiful itself" with the violent transcendental (*exaiphnês*) intrusion of a drunken Alcibiades in the *Symposium*; and (b) by the contradiction of terms; that is, the conscious violation of the principle of non-contradiction.

How and why should Plotinus develop a meaningful language based upon such forms of negation or even contradiction? Let us consider each of the above points in turn because we cannot even begin to understand the works we are reading unless we see them a little more deeply.

First, the contradiction of epistemic thinking. The presence of the One in, with, and to us is likened to simple infinitival forms either of being, such as "to exist," or of activities, such as sight and desire, as we have seen. Even pure thinking has this infinitival, unrestricted character, and in several cases Plotinus explores its purely self-dependent, creative capacities (cf. VI, 9 [9] 6, 50–57; VI, 7 [38] 40; VI, 9 [9] 11, 24–25). But more often than not, this involves awakening "another form of seeing" (VI, 9 [9] 11) more akin to the simplicity and foolishness of lovers. The famous closing words of VI, 9 (9), the "flight of the alone to the alone," should be understood in this way and not as solitary, self-absorbed mysticism in the way Julia Kristeva mistakenly understands them.[85] When vision is intense, no otherness separates lover and beloved. They are "alone" (cf. V, 1

---

it is *not looking at anything* will see a light, not a distinct light *in something different from itself*, but suddenly appearing alone by itself in independent purity . . ." (5–35).

85. J. Kristeva, 1983, 110–11; for criticism see K. Corrigan, 1996c, 29.

[10] 6, 50–54). This is not isolation but its opposite, pure intimacy, described in daring terms of intellect by Plotinus in VI, 7 (38) 35. To see the One so intimately, he says, intellect must not only become "loving" but it must become a "daft" intellect, and the mingling of "subject" with "object" in such vision he describes in erotic terms as "mingling his seeing with what he contemplates" (cf. I, 6 [1] 7, 13).

But simplification and intimate togetherness simultaneously involve augmentation. The One is not a point or a monad. "When you see him," Plotinus says in V, 5 (32) 10, "look at him *whole*." The One is not in need of anything as other things need it, but this does not mean that it is pure isolated self-sufficiency, for the One's presence is not only "in" us; it already embraces everything in itself. The "extension" of soul and intellect are less than that of the One: "not all things desire intellect, but all things desire the Good" (VI, 7 [38] 20, 18–19). What this means in practice will sound strange at first. The presence of the One even to us is the most immense presence there is, so that whether we intellectualize, reason, distort, or pervert that presence we cannot make it simply a subjective preference of our own being. This is the insight with which Descartes wrestles in *Meditation* III, the prior presence of the infinite in the finite (or the "Cartesian circle"). But for Plotinus this insight is not necessarily reached by introspection. True, he says, the Good is the most familiar and the most foundational presence in us, which is why we are not aware of it. But this presence is as outward as it is inward, "accessible to anyone when anyone wants," or in III, 8, 9, "wherever you are" (23–29). So the presence of the One, so to speak, reaches where the intellect and soul do not quite extend: into basic experiences to which we do not pay attention, like bare existence, instinctive desire, shapelessness, even pure possibilities. When Thomas Aquinas a thousand years later writes that the divine self-knowing must include everything in the universe, even future contingencies and the barest possibilities (which can never be recognized even as possibilities by the human mind), he is developing a line of thought that he encountered in Pseudo-Dionysius, Proclus, and Boethius[86] but that goes back to Plotinus' designation of the One as *dynamis pantôn*, the power-possibility-potency of all things—not in the passive fashion of matter, as Plotinus takes care to point out (V, 3 [49] 14, 33–35) but in the inclusive, simplest way of all beginnings. In such a context, *dynamis*, which we have to translate as "power" because there are no other options for a determinate language, bears *all* of its meanings: not *in*determinately, but *hyper*determinately.

For the development of a language about the One, therefore, the simplest images relating to the simple beginnings of things become paradoxically the most appropriate; the most *physical, ordinary*, down-to-earth images are in their context more appropriate as images than theological conventions because they de-

---

86. Cf. chapter 2, part II; n. 42; for Pseudo-Dionysius, Proclus, and Boethius see chapter 5.2, *Afterlife*.

stroy the merely accepted yet renew meaning with their own immediacy and yet shapelessness. *"Ego vermis sum,"* "I am a worm," the Psalmist sings, and even this dissimilar image, Pseudo-Dionysius will argue, is more appropriate for the divine than supposedly similar images.[87] According to the same logic, Dante's similes in the *Paradiso* become, in part, more earthy the higher he ascends. In Canto XXVI, form and content in the soul of Adam are like feeling transmitted immediately by the cover over a wriggling worm: "Sometimes an animal that is covered so stirs that its impulse must needs be apparent, since what envelops it follows its movements: in like manner that first soul showed me, through its covering, how joyously it came to do me pleasure."[88] The closer one comes to the divine, the simpler, more effective, immediate, and yet pervasive is the experience.

3.22.4. *Power and the language of hyperdeterminacy*

The consequences of this for our enquiry here are far-reaching. The perspectives of power (preeminently the One) and potency (matter), which I have called here hyperdeterminate and purely indeterminate respectively, do not deal with universes of fully realized things. Matter is a universe of the infinite postponement of being; as purely indeterminate, it is all things potentially but none actually. Conversely, the One is "all things and not a single one of them" (V, 2 [11] 1, 1). What sense can we make of these ways of speaking? In the realm of pure indeterminacy as matter there is no truth because the notions of true and false can only apply to a determinate world of things. So Plotinus will call matter "the truly false," consciously applying contrary predicates to an indeterminacy that is always going to be x or y but never is either. Aristotle himself recognizes that in cases of genuine indeterminacy (like pure potentiality—*De Interpretatione* 23 a 21–6, or the interesting problem of in what sense we can say that there will or will not be a sea-battle tomorrow—*De Int.* 19 a 29–35) "it is clear that it is not necessary that of an affirmation and a denial one should be true and the other false . . . for in the case of these things that can be or not be, the rule for the things that are does not hold" (*De Int.* 19 a 39–19 b 4). In later antiquity, Alexander of Aphrodisias implicitly and Ammonius explicitly took this to mean that statements about future contingent events are either true or false but neither "definitely."[89] The Skeptics in suspending judgement about the nature of phenomenal reality were prepared to admit contrary predications simultaneously (Sextus Empiricus, *Outlines of Pyrrhonism*, I, 7). But what of pure indeterminacy? It will never be true to say definitely that anything is in this respect true or in that respect false, for to make any actual

---

87. Psalms 22:6 ; and Pseudo Dionysius, *Celestial Hierarchy*, c. II.

88. "Tavolta un animal coverto broglia,/sì che l'affetto convien che si paia/per lo seguir che face a lui la 'nvoglia;/e similmente l'anima primaia/mi facea trasparer per la coverta/quant' ella a compiacermi venìa gaia" (*Paradiso* XXVI, 97–102).

89. See R. W. Sharples, 1992, 23–38.

predications of anything indeterminate will be false. So the best one can do is to say that indeterminate x is both y and −y in the sense that it "can be" or "will be" both, but that it will never actually *be* both simultaneously.

The perspective of power, however, is rather different. In fact, we could rightly use the phrase physicists apply in the Big Bang theory to the conditions of such power. It is a unique "singularity" in which the totality of the universe that will be is dynamically emerging, and the wonder is that, for all the explosive power, a "heap" does not result. But Plotinus' view of the Good is very different. For one thing, it is possible to speak the truth about it. We can, for instance, call it the Good and this is true, he says in III, 8, 9; only it is not informative for us on the level at which we make the predication because the discursive reason has nothing concrete to "lean on" (9, 16–19). In other words, the perspective of power is true beyond the capacity of reason or even thought to determine it. As he says elsewhere, "That is why it is also *truly* unspeakable [*arrêton tei alêtheia*]"(V, 3 [49] 13, 1). So how are we to take this?

3.22.5. The principles of identity and non-contradiction

We can translate into our own terms something that Plotinus suggests at the beginning of his second work on the omnipresence of all being, VI, 5 (23). The One is the principle of truth; that is, the principle of identity, which establishes intellect and everything else in being and thus gives intellect to be substantial truth in its totality, the image of which, soul, nature, and bodies possess in their own ways by substantial or qualitative reflection. But such a principle is prior to all subsequent principles, such as the principle of non-contradiction or again the so-called first principle of practical reason (that all things desire the good), Plotinus argues. It establishes those principles but is not subject to them since it is the power for determinate things but not their actuality. From the perspective of power, therefore, which is the One or pre-intellect or pre-soul (as opposed to the perspective of the highest activity, which is not so much pre-anything as it is hyper- or beyond-anything), everything is precontained as pure dynamic possibility, and the only thinkable and reasonable language we can employ is a language that appears to break the law of non-contradiction. But that language does not actually break the law of non-contradiction because a genuine power for contraries or for apparently opposite predications simultaneously can be described in no other appropriate way: "For that One is not absent from any, and absent yet from all, so as in being present not to be present . . ." (VI, 9 [9] 4, 24–25). Or: "It is indeed a wonder how he is present without having come and how though being nowhere there is nowhere where he is not" (V, 5 [32] 8, 23–24). Therefore Plotinus' language about the One, curiously enough, is not only reasonable—though not discursively reasonable; it is the *only appropriately thinkable* language for him to develop.

Treatise VI, 5 (23) chapter 1 is an important and rather striking chapter but is too long to cite here. Plotinus appeals to the common experience of humankind (*koinê*

. . . *tis ennoia*) that the god in each and every one of us is the god we are "spontaneously moved" to say is "one and the same." This, at any rate, he goes on to say, is what everyone simply assumes and what everyone instinctively, without discursive analysis, rests upon by "leaning" themselves upon what is one and the same. Discursive reasoning might have nothing to "lean upon" (cf. III, 8, 9, 18–19), but people are somehow spontaneously able to ground themselves in the principle of pure identity (cf. VI, 5 [23] 2 passim). At any rate, it is "the firmest principle of all, which our souls utter, as it were, not summed up from individuals, but before all the individuals and coming even before that principle that posits and says that all things desire the good. For this would be true if all things press on to the one and are one, and their desire is of this" (1, 8–14). Of course, the god who is "one and the same" here could well be intellect (and perhaps lines 14 and following might support this), but the Good is nonetheless implicit, and since the same power of unity runs also through intellect, it almost makes no difference what Plotinus refers to precisely, for the major point is clear: truth is established by the One before all individuals and before subsequent principles.

3.22.6. Intellect and language

How does this apply to intellect? Is not the way Plotinus speaks about intellect and the One ultimately the failure of rational thinking and an abandonment of the philosophical foundations of earlier thought in favour of religious irrationality? I have argued above that Plotinus' language about the One (as also about matter's indeterminacy) is a highly innovative, inherently philosophical way of speaking about relations in a nondeterminate universe of discourse. Such a language is, of course, not that of discursive reason, for it appears to break the principle of non-contradiction and opens a universe of discourse to its broadest possible extent to include maxima and minima as well as the barest possibilities. But it is a *reasonable* language. What then of intellect? The remarkable description beginning at III, 8, 11, 22 is not unique:

> It has, therefore, given a trace of itself upon intellect to intellect to have in seeing, so that in intellect there is desire, and intellect is always desiring and always attaining what it desires . . .

Here, as earlier in chapter 9, 32–9 ("life in outward passage"), the unchanging character of eternal life seems fundamentally compromised by the introduction of transition, duration, and so forth, so that the very coherence of Plotinus' descriptions is seriously threatened. But Plotinus' thought seems to be impaled upon both horns of the same dilemma: if the introduction of discursive language into a nondiscursive universe undermines coherence from one side, the very idea of nondiscursive thought has been regarded as utterly incoherent on the other side (by

Lloyd, for example).[90] So let us briefly look at the major aspects of this problem and suggest a means of thinking it through coherently along the lines we have developed above.

3.22.6.1. Propositional versus non-propositional language

A. H. Armstrong has raised some important questions that have helped to define the parameters of the problem: on the one hand, Armstrong points out that Plotinus never seems enthusiastic about discursive reason, though he admits its necessity and place in the hierarchy of mental activities (Armstrong-Ravindra, 1982, 79); on the other hand, Armstrong observes that Plotinus' accounts of the intelligible world or of the indefinite life of pre-intellect "are not fully consistent or coherent." Plotinus "is not always successful in confining his descriptions . . . within the limits imposed by the concept of non-durational eternity" (1971, 74). T. Szlezák holds a similar view that Intellect can be termed needy of the One only by a mental abstraction. So Plotinus' attempts to bring intelligible matter into the conceptual world of Plato's dialogues lead both to unanswered problems in the *Enneads* (e.g., can intelligible matter be undetermined without being potential?) and to contradictions in Plotinus' interpretation of Plato (1979, 82–5). But it is A. C. Lloyd who has set the baseline for the problem. Intellect is a nondiscursive transcendent Reality, but we, the describers, are necessarily discursive. Intellect's nondiscursive thought, then, is simple, nonpropositional, nonselfconscious, described in terms of contact, but fundamentally incoherent for us discursive thinkers (1969–70, 261–75). Partly against Lloyd, Sorabji has argued that while nondiscursive thought might involve no chronological transition from object to object, and while it clearly excludes concepts taken in isolation, it is nonetheless complex and can be propositional in the sense that (a) the route by which we attain to nondiscursive thought is through discovering the definitions of things in terms of genus and difference, and (b) intellect seems to involve a contemplation of these definitions arranged into a unified network (1983, 152–163).[91]

3.22.6.2. Discursive reason and understanding in Plato and Plotinus

Plotinus' approach to this problem is very much in the spirit of Plato. *Dianoia*, or discursive reasoning, is propositional; *noêsis*, thinking or understanding, is nonpropositional; but *both* are complex in different ways. We should not make the mistake, according to both thinkers, of thinking that *any* of our representations (propositions, myths, images, names, etc.) are "the real thing" (i.e., the "what" x is). Representations, explanations, plausible accounts, cogent scientific theories can blind us to reality if we take them uncritically as the absolute truth, but they can also open us up to reality if we are prepared to shatter them and see through

---

90. A. C. Lloyd, 1955–6, 1969–70.

91. Compare also on this question K. Wurm, 1973; A. Smith, 1981; K. Corrigan, 1987a; J. Bussanich, 1988, 103–4; and M. Alfino, 1988.

them. This does not necessarily downgrade the level of discursive reason; it just means that reason is not the same as understanding or as the truth of the thing in question. As Plotinus accurately puts it, we should not confuse our explanations of why things are so with their being so. This does not mean that we are wrong, only that *noêsis* and *dianoia* are different, and thus our explanations are always *provisional* (i.e., in terms of Plato's *Seventh Letter*, always subject to "being refuted through well-meaning refutations" [344 b]). Another way of putting this might be to say that we can determine whether someone really understands x (i.e., knows x) by getting him to give an account of some sort of what he says he understands, but in terms of the *Theaetetus* we might still want to say that *epistêmê*, science or understanding, is not simply a sort of linear addition, or justified belief (if we can translate *orthê doxa* into contemporary analytic terms), *plus* an account. No, it is actually *understanding*.

Plainly too there should be no reason why understanding cannot be complex yet simple too. I can see and think a face all at once, with everything distinctly within it and perfectly articulated. To borrow Plotinus' example, it is as if all the intellectual acts of the soul are all together, for "since its object of contemplation is richly varied [*poikilos*], its act of thinking too is richly varied and multiple, and there are many acts of intelligence, as there are many acts of perception of a face when the eyes and the nose and the other features are all seen at once" (IV, 4 [28] 1, 20 ff.). Nor should there be any reason why I should not be able to represent the profoundly complex unities that seem to haunt us in a host of different ways, not just in arguments or propositions that are only meaningful to one or two departments on campus, but in as many ways as people are human—as Plato, for example, makes story, example, prayer, myth, and argument fundamental parts of philosophical dialectic. This may be a controversial view of Plato's dialectic, but for Plotinus there is simply no question: *mythos* and *logos* are *both* essential to dialectical thinking. Again there is no reason not to develop different forms of representation for entirely new landscapes where determinate forms of thinking are in fact inadequate. These new representative languages finally will be inadequate also, but their very strangeness—their ability to provoke under-thought (*hyponoia*, cf. 10, 28: shall we *under-think* it to be the nothing?)—may by that very token be more appropriate to the question at issue than more linear forms of representative enquiry.

This view of Plotinus' developing new ways of speaking about the One is also true of intellect in this perspective. First, if thought essentially involves movement at rest and an intelligible "interval," and if no organism is really intelligible without some understanding of the termini of its being, then Plotinus is committed to representing the unity of opposites in intellect *dynamically*, just as Aristotle indicates in the *De Anima* that there may be other modes of transition from power/ potency to act than physical movement or qualification (cf. I, 1 [53] 13). So Plotinus represents such unity in movement as vivid, provocative oxymora (e.g., VI, 7 [38] 13: the "abiding wandering" of intellect [*menousan . . . planên*]). What is inappropriate for a determinate propositional world of concepts and things can be a useful linguistic tool for expressing the possibilities, potentialities, and the waking up to differences in an indeterminate universe.

Second, if intellect is pervaded dynamically by the One's *dynamis* (as in VI, 7 [38] 13), and if the One is the purest extension comprising everything from potency to power, then the phrase *dynamis tôn pantôn* (power for all things) includes the potency of other things (even if this is untranslateable, although Plotinus gets as close as he can to making it explicit in III, 8, 11, 1 ff.). The term *dynamis* includes both passive and active aspects in Aristotle's usage and is developed from Plato (*Republic* 509 b 8–10, of the overwhelming power of the Good; *Sophist* 247 e 3–4). We can compare the use of the phrase *dynamis pantôn* elsewhere in the *Enneads* (e.g., V, 4 [7] 2, 36–38; VI, 9 [9] 5, 35–38; 6, 7–8; V, 1 [10] 7, 9–11; VI, 8 [39] 9, 45). In this perspective, passive and active are necessary correlatives in the life of intellect: for example, in a remarkable first-person account, Plotinus says: "Often I have woken up out of the body into myself . . . and activated the best life and come to identity with the divine; and *having been set firm in it* [passive: *hidrytheis*], I have come to that activity above every other intelligible object *setting myself* [active: *hidrysas*] . . . then when I come down to reasoning from intellect, I am puzzled" (IV, 8 [6] 1, ff.). Here too in intellect (a) the language of desire[92]; (b) precise nuances of voice, mood, and tense in the derivation and articulation of intellect's nature (as we have seen in section 3.19.6); (c) the precise use of the future tense especially[93]; (d) the language of "more and less"[94]; as well as (e) gradational unities (III, 8, 10, 20 ff.: "That is also why the ascent is everywhere to a one . . .")—all of these different linguistic forms are just as appropriate a representational language as more determinate propositional forms might be in their own universes of discourse. Indeed, we have to go somewhat beyond this. For if the power of the Good is that by which we see ourselves and others and are also seen, such reflexive power *cannot* be represented as a determinate proposition, axiom, or anything else. Yet it is also the most intimate and fundamental *practical* good in every activity but one that can be glimpsed only in the self-reflexive activity itself. This aspect of dialectic (and it is surely Platonic to its roots) Plotinus seems to have in mind at the end of chapter 10 and

---

92. Cf. V, 3 (49) 17, 15–38; III, 8 (30) 11, 22 ff.; V, 5 (32) 12, 15.

93. From the perspective of power *before* the actualization of determinate things, everything must be future-tense. Cf. V, 2 (11) 1, 1–3: "all things . . . are not yet there but they will be"; III, 8 (30) 10, 7–10: "but each knows, as it were, where they will let their streams flow to"; VI, 7 (38) 16, 20–21; VI, 6 (34) 10, 4.

94. Cf. VI, 9 (9) 1, 26–30 (chapter 2, part II, passage 2); 9, 11–13; V, 5 (32) 7, 18–30.

throughout chapter 11 (e.g., 10, 34–5: "by bringing together into one view its greatness from the things that exist after it but through it").[95]

Jean Trouillard, therefore, rightly pointed out that Plotinian thought is "oriented to the future" (1961, 132) since from the perspective of such power the entirely new is always susceptible of jumping into full existence or, as Plotinus intimates, even of walking into language.[96] In this sense, Plotinus is the major developer (on the basis of Plato, Aristotle, Alexander of Aphrodisias, the Skeptics, and others) of significant new forms of discourse, reasonable and appropriate in their own domains, though not discursively reasonable if discursive reason is supposed to deal with a world of determinate things and the binary opposition of truth and falsity.

3.23.   Infinity and number (III, 8, 9, 1–6)

Let us return to III, 8, 9–11. Plotinus' argument is precise throughout, if highly compressed. Bussanich (1988, 40) thinks that 9, lines 5–11 offer no argument, but Plotinus certainly conducts an internal argument with *himself* throughout the chapter. The transcendent One is the goal of the whole dialectic (9, 1–3). Intellect remains a number; a substantial number, that is, which means, as we have seen, that it is the totality of number in one (a one-many), not quantitatively many units. Plotinus' friend and colleague Amelius apparently thought that the intelligible forms were infinite, but Plotinus is of the view that they are finite and that infinity is limited by "the really one" (9, 4; for similar phrases see V, 5 [32] 4, 1–7), which is no longer number in any sense, substantial or quantitative, but the origin of number. *Archê* can mean origin, beginning, or "originative" principle (see Sleeman and Pollet, and Aristotle *Metaphysics* V; for number, see VI, 6, [34]).

3.24.   Neither intellect nor intelligible object nor ignorant (III, 8, 9, 6–16)

If the One is neither intellect simply nor intelligible object simply (because intellect is the paradigm of a "yoking together"[97]—that is, if the intellectual subject and object are always coupled or yoked together like the charioteer's horses in the myth of Plato's *Phaedrus* (246 a ff.; see Appendix A, 2)—what sort of thing shall

---

95. For this question in Plato and further bibliography, see K. Corrigan, E. Glazov-Corrigan, *Plato's Dialectic at Play* (University Park, Pa.: Penn State Press, forthcoming).

96. Cf. V, 5 (2) 5: "For this that we call primary being walked forward, so to speak, a little way from the One, but did not wish to go still further, but turned inward . . . it is like what happens in the utterance of the sound: when the speaker leans in upon it *hen* [one] is produced that shows the origin from the One and *on* [being] signifying what uttered, as best it can . . ."

97. Cf. *syzygy*, a Gnostic entity (literally, yoke, pair, or conjunction of entities) that Plotinus may have in mind indirectly).

we imagine it to be (9, 6–14)? The verb *to imagine* used here is not accidental but an indication that we have to enter upon a simpler form of discourse (cf. 9, 17). At V, 3 (49) 11, pre-intellect is described as an indefinite desire "having in itself a *phantasm* or mental imagination" of the One. Note, too, the phrase, "If [the One] is not intellect then, but is going to escape the two [*ekpheuxetai*]" (8–9). Again, the future tense is appropriate to the perspective of a power beyond determinate being.

Elsewhere the *Enneads* appear to present a different view. In an early work, V, 4 (7) 2, Plotinus seems to envisage the One precisely as an intelligible object.[98] However, the two contexts are different; the description in V, 4, 2 is intellectual but ambiguous in the unfolding of intellect until intellect has explicitly become formed and the complete transcendence of the One is then affirmed. Plotinus says this intelligible object is not "senseless" (*anaisthêton*), but completely self-discernible (*pantê diakritikon heautou*) with life and everything in it and with an intimate self-perception (*synaesthêsis*) and a thinking different from that of intellect (V, 4, 2, 12–19). So the abiding intelligible object cannot be the One simply but rather *the One as intelligible object for intellect*, which is the highest aspect of intellect (as, for example, in VI, 7 [38] 40, 6–20). Thus, Plotinus does not ascribe *synaesthêsis* to the One here in V, 4, 2 or, for that matter, at V, 1 (10) 6, 18–19 and 7, 1–17.[99]

The problem for Plotinus in III, 8, 9 is that imagination confronts a dilemma, discursive reason an indeterminacy with which it cannot deal, and knowledge (*gnôsis*) its own restriction to intellect (9, 13–22). For we can only imagine the One to be intellectual or unintellectual, but if the first alternative is already excluded, we may have to accept the second horn of the dilemma—a principle that is ignorant of itself. Such a form of "unknowing" is incompatible with any philosophically authentic tradition of understanding divinity, Plotinus implies (16: *ti semnon*; see also Aristotle, Appendix A, 4 b), and so he excludes the Gnostic notion of a divine ignorance or even perhaps a Pythagorean intelligible "chaos" in the elements of things (which Sethian Gnostic texts appear to include [cf. *Zostrianus* VIII, 1, 117, 5–12; compare Proclus, *In Timaeum* I, 176, Diehl). The One does not think, but this does not mean it is asleep (cf. Aristotle, *Metaph.* XII, 9, 1047 b 17) or simply senseless (cf. V, 3 [49], 13, 6–8).

3.25. *Simple, instantaneous awareness (III, 8, 9, 16–24)*

So we have to seek a power that "has passed beyond the nature of intellect": a simple instantaneous awareness (*epibolê athroa*) (9, 19–22) (*"per quale improvvisa intuizione,"* Cilento; *"durch welche plötzliche Intuition,"* Theiler; *"par quelle*

---

98. Cf. V, 6 (24) 2.

99. On these questions generally see Corrigan, 1984, 1987 (a and b, for references); Beierwaltes, 1967, 1991; J. Bussanich, 1988; Schroeder, 1986.

sorte d'impression," Bréhier; *"by what sort of simple intuition,"* Armstrong). *Epibolê* indicates some form of direct apprehension, a "throwing upon" or casting off toward. *Athroos* means "all-at-once," "together," "concentrated" (see *LSJ*). My translation tries to convey simplicity and all-at-onceness as a form of immediate perception. I avoid "intuition" because of its unfortunate philosophical overtones and because the Latin root of the English word, *intueor*, implies a distinct object.

Epibolê perhaps reflects Epicurean usage (cf. Rist, 1967, 49–50) and is related to the comprehensive apprehension of images in the mind and of sense-data (Vlastos, 1955, review of F. M. Cornford, *Principium Sapientiae, Gnomon* 27,70–1; cf. Diogenes Laertius X, 35). The phrase *epibolê tês dianoias* is used of the simple mental apprehension of matter in II, 4 (12) 10, 4–11. *Epibolê athroa*, comprehensive apprehension, is used of soul at IV, 4 (28) 1, 20 and 8, 6: "what prevents soul too from having this unified grasp of all its objects at once (*tautên tên epibolên athroan athroôn*)?" But *epibolê* (and *prosbolê* too) is chosen perhaps for its reference to simple direct perception (internal or external), but more obviously still for its nontechnical simple "material" force, as in III, 8, 10, 32–5: "throwing [*balôn*] yourself upon it" and "knowing it by simple contact [*têi prosbolêi syneis*]." So in VI, 7 (38) 35, intellect is said to have one power for thinking, by which it looks at the things in itself, and one by which it looks at what transcends it "by a simple awareness and reception" (*epibolêi tini kai paradochei* [19–22]. Receptive awareness also characterizes III, 8, 9, 29 below.

The power in question connotes the directness of material impact or contact, as in perception (but without the medium, as it were), and the inclusion of everything simultaneously in unity, as in the later injunction, "When you see him, look at him *whole* [*holon*]" (V, 5 [32] 10, 9) or as in the description of the direct apprehension of the medium of light "by an instantaneous immediate perception [*athroai prosbolei*]" (V, 5 [32] 7, 8). *Prosballein* and cognates are used by Plato, for example, of perception. Given the immediacy in question, Plotinus even uses *epibolê* of the One itself. In VI, 7 (38) 39, 1–4 he argues that since nothing else is present to it (it rather is present to everything else) "there will be a simple awareness in it in relation to itself [*haplê tis epibolê autôi pros auton*], but since there is no distance or difference in relation to itself, what could its activity of awareness to itself be [*to epiballein heautôi*] except itself?"

Plotinus' language, then, very carefully links (a) two different sorts of capacity or power, one in intellect and one beyond intellect, (cf. VI, 7, 35, 19–22); (b) hyperdeterminacy (*hyperbebêkos*, "What has passed beyond" at line 21; again, a simple material image of walking); (c) immediate perception or awareness; and (d) receptive power ("by setting to it what is *able* to have it . . . you will receive all the voice and yet again not all of it" [25–28]). The curious appropriateness of these material images ensures that terms such as *epibolê* will continue to be used of intellect's mystical apprehension of the One by later Neoplatonists, as by Proclus for example (*In Parm.* VII, 92 and J. Bussanich, 1988, 95).

We should note here how at the summit of direct mystical apprehension Plotinus draws attention to the supreme responsibility of any authentic Platonism to point the way (*sêmainein*) in conversation or dialectic for others: "We shall say to the person to whom we *must* indicate how it is possible, that it is by virtue of what is similar in us" (22–3).[100] Care of the soul and care for others are dialectically related for Plato since we cannot really care for others unless we have ourselves been liberated from the cave and turned the "eye" of the soul to the Good in living, philosophical conversation. We risk our lives, as Socrates points out, if we return to the cave to free our fellow prisoners (*Republic* VII 517 a), but the responsibility to do so is so fundamental that Socrates even envisages the possibility of having to compel the philosopher to return. This Platonic duty evidently makes Plotinus think again of one of his favourite passages, namely, that in "fleeing" from here to the Good we should become as like to god as possible (*Theaetetus* 176 b: *homoiôsis theôi*; compare "what is similar in us," *homoios*, 9, 23). But he goes on to make the following concrete precisions: "For there is *something* of it in us too [*ti kai par'hêmin*]" or rather, because we are really *in* it: "there is nowhere where it is not for the things that participate in it" (9, 23–4). This linking of the intensive and extensive omnipresence of the One is again fundamental to later Neoplatonism. At the end of his commentary on the First Hypothesis of Plato's *Parmenides* preserved in William of Moerbeke's Latin translation, Proclus argues that we know the One by virtue of an interior understanding of unity in ourselves (54, 3–14, Klibansky-Labowsky). Does this mean that the One is purely subjective? No, it is present in us in an unnameable way because it also extends to and beyond everything: "And much less does everything participate in life or intellect or rest or movement. But in unity, everything."

3.26. Sound and omnipresence (III, 8, 9, 24–29)

The sound image (a favourite in Plotinus' treatments of omnipresence, VI, 4–5 [22–23]) is highly concrete and yet problematic, as are all the subsequent images. The text has caused difficulties (on which see Bussanich, 1988, 96–97) but the manuscript reading can be retained. What is striking about some of these images is what they include, as well as the direct dialectical form of address, "you" (9, 24–8), which then switches to "we" (29). The voice (*phônê*) reaches everywhere in the empty space, and Plotinus takes the trouble to include "human beings there too"—surely an oxymoron. Why the attention to an apparently incongruous and inconsequential detail; is it because Plotinus needs at least two sets of human ears to complete the structure of the analogy, that is, in order that "you" (and at least one other person) will receive all the voice and yet not all of it since the voice oc-

---

100. Cf. again Heraclitus, *DK*, fr. 93; Apollo "neither speaks nor hides but indicates."

cupies the whole space and can be received at any point? This detail does not appear in his use of the analogy elsewhere (cf. especially VI, 4 [22] 12) and is probably intended to emphasize indefinite multiplicity in that the voice can be received from *any* point (in the Greek text the two ideas are immediately adjacent: "human beings at any point" (*anthrôpous en hotôoun*) [9, 27]). What appears to be merely contingent and incongruous in empty space can be complete (and yet not entire) receptive awareness in the power of the spoken word. Or at least this is one conclusion we might draw in the circumstances since indefinite multiplicity crops up again, and very differently, in 9, 29–32.

3.27. A "backward" intellect (III, 8, 9, 29 ff.)

The thought and text of III, 8, 9, 29 and forward are difficult. First, just the idea of an intellect that retreats backward and has to let its hair down, as it were, looks somewhat incongruous. Then too, how can intellect be double-fronted like a *Janus bi-frons?* The statue of Janus possesses two faces looking in opposite directions, a symbol of intelligence in Homer (i.e., to look in front of and behind oneself), and Janus is depicted of *prudentia* (pro-videntia) in Medieval times. This may therefore be an appropriate image, but how can there be plurality "behind" intellect?[101] How should we understand this passage?

Intellect's retreat, its giving up of itself to what is behind it, and its not being completely intellect intimate a hypernoetic state that Plotinus elsewhere describes as the "pure intellect and the first of intellect" (VI, 9 [9] 3, 26–27), "its own not

---

101. I shall simplify the textual problems for convenience's sake here. The ms. *kakeina* (9, 31) looks suspicious. I have translated it here "and in relation to those things behind it." Kirchhoff, Bréhier, Cilento, Henry-Schwyzer (1), all thought *kakei*, "and there," should be the correct reading. Theiler suggested *ekeino*, "that," instead of *kakeina*. Dodds argued that the *kai* in *kakeina* (=*kai ekeina*) was redundant but that the whole phrase might be construed, on the analogy of Numenius' double intellect (which he saw as an important influence on Plotinus), along the lines of the following: "intellect is double-fronted (in the direction of the things that proceed from it) and in the direction of those things (sc. behind it)." But Dodds argues his case partly on the grounds of a text (VI, 9 [9] 3, 33–34) where the ms. reading has been bracketed by Henry-Schwyzer (2) (see also Bussanich, 1988, 99). There are verbal echoes of a Numenian phrase, *en diexodôi*, "in outward passage," (fr. 12, 16) in our passage. The passage perhaps also echoes the *Chaldean Oracles amphistomos*, "double-fronted," or *amphiprosôpos*, "double-faced," but the thought is distinctly Plotinian here (cf. J. Dillon, 1992). Anyway, Henry-Schwyzer (3) (i.e., *emendationes probandae* at the back of vol. III of *Plotini Opera*, p. 382) marked *kakeina* with a dagger to show that we just do not know what to do with it.

The line I take is as follows. Dodds' suggestion is too unwieldy to support. Theiler's *ekeino*, "that," does not help. *Kakei*, "and there," is possible, but it leaves the problem of what exactly is the plurality "behind" intellect anyway, and so, again, does not really help. If we can make sense of *kakeina* in context, as I suggest, then we should retain the ms. reading.

intellect" (*tôu heautou mê nôi* [V, 5 (32) 8, 22–23]), a loving, or rather "daft intellect" (VI, 7 [38] 35, 24), or "the intellect within" (*ho endon nous,* V, 3 [49] 14, 14–15:). The description is startling because it connotes an experience of letting oneself go into the power of the other, and it looks ridiculous because vulnerability of this sort is too radical for normal thought (just as the prisoner freed from the cave and blinded either by light or darkness in ascent or return looks foolish to observers[Plato, *Republic* VII]).[102] Elsewhere in Plotinus the would-be mystic leaves perception, or "the statues in the outer shrine," "behind to enter more completely into union" (cf. V, 8 [31] 11, 12; VI, 9 [9] 11, 18). But here intellect backs unknowingly, as it were, into that mystery (see also chapter 4, part II, 4–10); and yet instead of pure unity or nothingness, there is highly unified or hyperdeterminate *plurality* in what is a nonintellectual experience of a seedlike origin.

There are parallels. Such a hypernoetic plural occurs in an earlier work (again, in the context of power): "But we must take our report from intellect on the basis of the things for which it has power [*hôn dynatai*]. And intellect *can* [*dynetai*] see its own things and the things before it. The things in it also are pure, but still purer and simpler are those before it—or rather that which is before it" (VI, 9 [9] 3, 32–36). Other passages appear to contradict this hypernoetic distinctness. For example, V, 3 (49) 15, 29–32. How did the principle of all things bring them into being? Plotinus asks. "By possessing them earlier. But it has been said that this will make it a multiplicity. But it has them in such a way as not to be distinct [*hôs mê diakekrimena*]; they are distinguished in the second principle by *logos*." So formal distinctness, or what Plotinus terms *diakrisis,* separation, in V, 3, 15, is different from the One's "possessing them earlier." What it means to be "possessed earlier" apparently is taken up in Plotinus' subsequent description of life in outward passage. Even life as the first moment of procession (which must in some sense here correspond to the state of "not being altogether intellect") has everything accurately and unconfusedly; even in the seed-like state, as it were, things are already articulated. Aristotle applies the term *adiathrôtôs,* "non-articulatedly" in his biological works to the newborn of certain animals (*Historia Animalium* 579 a 24; *De Generatione Animalium* 774 b 15 ff.; Bussanich, 1988, 102), but the real point here is that we should not conceive of power (*dynamis*) as an incomplete activity (*atelês:* cf. 9, 36–7) or inarticulate movement without a goal (*telos*). Even if the origin is not substance or determinate being in this case, nonetheless the cardinal principle of Aristotle's biology, that the development or generation of any organ-

---

102. One may usefully compare here three very different approaches: (a) that of Plato in *Rep.* VII (the cave analogy); (b) that of Plotinus in VI, 7 (38) 35, cited above; and (c) that of Pseudo-Dionysius (late 5th or early 6th century A.D.—on which see 5.2 below) from the *Divine Names* (e.g., 712–13; *PG* 3, Migne) and—on the Trinity and divine darkness (*Mystical Theology,* 997 a 6).

ism flows out of its proper nature and does not come about haphazardly, should be applied appropriately in this context *above all*.[103]

The thought process in this difficult passage is rather like this: how are we to conceive of the source or first principle as well as the derivation of multiplicity from it *if*—as in Aristotle's biology—*genesis* follows upon and articulates *ousia* (nature, substance) *without* any process of deliberation (as earlier in III, 8) or *thought* (which is now in question) and *without* indiscriminate formation but *with* the sort of whole-formation of intelligible or physical organisms in which both Aristotle and Plotinus (and Plato in the *Timaeus*) believe? This presents the same problem of whole-formation from the One that we had at the level of nature and soul before. The answer turns upon the problem of the origin's nature at 9, 39–54, which implicitly takes up again the "heap" problem about substance (from the end of chapter 8) and seeks to establish the only grounds upon which any whole-formation theory can be based; that is, the nature of the organizing principle.

First, the origin has to be simpler than intellect (9, 42–4). One might argue that "simpler" is a much more promising hypothesis than "more perfect" for two reasons: it seems to be able to account for development from less developed to more developed forms; and it forces us to think about the nature of the origin in less determinate terms than glory or exercise of power. Proclus would accurately refer to this in his *Platonic Theology* III, 9, as "the *hidden* power of the *hidden* many" (9, 39, 2–13) Second, even if it is somehow simpler and yet coextensive with all things, then either it is each one individually or all together (and we are committed to a form of pantheism) (9, 46–7). On one meaning of "all together," everything makes up a collection of things, so that the elements are prior to their collection. On this view, the One will be later than all the elements of the collection, whereas if the One is earlier, it will be different from them. On a second meaning of "all together," simultaneous, it will not be an origin, source, or beginning. And if it is each individually, there will be an identity of indiscernibles (i.e., we will not be able to tell the One and the everything apart) which can account for nothing and there will be no principle of organization.

3.28.   A power for all things (III, 8, 10, 1–26)

Only if the One is a transcendent power for all things, Plotinus concludes, is there any basis for the complex articulate organization of biological, cosmic, and psychic life (10, 1–26). Here Plotinus bites the bullet on the hyperdeterminate multiplicity issue: not only, in his view, is there articulate multiplicity in the highest unity of life in outward passage. Even in the unity of all things together with their source, there is still a kind of individual identity in each and even a kind of instinctive knowledge. According to the remarkable image in 10, 5–10, the fountainhead gives all of itself to rivers and yet is unconsumed by them, remaining

---

103. On this see K. Corrigan, 1996a, 362–64.

quietly itself: "and those that have gone forth from it, before each of them flows in their different directions, are still together with each other, but already each knows, as it were, where they will let their streams flow to."

What a strange passage and image this is! The basic image can be found in Macrobius' *Dream of Scipio:* "A fountainhead . . . which is a principle of water in such a way that since it procreates rivers and lakes out of itself, it is said to be born from no one" (16, 23) and applies to the soul[104]; and in Numenius, fr. 3, 11–12, of matter and the indefinite dyad: "matter is a headlong and quickly turning river, in depth and breadth and length indefinite and endless." But nothing here is quite like the image in Plotinus. Rivers in normal experience (even ancient philosophical experience) do not generally know their future courses, yet they certainly may be described as possessing a fairly good knack of finding the most favourable water courses even if they have to move their beds a few hundred miles to the east or west over a hundred years or less to find them. In other words, from one perspective rivers know nothing, but from another perspective in which they are connected symbiotically with everything else, their power is simply divine. As T. S. Eliot so aptly put it: "I do not know much about gods, but I think the river is a strong, brown god" (*Four Quartets).* For Plotinus, of course, neither water nor any other elemental force is simply inanimate (cf. VI, 7 [38] 11, 4–10, 48–49). He is fully aware too of the metaphorical force of his words; the "as it were" (*hoion*) at 10, 9 makes this clear. But in such power, natural instincts (even, as here, images of *matter* in traditional thinking) achieve their proper focus, and pure future-tensed possibilities are knowable, according to Plotinus' peculiarly appropriate way of speaking about the One.

3.28.1 A theory of henads

Plotinus' arguments for a unified hyperdeterminate multiplicity are the source of Proclus' (or Syrianus') later development of a doctrine of divine "henads" (or "unities" beyond being, life, and intellect).[105] The term "henads" comes from Plato (*Philebus* 15a), but Plotinus uses it in his treatise on numbers in the context of a purely unified being that serves as a kind of preliminary sketch or outline for determinate beings "like unities [*henades*] keeping a place for the beings that will be founded upon them" (VI, 6 [34] 10, 1–4; cf. 9, 29–30). Again, the future tense characterizes the perspective of power. But if such henads are for Plotinus a logical result of the One's organizing power that can unite opposites, embrace the maximum and the minimum, and provide a dialectical path back to itself through the unities in nature, soul, and intellect (by virtue of power: "you take in each case

---

104. Macrobius: "fons . . . qui ita principium est aquae, ut cum de se fluvios et lacus procreet, a nullo nasci ipse dicatur."

105. See Proclus, *The Elements of Theology,* propositions 113–27, ed. E. R. Dodds, 1963, and commentary, 257 ff.)

what is most powerful" [10, 25–26]), then for later Neoplatonism too it seems to have made that power too close for comfort, everywhere and anywhere "accessible to anyone" (V, 5 [32] 12). Thus it has risked its transcendence, for Iamblichus and Damascius will take the further decisive step of positing an absolutely unknowable, unspeakable One beyond the One itself to ensure its inaccessibility. Imagine: two supreme Ones in order to prevent insidious forms of language and image encroaching upon the supreme principle! Yet in this, Iamblichus and Damascius remain true to the fundamental speech-skepticism of Plato and Plotinus.[106]

3.29. Negative theology and dialectic (III, 8, 10, 26–35)

Chapter 10, lines 26–35 pose several difficulties. Line 28 has *to mêden* twice, which I have translated in each case as "the nothing." Ficino deleted the second *to* ("the"), so that one would read as in VI, 9 (9) 7, 1: "certainly it is none of those things." There is no extra significance here in Plotinus' use of this phrase. No hint of a "divine darkness" (as in later mystical writings) or of a Heideggerian "das Nichts" (the Nothing). The fear for the soul, Plotinus tells us elsewhere, as she moves towards the formless but is not able to get a grasp on the One and be defined and so "slips away," is that "she may have nothing at all" (VI, 9 [9] 3, 1–6).

In context, the precise force of "But if you grasp it by removing being from it . . ." (10, 31) is difficult to see since "being" has already been removed, but the sentence does move to a new thought. What has been removed at line 30 is, first, "being" in the sense of the whole substance of intellect (*ousia*). What Plotinus proposes at line 31 is removing "the to be" (*to einai*); that is, any sense of infinitival "to be." This may seem to the modern reader like splitting hairs, but it is clearly important for any negative theology. The participle "removing" (*aphelôn*) and other forms of the verb are frequent in the *Enneads*, and the most well-known instance is at the end of V, 3 (49) 17, 38: when asked how we see the One's light that is also the soul's means of seeing, Plotinus replies, "Take away everything" (*aphele panta*).

Lines 10, 32–5 are striking. In 10, 33, the phrase "within it" ("taking your rest within in") is an emendation proposed by Henry-Schwyzer (2) and adopted by Armstrong for the manuscripts' *en tois autou*, "taking your rest *in its things*," which may mean no more than *"reposez-vou en lui"* (Bréhier), *"nella sua dimora"* (Cilento), or *"dass du in seinem Bereich zur Ruhe kommen kanst"* (Beutler-Theiler) (and by analogy with V, 8 [31] 10, 10: "all those who have the power to see look to him and to what belongs to him (*to autou*)"). So Bréhier, Cilento, and Beutler-Theiler retain the manuscript reading, and I should also prefer to retain *en tois autou,* "in what belongs to him," as I would also on the grounds not

---

106. For Plato see especially *Phaedrus* 277 d ff. and the *Seventh Letter* 344 c ff.; for Plotinus see also IV 3 (27) 18, 13–20). For Iamblichus and Damascius see Damascius, *De Principiis* 1, 86, 3 ff.

simply of V, 8, 10, 10, but of the several hyperdeterminate plurals in the chapters above (and the comprehensive extent of the One).

The "with" (*syn-*) prefixes in 10, 32–5 are virtually untranslatable, so I have tried to emphasize them, where possible, since they are striking enough: "meditate more deeply in company with it [*synnoei mallon*]," "knowing it [*syneis*]," "bringing together into one view [*synorôn*]." Two points should be made: (1) The verb *anapauesthai*, to rest, is the last word in Plato's *Symposium*. Socrates finally goes home after all the day's activities and *rests*, followed by his disciple, Aristodemus, who wants to know everything he says and does. Socrates' rest, in the context of Alcibiades' speech and its subsequent events, is not the slumber of the rich and famous but the symbol of contemplative thought "standing seeking," which Plotinus, I think, has in mind here in his use of this verb. (2) The verb *synoran*, to see together, is conspicuously Plato's verb in the *Republic* for what dialectical conversation should do, though *syn-* prefixes are striking too in the *Symposium's* corresponding discussion (cf. 211 d 8, 212 a 2). This is not just the image of dialectic that grasps the kinship in all sciences and pursuits, as earlier in the soul here in III, 8, but a living dialectic that is able to see by virtue of the good or the beautiful itself. Plotinus also emphasizes the reflexive dependent character of all things at line 34; they "exist after it, but through it." Living dialectic brings everything (oneself included) together in the living medium of vision. The verb *tychôn*, "attaining to it," seems here to describe simple, mystical contact (as opposed to 11, 16 and 24, where it includes the whole range of intellect). The imagery from the *Republic* (509 a) is picked up again in 11, 16, and following: knowledge and truth are good-formed by virtue of the Good's light, and this light creates intelligible and sensible beauty (11, 26 ff.). This anticipates the theme of the next dialectical enquiry into intelligible beauty (V, 8 [31]).[107]

3.30. The simplicity and playfulness of the image (III, 8, 11)

Chapter 11 moves to a new level of simplicity: seeing and the movement of potency to act (1–6); filling (6 ff.; 39 ff.); uttering (12; and the theme of no addition to the Good, which complements that of removal or abstraction earlier in negative theology); needing, desire, and attainment in the context of the light-trace from the Good and its giving (15–26); entering into and becoming one with it; the shock of amazement (32–3); interior seeing and fullness (36–44). All forms of desire and potency based in some way or other upon the Good and internal to the ordinary activities of life (from perception, speech, wandering meditation, natural curiosity, and amazement) are expressive in their different ways of an experience that goes together with intellect's convergence on form. And they have a kind of contingent but powerful playfulness: the trace (*ichnos*)—the sort of thing one has

---

107. On dialectic, cf. *Ennead* I, 3 (20), and V. Jankélévitch, 1998.

to hunt or track down (cf. latin, *vestigium*: footprint)[108]—"runs over" intellect (21) while the "fullness" (*koros*) of intellect becomes in the wordplay of dialectic a "child" (*koros*) of the One like a "toy" or "doll" (again, *koros*) in which everything is included (cf. III, 8, 5, 7; and perhaps an additional argument for the reading *koroplathai* "doll-makers" at 2, 7). At any rate, this situates the human playfulness of dialectic that opens the treatise within the divine playfulness of the Good that concludes it.

Three final points need to be made here. First, the interpretation of myth. Plotinus' reference to intellect as *koros* (child, fullness, toy) is part of his interpretation of the ancient Hesiodic myths about the generation of the gods Ouranos, Kronos, and Zeus.[109] The interpretation of poetic and philosophical myth is itself a philosophical enterprise and must have been a bone of contention among the Gnostics who appropriated and developed the whole field of mythical discourse.[110]

Second, the problem of intelligible matter. Since intellect is complex, there must, Plotinus thinks, be a distinction between matter and form in it. Whereas form in the sensible world merely covers or adorns the matter, form in the intelligible world expresses entirely what the matter is so that both are one "whole, illuminated substance" (cf. II, 4 [12] 5, 12–23). Scholars are divided about Plotinus' view of intelligible matter. Some are of the view that it marks a departure from his usual accounts of the intelligible world or that it is an earlier kind of description that disappears in later works. Others are of the opposite view that it remains integral to Plotinus' thought but are most persuaded that it brings together too many different philosophical strands—Platonic "greatest kinds" (being, sameness, otherness, motion, rest from the *Sophist*); "unwritten doctrines" (the One and the indefinite dyad); Aristotelian potency—and so creates terminological confusion.[111] However, intelligible matter seems to be so essential to Plotinus' complex language about intellect's origin, return, termini of being, and need, that it would be incoherent if it were *not* to include indefiniteness and potentiality (or as he puts it in an important passage, "shapelessness" like the maker [VI, 7 (38) 32, 31–39; cf. 33, 28–38]) (cf. Corrigan, 1996a, 273 ff.; 281 n 58). So chapter 11 consciously brings together the Platonic and Aristotelian sides of this first treatise in the big work: in the medium of good-forming light, the movement of potency to act is perhaps the simplest form of procession and conversion: "intellect is a kind

---

108. Cf. Bonaventure's usage, i.e., *vestigia Dei*, in his *Itinerarium mentis in Deum* (written in the 13th century A.D.).

109. On this theme generally and in the *Großschrift* see Hadot, 1981, and Pepin, 1976, 190–209.

110. For Plotinus' understanding of mythical exegesis see III, 5 (50) 9, 24–29, and V, 8 (31) 10–13 below.

111. E.g., Merlan, 1975, 125, 133–5; Heinemann, 1921, 174–6; Armstrong, 1955, 278; Rist, 1962, 99–107; Szlezák, 1979, 82–95; Bussanich, 1988, 118–20.

of sight ... a potency/power (*dynamis*) that has come into actuality" (11, 1–2). Plotinus otherwise fastidiously avoids any notion of a potential intellect (though in III, 8, 11, plainly he does not mean potency in the Aristotelian sense). In his *De Anima*, Alexander of Aphrodisias identifies three phases of ordinary development in intellect: (1) the material (*hylikos*); (2) the dispositional (*en hexei*); and (3) the actual (*en energiai*).[112] Plotinus avoids such developmental terminology because intellect for him is not like a material developmental progression but whole-formed: "actual seeing also has a doubleness to it; before seeing at any rate it was one. So the one has become two and the two one. In seeing, then, filling and a kind of perfection come from the sensible object, whereas for the sight of intellect the good is that which fills" (11, 4–8).

3.31. Conclusion: Some answers to frequently asked questions about Plotinian Neoplatonism

At this point in our reading of III, 8, we are in a strong position to answer some frequently asked basic questions about Neoplatonism. These are: (1) Is Plotinian Neoplatonism pantheistic? (2) Is emanation or derivation-theory just a sort of divine reflex-action? Or, in other words, does the One produce simply out of necessity? (3) Is there a genuine doctrine of creation here—at least in something resembling the notions of divine creation that we find in the Jewish, Christian, and Islamic traditions? (4) Even if Neoplatonism avoids pantheism, does it not really obscure the problem of identity so that it is really the One that is the true subject of everything?

3.31.1. Is Plotinian Neoplatanism pantheistic?

The answer to (1) above is clear. Plotinus' thinking can in no way be described as pantheistic. If the One is neither a single individual—whether intelligible or physical, nor all the individuals together, whether collected or simultaneous, nor the unity in anything else, whether the "one" of intellect, soul, or nature—then the One is not everything and everything is not "god." Yet Plotinus does say conspicuously: "The One is all things and not a single one of them" (V, 2 [11] 1, 1). But this is an appropriate way of speaking from the perspective of *power*, which is not the perspective of determinate reality and therefore not pantheistic. The very next words in V, 2 (11) 1, indicate the indeterminate, future and past-tensed (and double-fronted) forms of language intended: "it is the origin of all things, not all things, but all things according to the way of that (*ekeinôs*); for in a special way all things ran in the One; or rather not yet are they, but they will be." For Plotinus, of course, *god* is a term used not only of the One but also of intellect and the heavenly, visible gods of this universe (the sun, stars, etc). Here too it is clear

---

112. Cf. Alexander, *De Anima* 84, 24 ff. (Bruns).

that while everything is indeed dynamically interconnected and from within "I," "you," and "cats" and "trees" are precisely these substances and not the "visible gods." But what about the case of intellect itself? In V, 8 (31) 4, Plotinus says strikingly that each thing *is* everything else: "and the sun there is all the stars and each is the sun and everything else." But the point to understand here is that each thing is not *simply* everything else, i.e., one-on-one in unit form. It is "everything," but also itself: "and in each a different thing stands out, but all things are manifest too" (V, 8 [31] 4, 10–11). This, as I have argued above, is Plotinus' way of speaking about substance, and it certainly does not commit him to any form of pantheism.

3.31.2. Does the One produce out of necessity?

The answer to (2), does the One produce out of necessity, again has to be negative. In the sense that this question is posed, *necessity* usually means either simple or brute necessity or some form of determinism (the One just has to overflow in this way). But simple or brute necessity is more the characteristic of matter for both Plotinus and Aristotle and the sort of necessity that is really interesting for either thinker is what we might call "conditional necessity"; that is, the view that the matter has to have a certain kind of structure or condition *if* a certain goal or mature form is to be realized.[113] Conditional necessity, therefore, is conducive to finality or intelligibility and involves the matter being so structured as to be already included within the form. But clearly the One does not produce either by brute or conditional necessity. Does it then provide by epistemic necessity or a form of determinism? Plotinus, for instance, characterizes scientific thinking belonging to intellect as *necessary* and the sort of thinking that is appropriate to soul as *persuasion* or *faith*.[114] The principle of non-contradiction, for instance, or that of identity, we might consider to be necessary epistemic truths that we simply have to accept. So maybe it is in this sense of necessary as inexorable determined laws that the One produces.

Again, however, this is clearly not Plotinus' view for the following reasons. First, the One establishes everything else and is not determined or necessitated by anything outside or inside itself. Pure singularity is free self-giving. Second, Plotinus appears to be of the view that while soul can doubt everything and therefore always needs persuasion and the "charms" of speech and dialectical argument, intellect cannot really be a self-doubter because its very being is self-authenticating. Since its truth is not an image (as it is for soul), it literally *is* its own epistemic necessity. The case of the One, however, is different again, for it clearly can be doubted. Its very simplicity, indeterminacy—its hidden nature—seem to invite doubt. Ennead III, 8, 10, lines 25–35, make this clear. Epistemic necessity or de-

---

113. For the notion itself see Aristotle, *Physics* II, 9.
114. V, 3 (49) 6, 9–10; cf. VI, 7 (38) 40, 3–5.

terministic certainty are not characteristic of our approach to the One. Yes, we can ask, if it is the foundation "of things that really exist in truth, shall we lose trust and suspect it is nothing?" (10, 27–8). Hardly, but Plotinus freely admits there is a problem here since if nothing can be predicated of it and if one must relinquish everything, including self-possession and self-determination, if one is to attain to it in the simplest but deepest form of with-ness, then doubt, vulnerability, perplexity, pain, and desire more characterize such union than self-certainty and automatic reflex. "You will be amazed" (10, 32) would be a better characterization of how Plotinus regards the One's production.

Finally, this analysis is borne out by one of Plotinus' most important theological works, "On free will and the will of the One" (VI, 8 [39]; see chapter 1, part II, 1.2), in which while emphasizing the One's transcendence, Plotinus shows how the analysis of human freedom can help to illuminate what we mean when we speak of freedom, judgement, and constraint in other contexts and how the One can thus be said in the highest unrestricted sense to will freely both itself and everything else it produces (see especially chapters 13 and 18, and Leroux, 1990; O'Meara, 1993, 68–9). So unrestricted, generous freedom and will characterize the One's production. Consequently, while a host of environmental and external influences have a bearing upon the limitations of human freedom, in our essential natures, which have come to us from soul, intellect, and the One, we are capable of freedom, and providence too only assists the working out of that freedom: wicked action is done neither by providence nor in accordance with providence, Plotinus argues in the second of his two works on the topic, III, 2–3 (47–48), but the action of the temperate person "is not done by providence, because it is done by the person himself, but is done according to providence" (III, 3, 5, 46–49).

3.31.3   Do the Enneads contain a doctrine of creation?

If the above is true, it should follow that Plotinus' work offers a genuine doctrine of creation, not in the sense that the world comes into being at a definite moment in history or that there is any first moment of time, for time unfolds as such, for Plotinus, out of eternity in the soul's movement between two different dimensions (the intelligible and physical worlds) (III, 7 [45] 11). So the world is eternal in the sense that there was never any moment when it was created, but it is created in the sense that there is no moment in which the divine creativity ceases to act. If creation is not a reflex but a freely willed outpouring or undiminished self-giving out of the One's *in*-finity, or *no*-thingness, then Plotinus' theory can, of course, be critically compared with some of its more favoured Western cousins, as its apophatic side has rightly been compared with some of its Eastern counterparts.[115]

---

115. For a balanced assessment of the problem in context, see R. T. Wallis, 1972 (new ed., 1995), 102–3 (and 64, 86).

3.31.4. Is the One the only true subject of everything?

In the light of III, 8 (and the rest of the *Großschrift*), too, it is clear that the One is not the real hidden subject of everything that annuls any other genuine subjectivity or real agency in the *Enneads*. This is a misunderstanding, I think, not only about Neoplatonism but also about the nature of a Platonic "Form," the *auto*, "itself," or *auto kath'auto*, "itself in itself." The Platonic Form is not a type or a universal or a bland homogeneity (as the term *monoeides* [*Symposium* 211 b 2] might suggest if translated with the English "uniform"). Rather, it is the unique unrepeatable individual that is capable of transforming the far less unique individuals that participate in it into what they could be. In a similar fashion for Plotinus, the One does not annul other individual identities or freedoms; it establishes them (even to the extent in III, 8, as I have suggested, of preserving hyper-determinate individual identities).[116] Mystical union might, perhaps, be a different case in which the extinction of any form of identity or individuality is necessitated (for one view of this see Bussanich, 1988). But if the One is "more," not less or a unit, then it is not an extinction like any other—except perhaps the extinction that the passionate lover longs for; that is, as Plotinus and Ps. Dionysius put it, the desire of the lover to belong totally not to themselves but to the beloved. Unconditional erotic love of one person for another, just for the other's sake and with no other utilitarian, moral, intellectual, or spiritual baggage at stake is, for Platonism, only a divine option, for human examples (despite Dover's criticism of "Platonic" love in the *Symposium*) are unfortunately either shot through with the tragic pathos of comic illogicality (as in Aristophanes' divided halves) or pervaded by opposition (as in Alcibiades' love-hate for Socrates).[117] At any rate, for Plotinus, while the "fall" is characterized by soul's wish "to belong only to herself" (cf. V, 1 [10] 1, 1–5), the One's creativity is characterized by the will "to let them exist by themselves," a kind of deeply gracious respect for others: "since he walks above all things [*hyperbebêkôs*], he can make them and let them exist by themselves" (V, 5 [32] 12, 48–49).

---

116. See 3.28 and 3.28.1 above.
117. Cf. Dover, 1980.

Chapter 4

A World of Beauty: From Beautiful Things to Intelligible Shapelessness

Text: Ennead V, 8: On the Intelligible Beauty

1. Since we say[1] that the person who has come into contemplation of the intelligible world and understood the beauty of the true intellect will also be able to form a notion of the father of this world who is beyond intellect, let us try to see and to say to ourselves, [5] as far as it is possible to say such things, how anyone might contemplate the beauty of intellect and of that world. Let us suppose, if you like, that there are two blocks of stone lying close to one another, the one undressed and without a share of art, the other already fashioned by art into a statue of a god or even of some [10] human being, of a Grace or of some Muse, if it is a god, but if of a human being, not of some particular human being, but of one whom art has made from every beautiful human being. The stone that has been brought by art to beauty of form will appear beautiful not from being a stone—for the other stone would have been just as beautiful—but because of the form that art has put into it. [15] This form, then, the matter did not have, but it was in the person who conceived it even before it came into the stone; and it was in the craftsman not inasmuch as he had hands and feet, but because he had a share of the art. This beauty then was in the art, and it was better by far there; for the beauty that was in the art did not come into the stone, [20] but that beauty remains in the art and another came from it that is lesser than it; and not even did this remain pure in itself, nor again did it remain as it wanted to be, but only inasmuch as the stone yielded to the art. And if art makes its product to be of the same quality as what it is and has—and it makes it beautiful according to the forming principle of that which it makes—it is far more beautiful, and truly beautiful [25] since it has the beauty of an art that is indeed greater and more beautiful than anything in the external thing. For to the extent that a thing has been drawn out on its way toward the matter, so much is it weaker than what remains in unity[2] For everything divided departs from itself: if strength, it departs from its strength, if heat, it grows less hot, if power in general, it becomes less powerful, if beauty, [30] less beautiful. And every primary maker must in itself be stronger than what is made; for it is not lack of music that makes a human being musical, but music, and music in the sensible world is made by the music prior to this. But if anyone does not value the arts because they make by imitating nature,[3]

---

1. III, 8, 11, 36–8.
2. Cf. Plato, *Timaeus* 37 d 6.
3. Cf. Plato, *Republic* X 597 b ff.

first we must say that natures also imitate other things, and then one must [35] know that they do not simply imitate what is seen, but they run back up to the forming principles, from which nature comes. Then too one must know that they make many things from themselves and in fact make up by addition whatever is defective in things, since they have beauty. Pheidias also made his Zeus with reference to nothing perceptible, but he grasped what Zeus would be like [40] if he wished to make himself visible to us.

2.   But let us leave the arts, and let us contemplate those things whose works they are said to imitate, natural things which come into being as beauties and that are admitted to be so, all rational and irrational living creatures and, most of all, those of them that have been made successfully, since the one who moulded and crafted them [5] controlled the matter and provided the form he wanted. What then is the beauty in these? It is certainly not the blood and the menstrual fluid; rather, the colour of these is different and the shape is either no shape or something without shape or like that which contains something simple [like matter].[4] Where indeed did the beauty of Helen [10] who was so fought over shine out from or that of all those women like Aphrodite in beauty? Then, too, where does the beauty of Aphrodite herself come from or of any beautiful human being at all, or of any god, of those who have come into our sight or even of those who do not, but have in themselves a beauty that would be seen if we could see it? Is not this beauty a form everywhere that comes [15] upon what has come to be from the maker, just as in the arts we said[5] it came upon their products from the arts? How so? Are the things made and the forming principle upon the matter beautiful, while the forming principle that is not in matter but in the maker is not beauty, that is, this first, immaterial forming principle? But if the mass was beautiful [20] insofar as it was mass, then the forming principle that was the maker, because it was not mass, was beautiful; but if the same form, whether in something small or in something large, moves and disposes the soul of one who sees it in the same way by its own power, then we must not attribute beauty to the size of the mass. And further confirmation is this, [25] that as long as something is external, we do not yet see it, but when it becomes internal, it has moved us. But it comes in through the eyes as form alone; how else could it enter through so small a space? But the size is also drawn along together with it, though it has not become large in mass but large in form. Then again, the maker must be ugly, indifferent, or beautiful. Now, if ugly, it [30] would not make the opposite, and if indifferent why should it make something beautiful rather than something ugly? But, really, nature that crafts such beautiful things is also beautiful much earlier than they, but since we are not accustomed to see any of the things within and do not know them, we pursue the external without realizing that it is the inner which moves things: just as if someone were to look at his own image [35]

---

4.   On this see chapter 4, section 4.3.
5.   V, 8, 1, 18–21.

and without realizing where it came from were to pursue that image.[6] But the beauty of studies and of ways of life, and generally the beauty in souls,[7] makes it clear that what is pursued is different and that beauty does not reside in magnitude. Indeed, it is truly a greater beauty than that, when you see practical intelligence in someone and take delight in it, not looking to [40] his face—for this might be ugly—but letting all shape go, you pursue his inner beauty. But if it does not yet move you, so that you say such a person is beautiful, not even when you look right to the interior at yourself will you take pleasure in the fact that you are beautiful, so that it would be pointless to seek that beauty if you are so disposed; for you will be seeking with something ugly and impure; [45] that is why arguments about these sorts of things are not for everybody; but if you have indeed seen yourself as beautiful, recollect it.

3.   There is therefore in nature a forming principle of beauty, archetype of that in body, and of that in nature a more beautiful archetype in the soul from which the forming principle in nature has also come. Clearest, however, is the forming principle in the serious soul and already advanced in beauty; for it orders the soul [45] and provides light from a greater light that is primarily beauty; and since it is in the soul, it makes us infer what the forming principle before it is like, that which is no longer even in anything else but in itself. That is why it is not even forming principle, but a maker of the first forming principle that is beauty in psychic matter; and [10] this is intellect, always intellect and not sometimes intellect, because it is not brought in from outside to itself. So what image could one take of it? For every image will come from something worse. But, in fact, the image must have come from intellect, so that one apprehends it not by means of an image, but just as if one were to take a particular bit of gold as a sample of all gold, and if the bit that has been taken is not pure, one purifies it [15] in deed or word by showing that this sample is not all gold, but only this bit in the whole mass; so also here it is from the intellect that has been purified in us or, if you wish, from the gods that we grasp what kind of thing is the intellect in them. For all the gods are exalted and beautiful and their beauty is irresistible.[8] But what [20] makes them so? It is intellect, and because intellect is more active in them so that it is visible. For it is certainly not because their bodies are beautiful. For even in the case of those who have bodies, it is not this in which their divine being consists, but it is because of their intellect that these also are gods; they are beautiful precisely in being gods. For indeed they are not thinking sensibly at one time and being foolish at another, [25] but they are always thinking in the impassibility, stability, and purity[9] of intellect, and they know all things and they recognize not human affairs but their own divine things and all that intellect sees. And those gods in heaven—for they have the leisure for it—are al-

6.   Plotinus refers to the Narcissus story. Cf. I, 6 (1) 8, 9–12.
7.   Plato, *Symposium* 210 b–c (see Appendix A, 1).
8.   Plato, *Symposium* 218 e 5.
9.   Plato, *Phaedrus* 247 a–b; 248 a 2–3; 249 a 3–4; *Phaedo* 109 d–e.

ways contemplating, though as if from afar, the things in that higher heaven into which [30] they raise their heads;[10] but the gods in that heaven, all those who have their dwelling place upon it and in it, contemplate as dwelling in the whole of that heaven there—for all things there are heaven, and earth is heaven and sea and plants and animals and human beings, everything of that heaven is heavenly—and the gods in it do not consider human beings [35] or anything else unworthy of the things there because they belong among the things there, and they traverse all the country and region there, while taking their rest.

4.   —For it is to live a life of ease there—[11] and truth is their mother and nurse and substance and nourishment—and they see all things, not those to which coming-to-be is added[12] but those to whom substance belongs, and they see themselves in others; for all things are transparent and [5] there is nothing dark or resistant, but everything is clear to everything right to the interior and all things are clear; for light is transparent to light; everything in fact has everything in itself and then again sees everything in another, so that all things are everywhere and all is all and each is all and infinite the glory; for each of them is great, since even the small is great; and sun there [10] is all the stars, and each is sun again and all things. And in each a different thing stands out, but all things are manifest too. And movement also is pure; for the principle that moves it does not confuse it, as it goes, by being different from it. And rest is not disturbed because it is not mixed with the nonstable;[13] and the beautiful is beautiful because it is not in what is [not?] beautiful. [15] And each walks not as upon alien earth, but the place of each is its very self, and the place from where it came runs together with it, so to speak, as it ascends, and it is not one thing itself and its place another. For the substrate too is intellect and it is itself intellect; it is as if someone were to think in the case of this visible heaven [20] which is in the form of light that this light that is from it grew the stars. Here, however, one part would not come to be out of another, and each would only be a part; but there, each comes along out of the whole and it is simultaneously each and whole; for it appears to be a part, but for one who is sharp-sighted the whole is seen in it, as if someone were to have [25] the kind of sight that Lyncaeus[14] was said to have, even to see into the insides of the earth, a story that talks in the form of riddle of the eyes that exist there. But of the vision there, neither is there weariness nor a filling as would lead to an end of contemplation, for neither was there emptiness so that they might be satisfied in

---

10. Plotinus is thinking of the *Phaedrus* myth, 247 ff., throughout this passage (see Appendix A, 2) as well as the description of the "true heaven and earth" in the *Phaedo*, 109 d ff.

11. Homer, *Iliad* 6, 138.

12. Plato, *Phaedrus* 247 d 7.

13. On the difficulties and interpretation of the text see chapter 4, section 4.8.

14. For the legend of Lyncaeus see *Cypria*, fr. 9, Allen, and Apollonius Rhodius I, 153–55; cf. Plato, *Seventh Letter* 344 a.

coming to fulfillment and their goal; and neither is one thing different from another [30] so that what belongs to one is not pleasing to another with a different content; and things there are untiring. But there is the state of being unfilled, in the sense that fulfillment does not bring contempt for the one who has given fulfillment; for in seeing the subject sees still more, and in beholding itself and what is seen as infinite it follows along together with its own nature; and life has no weariness for anyone, [35] when it is pure; and how could that which lives the best life be weary? Its life is wisdom, not a wisdom provided by reasonings, because she was always all and lacking nothing that would make her need enquiry; but she is the first and does not come from another wisdom; indeed, intellect's very substance is wisdom, and intellect is not itself first, and then wise. And because of this there is no wisdom greater, [40] and science-itself sits here beside intellect as they are manifested together, just as they say in imitation that Justice sits beside Zeus.[15] All such things there are like images, seen in their own light so as "to be a sight for supremely blessed spectators."[16] One might then behold the magnitude and power of wisdom [45] if one sees that she has with her and has made the real beings and all things have followed her, and she is herself the real beings, and they came to be together with her, and both are one, and substance is wisdom there. But we have not come to an understanding of this because we have assumed that the sciences too are theorems and a collection of propositions; but this is not even so [50] in the case of sciences here. But if anyone disputes these matters, we must let these sciences be for the present. And about the science there, which Plato in fact also surveyed and said "it is not one thing in another,"[17] but how this is, he left us to seek and discover, if we say that we are worthy of what we are called [Platonists]—perhaps then it is better [55] if we make our start from here.

5. Everything, in fact, that comes to be, whether products of art or nature, some wisdom makes, and everywhere a wisdom guides the making. But if anyone really makes in accordance with wisdom herself, let us grant that the arts are like this. But the craftsman goes back again to [5] a wisdom in nature, according to which he has come into being, a wisdom no longer composed of theorems but a single whole not compounded from many into one but rather loosened from one into multiplicity. So if one puts this first, it is enough: for no longer is it from another or in another. But if they are going to say that [10] the forming principle is in nature, and that its origin is nature, from where shall we say that nature has it, and does it come from that principle which is different from it? If it is from itself, we shall come to a stop; but if they are to go on to intellect, here we must see if intellect generated wisdom; and if they agree, from where did it generate it? And

---

15. Sophocles, *Oedipus Coloneus,* 1381–2. Plato, *Laws* 716 a 2.
16. Plato, *Phaedo* 111 a 3.
17. Plato, *Phaedrus* 247 d 7–e 1.

if from itself, it is impossible in any other way except if intellect is itself wisdom. [15] So true wisdom is substance, and true substance is wisdom, and the value even of substance is from wisdom and, because it is from wisdom, it is true substance. That is why all those substances that do not have wisdom, insofar as they have become substance because of some wisdom but do not have wisdom in themselves, are not true substances. [20] One must not presume, therefore, that the gods or the supremely blessed see axioms there, but each of the things we speak about there are beautiful images of the kind someone imagined to exist in the soul of the wise man,[18] images not drawn, but really existing ones. That is also why the ancients used to say that the ideas are beings and substances.[19]

6.   And I think that the wise men of Egypt grasped this, whether by precise or native science, and when they wanted to signify anything in a wise way, they did not use the imprints of written letters, which move on outward through words and propositions and imitate sounds and the articulation [5] of axioms, but by drawing picture-images and inscribing in their temples one individual image for each thing, they manifested the non-outward-going nature of that [intelligible world], that is, that each image is a science and a wisdom and a subject and togetherness in one and not discursive reasoning or even deliberation. But later [10] they discovered from out of its togetherness in one an image enfolded already in another and speaking of itself[20] in its outward passage and telling the reasons why things are so, with the result that since what has come into being is disposed so beautifully, if anyone knows how to wonder at it, he says he wonders how this wisdom, which does not have the causes why substance is so, provides them [15] to the things that are made according to wisdom. What is beautiful then in this way and what could only be revealed with difficulty or even not at all by enquiry to be necessarily like this, if indeed anyone could discover it, exists in this way before enquiry and before reasoning; just as—for let us take just one great example of what I mean, which will also fit all cases—

7.   This all then, if we agree that its being and its being of such a kind come from another, are we to think that its maker thought up earth in his own mind and that it had to stand in the middle, then water and its place on earth, and the rest [5] in order right up to the heaven, then all living creatures and the various sorts of shapes for each of them such as they have now and the inner organs for each of them and their other parts, and when each was disposed in this fashion in his own mind, he then set to work? But neither was this kind of conception possible—for

---

18.   Cf. the divine images in the Silenus-figure of Alcibiades' speech in praise of Socrates from Plato's *Symposium* 215 b; 216 e–217 a.

19.   Plato, *Republic* 507 b; 509 b.

20.   In this passage Plotinus is thinking not of sacred writings, but of the purely ideogrammatical symbols on temple walls, which in an ancient way manifested the nondiscursive nature of the intelligible world. The later discovery of writing and of discursive scientific explanation is what is at issue here. Compare Plato, *Phaedrus* 274 b ff.

where did it come from for one who had never seen it?—[10] nor was it possible for one who took it from somebody else to put it into production in the way that contemporary craftsmen make by utilizing their hands and tools, for both hands and feet come later. There remains, therefore, only the possibility that everything exists in something else, and since there is nothing in between, because of the closeness of that world to something else, suddenly, as it were, there appeared a likeness and [15] image of that, whether directly from itself or through the service of soul—it makes no difference at present—or of a particular soul. At any rate, all of these things here together were from there and exist there more beautifully; for what is here has been mixed, while those are not mixed, but then this universe is covered by forms from beginning to end: and first, matter [20] by the forms of the elements, then other forms upon forms, then others again, so that it is even difficult to find the matter hidden under the many forms. And since matter too is a last form, this world is all form, and all things in it are forms; for its paradigm was form; and they were made noiselessly, because the maker was all substance [25] and form; that is also why the craftsmanship of intellect is without toil; and it was the craftsmanship of an all so that it would be an all.[21] There was therefore nothing to obstruct it and even now it has control, even though different things have come to obstruct one another, but not in its craftsmanship, not even now; for it remains as an all. And I think that if we were archetypes and substance and forms simultaneously and [30] if the form that makes here were our substance, our craftsmanship too would have control without any trouble. And yet the human being also crafts a form other than himself since he has become other than what he is; for he has fallen away from being the all now that he has become human being; but when he stops being a human being he "walks on high," he [Plato] says, "and directs [35] the whole universe"[22]; for once he has come to belong to the whole he makes the whole. But the argument has this goal, to show that you can explain the cause why the earth is in the middle and the reason why it is round and why the ecliptic is slanting in the way it is; but it is not that things were planned in this way because it was necessary for them to be so, but because things there are so disposed as they are that even these things [here] [40] are beautifully disposed; just as if before the syllogism that showed the cause the conclusion was there, not derived by way of the premises; for it is not the result of a chain of rational consequences or of purposive thought, but is before rational consequences, and purposive thought; for all these are later, reasoning, demonstrations, and conviction.[23] For since it is an originative principle, all these things spring directly from itself and in their own way; [45] and that we should not seek the cause of a principle is

---

21. I.e., the sensible world. Ficino takes this differently: *sicut et ipse faber est universum;* and Armstrong differently again: "And it is the fashioning of an All, so an All is the maker."

22. Plato, *Phaedrus* 246 c 1–2. For Plotinus' anthropology see chapter 2, section 5.

23. Compare VI, 7 (38) 1–2.

well said[24] in just this sense, and of an originative principle of this kind, the complete originative principle that is identical to the goal;[25] and that which is origin and goal, this is the all, completely together and without deficiency.

8.   Beautiful therefore primarily, both as a whole and everywhere as a whole, so that no parts fail by being deficient in beauty—who will then deny it is beautiful? For one would definitely not call beautiful that which is not beautiful as a whole itself, but has a part of it or not even any of it; or if that is not beautiful, what else is? [5] For what is before it is not even willing to be beautiful; for what primarily passes into vision by being form and spectacle of intellect, this too is a delight to see. This is also why Plato, wanting to point this out with reference to something more active in relation to ourselves, makes the demiurge approve his completed product,[26] thereby [10] wanting to show how delightful is the beauty of the paradigm and the idea. For whenever someone wonders at anything modelled in something else, he directs his sense of wonder to that model in whose likeness the thing has been made; but if he does not know what he experiences, this is no wonder, since lovers also[27] and in general those who have a sense of wonder at the beauty here do not know that it is because of that intelligible beauty; [15] for it is because of that. And that he refers the "was delighted" to the paradigm, he (Plato) deliberately makes clear by what he says in the following passage; for he says: "he was delighted and wanted to make it still more like the paradigm,"[28] showing what the beauty of the paradigm is like [20] by saying that what has come to be from this is also beautiful itself as an image of that. For if that were not supremely beautiful with an irresistible beauty, what would be more beautiful itself as an image of that. For if that were not supremely beautiful with irresistible beauty, what would be more beautiful than this visible world? So those who censure this world do not do so correctly, unless perhaps on the grounds that it is not that world.

9.   Let us therefore take by discursive thought this world, each of its parts remaining what it is without confusion, taking all together into one,[29] as far as possible, so that when any one part shines forth, for example, the outer sphere, there follows immediately [5] the imagination of the sun and together with it the rest of the stars and earth and sea and all the living creatures are seen, all as could in fact be seen within a transparent sphere. Let there be, then, in the soul a shining imagination of a sphere that has everything in it, whether moving or at rest or some things [10] moving and some at rest. Keep this and take another from yourself removing the mass; and remove too the places and the imaginative picture of

24. As Aristotle says, *Physics* 188 a 27–30.
25. Cf. Aristotle, *Nicomachean Ethics* 1143 b 9.
26. Plato, *Timaeus* 37 c 7.
27. Plato, *Phaedrus* 250 c 7–b 1.
28. Plato, *Timaeus* 37 c 7–d 1.
29. Anaxagoras, *DK*, fr. 31.

matter in you, and do not try to take another sphere smaller in mass than it, and calling upon the god who made that of which you have the imaginative picture, pray him to come. [15] And may he come, bearing his world with all the gods in him, he who is one and all of them, and each god is all the gods united in their being together, and different in their powers, but by that one, multiple power they are all one; rather, the one god is all; for he does not himself fail if all those gods become him; and they are all together and [20] each is separate again in a rest without interval, possessing no perceptible shape—for already one would be in one place and one in another, and each would not in fact be all in himself—nor even does each have different parts in different gods from himself, nor is each like a power cut up into pieces that is as large as the measure of the parts. But it is [25] all power, going on to infinity and powerful to infinity; and that god is so great his parts have also become infinite. For what place can we speak of where he is not already there? Great then also is the heaven and all the powers together in it, but it would have been greater, and how much greater [30] it would not have been possible to say, if some small power of body did not dwell together with it. And yet one might say that the power of fire and the other bodies are great; but already it is by inexperience of this power that they are imagined burning and destroying and squeezing and assisting in the generation of living creatures. [35] But these things destroy because they are also destroyed and they work together to generate because they are also themselves generated; but power there has only its being and only its being beautiful. For where could its beauty be if it were stripped of being? For in being deficient of beauty, it would also be lacking [40] in substance. That is why being is something longed for because it is identical with the beautiful, and the beautiful is lovable because it is being. And why must we seek which is the cause of the other when they are one nature? For this false substance needs an image of beauty to be brought in from outside itself so that it may appear or be beautiful in any way at all, and it is beautiful [45] in proportion as it has shared in that beauty which is in accordance with form, and when it takes this, to the degree it manages to take it, it is still more perfect; for it is more substance insofar as it is beautiful.

10.   For this reason too Zeus, although the oldest of all the other gods whom he himself leads, goes forth first to the vision of this god, and the rest of the gods, spirits, and souls who have power to see these things follow him.[30] But he [5] appears to them out of some invisible place and rising from on high upon them he illuminates everything and fills them with his radiance and dazzles those below, and they turn away since they do not have the power to see such things as the sun. Some there are who endure him and look; but others are thrown into confusion in proportion to their distance [10] from him. But those who see, that is, all those who have the power to see, look to him and to what belongs to him; and each does

---

30. Plato, *Phaedrus* 246 e 4–6; 247 a 7; 248 a 1 (Appendix A, 2).

not always take the same vision, but one who looks intently sees the fountainhead and nature of justice shining out and another is filled with the vision of self-control, not the sort human beings [15] have from themselves when they have it; for this is in some measure an imitation of that; but that self-control, seated over all, and running all over the magnitude of intellect, as it were, is seen finally by those who have already seen many clear visions, the gods individually and every one together, the souls who see everything there and have come to be from everything, so as [20] to embrace everything themselves too from beginning to end; and they are there insofar as they have a nature to be there, but often, in fact, the whole of them is there when they were not divided. So Zeus sees these things, and in his company any of us who share his love, and finally he sees, abiding over all, beauty as a whole, even as he participates in the beauty there; [25] for it gleams out upon all and fills those who have come to be there, so that they themselves also become beautiful, just as, it often happens, people who go up to high places where the earth has taken on a golden-yellow tinge are filled with that colour there and made like that earth upon which they have walked. But there the colour [30] that comes into bloom upon it is beauty, or rather it is all colour and beauty from its depths, for what is beautiful is not other than itself, like a bloom upon something different. But the exterior impression is the only concern of those who do not see it whole, while for those who are completely drunk, so to speak, and filled with the nectar,[31] since the beauty has permeated the whole soul, it is not possible simply to become spectators. [35] For there is no longer one thing outside and then another in turn outside looking at it, but the sharp seer has what is seen in himself, although since he has many things, he does not know that he has it and looks at it as if it were outside, because he looks at it as if it were an object seen and because he wants to look at it. Everything one looks at as a spectacle one looks at from outside. But one must already transfer what is seen into oneself [40] and look at it as one and look at it as oneself, just as if someone possessed by a god, taken over by Phoebus or one of the Muses,[32] could make the vision of the god in himself if he had the power to look at god in himself.

11.   And further, any one of us who is unable to see himself, when he is possessed by that god and brings forth the object of vision to see it, brings forth himself and looks at an image of himself rendered beautiful; but letting the image go, beautiful though it is, and coming to unity with himself [5] and no longer making any division, he is all one together with that god noiselessly present and is with him as much as he can be and wants to be. But if he returns again to two, while he remains pure he is close to him, so that he is present to him again in that way if he turns back to him again. And in the turning he has this to gain; [10] as he begins, he perceives himself while he is different from the god; but running inward he has

---

31. Plato, *Symposium* 203 b 5.
32. Plato, *Phaedrus* 245 a 1–2.

everything, and leaving perception behind him in his fear of being different from god, he is one there; and if he desires to see by being different, he makes himself external. But he must, in coming to learn about the god, remain within an imprint of him and [15] exercise discrimination in seeking him [i.e., the god] to determine[33] what he is entering into; and when he has learned in good faith that he is entering into the most blessed thing, he must already give himself to what is within and become, instead of one who sees, already an object of vision of another who contemplates him shining out with such thoughts as come from there. How then will anyone be in beauty [20] if he does not see it? No doubt, if he sees it as different he is not yet in beauty, but when he has become it, in this state he is above all in beauty. If seeing then is of something external, there must not be seeing or only a seeing as to be identical with its object. This is a kind of understanding or intimate perception of itself that takes care not to stand off from itself by wanting to perceive too much. And one must [25] reflect upon this too, that the perceptions of evils have stronger impact upon us, but leave less knowledge because it is driven out by the strength of the impact; for sickness strikes us more, but quiet companionable health gives us a better understanding of it; for it comes to sit beside us since it is our own and is united with us. Sickness is something alien and not our own, [30] and so thoroughly obvious because it appears to be very different from us. But we have no perception of what belongs to us, and since we are like this, we are comprehensible to ourselves when we have made self-knowledge one with ourselves. So there too, when we are most in accordance with intellect, we seem to know nothing because we await the experience of perception, [35] which says it has not seen; for it did not see nor ever would see such things. That which lacks trust then is perception, but it is the other who sees; certainly, if that one were to distrust as well, not even would he trust in his own existence; for he certainly cannot place himself outside and look at himself as an object of perception for the eyes of the body.

12. But we have said how he can do this as another and how as himself. At this point when he sees, however, whether as another or as remaining himself, what report does he bring back? He reports, no doubt, that he has seen a god labouring to give birth to a beautiful offering, a god who has indeed generated everything in himself and who has the child of his painless [5] birth labour in himself; for he has been pleased with what he has given birth to and takes delight in his offspring and so has kept everything with him[34] in his gladness to receive his own and their splendour; and while the other beautiful and still more beautiful children have remained within, Zeus was the only child among them to appear to the external world. Though he is the youngest[35] son, [10] it is from him that one

---

33. Plato, *Republic* 516 e 8.
34. Hesiod, *Theogony* 459.
35. Hesiod, *Theogony* 478.

can see, as if from some likeness of him. But he says that it was not in vain that he came from his father; for his other world that has come to be beautiful had to exist, as an image of beauty; for it was not at all lawful that there should not be a beautiful image of beauty and [15] substance. Indeed, it imitates the archetype in every way; for it also has life and what belongs to substance, as an imitation, and it has its being beauty, since it is from there; and it really has in fact its eternal being as an image; otherwise at one time it will have an image and at another it will not since the image has not come to be by means of art; but every natural image exists as long as the archetype [20] remains. That is why those who destroy the image while the intelligible remains and generate it in such a way as if its maker deliberately planned to make it are not right[36]; for they are not willing to understand the mode of such making and not even do they know that as long as that shines out, the rest of things will never fall short; as long as it exists, these also exist; but it was [25] always and will be. For we have to use these words out of the necessity of wanting to signify what we mean.

13.   The god, therefore, who has been bound so as to remain the same and who has given up rule of this universe to his son[37]—for it was not in his character to give up his role there and go after a younger and later role than his own, when he had a surfeit of beautiful things [there]— [5] letting these things go, has established his own father[38] in himself, and extends upward as far as him; and he has established also again on the other side what begins from his son to be after him, so that he has come to be in between both, by the otherness of his severance from what is above, and by the bond that holds him up from what comes after him on the side below; [10] he is in between a better father and a lesser son. But since his father was still too great to be ranked according to beauty, he himself remained primarily beautiful, though the soul is also beautiful; but he is still more beautiful than soul, because there is a trace of him in soul and by virtue of this trace, soul is beautiful by nature, but more beautiful still [15] when she looks there. If the soul of the all, then, to speak more familiarly, that is, Aphrodite, is herself beautiful, what is that?[39] For if her beauty is from herself, how great must that beauty be? But if it comes from another, from whom does soul have the beauty that comes to her from outside and that is native to her substance? For, when [20] we ourselves

---

36. Perhaps the Gnostics or the Stoics; cf. *SVF* 98. Theiler cites Aristotle, fr. 19 Ross; fr. 20 from Cicero, *Lucullus*, 119.

37. Kronos is "the god" and Zeus is his son.

38. I.e., Ouranos.

39. So far in this treatise Plotinus has identified Zeus with soul, but here (as in III, 5 [50] 2 ff. and VI, 9 [9] 9, 13) he slips into what is probably a more natural way of understanding soul as Aphrodite (from Plato's *Symposium* and originally from Pausanias' speech). To interpret or use the *Symposium* in this way looks like a highly uncritical use of texts, but the question really turns upon how Plotinus might reasonably interpret the *Symposium* as a whole.

too are beautiful, it is also by belonging to ourselves; but we are ugly when we pass over to another nature; and in knowing ourselves we are beautiful, but ugly when we do not know ourselves. Beauty then is there and comes from there. Is what we have said, then, sufficient to lead to a clear understanding of the intelligible place[40] or must we go back again and take up another path,[41] in this way?

---

40. Plato, *Republic* 517 b 5.
41. This leads into the next part of the work: V, 5.

Part II: Commentary

4.1. Introduction: The importance of V, 8 and its major issues

Treatise V, 8 is no simpler than III, 8, and we would be mistaken to assume that Plotinus simply says much the same sort of thing everywhere. These two treatises, it is true, are part of the single "big work" divided by Porphyry into four parts, but each treatise does something rather different. Treatises V, 8 (31), *On intelligible beauty*, and V, 5 (32), *That the Intelligibles Are Not Outside the intellect and on the Good*, are new beginnings of a dialectic designed to deepen, amplify, and change our understanding so far, as well as to provide a theoretical framework for the explicit critique of the Gnostics that follows in II, 9 (33), *Against the Gnostics*, or according to Porphyry's more revealing title in the *Life of Plotinus*, chapter 24, *Against those who say that the universe and its maker are evil*. Why is V, 8, important? What other treatises in the *Enneads* are useful companions to this work? What are the problems at issue in the work? Against whom, for example, is Plotinus arguing and upon what forms of thought is he building?

Why is V, 8, important? (a) Because it creates an entirely new way of looking at beauty in nature, art, self, soul, and intellect—a way indicated certainly in Plato, Aristotle, and the Stoics, and prepared for in III, 8, and other treatises but a way that might never have been predicted from a reading of III, 8, or earlier treatises. (b) Because it gives such a vivid picture of the nature of philosophical dialectic: the work of conversation is never self-satisfied or completed. In a universe of infinite possibilities, it always has to start anew. (c) Because in a very concrete way it charts the strengths and limitations of any positive aesthetics and shows at the same time that the theory of intelligible beauty that grounds such aesthetics is not a private universe of religious or apocalyptic persuasions but is open in principle to any scrutiny. And (d) because it helps to establish later, highly important traditions of frequently very different thinking; not only, for example, the immediate Neoplatonist philosophers like Porphyry, Iamblichus (c. 245–325), Proclus (c. 410–485), Synesius (fourth–fifth centuries), Damascius (fifth–sixth centuries), or Boethius (c. 480–525), Pseudo Dionysius (fifth–sixth centuries), Simplicius (sixth century) and Augustine (354–430), but also those later thinkers whose theories of light and beauty, image and architecture, helped both to build the great cathedrals of Europe and to develop the foundations of empirical science; for example Eriugena (c. 800), and Bacon (c. 1214–1294), Grosseteste (c. 1168–1253), and Bonaventure (1221–1274), in the Franciscan tradition, who saw the world as saturated with the traces of divine beauty; also for example, thinkers like Aquinas (1225–1274) and Dante (1265–1321), for even in the aesthetics of Aquinas, the influence of Neoplatonism is clearly discernible in the three qualities of integrity, order, and clarity required for the beauty of real things in the world and in the ultimate character of beauty as a transcendental (still a topic of modern scrutiny in the adolescent conversation of Stephen Daedalus and Cranly in Joyce's *Portrait of the Artist as a Young Man*). In modern times, too, Goethe (1749–1832) translated the beginning of V, 8 (*Letter to Selter*); German Romanticism generally was influenced by Neoplatonist aesthetics, and Kant (1724–1850) and Schelling (1775–1854)[1] particularly saw the question of the beautiful in nature and art as the completion or arch stone of their philosophies (Kant in the third *Critique* and Schelling in the *Philosophy of Art*). In the English tradition, Wordsworth (1770–1850), Coleridge (1772–1834), Shelley (1792–1822), and Keats (1795–1821) transformed Plato and Plotinus into new forms of expression, Shelley (particularly, but not exclusively) in his "Hymn to Intellectual Beauty," as also Keats in the "Ode on a Grecian Urn" ("Beauty is truth, truth beauty . . ."). Coleridge proclaimed Plotinus' definition of beauty "that which is partless, imagined in many" (which he cites in Greek as usual and which he paraphrases in the strangest language as "exciting an immediate and absolute complacency . . .") as the safest and the oldest definition (in *On the Principles of Genial Criticism*, third essay). Finally, in the North American tradition, so-called transcendentalism flourished and one of its major exponents, Emerson (1803–1882), wrote two works about intellectual beauty. If this seems like a long list, it is nonetheless only representative of much larger fields of influence.[2]

What other treatises are useful companions to this work? The first treatise Plotinus wrote, I, 6, *On Beauty*, is interesting in its own right and had a major influence in the Renaissance, partly due to the translation and commentary by Marsilio Ficino (which is collected today in the Creuzer edition). Chapters 20–34 from one of Plotinus' greatest works , VI, 7 (38), *On how the multitude of the forms came into being, and on the Good*, are also useful supplemental reading, as is also the treatise that follows, V, 5 (32), as we shall see below.

What are the problems at issue in the work? Against whom is Plotinus arguing and upon what thought is he building? In I, 6 (1), Plotinus refers to the Stoic definition that beauty consists in the symmetry of the various parts to each other and to the whole and that beauty also depends upon a certain excellence of colour

---

1.   On Schelling and Neoplatonism see especially Gabriel Marcel, 1971, 166–7, W. Beierwaltes, 1972, 100 ff.; 1980a; 1985; 2002.

2.   On Plotinus' influence generally see A. H. Armstrong, 1967, 1990; W. Beierwaltes, 1972, 1985, 1988; P. Hadot, 1968; D. J. O'Meara, 1974, 1983; R. T. Wallis, 1972 (new ed. 1995). See chapter 5.2 below.

(*SVF* 3, 278–9; cf. I, 6, 1, 21). So I, 6 (1), may be taken in part (together with IV, 7 (2), "On the immortality of the soul") as part of Plotinus' refutation of Stoic materialism. Treatise V, 8 (31), is more difficult to determine directly. The occasion for the treatise is Plotinus' remark at the end of III, 8, that as the person who looks up to our visible heaven and sees the splendour of the stars thinks about and seeks their maker, so the one who contemplates the intelligible world must seek its maker (11, 33–7). The "maker" or "craftsman" of this world is, for Plotinus, Plato's demiurge in the *Timaeus* (i.e., intellect or intellect inclusive of soul), but the analogy between the two worlds arises out of the cave image in *Republic* VII. Socrates likens the prison-world and its fire to the visible world, and the upper world of physical things to the intelligible world, illuminated by that which is last to be seen but is the source of truth and intellect, namely, the idea of the good itself (*Republic* 517 a 8–c 5). Aristotle's cave-image (from his lost dialogue *On Philosophy*, a fragment of which is cited by Cicero, *De Natura Deorum* 2, 37), represents industrious, artistic, and technologically competent cave-dwellers who have heard reports of divine power but have never been on the surface of the earth. One day, the earth is opened up unexpectedly and they look upon the magnificence of earth, sea, and heaven, but at night gaze directly upon the whole sky, the stars, the moon waxing and waning, and the heavenly orbits "in all eternity." As soon as they see these things, immediately they think that there are gods and that these are their mighty works. I cite Aristotle's cave-image for two reasons: it is an unforgettable image, as is that of Plato, and it suits Plotinus' positive view of nature and art here in some respects much more than the sedentary chained state of the prisoners in Plato's cave. Plotinus' starting point, however, is not the cave, but two blocks of stone "lying close to one another, the one undressed and without a share of art, the other already fashioned by art into a statue of a god or even of some human being."

What is the particular problem? Plotinus has told us in the lines immediately above: "let us try to see and to say to ourselves, as far as it is possible to say such things, how anyone might contemplate the beauty of intellect and that world" (1, 4–6). We expect something apocalyptic and magnificent but are given instead two stones. What is perhaps at issue is the external, apocalyptic revelations and essentially private world-views, communicated to spiritually gifted individuals by demonic or divine figures that seem to characterize the visions of some Gnostic texts. Plotinus characterizes the Gnostic claim to contemplation as private revelation later in II, 9 (33) 18, 35–6, or, again, as a "private philosophy" (*idia philosophia*)—by contrast with the "ancient philosophy" (*archaia philosophia*)—that is "outside the truth" (II, 9 [33] 6, 11–12). Unlike the action of an ignorant, fallen *Sophia,* or Wisdom (cf. II, 9 [33] 8, 36–9; 43–6; 1, 19–33), which makes piecemeal with a sort of faulty deliberation, Plotinus argues here (as in the case of contemplation in III, 8) that wisdom, far from being private or external to the world, is *the* fundamental form of all natural making, insofar as all artistic and natural objects contain within themselves the seeds of their own whole-formed making in accordance with a *physical Sophia* (cf. V, 8 [31] 5, 1–8). In the account he develops here, this has to be traced back internally to intellect so that one can appreciate the beauty of both worlds in each other, as it were, namely, the *intelligible beauty* of the *aesthetic, actually visible* star-gods (cf. V, 8, 3, 20–36), which the Gnostics, in Plotinus' view, disparage (cf. II, 9 [33] 16, 1–2). So at issue from the start, is the shared world of ordinary experience, language, and thought, distilled into an image of two forms of nonapocalyptic *mass* (1, 7–8: *lithôn en oykôi*).

4.2. What does "the beautiful" mean?

What does *to kalon* ("beauty," or "the beautiful") mean and what range does the term have in earlier thought? *Kalon* means something "fine," "noble," "admirable," "beautiful," and contrasts with *aischron*, "ugly," "shameful," as in Pausanias' speech in Plato's *Symposium*: "if an action is performed in a fine way [*kalôs*] and correctly [*orthôs*] it becomes fine [*kalon*], and if incorrectly, shameful [*aischron*]" (181 a 4–5). Any ordinary distinction between *kalos* and *agathos*, "good," "fine," tends to blur; both are used together generally of the admirable person who sets the right tone: *kalos kagathos*, literally, "beautiful/fine and good." This lack of distinction in ordinary speech provides a subtle irony, again in Plato's *Symposium* when Agathon under cross-examination admits, like the fine gentleman he is, that he did not have the foggiest idea what he was talking about, and Socrates replies: "And yet you said it so beautifully (*kalôs*) . . . but tell me one little thing more; don't you think that the good is also beautiful?" (201 c 1–2). The question has already been answered, for if Agathon spoke *beautifully* (*kalôs*), but not *well* (i.e., not "goodly" or incorrectly), then the beautiful and the good must be different.

So Plato speaks of the beautiful and the good together, but also distinguishes them, conspicuously in the *Republic*, less so in the *Symposium*. In the former dialogue, the form of the good is the ultimate self-disclosing reality, while in Socrates-Diotima's speech in the *Symposium*, though the search to have the "good" forever plays an important heuristic role, it is the beautiful (in the context of speeches on Eros) that ranges in meaning from the beautiful in bodies, souls, pursuits, observances, institutions; that is, the progeny of soul, sciences, the single science of dialectic, and ultimately to the self-disclosing form of the beautiful itself (210 a–212 a).

In the *Phaedrus*, love of beauty is a form of divine madness (249 d–e), so that as soon as the lover of beauty sees the beautiful in this world he falls so desperately in love with it that he wants even to worship his beloved. His soul's wings, which had shriveled into stumps start to throb with the pain of new growth (a highly erotic, psychic image), as he is reminded of the true beauty of the world above, which he saw before birth in the company of the gods (see Appendix A, 2). This context is crucial for Plotinus in V, 8, and particularly for his description of the intelligible world in V, 8, 4,[3] but the overwhelming erotic power of the beautiful (from the *Phaedrus* myth) is more in evidence in I, 6 (1) (e.g., 4, 15–17: "for these experiences must happen [i.e., the experience of passionate excitement in spiritual beauties] whenever there is contact with any sort of beautiful thing, wonder, sweet delight, longing, love, and pleasurable excitement"). In fact, the early treatise seems to take its striking start from *Phaedrus* 250d: beauty in this world is perceived by the "clearest" of the senses, "for sight is the sharpest of the perceptions that come through the body." Compare Plotinus: "The beautiful is mostly in sight. . . ." (I, 6, 1, 1).

So the range in meaning of the term *kalos* that Plotinus inherits comes principally from Plato, but one other related usage in both Plato and Aristotle is important for understanding V, 8, though to my knowledge it is never mentioned. Beauty first strikes us through the senses, makes us notice the world in entirely new ways, especially the beauty of individual things and persons, and helps (or hinders) the ordering of perception and desire. In this sense, beauty of form by its presence or absence can make the world full of intelligibility or empty of meaning, so that we come to ask not just what things are made of but what they are and why it is "good" or "beautiful" for them to be so. This is the substance of Socrates' famous complaint in the *Phaedo* about the earlier philosophers of nature. Anaxagoras, he says, introduces "mind" and then explains everything by purely physical causes, as if we were to explain Socrates' presence in prison on hemlock row by giving a physiological description of his sitting right in front of us rather than by saying what seemed "good" (99 c 5), "best" (98 b 2, 99 a 2, b 1, c1), "better" (98 e 3), or "finer," "more beautiful" (99 a 3: *kallion*) to him. In Aristotle's later language, we could say that a material cause cannot sensibly be substituted in most cases for a formal (not what it is made of, but *what* is it?) or final cause (where is it tending and why should it be so?). Indeed, when Aristotle expresses final causes by the formula "that for the sake of which" or "for the sake of something," he explicitly includes the beautiful in the notion of finality, that is, a notion of inner, nondeliberative purposiveness. In the biological works such as *PA* 645 a, in fact, he argues that in all natural things, even the meanest parts of animals, there is an "amazing" beauty: "the end or goal for the sake of which they have been constructed or come to be has the place of the beautiful." Beauty, therefore, is intrinsic to any consideration of causality, formal or final, but particularly to the final causality that moves all things from within, as Aristotle's intellect is said to move all things "in the sense of being loved" (*Metaphysics* XII, 1072 b3).

---

3.   Compare the less powerfully philosophical versions of this to be found in some of the Sethian Gnostic texts of the Nag Hammadi library, e.g., *Allogenes* XI, 3: 48, 6–49, 37; *Zostrianos* 64, 7–75, 11; trans. in J. Robinson (ed.), 1977.

Formal and final causality, therefore, are like windows open to the beautiful in ordinary things, windows essentially expressive of intellectual beauty,[4] and this insight Plotinus will develop in quite revolutionary ways in V, 8. So now let us turn to Plotinus' examination of the beautiful and first to the question of why beauty is not just harmony or structure of parts in relation to the whole (I, 6 [1]).

4.3. Why is good proportion and structure not "the beautiful"?

Why does Plotinus reject good proportion and colour as an adequate account of beauty? In I, 6 (1) 1, his arguments do not seem very convincing. On the Stoic account, he says, nothing simple will be beautiful. By "simple" (*haploun*), he appears to mean anything taken just in itself—for example, light, gold, lightning, individual sounds, colours, or soul (cf. 1, 32–8). One might reply that these are composite in different ways, but if Plotinus means "simple" in the way we experience them (a single note just in itself, for instance, though an integral part of a larger whole, can be intensely beautiful), then maybe he has a point. But this means, he goes on to argue, that it is wholes—composite things—that are beautiful and not the simple elements of which they are composed. But surely the parts or elements must also be beautiful, he insists, hardly a telling point since he allows elsewhere, as do the Stoics, that some parts of a beautiful play do not have to be beautiful themselves (cf. III, 2 [47] 1) and he argues that opposition, and even apparently deviant forms, are included in the beautiful, providential *logos* (cf. III, 3 [48] chapters 1 and 7; III, 2 [47] 16). The contemporary French notion of "*une belle laide*" (a beautiful ugly face) would seem an obvious counterexample. It is possible for every feature in a face to be individually ugly and yet for the face as a whole somehow to be beautiful. Or conversely, a face can be ugly and yet transfigured by beautiful eyes (e.g., Maria Bolkonsky in Tolstoy's *War and Peace*). I am not sure that we can extricate Plotinus from these difficulties. He is certainly aware of them in other places (the indefinable quality of living beauty in a face, for example). A difficult passage in V, 8, 2 seems to imply that a complex shape is necessary for beauty, in opposition to what Plotinus says in I, 6, 1–2, about the beauty of simple things. The beauty in natural things, he says, "is certainly not the blood and the menstrual fluid" (by which he appears to mean, according to his outdated view of reproduction and embryology, the "matter"); "rather, the colour of these is different and the shape is either no shape or something without shape or like that which contains something simple [like matter]" (2, 6–9). The text and meaning of the passage are doubtful, so much so that we might read it the other way round as implying that form is something simple while matter as the container is amorphous and multiple. Nothing solid, however, can be based on either reading.

---

4. On causality in Aristotle see H. H. Joachim, 1951; M. Nussbaum, 1978; R. Sorabji, 1980; J. M. Cooper, 1982; J. Lear, 1988.

What, then, do Plotinus' objections amount to in I, 6 (1) 1? If beauty is only a question of the symmetry of parts to one another and to the whole, with a little colour thrown in for good measure, then only a compound can be beautiful (which cannot account for our experience of the beautiful as something simple), but also its parts will have to be beautiful if the whole involves the symmetry of the parts. This second part of the argument is not Plotinus' own view but that to which he thinks the Stoics are implicitly committed in their structural account of beauty; that is, a sort of dialectic of consistency between wholes and atomistic parts. The same problem, Plotinus argues, occurs with the Stoic view of soul. If beauty of soul (virtue, knowledge) is a question of proportion, what is the formula for this consistency? As he points out, there can be just as much consistency in bad ideas as in good. So simple consistency is not a sufficient criterion of beauty, goodness, or truth (I, 6, 1, 45–9). In fact, as Plotinus indicates elsewhere, symmetry can be downright boring; the beautifully structured face that once moved us can leave us absolutely cold upon closer or too long acquaintance.

4.4. Is beauty in the eye of the beholder?

What is it we see or sense in the beautiful object (the two stones, for instance) that accounts for the beautiful? Is beauty in the eye of the beholder or is there something more at issue? To a certain extent, beauty always *is* in the eye of the beholder. Plotinian thought could be characterized as "reception or participation according to the mode of the receiver." Furthermore, Plotinus admits the major environmental and social influences, hereditary traits, and so forth that prevent us from getting beyond our own preferences.[5] In fact, what it means to see beyond our own preferences is a major preoccupation of all Platonic thinking. Plato appears to be of the view that, though such a seeing beyond what we want to see, or are conditioned to see, is always possible and is the condition of any intelligent self-conscious life, most of us are demonstrably incapable of doing so most of the time. In the *Symposium*, Agathon is a rarity: a human being who will admit that he has no idea what he was talking about (201 b 10–11). But it is not as if the other speakers are Phaedrus, Pausanias, Eryximachus, Aristophanes, or anyone else for that matter queuing up to admit to their own preferences. The problem, as Diotima so aptly puts it, is that ignorance, a little like Divine wisdom, is not in search of the truth: it thinks it is the truth. So someone who really holds the view that beauty is in the eye of the beholder is constitutionally incapable of accepting any different view. Extreme subjectivism, like relativism, is obviously self-defeating, but less extreme forms of aesthetic subjectivism are more plausible because tastes, times, receptive capacities, and educated minds really do differ and make an enormous difference. "[J]ust as in the case of sense beauties it is impossible for those who have not seen them or grasped their beauty . . . to speak about them, in

---

5.   Cf. K. Corrigan, 1996a, 360 ff.

the same way only those can speak about the beauty of ways of life who have accepted the beauty of ways of life . . ." (I, 6 [1] 4, 4–12).

4.5. What is the beauty of art? (V, 8, 1–2)

Where, then, is the beautiful in the stone fashioned into a statue? And what is
Plotinus' view of art? Like Plato and Aristotle, he tends to come at the inner relation between a thing and its form by the analogy of *techne,* or art, which permits
us to view it in terms of an external transmission. If art is a more external relation
than the working of nature, it can reasonably serve as an analogy for the understanding of nature.

In I, 6 (1) 2, 2–7, Plotinus says that something beautiful is perceptible at the
very first glance, and the soul recognizes and adapts herself to it. In the case of art
in V, 8, 1–2, Plotinus argues that beauty is not a function of matter but of the form
since the form is evidently transmitted by the artist and was therefore "in the person who conceived it even before it came into the stone" (1, 15). The nature of the
form is also of special interest because it can so obviously not be a product of individual imitation but must rather involve imaginative projection, universalized
(yet also perfectly individual) on the basis of experience and crystallized in a particular form ("of a Grace or of some Muse, if it is a god, but if of a human being,
not of some particular human being, but one whom art has made from every beautiful human being").[6] The artistic form does not have to imitate or represent individual physical things since it naturally has an imaginative and intellectual source.
The form is not in the artist as an expression of his or her material nature ("not inasmuch as he had hands and feet"), but rather because the artist "had a share of
the art." In this case, then, beauty is a function of art that expresses itself within
the limitations of a particular medium, dwells in the craftsman not simply as an
expression of his feet or hands, no matter how brilliant the performance, but as art
yet remains more beautiful than either the product or the artist. Plotinus' view

---

6. The German poet Rilke evokes the deeper significance that Plotinus' example suggests. In a poem about reflexive conversion, "Wendung" ("Turning-Point"), Rilke captures
precisely the inner feminine quality ("Grace" or "Muse" in Plotinus) attained from a thousand faces by the "heart-work" and yet still looked at even in an interior way as an art-
object, not yet *known,* "not yet beloved form" (i.e., as one's own other self): "Denn des
Anschauns, siehe, ist eine Grenze./Und die geschautere Welt/will in der Liebe gedeihn./
Werk des Gesichts ist getan, tue nun Herz-Werk/an den Bildern in dir, jenen gefangenen;
denn du/überwältigtest sie: aber nun kennst du sie nicht./Siehe, innerer Mann, dein inneres
Mädchen,/dieses errungene aus/tausend Naturen, dieses/erst nur errungene, nie/noch ge–
liebte Geschöpf" ("For there is a boundary to looking./And the world that is looked at so
deeply/wants to flourish in love./Work of the eyes is done, now/go and do heart-work/on
all the images imprisoned within you; for you/overpowered them: but even now you do not
know them./Learn, inner man, to look on your inner woman,/the one attained from a thou-
sand/natures, the merely attained but/not yet beloved form"), *The Selected Poetry of Rainer
Maria Rilke,* ed., trans., Stephen Mitchell, Vintage, New York, 1982, 134–35.

may look idealistic, but his speaking of the artist's having "a share of the art" (1, 18) makes sense, for the forms we see or experience in art do seem to speak of something much more beautiful than this particular time, place, or artist. Yeats, for instance, writes of the capacity of physical forms to provoke a deeper sense of intelligible power: "all sounds, colours, forms . . . call down among us certain disembodied powers, whose footsteps over our hearts we call emotions" (*Ideas of Good and Evil: The Symbolism of Poetry*). Plotinus goes on to argue that the movement into matter and spatio-temporal extension (as in the case of soul from eternity in III, 7 [45] 11, 23–7) involves a weakening of power and unity, and since the power for the beautiful does not come from the matter alone or from its privation in just this material context, then it must come from the art that is not squandered or used up in its material expression: "for it is not lack of music that makes a human being musical but music, and music in the sensible world is made by music prior to this" (V, 8, 1, 31–2; I, 6, 3, 28–36). Or as Keats puts it, "Heard melodies are sweet, but those unheard/Are sweeter; therefore, ye soft pipes, play on; Not to the sensual ear but more endear'd/Pipe to the spiritual ditties of no sense" ("Ode on a Grecian Urn"). Compare I, 6 [1] 3, 28–31: "The melodies in sounds too, the imperceptible harmonies that make the perceptible ones, make the soul become aware of beauty in this way, showing the same thing in another medium."[7]

Plotinus suggests then that the beauty of form is itself more beautiful than the things that participate in it because (a) the matter and the medium are not the simple sources of the beauty they express but a limitation and privation rather of what they attempt to express and (b) the artist has access to intelligible being and can therefore *create* the more-than-individual, the improvement upon nature, and the divine-which-should-be in concrete visible form. Art therefore has a natural anagogical function. For all its indirectness, the call to return to intelligible being is in some respects more direct in art than in nature. Plotinus' positive view of art certainly anticipates its reception in the Renaissance, but his way of indicating a departure from the Platonic criticism of mimetic art ("But if anyone does not value the arts . . ."; 1, 32–3) as the sole criterion of artistic sensibility shows that he does not believe this to have been Plato's only view of art itself (on which see 3.12 above).

4.6. Why is intelligible beauty bound up with the perception of natural things? (V, 8, 2)

Why is intelligible beauty so bound up with the perception of natural things (V, 8, 2)? Our emphasis upon the visible product tends to skew our judgement and make us discount the beauty of the forming principle in the artist just because we cannot

---

7.   Cf. Heraclitus, *DK*, fr. B 54: "The imperceptible melody is greater than the perceptible one."

see it. But when it comes down to the mind or soul, beauty is not a question of mass. The forms of anything, large or small, have the power to enter into us and change us (2, 21–4), which makes it clear that mass is not the criterion of beauty. We can resist a form's power or just fail to notice it (24–5), but when a form really reaches our attention, "becomes inside" (25), it moves us. This is because its beauty springs from nature, a dynamic internal principle itself (or together with nature, *from us* by virtue of soul). So like Narcissus attempting to become one with his reflection in water, we pursue external objects without realizing that we cannot grasp them except superficially in that way. Instead, we have to grasp them by what links us, the reflexive immaterial medium of soul (or as Plotinus calls it in 3, 9, "psychic matter"), rather than by what separates us, the reflective medium of matter.[8] There is nothing mysterious or ghostly about this because we experience it all the time in the beauty of studies, ways of life, and souls, as Plato puts it in Diotima's ladder of ascent (Appendix A, 1). Or when we *see* practical intelligence in Socrates, we take delight in it and just do not notice the ugly face. But the proper form of this reflexive medium, Plotinus goes on to suggest, is the inner beauty not of other things but of oneself. This apparently is a question of *recollection;* that is, of recalling an intelligible form: if one is not yet moved by the interior beauty of another, one will not take pleasure in one's own beauty, "but if you have indeed seen yourself as beautiful, recollect it" (2, 45–6).

In I, 6 (1) 8–9 Plotinus speaks of shutting one's eyes and of waking up to a different, interior form of seeing in order to grasp the beauty of a good soul. There follows a famous passage inspired by Plato's *Phaedrus*, which was in turn to inspire the Christian writer Gregory of Nyssa in the next century[9]:

> Go back to yourself and see; and if you do not yet see yourself as beautiful, then, as the maker of a statue that has to be beautiful cuts away here and polishes there, makes one part smooth and another clear until he has shown a beautiful face in his statue, so you also cut away anything that is superfluous

---

8.   Cf. Rilke: "Durch den sich Vögel werfen, ist nicht der/vertraute Raum, der die Gestalt dir steigert./(Im Freien, bist du dir verweigert/und schwindest weiter ohne Wiederkehr.)/Raum greift aus uns und übersetzt die Dinge:/dass dir das Dasein eines Baums gelinge,/wirf Innenraum um ihn, aus jenem Raum,/der in dir west. Umgieb ihn mit Verhaltung./Er grenzt sich nicht. Erst in der Eingestaltung/in dein Versichten wird er wirklich Baum" ("What birds plunge through is not the intimate space/in which you see all forms intensified. [Out in the Open, you would be denied/your self, would disappear into that vastness.]/Space reaches from us and construes the world: to know a tree, in its true element,/throw inner space around it, from that pure/abundance in you. Surround it with restraint./It has no limits. Not till it is held in your renouncing is it really there"), *The Selected Poetry of Rainer Maria Rilke*, ed., trans., Stephen Mitchell, Vintage, New York, 1982, 262–3.

9.   See *The Life of Moses* 313, *Patrologia Graeca* 44, ed. Migne, 428 a; also 544 a–d; 1069 b–c.

and straighten what is crooked, purify the dark and make it shine, and do not stop "working on your statue" [*Phaedrus* 252 d 7] until the divine glory of moral virtue shines out on you, until you see "temperance enthroned on its holy seat" [*Phaedrus* 254 b 7]. (I, 6, 9, 7–15)

In the *Phaedrus*, it is the lover who works upon the soul of his beloved, making him "like a statue for himself as though the beloved were a god . . ." (252 d). Plotinus has adapted the image to express the quality of one's own self-relatedness, but this should not be thought to exclude interpersonal relations or to promote a form of self-absorption; this self-relatedness is utterly different from that of Narcissus, as Plotinus has made clear in his allusion to the Narcissus story in the previous chapter (I, 6 [1] 8, 8–16). Plato had explored in the *Republic* what it meant for a human being to be master of himself in terms of the integration of all the parts of the soul: "he binds them all together, and from many becomes altogether one" (IV, 443 d 7–e 1). And Aristotle had subsequently argued in the *Nicomachean Ethics* that in friendships of the deepest kinds (namely, in those friendships based upon the good, in which friends actually recognize one another as other subjects and selves and therefore look out for the deepest good of one another) we glimpse the necessity of developing a better, more authentic self; that is, of becoming lovers of self in a nonegoistic way.[10] So the noble self-relatedness of the good person (his or her concern for goodness, nobility, and justice) is a precondition for the mutuality of a true friendship based on goodness; that is, for the sharing of a single soul in which two human beings can become better together.

Plotinus' view in V, 8, is a little different from I, 6, 9. To recognize the beauty of another thing, he suggests, is to be moved and so disposed in one's own being. To recognise the beauty of another person is, even more so, not to see an object somehow external or indifferent to oneself but to recognize another in and as oneself. Thus, he suggests, we take such delight in seeing the inner beauty of another person (or thing) *for its own sake* because we recognize the ground of that beauty simultaneously in ourselves. What we experience, he argues, is a sheer delight in intelligible beauty for its own sake. This is why he uses the (Platonic) imperative "recollect it." Such beauty overflows a subject/object relation or even the physical divide of two selves seeing each other.

This is important because it demonstrates that the love of such beauty is neither the hankering after an abstract universal nor self-absorption and the refusal to love others as they actually are (charges sometimes levelled, as we have seen in chapter 3 above, against Plato and Platonism generally). If self-recognition is the proper reflexive form of intelligible beauty (i.e., I delight in myself spontaneously as the shared form of delight in the other), then such experience is not abstract universalism or the postponement or manipulation of earthly beauties but the intelligible form of loving the other for the other's sake; that is, *spontaneously* and

---

10. See especially *EN* VIII, 1–9; XI, 8.

not *because* of anything else at all. Plotinus is therefore of the view that when we pursue the external form alone, what we really want cannot be achieved on the level we want it (i.e., ego-object consciousness or Narcissus' attempt to become one with an image) because it is only an image reflected in matter and not integrated yet in the reflexive medium of soul.

What *is* this intelligible beauty we see reflexively in art, nature, and souls? The problem for Plotinus is what sort of image we are to use, since we cannot understand such beauty by anything other than itself. A means of tackling this problem is presented already by the spontaneous delight we take in the inner beauty of another person as our own. Plotinus calls this "the serious soul . . . already advanced in beauty" (3, 4), which does not perhaps sound too enchanting. What he means is that here we find the opening up of light upon light ("for it orders the soul and provides light from a greater light that is primarily beauty"); that is, not only what organizes and orders this shared soul but also what the soul is rooted in (3, 4–8)—intellect, a landscape bigger than that of soul. The organizing principle in the soul "makes us infer" what the one before it is like (3, 6), so we can get an idea of intellect from ordinary reflexive experience and from reflection upon that experience "of the purified intellect *in us*" just as we can, conversely, form a concrete notion of the divine intellect by looking at the sky and *seeing* what intellect means from its activity in the heavenly gods (3, 20 ff.).

What is the purified intellect in us? It appears to be what we essentially are as intelligible beings once the inessential additions and accretions have been stripped away. But we should not conceive of this as a straightforward division between intelligible existence and historical, sensible experience because the purified intellect is at the root of all our existence. Still, we cannot reach it as it is from any perspective but its own, though according to IV, 3 (27) 18, it includes reasoning, if reasoning is an active reflection of intellect, and though according to V, 8, 3, it also includes our ability to see the activity of intellect in the heavenly bodies. Nonetheless, to reach it from its own perspective involves purgation (V, 8, 3, 14–15) and stripping (i.e., taking away). Treatise IV, 7 (2) 10 should be compared with V, 8, 3, (and the gold image):

> It is necessary to examine the nature of each thing in looking to its pure form, since what has been added is always a hindrance to a knowledge of that to which it has been added. Examine it then by stripping away, or rather let the person who has stripped away look at himself and trust that he is immortal when he contemplates himself as he has come to be in the intelligible and pure. . . . For it is certainly not by running around outside that soul sees temperance and justice, but herself by herself in understanding of herself . . . seeing them seated in her like statues rusted with time that she has made pure [cf. *Phaedrus* 247 d ff.]; as if gold was ensouled, then knocked off what was earthy in it, being in ignorance before of itself, because it did not see gold, but then seeing itself already on its own was amazed at its worth. (9, 27–50)

4.7. How are beauty, science, and wisdom related?

There is a problem in the chief account of intelligible beauty (V, 8, 4): Plotinus does not mention beauty at all except once in passing (4, 14–15). In fact, after 3, 23, this is the only reference to beauty in 100 lines. It is not as though chapters 5–7 are full of the subject either. Here again only four mentions of beauty in over 90 lines (5, 22; 6, 12, 15; 7, 40). What does Plotinus have in mind?

For all its possible shortcomings, Plotinus' theory of intelligible beauty offers an alternative way of configuring the relationship among science, wisdom, and beauty. We think of these as separate qualities, but they are expressions for Plotinus of what self-understanding or intellect really is: that is, the complete and inclusive life of all beings in self-understanding, a life in which everything is transparent to everything else, where to understand is to be simultaneously understood and where each is everything yet each is also itself (V, 8, 4 *passim*; see also IV, 3 [28] 18). We might say that each is more itself by being everything, while everything is more because of the each, and this is because each is not a divided part, like a piece of pie), but a new and distinctive form of mutuality in the whole. So when Plotinus says that the visible heavenly gods are beautiful not because of their bodies but because of the visible activity of intellect in them (3,19–23), he apparently means that they are living manifestations of a higher intelligible order. But they are beautiful, he goes on to say more plainly, because they are not silly one moment and thinking intelligently the next (like us most of the time). You can count on them, in other words. Or as Plotinus puts it: "they are always thinking in the impassibility, stability, and purity of intellect" (3, 25). Their beauty as a community of what being means to each other, and presumably as a higher expression even of what a solid friendship will come to mean for us, is already completely open and transparent before we begin to see it. We "have" intellects, but we are not just intellects, so the ways that we make and become our worlds are invariably partial, sometimes self-seeking, but occasionally even we see more holistically, as if by virtue of a beauty that already is everything "irresistibly," to use the word Plotinus cites of the "beautiful itself" from Plato's *Symposium*.[11] The experience of such beauty is not the experience of a fore-ordained blueprint or a menu but more that of divine madness or ecstasy in which one discovers and becomes something new.

Such beauty, Plotinus says in 4, 44–5, is beautiful because it is not dependent upon something other than itself. Unfortunately, the text is corrupt at this point because a negative has crept in that probably should not be there. With the negative included, we could understand Plotinus to say that the beautiful is beautiful because it is not in what is (not) beautiful, which is to say that it is in or is itself. Without the negative, Plotinus would simply say that the beautiful is beautiful because it is not in the beautiful, which is a very dark saying indeed but probably

---

11. Cf. V, 8, 3, 19; 8, 21; *Symposium* 218 e.

only means that the beautiful is not *in* the beautiful because it *is* the beautiful, which amounts to saying the same thing.

The distinction is lost on most and probably escapes even seasoned readers, but it might be helpful to clarify the point further. As we have seen, physical substances are images in the sense that they express a relationship of one "thing" in "another," not literally of two different things but a relationship of dependence—form in matter. We express this relation in propositions by predicating qualities, quantities, and relations themselves of subjects, be they either material, linguistic, or logical. In such cases we try to say what something is like rather than what something really is. There is, however, another form of predication, substantial predication, in which again we express a likeness or dependence of one thing on another, but we *mean* that the subject in this case is essentially characterized by or *is* simply the predicate. In the case of physical substances our essential predications tend to fall short, however: "John is a rational animal (most of the time)," for example, or "she is the heart of the class." We tend to see things in their divided forms, so we take what they are like to be the truth of what they are, but not always: sometimes we *mean* what we say, as when we discover the causes of something and for a moment see the thing in a wholly new, beautiful light because we see it more completely than we have ever seen it before. This is, in fact, what Plotinus means when he says that we can perceive things without their moving us; we can because we have neither feeling for nor understanding of them. When they move us, it is because we come to understand and feel for and through them; this is already an intelligible relation in the soul, yet it is also a real relation in the world, which Plato and Aristotle called causality. To understand what something is and what inner purpose or goal it expresses is already to be moved by its beauty in what is beautiful in us. As Plotinus says elsewhere, "things are beautiful with their cause; since even now something is beautiful because it is everything" (VI, 7 [38] 3, 9–10). Causality, as we experience it, is piecemeal, hit and miss, but the meaningfulness of things that sets up a resonance in our souls is already intelligible beauty; that is, a kind of partial glimpse of everything.

When we come to intellect, we speak of substance *directly*, not of one thing in another but of all things in each other. Leibniz expressed this in his *Monadology*, proposition 56: "each single substance has relations which express all the others, and consequently each is a perpetual living mirror of the universe." The 1948 Latta edition attributes this to the influence of Nicholas of Cusa (which is probably partially true), but Leibniz knew Plotinus' work, and V, 8, 4, is a conspicuous text for the whole subsequent tradition. However, Plotinus' language about intellectual beauty is still more direct than that of Leibniz, for substance does not just *have* such relations; it *is* those relations. In other words, causality in intellect is not an external relation or a dependent relation but its very self.

Plotinus expresses this in V, 8, 4, in several curious ways: (1) "And movement also is pure; for the principle that moves it does not confuse it, as it goes, by being different from it" (12–13); that is, intellect is a *self-mover* whose motive form and moved matter completely express each other as a unity. (2) "[A]nd rest is not disturbed because it is not mixed with the non-stable" (13–14); that is, its *nature* or *form* does not fluctuate in matter but is eternally itself. (3) The next sentence is the one we have translated above with the creeping negative, but now we will exclude the negative as unnecessary: "and the beautiful is beautiful because it is not in the beautiful" (14–15); in other words, its beautiful causefulness is not dependent upon anything else—it is *final*. (4) "And each walks not as upon alien earth, but the place of each is its very self, and the from where it came runs together with it . . . and it is not one thing itself and its place another" (15–18). The word for *place (chora)* is Plato's term in the *Timaeus* for the receptacle or material principle, the word Aristotle uses in the *Parts of Animals* when he says that purposiveness even in the least significant parts of animals is the *place* of the beautiful.[12] Here Plotinus means that *form* and *matter* are one, pure self-expressive, purposeful, self-dependent being. We recall the termini language in III, 8, 8: the "from where" and "to which." Such language denotes causality. Here this means that intellect's causality or termini are itself. And so, Plotinus concludes, (5) the *substrate* (the matter or material subject) is intellect and its *form* is intellect (18–19), as if, he goes on to say, we were to think even in this visible universe that physical light grew the stars out of itself.

Intelligible beauty, it turns out if we follow Plotinus' otherwise rather puzzling account closely, is literally *sophia,* or wisdom; that is, a totally transparent, intelligible causality that is not, as Plotinus says, derived from reasonings or from anything else but itself. In fact, this is the real point of his whole description, for not only does he make "science-itself" (*autoepistêmê*) sit substantially beside intellect(as if for a moment intellect moves over on the bench and becomes a team-player instead of the whole show), but he then goes on to say that wisdom "has with her, and *has made* the real beings . . . and substance is wisdom there" (45–7). If wisdom is the dynamic *causality* of the divine intellect, it is much easier to see the essential connection between intelligible beauty and wisdom in Plotinus' mind, and that connection may be expressed as causality: in the physical world, a thing is beautiful in and through its causes, which we express by breaking them into different perspectives (motive cause, formal, final, material causes, etc.). In the intelligible world, causality is simply beauty: "origin is identical with the goal; and what is origin and goal this is the all, completely together and without deficiency. Beautiful therefore primarily . . ." (7, 46–8, 1).

4.8. The form of the beautiful?

We should note here an apparent major difference between Plato and Plotinus. According to Diotima, the final revelation in love matters culminates in the vision

---

12. *Timaeus* 52 b; *PA* 645 a.

of the beautiful "itself by itself with itself always being of a single form" (211 b; Appendix A, 1). For Plotinus, by contrast, there is no individual "Form of the Beautiful" in V, 8.[13] The whole of intellect is beauty. Why should this be so?

Plato, of course, distinguishes the beautiful from the good, at least in terms of individual things, though the line between *kalon* and *agathon*, beautiful and good, as we saw above, is not easy to draw (cf. *Republic* 506 a; *Symposium* 201 b 10–c 2). The "Form of the Good" is the highest form beyond being and intellect in the *Republic*. The "Form of the Beautiful" is the highest form in the *Symposium*, though the question of the good is very much a part of Socrates-Diotima's speech (see 204 e ff.). Plotinus seems to hold a rather nuanced view of all this. Plainly, from the way he cites the *Symposium*'s ascent to "the beautiful itself" in I, 6 (1) 7, 9–10, 21–24 (cf. 8, 1–2), we can have no doubt that the Good is the "primarily beautiful," which may seem to contradict what he says elsewhere about beauty's capacity to draw us away from the Good (e.g., in V, 5 [32] 12). Yet at the end of this work, first in the chronological order, he adopts a rather characteristic solution of the "well, it depends on your viewpoint" variety. First, all things are beautiful by virtue of the products and substance of intellect (I, 6, 9, 36–37). But then the Good "holds beauty set before it as a screen so that in a general way of speaking the Good is the primary beauty" (37–40). Plotinus then offers an alternative: either the place of the forms is intelligible beauty and the Good is that beyond, or the Good is primary beauty. But even in this case, he adds, beauty is in the intelligible world. We shall take up the question of what Plotinus thinks in other passages in section 4.12 below. On the whole, however, we might say that in interpreting Plato he not unreasonably wants to have it both ways. The really "irresistible" beautiful *is* the Good, yet at the same time the beautiful is like the light or grace of the Good *in* intellect and therefore a characteristic of the whole intelligible world of forms. If this is so, then intelligible beauty is really the form of the whole or, at least, the shapelessness of the Good that lies at the root of intelligible beauty.

4.9. Intelligible beauty and concrete physical things (V, 8, 4–8)

How is this intelligible beauty related concretely to the physical things we experience and the way we think about science? This whole of section V, 8, 4–8 should be compared with VI, 7 (38) 1–11 (and VI, 8, [39] 14). The essence of Plotinus' view is that intelligible science is not a construction or even a preconstruction like discursive sciences, but a preexisting, organic whole that the artist taps into in creating works of art and that is a living reality in nature, "a wisdom no longer composed of theorems . . . but loosened up from one into multiplicity" (5, 5–8). Nonrepresentational, nondiscursive forms of art, according to Plotinus, are ancient ways of signifying this creative beauty that is there before enquiry "in a wise

---

13. See S. Stern-Gillet, 2000, 38–63 more generally on this question.

way" (6, 1–9); it creates nondeliberatively in such a way that the physical universe springs spontaneously out of it as a partial, mixed image of its complete wisdom—mixed, that is, with matter, but even the matter, Plotinus says, is a "last form," hard to find because "hidden under the many forms" (7, 36–47).

This passage has been much misunderstood either as committing Plotinus to a view that is hard to reconcile with his "normal view of matter as the principle of evil" (Armstrong, Loeb) or as involving a crucial difference between Platonism and Aristotelianism—specifically, the plurality of substantial forms, which means that for Platonism the individual star, human being, dog, cat is never really *one,* an error that Aquinas later sees clearly (in *De spiritualibus creaturis* a-3; see in Cilento, 1971, 175–6). I shall deal with both of these problems briefly below. What is crucial here, however, is how Plotinus is implicitly trying to think through what the beauty of causality is in such a way that his argument will include and interpret Aristotle. He first cites Plato (7, 34–35; "he walks on high and directs the whole universe," *Phaedrus* 246 c 1–2) and then concentrates upon the scientific language of Aristotle (7, 36–47: "you can explain the cause why the earth is in the middle and the reason why it is round . . ."; cf. VI, 7 [38] 2, 12; Aristotle, *Posterior Analytics* B 2, 8, etc.). He prefaces this by indicating that the goal of the argument is Aristotle's view of causality and science (e.g., in the *Posterior Analytics*) in the light of real philosophical problems inherited from Plato. We can provide the causes of events syllogistically, but the epistemic necessity of which we speak is not the result of a process of planning (7, 37–40). Causal beauty here ("even these things are beautifully disposed," 7, 39–40) depends upon the beauty of wisdom there, as if the conclusion preceded the causal syllogism (7, 40–1). For when Aristotle says that we cannot seek the cause of a first principle (e.g., at *Physics* 188 a 27–30), Plotinus thinks he is ultimately committed to a living, comprehensive, and supremely beautiful wisdom that makes everything else beautiful in its own way. Of course, this is not a view Aristotle anywhere holds. But Plotinus apparently thinks that what Aristotle says about such wisdom in the *Nichomachean Ethics* (VI) and *Metaphysics*, as well as about the "origin" and "goal" of action, thought, and substance leaves room for a significant reconsideration of the merits of the case.

Thus, Plotinus' theory of intelligible beauty involves (a) a rethinking of the notions of science and causality and (b) a holistic and integrative view even of physical beauties in the light of form and its radiance or splendour (not unlike the view of Aquinas' aesthetics mentioned above).

But why, we might ask, is the integrity of physical things important for any consideration of their beauty? Plotinus does not use the word *integrity* himself, and we know both from here and elsewhere that physical substances are "not true substances"; they may spring spontaneously out of wisdom, but they do not themselves "have" wisdom (cf. 5, 17–19). Part of the answer is that to speak in terms of causes at all, for Plotinus, is *already* to be moved by the meaningful beauties reflected but also living within physical things. Even in perception, the organizing form in both the perceiver and the perceived becomes a proportion or confluence of mutual beauties that cannot even in the deepest perception, as it were, capture the wholeness of the intelligible beauty manifested already in truly symbiotic seeing. So although physical beauty is only an image itself "in something else," science can exclude no part of such beauty (even if science finds it in the most unlikely places—fangs, teeth, claws, hooves—as is the case in both Aristotle's biological works and in *Ennead* VI, 7 [38] 9, 1–14).

4.10. Elements of a reflexive aesthetic theory (V, 8, 1–11)

If beauty involves "everything," then how does Plotinus avoid the trap of false universality or the projection of his own preferences onto the transcendental plane? Perhaps he does not and cannot entirely. His move from the visible heavenly gods to the complex transparency of intellect in V, 8, 3, for instance, looks impossible to accept unless we are to change entirely our typically modern ways of thinking. Plotinus' view, however, includes elements of a different sort of realism that we might uncritically and unfairly discount from more "academic" considerations:

a. For Plotinus, conformity of eye to object is crucial or else we will not see anything. Waking up and training the organs of reception is a basic task (cf. V, 8, 2, 32–4; I, 6, 3, 3–5: "or perhaps . . . the soul pronounces the judgement by fitting the beautiful body to the form in itself and using this for judging beauty as we use a ruler for judging straightness"). Form itself is active, both the form at work in physical compounds ("it approaches and composes what is to come into being . . . and makes it one by conformity of parts," I, 6, 2, 18–22) and the inner form ("which moves things," V, 8, 2, 34). *Logos*, Plotinus says in III, 3 (48) 4, 9–13 has a double function in the universe: there is one *logos* or forming principle that is productive and another that is "connective [*synaptôn*] of the better principles with the things that have come into being." The capacity for connectiveness is everywhere. But this conformity or intelligible connectiveness awakens the soul's deepest emotions and passions ("for this is what true lovers *feel* [*paschousi*]. But what is it that makes them *feel* like this? Not shape, not colour . . . but you *feel* this way when you see in yourselves or in another greatness of soul . . ." I, 6, 5, 8–13). Consequently the soul has to be trained (cf. I, 6, 9, 2 ff.).

b. A proper humility and recognition of the limitations of vision are essential: we cannot look into everything as though it were an object or even a subject, but we have to see beauty by the appropriate organ: "there must be those who see this beauty by that with which the soul sees such things" (I, 6, 4, 12–13; cf. Plato, *Symposium* 212 a "and contemplates that [beauty] by means of the power he should employ . . .").

c. It is perfectly possible to be the world authority on a particular subject and yet to remain a moral, intellectual, and spiritual newt (unfortunately); that is, to be the least self-aware or self-integrated person of all. For Plotinus, to know oneself and to know oneself as beautiful, as we have seen above, is the concrete practical ground implicit in any partial recognition of intelligible beauty (V, 8, 2). The return to oneself is simultaneously the capacity to go beyond oneself, a capacity for shared experience.

d. As P. Hadot has so convincingly argued, the ancient philosophy we have on the pages before us has itself to be understood as a practical, spiritual exercise; that is, as a means of our recollecting a bigger world than that of our own preferences.[14] Occasionally, the voice of a very human, vulnerable Plotinus breaks through the rest of the text and we glimpse what appears to be missing elsewhere. Treatise V, 3 (49) chapter 17, is a striking example. If birth and its pains are a model for creativity in Plato and Plotinus, then self-knowing on this scale is bound to be a painful, even messy business.

e. The sort of vision of the world that is in any sense going to be adequate cannot be achieved without the proper form of address since it is not entirely within our power. Prayer, therefore, in V, 8, 9, is the natural extension of the reflexive recognition of beauty into the power of the genuinely other, without which the beauty of knowing and being known in intellect, of which Plotinus speaks, is impossible. If we look at this beautiful passage for a moment, we can see its inclusive and integrative character. Nothing gets left out, except ultimately the "matter" (on which see below). Let us take everything transparently in the *discursive reasoning* (9, 1–7): *this* world (i.e., the world we *see*). Let there be a *shining imagination* of it in the soul (7–10). *Keep this* and take another from yourself, Plotinus enjoins; do not make it smaller but dematerialize it: remove the mass (10–13). In other words, to prepare the eye to see intelligible beauty, expand the range of the eye and leave no beauty behind. Plotinus continues: "And calling upon the god who made that of which you have the imaginative picture, pray him to come. And may he come, bearing his world with all the gods in him . . ." (13 ff.). Inclusiveness (with negation or removal) and prayer are the proper forms of dialogical address in both worlds, for intelligi-

---

14. On evil see 4.11 below, together with: B. A. G. Fuller, 1912; E. B. Costello, 1967; J. M. Rist, 1961, 1974, 1983; D. O'Brien, 1971, 1977, 1991; J. M. Narbonne, 1993; K. Corrigan, 1996a.

ble beauty is the reflexive medium of both, not a property, but the divine world itself. Treatise V, 1 (10) chapter 6, is a striking example of prayer in this sense. "Let us speak in this way calling upon god himself not in spoken word, but by stretching ourselves out with the soul into prayer to him, being in this way able to pray alone to him alone" (6, 8–11).[15]

f. Plotinus emphasizes that to attain to any identity with intellect we must change from being spectators: "The sharp seer has what is seen in himself"; on the one hand, this is "to see whole" since "the whole soul" is with beauty and is completely drunk on nectar (10, 32 ff.); lovers recognize this straightaway, Plotinus says; on the other hand, even the sharp seer, "because he has many things," does not know he has the object of vision as subject inside him "and looks at it as if it were outside, because he looks at it as if it were an object seen and because he wants to look at it" (10, 35–8).

g. This scrutiny from outside is also important, for visions have to be *tested*: But he (the sharp seer) must, in coming to learn about the god, "remain within a particular imprint of him and exercise discrimination in seeking him to determine what he is entering into; and when he has learned in good faith that he is entering into the most blessed thing, he must already give himself to what is within and become instead of one who sees already an object of vision of another who contemplates him shining out with such thoughts as come from there" (11, 13–19).

Such a view balances image, experience, intelligent discrimination, and good faith. It also integrates implicitly several different standpoints within the learning experience: the third person standpoint of objective scrutiny (he, she, it), the first person standpoint of reflective discrimination (I, we), and finally, the second person standpoint (I, you) in which I see myself through your eyes—from the perspective of the eyes of the other *as a subject*. Can we think of this as an experience of "divine loving"? This will always be a vexed question for Neoplatonism. It must however, be an experience in some sense of being delighted in and beloved just for oneself, the culmination of the habit of good faith and an experience of pure loving delight (cf. V, 8, 12, 5: "for he has been pleased with what he has given birth to and takes delight in his offspring and so has kept everything with him").

So the apprehension of beauty as wholeness of causality in this world and as self-reflexive being in intellect does not occur without a series of practical qualifi-

---

15. Compare the well known saying of Theodorus of Asine, a pupil and rival of Iamblichus, often quoted by Proclus: "all things pray except the First" (*In Timaeum* 1, 213, 2–3).

cations: (a) preparation of the organs of reception, the awakening of the deepest feelings and consequently the need for a proper training of the soul; (b) the recognition of the limitations of the subject percipient (and the object perceived); (c) the call to integrative self-knowing; (d) practical, spiritual exercise; (e) inclusiveness, removal, and prayer; (f) transformative identity; and (g) a balance between analytic testing of experience and good faith.

Several final questions remain to complete our brief account of this topic.[16] How does evil fit into this picture? Is beauty truth and truth beauty, as Keats has it? Or, in other words, what are the limitations of beauty, and what role does the One play? Why should shapelessness, as Plotinus ultimately suggests elsewhere, be the supremely beautiful?

4.11. How does evil fit into this picture? (V, 8, 11)

How does evil fit into this picture?[17] It belongs to the same science to know the contraries that fall within its sphere, Aristotle holds. Plotinus too approaches the beautiful with the ugly in mind (cf. I, 6 [1] 5, 22 ff.: a knowledge of what one finds distasteful will perhaps be a help in recognizing what is aesthetically pleasurable). The soul "shrivels up and rejects" the ugly, he argues in I, 6 (1) 2, as something foreign to its essential being, which is to be a forming power. Ugliness is shapelessness in the sense that the matter has somehow resisted being shaped by form (2, 3–18). Now this is curious, because Plotinus is also going to argue that beauty in the highest sense is shapelessness. How can he coherently maintain both views? And what does he mean by attributing a kind of resistance to matter? Is ugliness a kind of evil (Plotinus on one occasion uses the term *form* of evil) disclosed by matter's resistance to form, so that it is matter that is the ultimate principle of evil? But how could a supposedly "passive" matter be resistant? At

---

16. Where now are the stones we started with? The image of dressed and undressed stones started us on the ascent to intelligible beauty, but it seems as if by V, 8, 10, they have become a mountain: "Just as, it often happens, people who go up to high places where the earth has taken on a golden-yellow tinge are filled with that colour there and made like that earth upon which they have walked" (10, 26–9). So the beauty of undressed stone is just this: it does not have to be a planispheric vanishing point, for when it admits a world of sun and colour it is also a mountain. *Ennead* V, 8, 1–10 is, to paraphrase Wallace Stevens, the treatise that "took the place of a mountain"(according to the title of his famous poem "The Poem That Took the Place of a Mountain"): "There it was, word for word,/The poem that took the place of a mountain./He breathed its oxygen . . . /It reminded him how he had needed/A place to go to in his own direction,/How he had recomposed the pines,/Shifted the rocks and picked his way among clouds,/For the outlook that would be right,/Where he would be complete in an unexplained completion:/The exact rock where his inexactnesses/would discover, at last, the view toward which they had edged,/Where he could lie and, gazing down at the sea ,/Recognize his unique and solitary home."

17. On evil see B. A. G. Fuller, 1912; E. B. Costello, 1967; J. M. Rist, 1961, 1974; D. O'Brien, 1971; P. Pecorino, 1981; K. Corrigan, 1996a.

any rate, Plotinus has some interesting things to say about evil in V, 8, 11. The idea that we might "want to perceive too much," like wanting things only to belong to us or wanting to belong only to ourselves,[18] which he calls the beginning of evils for souls in V, 1 (10) 1, seems to provoke a rather profound meditation upon the effect upon us of what we might call physical and moral "evils":

> The perceptions of evils have stronger impact upon us, but leave less knowledge because it is driven out by the strength of the impact; for sickness strikes us more, but quiet companionable health gives us a better understanding of it; for it comes to sit beside us since it is our own and is united with us. Sickness is something alien and not our own, and so thoroughly obvious because it appears to be very different from us. But we have no perception of what belongs to us and since we are like this, we are comprehensible to ourselves when we have made self-knowledge one with ourselves. So there too, when we are most in accordance with intellect, we seem to know nothing ... (V, 8, 11, 25–34).

Our perceptions of evil—slights, injustices, earthquakes—have a stronger physical effect upon us than any normal sense of well-being. They "strike" us and drive good sense out of us. Sickness violates us, whereas we do not even notice quiet good health (like "science" in intellect above) sitting beside us. The irruption of the plague comes from outside, but we are so unaware of what and who we are that without self-knowledge we are simply incomprehensible to ourselves; even then, to know ourselves seems like knowing nothing. A remarkable psychological self-portrait of being human!

Why should this be so? Why should evil have such an effect? Why should it be alien to us? How could matter be resistant or evil when Plotinus plainly thinks that this visible world is created as a good and that matter too is a final form?

If we go back to our treatment of matter in chapter 3.8, we will recall that formed matter is a positive reality for Plotinus (just as it is here in V, 8, 7), but that the indefiniteness of matter requires also a negative analysis and a special language for speaking about the indeterminate. Matter's indeterminacy is such that it is potentially everything, while actually being no one thing. Its *positive* character (that it is potentially everything) is paradoxically a function of its very *negativity* (that it is actually no thing). Unlike the hyper-determinate power of the One, in this landscape there is no truth since there are no determinate things or forms as bearers of truth or falsity upon which we can "lean" our judgements. This is because pure indeterminacy, on a negative analysis, is privation of opposites, not, as on a positive analysis, a genuine potency for opposites. Therefore, any predications we might make of a negatively charged indeterminacy (i.e., matter as pure privation of everything) are false. So if we mean by matter "stuff" or any thing that is formed, matter is positive. But if we mean by matter privation, indefinite-

---

18. Cf. Augustine on *curiositas, Confessions 10.*

ness, and negative indeterminacy (we might catch the change of emphasis, for instance, in the two different phrases: matter lacks *shape*; and matter *lacks* shape), then matter in this sense for Plotinus is not bland nothingness or simple absence; it is an absence, negativity, or non-being that has real effects in the world and can even come to condition much of our thinking since absence can be experienced in as many ways as matter appears.

So matter in the negative sense is false, misformed, and evil (cf. II, 4 [12] 16). In his final work on this subject (I, 8 [51]), Plotinus argues (against the wholly positive Aristotelian and Stoic conceptions) that while individual substance has no contrary (i.e., "John" does not reflect "–John" in antimatter), substance in the widest sense of form is opposed to matter in the sense of privation and evil. Whatever is rooted in the nature of one of these principles is opposed to whatever belongs in the nature of the other (cf. I, 8 [51] 6 generally). Does this commit Plotinus to a radical dualism in his view of physical compounds? There may be some justification for supposing this, but his view is a little more subtle than doing so would allow. Matter is not an unconnected principle "separate" from form. When Plotinus says that there is no "middle" between form and matter (e.g., VI, 7 [38] 23, 13–14) as substance and antisubstance (I, 8, [51] 6), he does not mean (a) that matter is an independent or separate principle (it is, after all, generated by soul; cf. III, 4 [15] 1), or (b) that it somehow has independent power (matter is a "cause" or "principle" only in the sense of *deficiency*, not efficiency; matter is the *deficient* cause of the fall of soul, but soul provides the efficient power and freedom; cf. I, 8 [51] 14), or (c) even that form is not united with matter (for in physical compounds form is united with matter). He means rather that matter is different from form in a more extreme fashion than any other kind of formal contrariety. In this sense, matter cannot be fitted into a generic scheme of things.

Furthermore, when Plotinus calls matter evil, he does not mean that the "stuff" of which things are made is evil. All stuff in the physical universe is good except to the degree that it does *not have* what it should or might have. The divine heavenly bodies, for example, are *perfect*, and the same is true in different degrees of all physical compounds except that their matter is not mastered forever. Consequently, matter plays a thoroughly positive role (1) in form (a) insofar as matter comes already vested with some form (cf. III, 8 [30] 2, 23–24) or (b) to the extent that the material structure is already included in the forming *logos* as what Plotinus calls a *logos* of matter (cf. III, 3 [48] 4) and (2) insofar as it is shaped by the form, or *logos* (cf. III, 8 [30] 2, 25); III, 4 [15] 1, 14–16). To the degree that matter is not so shaped but is privative, corruptive, and indeterminate, however, it is a subordinate but *opposed* antiprinciple whose negativity is a real fact of ordinary experience not to be underestimated. Absence of what should be present, therefore, is not an indifferent or morally neutral condition or a simple non-existence but the intrusion of negative difference. Plotinus argues that this negativity both in us and in things is a facet of ordinary experience glimpsed in all sorts of minor forms of absence, ugliness, decay, and moral and physical failings, as well as in death and more extreme cases of moral corruption. It is a negativity that cannot be made into a thing or a substance, on the one hand, or simply thought out of existence by abstraction or romanticism, on the other.

The two sides of Plotinus' thinking about matter are present in his positive treatment of the physical world and its creation here in V, 3. On the one hand, from the perspective of wisdom matter is a "final form," but it is difficult to "find" hidden under all the forms. On the other hand, the "phantasm of matter" in ourselves is *not* included, along with perception, discursive reasoning, and imagination in the anagogic ascent of prayer in V, 8, 9. The substances that are "not true" in V, 8, 5, 19 (in the context of *sophia*) become "false substance" in 9, 43, when considered as being in need of a beauty that is not its own and, therefore, effectively destitute in its own right.

Matter is thus passive to form but resistant in its own negativity, and the weaker the form the less power it has over the negatively charged field in which it finds itself and to which it continues to clutch (like Narcissus to his reflection) out of fear that it may itself be nothing without the nothing it appears to be "in." This is why our perceptions of evils seem to knock the very stuffing out of us.

4.12. The limitations of beauty: What role does the One play?

Let us go finally to the other pole of Plotinus' thinking and ask what role the One plays in the beautiful. What are the limitations of beauty? Why should shapelessness turn out to be the supremely beautiful?

When Keats concludes his "Ode on a Grecian Urn" with the vatic pronouncement, "'Beauty is truth, truth beauty'—that is all ye know on earth, and all ye need to know," he seems to capture two timelessly tragic features of human thought and life: on the one hand, the eternally fresh, unfilled, always-about-to-be-realized power and potency of great art, which the poem powerfully intimates and, on the other hand, the ambiguity of determinate life itself in the equivalence of truth and beauty; that is, the ambiguity that the realization of anything in time leads to its death and to the vanishing of potency expressed in the fact, or even the ambiguity of the sublime enigma contained in the identity of truth and beauty in the intelligible world, which belies the fact that in this determinate world the true is not always the beautiful. Certainly for Plotinus in the world of false substance neither is beauty truth nor truth beauty. Only in intellect is there such identity: "That is why being is something longed for because it is identical with the beautiful, and the beautiful is lovable because it is being" (9, 40–1). But is there something about potency and power, as Keats perhaps suggests, that goes beyond even the intelligible truth of beauty?

In the next treatise of the big work, V, 5 (32), Plotinus extends his aesthetic model of light explicitly to include the self-dependent power of the One (see especially V, 5, 7) but distinguishes sharply between Beauty and the Good. He argues that the grasp of the beautiful and the awakening of love come to those who are already in a way awake to it, whereas the presence of the Good is so deep that we have it whether we are awake or asleep: it is always with us; we do not have to recollect it.[19] Beauty, on the other hand, causes pain and even draws those who do not know what is happening away from the Good "as the beloved draws a child away from its father; for beauty is younger" (12, 36–7).[20] So the gentle, mild, intimate presence of the Good (which is more familiar to us than ourselves) is the ultimate and broader goal of all desire.

On the other hand, in a still later work, VI, 7 (38), Plotinus makes it clear that the source of beauty is ultimately the Good. As we have seen above, he even goes so far as to suggest that for us the beauty of anything, including intellect, is boring or inactive "until it catches a light from the Good" (22, 10–14). This is the play of light that delights us: "For each is what it is by itself, but it becomes desirable when the Good colours it, giving graces as it were to them and passionate love to the desirers" (22, 5–7). Even the living light in an ugly person is a beauty to be preferred to the beautiful statue or a dead face, he argues, because the living light of soul is already transfixed by the power of the Good (22, 27–36). The pure shapelessness of the Good that gives colour to all determinate forms is the source of beauty: "Therefore, the power of everything is a flower of beauty, a beauty-making beauty. For it generates beauty and makes it more beautiful by excess of beauty" (32, 31–3). But Plotinus goes a little further still: this shapelessness is the Good's first gift to intellect, so that even the source of intelligible beauty *in intellect* is shapeless: "since it is the principle of beauty it makes that beautiful . . . not in shape; but it makes the very beauty that comes to be from it to be shapeless, but in shape in another way" (32, 24–6). Intelligible beauty is a mean between two faces of a single beauty: the self-identity of being itself and the shapeless gift of the Good in and from which that identity emerges.

Why should we suppose that beauty is shapelessness? Plotinus argues that in the desire of the Good there is something that goes beyond intellect and soul. Even when we desire life and to exist forever and to be active, he says, we are not desiring intellect for its own sake, or soul, but intellect precisely *as good* (VI, 7,

---

19. Cf. Levinas (in Peperzak, 1993, 107): "The transcendence of the infinite with respect to the ego that is separated from it and thinks it constitutes the first mark of its infinitude—It has been put into us. *It is not a reminiscence*" (emphasis added).

20. The ability of beauty to hide the good and to subvert the deeper but quieter value of the more ancient or primordial desire in favour of the attraction of the younger is explored by the German poet Hölderlin (of Socrates and Alcibiades): "Wer das Tiefste gedacht, liebt das Lebendigste,/Hohe Jugend versteht, wer in die Welt geblikt/Und es neigen die Weisen/Oft am Ende zu Schönem sich" ("Who the deepest has thought, loves/what is most alive/Wide experience may well turn to what's best in youth,/And the wise in the end will/Often bow to the beautiful").

20, 22–4). In seeing colour in bodies or light in intelligible forms, there is still a need for another light to give them "grace and passionate love to the desirers." In a simple metaphor from Plato's *Phaedrus,* he argues that we do not even want to see so much as just to be warmed, lifted up, increased, and strengthened (VI, 7, 22, 14; *Phaedrus* 251 b). The grace of the Good deepens and expands our being, and so this grace is supremely beautiful (VI, 7, 22). To grasp a shape or form is still only part of the experience of love: "when you cannot grasp the form or shape of what is longed for, it would be most longed for and most lovable, and love for it would be immeasurable" (32, 24–6).

Thus Plotinus does make a case for the supreme shapelessness of beauty, even the shapelessness of intelligible beauty. In doing so, he brings together the Good of Plato's *Republic* with the Beautiful of Plato's *Symposium* in an inventive and not unpersuasive way.

Chapter 5

Conclusion

Assessment and Afterlife

We cannot recreate or return to the past, so in order to recover what may still be living in the thought, art, and lived experience of bygone ages, we are forced to transform that heritage and to find something entirely new within it, something that points to our own future. This transformative creativity was a feature of Plotinus himself, as we have seen. Plotinus the reader quickly absorbed what he read and took a distinctive personal line, stating what he himself really felt about the issue at hand (*Life*, 14). His personal, creative, yet comprehensive and often indirect transformation of earlier Greco-Roman philosophies into a new form of thought is undoubtedly a major part of his heritage. Plotinus writes no commentaries and does not try to reconcile Plato and Aristotle. Instead, he shows how one can think creatively through philosophical puzzles by means of ideas, problems, and suggestive images in Plato, Aristotle, the Stoics, and others in a way that synthesizes and illuminates ancient thought as a whole while also providing a coherent and compelling interpretation of Plato.[1] At the same time, Plotinus' thought is very much "oriented to the future," as Jean Trouillard observed, at least in the sense that so many elements in it seem to look forward to later important developments in the history of Western thought as well as to be congenial with important features of Eastern thought.[2] Let me first assess some of those elements before closing with a brief account of the strange but fascinating subsequent history of the reception of the *Enneads*.

5.1. Assessment

Plotinus' anthropology breaks new ground in so many different ways. Plotinus provides a new understanding of the soul-body relation that puts an end to the unresolved conflict between Platonic dualism and Aristotelian entelechism in a manner unparalleled until Aquinas' rather different Aristotelian-type approach in *Summa Theologiae* I, Question 75 and following. Not only that, but he also provides a coherent picture of soul's own nature as a unified, indivisible power in

---

1. The question of the interpretation of Plato and Aristotle is fundamental in different ways for all of subsequent Neoplatonism whether in Porphyry, the subsequent Athenian and Alexandrian schools, the later Islamic world, and so on (see 5.2 *Afterlife* below); however, there is no space to develop the issue in this brief concluding chapter.

2. Jean Trouillard (1961) "The Logic of Attribution," *International Philosophical Quarterly*, 132.

herself and yet also a power to animate bodies by her presence. This means that Plotinus can both maintain the substantial unity of what it means to be human and yet explore the great range of different foci possible, from the "beast" to intellect, with a precise account of how man is related to both soul and intellect (cf. I, 1, 8 and 13; V, 3 [49] 3–4). Of course, much of Plotinus' emphasis upon the reality of the human soul, our inner self, and the need for a genuine return to oneself and to God (by virtue of the interior life of purgation, illumination, and unification) had an immense influence upon later Christian thought and ascetic practice. But his philosophy of the multidimensional self, his sense of the difficulties involved in any genuine self-knowledge, his conviction that the deepest source of desire lies in the soul and intellect for something greater than themselves, and his view that even this desire has to be tested by the ambiguity between the attractive pull of beauty and the gentler yet more primordial presence of the good—all this, together finally with his belief in the unconscious and preconscious, seems to anticipate contemporary concerns in cognitive psychology and in various forms of psychotherapy from Freud to Jung and Frankl.

Perhaps most striking of all for the modern reader of III, 8, is Plotinus' vivid sense, developed from Plato and Aristotle, that we are parts of a great living organism (not a mechanism arranged by pulleys and levers) whose living contemplation springs from the deeper and more intensive contemplation of an intelligible organism. The latter is where truth really resides, but since intellect is omnipresent, such truth is open to anyone and to anything at any point yet at the same time is never to be instantiated anywhere. In our own times we have become increasingly aware of the interconnectedness of everything and of the need to respect even apparently unliving things as complex entities in their own right and not simply as manipulable properties for our own consumption. We are also aware that in order to take proper account of the sheer diversity of the sciences and arts we can no longer continue to adopt a single scientific paradigm, such as that of physics or chemistry or even mathematics. Biology needs its own paradigm, for instance, and any philosophy of science in a broader sense needs also to include the subject doing the investigating. Plotinus' reflexive model of living contemplation with its rather startling insistence that reality is fundamentally holographic (i.e., that all the parts contain the whole, but each part in its own way) and that all being must be able to return to itself in an inclusive, multidimensional subject-object duality in which each is reflected in the other seems light-years ahead of some of the simpler modern scientific paradigms based upon an uncritical, supposedly objective, third-person standpoint. Perhaps even more important for human beings is Plotinus' balanced view of humanity in relation to other species. Humanity is not the most important species but a part of something much larger. Other species too have claims to thought and intellect, and even where no such claims can be made, existence and life are given to things by the Good. So, even if the notion of the whole is somewhat unwieldy at times, Plotinus' works are imbued with a sense of respect for the whole a respect that extends very much to the parts. After our experience of the twentieth century, the bloodiest century of all centuries; of racial exterminations attempted on a larger scale than ever before; and of the rapidly multiplying problems we face with genetic engineering, it becomes even more important to continue to remind ourselves of the need to develop an inclusive yet realistic view of what it means to be human.

In this book, I have referred to Plotinus' theory of contemplative making as creation; undoubtedly some readers will baulk at this, some of them specialists in the field. What, after all, has the Greek verb *poiein*, "to make," in common with the Latin verb *creare*, "to create," if we also grant the total difference in signification for the Christian or Jewish view points of a creating, personal diety? I make no apologies for this. Plotinus was neither a Christian nor a Jewish thinker. Nonetheless in the *Enneads,* the One's free creative will generates all things out of the infinite, superabundant, no-thingness of its power—just about as close to "creation out of nothing" as one can get. It is hardly accidental, therefore, that when Thomas Aquinas one thousand years later came to frame his great unfinished theological masterpiece, the *Summa Theologiae*, he did so according to the three constitutive moments of Neoplatonic creation: abiding, procession, and conversion, or in Christian terms, the power of God, the procession of created things, and the return of created things through the incarnation, sacraments, the resurrection, and the last things. From a philosophical point of view, creative transformation is the surest mark of respect.

Another important feature of Plotinus' thought is his development of new forms of language to reflect different domains of discourse. In the case of matter as a negative field of indeterminacy, Plotinus fashions a discourse to reflect a domain in which there are no actual beings and therefore no truth or falsity upon which to rest discursive thinking. So his language about matter breaks the constraints of our normal thinking, not unlike the way the discovery of quantum mechanics in the twentieth century compelled physicists to develop entirely new ways of thinking and talking about indeterminacy. Plotinus' view of the negativity of matter was rejected both by subsequent Neoplatonic philosophers, and of course, by Christian thinkers; nonetheless, the major thrust of his view that evil is a form of absence, privation, or non-being with profoundly disturbing consequences in the real world had a major influence upon Augustine as well as on Aquinas much later (through Pseudo-Dionysius–on which see below) and has left its mark indirectly upon Sartre, Heidegger, and much modern literature (e.g., Dostoevsky).

In the case of the One, Plotinus' negative theology and the language he develops to speak about what is beyond determinate being is of immense significance.Through Plotinus the vocabulary, imagery, and methods of mystical experience are transmitted directly or indirectly to such different thinkers as Gregory of Nyssa (in Turkey in the fourth century), Augustine (in Africa in the fourth and fifth centuries), Dante (in the concluding vision of the *Divine Comedy, Paradiso,* canto 33, in the thirteenth and fourteenth centuries), the Rhineland mystics (Meister Eckhart, c.1260–1327, and his pupils Tauler, c.1300–61, and Suso, c.1295–1366), Nicholas of Cusa (1401–64), John of the Cross, Jacob Boehme, and on. This on its own would be important, but it is equally notable because it poses centrally the question of what such experience means and in what sense it can be compatible with philosophical thinking. It is significant also because of the "future" orientation that this gives to the whole of Plotinus' thought: "all things are not there yet, but they will be" (V, 2 [11] 1). The Good, or the One, is the property of none, but in different ways the experience of all. So none can claim him, yet none can avoid him. He, she, it—nothing can be predicated of such power that is always in the future of determinate beings and that can become manifest only from its own perspective. Here Plotinus is congenial to many Eastern forms of thought (as he is also in his views of the destiny of soul and the nature of intellect). We can talk, for instance, of theistic or nontheistic forms of Buddhism, but if even the word "god" is not suitably predicated of such experience, then the categories we employ pale into insignificance alongside the experience. In other words, for Plotinus there is a perspective beyond all determinate being that cannot be manipulated into derivative categories or into the divisions of race, religious denomination, fraternity, or otherwise. At the same time, this perspective is a unity about which we can speak meaningfully from our own experience of it. Far from abolishing difference, however, it establishes differences, according to Plotinus' view, though not the divisions that separate us from one another and block out the light of a shared sun. This is, of course, a major claim not at all accepted by the more parochial materialisms of our own age. But the question is this: can we be sufficiently inclusive without the transcendent dimension? If it is true that even intelligible levels of significance can be properly disclosed only from their own perspectives, then it might seem that we cannot prescind from the transcendent dimension without destroying the very ground on which we stand and without cramping the whole world into the conventional ego of our own preference. Are unity and universality simply the product of our own good judgement and will-to-community, or are they a part of our own being and of all things and yet a principle beyond all? Plato, Aristotle, and Plotinus were of the view that we human beings had to awaken a much larger way of seeing the world in order to be fully present to it. This formed one basis (with Scripture and the life of Christ) for understanding the later Christian anchoretic and monastic traditions. A Christian writer of the fourth century, Evagrius of Pontus, puts it in this way: "The monk is separated from all and united to all. The monk is one who regards himself as one with all because he sees himself appearing continually in each person" (*Treatise on Prayer*, 121–25). The ascetic withdrawal from the world and, even more so, the mystical life itself are paradoxically perhaps ways of being present to the world, just as in Plotinus and in Proclus later[3] the presence of the One is more extensive even than the presence of intellect and soul. If this or something like it is the perspective that can bring us closest to the world and to an inclusive respect for all its parts, then we need it more today than ever before.

Finally, Plotinus' work on intelligible beauty and his theory of art and artistic activity, which through many intermediaries (Pseudo-Dionysius, Augustine, Aquinas, Dante, and Ficino among them) had such an impact upon the Italian Renaissance, upon later German philosophy (especially Kant and Schelling), and upon the British Romantic poets, particularly Coleridge and Wordsworth, is far-sighted in so many ways that its significance is easy to overlook:

1. It overturns any simple, spatial dichotomy between the sensible and intelligible worlds, for such beauty is not only within the soul but springs out of form and soul everywhere, empowers our understanding, perception, and even our simple aesthetic delight in the beauty of people and things.
2. Intelligible beauty is the medium in which subject and object come to reflect each other's being. Delight in the inner beauty of another person as our own beauty is part of our immediate experience of being. Intelligible beauty, therefore, reveals the essential connectedness of self to others and of self to self in more immediate ways than our otherwise divided, more external experience of other things. Being is more immediately experienced than becoming.
3. The inner landscape of such beauty brings the philosophical imagination into a new and powerful focus.[4] "Each of the things we speak about there are beautiful images of the kind someone imagines to exist in the soul of the wise man" (5, 22). What the mind cannot conceive, the imagination attempts to penetrate by image-experiment, exercise, and prayer since the philosophical imagination is also aware of its own limitations. So in V, 8, 9, the sensible cosmos is literally offered up, through a discursive thought infused with the light of the imagination, to be transformed from "a shining imagination of a sphere" into an all-inclusive intelligible cosmos. The importance of this for art and literature cannot be underestimated. From this point on, the intellectual and religious imaginations would have a projective function linking sense to thought and beyond. This is the essence of the symbolic imagination: to cast together (sym-bolon), different modalities, different

---

3. See Proclus, *Elements of Theology*, props. 57, 71–2. But for Proclus this means that matter cannot be evil.

4. On imagination in Plotinus see H. J. Blumenthal, 1971; III, 8 (30), 4; IV, 3 (27), 28–32; IV, 4 (28), 13; I, 4 (46), 10.

worlds, and ultimately to unsay or shatter the image by transformation. Dante's l'alta fantasia ("high imagination"), whose power traverses all the landscapes of life and spirit and fails only before the highest vision of Love in Paradiso, canto XXXIII, 133–145, is part of the heritage of V, 8: "Here power failed the lofty imagination, but already my desire and will . . . were revolved . . . by the Love which moves the sun and the other stars." There comes a point in the intellectual and spiritual lives where the human sphere has to be revolved by another. In such cases one can only prepare and wait passively to be moved or changed. Nonetheless, the imagination—even in this affective, passive state— can go where our normal thought-processes cannot.

4. Finally, V, 8, develops a new view of science by paying close attention to the purposeful beauty of artistic and natural objects and by linking this beauty reflexively to the soul of the one who sees. Causality is a form of beauty-seeing, of unpacking into causes (i.e., into different accounts why things hang together "beautifully") a beauty that already precontains all its relations: "What is beautiful then in this way, and what could only be revealed with difficulty, or even not at all, by enquiry to be necessarily like this . . . exists in this way before enquiry and before reasoning" (V, 8, 6). Furthermore, V, 8, is an experimental work in the sense that it pays close attention to, and wants to test, its experience (cf. V, 8, 11, 13 ff.). This is exactly the vision that will give rise to the birth of empirical science in the Franciscan tradition a thousand years later. St. Francis himself might look an unlikely sponsor of this tradition, but he certainly possessed the mystical eye by which to see the intelligible beauty and kinship of all natural things. This spirit, developed in different ways by Bacon, Grosseteste, Bonaventure, and others, gave rise to experimental science, to the study of optics for the multiplicating power of natural light, to Light metaphysics, and much more. It is natural, after all, that the mystical eye, open to the transcendent in everything, should be compelled to test itself and all of its experience. In this sense, as we observed above, the mystic eye, though it must escape certain forms of attachment, is so close to nature that it is able to see in a new way. Here in Plotinus we observe the preconditions necessary for the birth of empirical science and a subtle attention to the psychology of experience springing precisely out of the mystic's awareness of all that is involved in seeing.

5.2. Afterlife

The history of thought is full of the unanticipated and the unlikely. Plato's dialogues have shaped much of the Western tradition, yet Plato himself considered his real work to be the living conversation of the soul and did not put much store upon the written word whose impotence to ask new questions and to come to its own defence he had outlined in the *Phaedrus*. Who could have anticipated anyway that a man with the nickname Broad (*platôn*) would have had such a decisive intellectual influence? Aristotle too wrote dialogues of which he was reputedly proud, yet they have all been lost except for fragments embedded in other writers' works; what remains are his unfinished lecture notes.

What then about Plotinus?[5] Plotinus started to write only in the later years of his life, and only because of the accident of Porphyry's arrival at the school in Rome have all of those writings been preserved. Yet the school itself did not survive Plotinus' death. Porphyry did his best to promote Plotinus' thought not only with his edition of the *Enneads* and the *Life* but also with summaries and commentaries on the treatises as well as an introductory manual (the *Sentences*) based upon the *Enneads*. He also wrote an introduction (*Isagoge*) to Aristotle's *Categories* that was later translated into Latin by Boethius and that provided a focus for the Medieval debate on the status of universals. From his other works, and from the testimony of later writers, we can see that Porphyry was interested in moral and religious matters as well as in a whole range of questions, from abstinence to avoid animal transmigration to the interpretation of traditional mythology.[6] In his metaphysics, Porphyry tended to do away with any absolute distinction between hypostases, a tendency to telescope hypostases that can be found on occasion in Plotinus too.

Porphyry's pupil, Iamblichus (c. 245–c. 325), who founded a successful school in Syria, criticized much in Porphyry and Plotinus and thus created a new form of Neoplatonism that helped to start schools in Athens and Alexandria. Iamblichus' criticisms were radical. He posited an absolutely ineffable One beyond the One itself to avoid any tendency to think or render it intelligible, and he rejected Plotinus' views of man as an intelligible cosmos and of the existence of an undescended part of the soul. Each entity reflects the whole but only from the appropriate perspective of its own fixed place. The human soul is, therefore, not consubstantial with those of the gods nor can she migrate into other animals. Salvation, then, is not within man's powers. Iamblichus also denied that pure thought or contemplation could bring about union with the divine. What was crucial was the performance of appropriate ritual actions or theurgy ("divine work"),[7] in the belief that one could attain to the divine by the incarnation of divine forces in either material objects or statues or human beings (by virtue of the divine power mirrored everywhere in the universe and in the natural sympathy of all parts), but not just by talking about the gods (*theo-logy*) or by philosophical contemplation

---

5.   For accounts of this subsequent history see A. H. Armstrong (ed.), 1967; R. T. Wallis, 1995, 94–178; D. J. O'Meara, 1993, 111–16; E. K. Emilsson, 1999, 356–87.

6.   For Porphyry generally see A. Smith, 1974; 1987, 717–73; 1993; and for editions and translations see L. P. Gerson, bibliography, in R. T. Wallis, 1972.

7.   On this see R. T. Wallis, 1972, 107 ff.; G. Shaw, 1995.

(*theôria*). In his metaphysics, Iamblichus developed a system of logical realism according to which objects of thought exist prior to and independently of our thinking about them (and so in intellect he supposes an intelligible order of being prior to an intellectual order of thinking) and logical distinctions imply ontological ones (and so a vast and complicated hierarchy is developed to articulate every possible distinction).[8]

Much of this was developed and systematized by the schools in Athens and Alexandria (particularly the former). The most famous representatives of the Athenian school were Syrianus (died 437) and Proclus (412–485). The latter was perhaps the greatest systematizer of all time. Among his many works was a commentary on the *Enneads* (a few fragments of which survive) and the most influential *Elements of Theology*, which condenses the whole of Neoplatonic metaphysics into 211 propositions (each deduced from its predecessors as in Euclidean geometry). This work anticipates the method of Spinoza's *Ethics* well over a thousand years later. In Proclus' great commentaries on Plato and, above all, in his *Platonic Theology,* the structural principles of logical realism are developed to their logical conclusion. Many features only implicit in Plotinus' thought are developed and transformed. Probably because of Christian influence, faith becomes the chief theurgic virtue, and a descending or providential love of the higher for the lower becomes integral to Neoplatonism.[9]

But the strangest turn of events occurred with a late fifth- or early sixth-century forgery that resulted in a new and surprisingly vital form of Christian Neoplatonism. Four works dealing with negative and affirmative theology, as well as with the mediation of divinity through the ranks of angels and the orders in the Church,[10] and essentially distilling Athenian Neoplatonism into new Christian form were passed off as the work of St. Paul's first convert at Athens, Dionysius the Areopagite, in an attempt aimed to provide Neoplatonism with impeccable Christian credentials. For these reasons, the author is now referred to as Pseudo-Dionysius, yet he was an original thinker of great subtlety in his own right, and his works were to have enormous influence, not least upon Medieval Western theology via the Latin translation made in 858 by the Irish philosopher John Scotus Eriugena (c. 810–c. 877), whose own original thinking in *On the Division of Nature* got him condemned by the Church for pantheism. Thomas Aquinas, in particular, was much influenced by Dionysian theology, and Neoplatonic elements both from Dionysius and other sources (especially Proclus, as we shall see) are creatively transformed in his works. So much, then, for the school of Athens,

---

8. Further on Iamblichus see J. Dalsgaard Larsen, 1972; J. Dillon, 1987, 862–909; D. J. O'Meara, 1989; H. J. Blumenthal and E. G. Clark (eds.), 1993.

9. See R. T. Wallis, 1972, 142–58 (and bibliography, 192–4); cf. also J. M. Rist, 1967, 231–46.

10. Respectively, the *Mystical Theology, Divine Names, Celestial Hierarchy,* and *Ecclesiastical Theology* (together with some letters).

which was silenced by a hostile Christian imperial state (Justinian) in 529, though some of its members continued to work in Persia.

Among the members of the Alexandrian school in Egypt were the mathematician Theon and his daughter Hypatia, who seems to have represented all that was gracious, gentle, and luminously intelligent in Neoplatonism but who was brutally murdered by a fanatical Christian mob in 415. A gentleman farmer and amateur philosopher, Synesius of Cyrene—not unlike the nobility who had turned to philosophy in Rome in Plotinus' time—was a member of the school and became Christian bishop of Ptolemais (in 410). So relations between paganism and Christianity were invariably problematic, though the Alexandrian school survived for a century beyond the demise of the Athenian school; about 720 it moved to Antioch and about 900 to Baghdad. Neoplatonism's entry into the Muslim world occurred on several fronts, but perhaps the most startling entry point of all was another forgery, as we shall see presently.

Meanwhile in the West, Neoplatonism was not just transmitted and transformed by the schools of Syria, Athens, and Alexandria. The *Enneads* were read by theologians writing in Greek, including Eusebius of Caesarea, Basil the Great and his younger brother, Gregory of Nyssa, and their friend Gregory Nazianzen (in Cappadocia or now the interior of Turkey) in the fourth century, and also by the great Latin bishops Ambrose of Milan and Augustine of Hippo (354–430). Augustine read Plotinus in the translation of Marius Victorinus, a Roman professor of rhetoric, and this (together with other "Platonic books") changed his life (cf. *Confessions* 7). Later as a Christian bishop, Augustine had an ambivalent attitude to pagan Neoplatonism, but his use of Neoplatonic elements in his many works demonstrates, in my view, that he understood Plotinus profoundly and transformed that understanding into something entirely new. According to his biographer, Possidius, it was the words of *Ennead* I, 4 (46) 7, 24–5 that consoled him as he lay dying in Hippo, with the Vandals surrounding the town and about to destroy his life's work: "He is no great man who thinks it a great thing that sticks and stones should fall, and that men, who must die, should die" (*Life of Augustine*, 28). The later Latin Neoplatonic tradition of translations and commentaries from the Greek also was built in part upon the work of the Christian Boethius, who translated Aristotle's logical treatises and a work by Porphyry (the *Isagôgê*) before he was arrested on a charge of treason by Theodoric, king of the Goths. While awaiting execution, he composed his most accessible and influential *Consolation of Philosophy*, a beautiful work that creates a new synthesis of poetry and philosophy but for whatever reasons never mentions anything Christian and instead restricts its scope entirely to pagan thought.

Plotinus' entry into the Arab and Jewish worlds was marked by another forgery with far-reaching consequences. Arabic paraphrases of *Enneads* IV–VI became available under the title (of all things!) the *Theology of Aristotle* (read by Al-Kindi [ninth century], Al-Farabi [c. 950], and Avicenna [Ibn Sina, 980–1037]), and with lesser authority since they lacked Aristotle's name, two other Plotinian paraphrases, *The Epistle of Divine Science* and the *Sayings of the Greek Sage.* Partly as a result of these works, Neoplatonism came to have a marked influence on Islamic mysticism (or Sufism). The *Theology of Aristotle* must have had an influence upon the Jewish *Cabala*, since it is cited by Moses de Leon, the supposed author of the *Zohar*. Another pseudo-Aristotelian work, the *Book Concerning the Pure Good,* became known in the West as the *Liber de Causis*. It is actually based on Proclus' *Elements of Theology* and was commented upon and much cited by Thomas Aquinas. The *Theology of Aristotle* was translated into Hebrew and thus not only influenced later Cabbalistic thinking, but in very different ways clearly left its mark on Ibn Gebirol (Avicebron, c. 1021–c. 1058) and Moses Maimonides (1135–1204).

So through the schools and their somewhat remarkable afterlives, Plotinus came to influence the birth of philosophy, theology, art, and science in the Byzantine, Islamic, and Jewish worlds as well as in the Latin West in the Middle Ages and on into the Renaissance.[11] Byzantium, the eastern half of the Roman Empire, which lasted until the Turkish capture of Constantinople in 1453, became a centre for Neoplatonic studies only in the eleventh century, especially under Michael Psellus (1018–79). Our earliest manuscript copies of the *Enneads* are from Byzantine scribes and scholars of the twelfth and thirteenth century. Just before the capture of Constantinople, George Gemistius Pletho (c. 1360–c. 1450), sent as a delegate to the Council of Florence in 1438, inspired Cosimo de' Medici to found his own Platonic Academy. The manuscripts collected by Gemistius' pupil Bessarion, when he soon after settled in Florence, were thus transmitted to the Western world.

We have mentioned already the complex Neoplatonic influences upon the Medieval world; for example, Aquinas and Bonaventure in the thirteenth century, the Rhineland mystics in the thirteenth and fourteenth centuries, and Nicholas of Cusa (1401–64), who escaped as a young boy from his abusive bargeman father to become a cardinal. Cusa was the first of his age (even before Galileo) to argue that neither the earth nor the sun was the centre of the universe, for the universe could have no centre but the infinity of God, in whom is the coincidence of opposites; since God was everywhere and nowhere, the centre of the universe must be nowhere and yet be found at every point. In the Renaissance in Europe all of these strands (and more) converged in the flowering of a new form of Platonism in the figures of Marsilio Ficino (1433–99), Giovanni Pico della Mirandola (1463–94), and the rather more pugnacious Dominican Giordano Bruno (1548–1600). On account of his development of Nicholas' coincidence of opposites doctrine, as well

---

11. For a restricted bibliography of Neoplatonism's later influence on Byzantine thought and history, Islamic and Jewish philosophy, Medieval thought in general as well as Renaissance and post-Renaissance thought, see L. P. Gerson in R. T. Wallis, 1972, 194–7.

as for other reasons, Bruno was burned at the stake. (Only very recently has a statue of Bruno been erected on the spot of his death.) Ficino, and Pico later, set out to demonstrate the essential harmony of Christianity with the various ancient traditions, Platonism and Jewish Cabalism (in Pico's case) included. After finishing his great translation of Plato in 1469, Ficino turned to the enormous task of translating and commenting upon Plotinus. This work was finally printed in 1492. His own major works, the *Platonic Theology on the Immortality of the Soul* (1474) and his commentary on Plato's *Symposium* (1469), show quite clearly that Renaissance Platonism was not a return from Neoplatonism to the "original Plato" (this was not achieved until the nineteenth century, if it is a realizable goal at all), but yet another major transformation of an already highly evolved Neoplatonic tradition. Ficino's translation now made Plotinus more widely available throughout Europe. Indeed, the great humanists of the late fifteenth and early sixteenth centuries, like John Colet, Erasmus of Rotterdam, and Thomas More, were versed in Platonic and Neoplatonic themes, as accessible works like More's *Utopia* and Erasmus' *In Praise of Folly* demonstrate. The latter work, *Encomium Moriae,* written for his friend More, unites many different scriptural, ascetical, and philosophical themes with the figures of Socrates and Christ in favour of a thesis not entirely dissimilar from that of Plotinus in VI, 7 (38), 35, namely, that in order to see God, intellect must become not only "loving," but "daft." In 1580 the first printed edition of the *Enneads* in Greek was published.

The subsequent history of philosophy in Europe owes a major debt to this foundation provided by the Renaissance. In his attempt to escape from the scholastic Aristotelianism of his upbringing, Descartes was moved by the spirit of Augustinian Platonism. Leibniz and Spinoza developed entirely opposite views of substance on Neoplatonic principles and methods. The word "monad," in Leibniz's *Monadology,* had been a favourite of ancient Athenian Neoplatonism. In a remarkable late work, *Siris,* the Irish philosopher George Berkeley begins with the virtues of tar-water, ends with the Trinity, and in between comments knowledgeably (and with much Greek) upon the whole course of ancient philosophy, especially Neoplatonism. Immanuel Kant was, of course, precisely interested in the relation between the sensible and the supersensible, which he spent his life developing over the course of three *Critiques.* Goethe, Schelling, Hölderlin, and Hegel all admired Plotinus' ideas and transmitted this admiration to the British Idealists. The developmental or evolutionary application of Neoplatonic notions was carried still further in the twentieth century by Henri Bergson, who brought together modern scientific ideas with Plotinus' philosophy of the soul. Plotinus and Neoplatonic influence upon Husserl and the subsequent phenomenological tradition is immediately evident to any reader of Husserl's *Ideas* (1913) or to anyone familiar with Heidegger's idiosyncratic interpretation of Plato's notion of truth or with the major notion in Heidegger's later works of the lighting up (*die Lichtung*) of being. In England, of course, Neoplatonism had an immense influence upon literature, not least in Shakespeare (though this is a much debated question) and Spenser (see Spenser's adaptation of the opening of *Ennead* I, 6, in his *Fowre Hymns: Of Beautie*, reprinted in Wallis, 1971, 174), and, of course, in the later Metaphysical poets. In part through Thomas Taylor's English translations and the Hegelian movement in the nineteenth century, its influence continued on the Romantics, such as Wordsworth, Coleridge, Blake, Shelley, Keats, and in the modern era, on Yeats especially but also the Christian imaginative literature of Charles Williams and C. S. Lewis.

As for the Anglo-American connection, Alfred North Whitehead, who coauthored the *Principia Mathematica* with Bertrand Russell, developed a process philosophy that resonates strongly with Plotinus' view of the intelligible universe. By emphasizing the importance not only of Aristotle's concept of potentiality but of the less examined notions of decay and privation, Whitehead takes up an important theme that Plotinus developed in his works on matter. Of course, earlier in North America, Ralph Waldo Emerson had developed a philosophy dubbed transcendentalism, based for the most part upon Plotinus' views of soul and of intelligible beauty. This understanding, when transformed through her own reading of Plato and (probably) Plotinus, as well as through her own considerable poetic genius, resulted in the many "Neoplatonic" poems of Emily Dickinson, whom Allan Ginsberg and the Beat poets proclaimed to be their sole Muse.

Hegel's colleague, F. Creuzer, with G. Moser, published a new complete edition of Plotinus in 1835, and Victor Cousin, a French contemporary and admirer of Hegel, did a similar service for the French-speaking world (cf. M. Bouillet's translation and notes, 1857–61). Thomas Taylor's translations of Neoplatonic texts at about the same time and, finally, the great translation by Stephen MacKenna (published 1917–30) made Neoplatonism accessible to the English-speaking world. This complex achievement formed the basis upon which modern editions (and scholarship) could emerge: (1) the French translation by E. Bréhier (1924–38), (2) the German by R. Harder (1930–37), (3) the Italian by V. Cilento (1947–49), (4) the English by A. H. Armstrong (1966–88), (5) the (unfinished) Spanish by J. Igal (1982–85), and (6) the great critical edition *Plotini Opera* in three volumes by P. Henry and H. R. Schwyzer emerging between 1951 and 1973 as the fruit of over twenty years' painstaking work and collaboration with many international scholars. If we consider for a moment the overwhelming odds against anything from any lifetime surviving more than the shortest period; if we reflect upon the obvious fact that most of us have no idea what we did or thought yesterday, much less a year ago, then the real achievement of this eighteen-hundred year transmission and transformation of a text and the wild improbability of its ever happening at all might strike us with amazement.

Appendix A

Some Key Passages from Plato and Aristotle

1. *Plato*, Symposium: *209 e 5–212 a 7*

"Into these love matters, perhaps, Socrates, you too could [210] be initiated; but as to the final revelatory rites, for the sake of which all of our conversation has been conducted, if one approaches them correctly, I do not know if you would be capable of being initiated. Well, I will tell you," she said "and try my hardest. And you try to follow, if you can. The one who proceeds rightly," she said, "in this matter must, while he is young, begin to turn to beautiful bodies, and first, if the one who leads him leads him rightly, he must love one body and there produce beautiful words, and then he must realize that the beauty in any [b] body is brother to that in any other body, and that if one must pursue beauty in form, it is very stupid not to think the beauty in all bodies one and the same; and having realized this, he must become a lover of all beautiful bodies, and relax this strong passion for one body, looking down on it and thinking it of little worth; and after this he must think that the beauty in souls is more to be honoured than that in body so that even [c] if someone has little physical bloom though is fair in soul, it will be enough for him, and he loves and cares for that one and gives birth to such words and seeks such words as will make the young better, so that he may be compelled again to contemplate the beauty as it is to be seen in activities and laws, and to see this, that all of it is related to itself, in order that he should think beauty of body a little thing; and after activities, he must lead him to kinds of knowledge, so that he may see in turn a beauty of different sorts of knowledge, and looking towards [d] a great beauty already, no longer loving, like a house-slave, the beauty of one thing, a young boy, or some one human being, or one activity, no longer being a slave, inferior and busy about little things, but instead turned to the great sea of beauty and contemplating it, he may give birth to many, beautiful and magnificent words and thoughts in a philosophy which grudges nothing, until there, strengthened and increased, he may come to look upon a single knowledge of such a kind which is of a beauty I shall now tell you about. [e] Do try," she said, "to pay as close attention to me as possible. Whoever is led along the way up to this point in love matters and contemplates the beauties in order and in the right way, and is already on the way to the final end of matters of love, will suddenly look upon a beauty wonderful in nature, that beauty in fact, Socrates, that all his earlier labours were for, a beauty, first, that always [211] exists, and neither comes to be nor perishes, neither increases nor diminishes, and then is not beautiful in one respect, but ugly in another, nor beautiful at one time, but not at another, nor beautiful in relation to this, but ugly in relation to that, nor beautiful here, but ugly there, since to some it is beautiful, but to others ugly; nor again will he imagine beauty to be like a face or hands or anything else in which body participates, or a word or a kind of knowledge, nor as situated [b] in some other thing such as a living creature or the earth or the heaven or anything else, but rather as itself by itself with itself always being of a single form, and all other beautiful things participating in it in such a way that when the rest come to be and perish, that does not become any greater or less or undergo any change at all. Certainly when someone goes up from these beauties through the right way of loving boys and begins to come within sight of that beauty, he would be just about to touch upon the goal. For this in fact is the right way of proceeding in love matters or to be led by someone else, beginning from these beautiful things here [c], one must always go up for the sake of that beauty, using them as stepping stones, from one to two and from two to all beautiful bodies, and from beautiful bodies to beautiful activities, and from activities to beautiful forms of learning, and from forms of learning to end up in that form of learning which is a learning of none other than that beauty [d] itself, in order that one may end up knowing what beauty itself is. It is here, my dear Socrates," said the stranger from Mantinea, "if anywhere, that life is worth living for a human being, contemplating beauty itself. If you ever see that, it will not seem to you to be the same value as gold or clothes or the beautiful boys or young fellows who now when you see them drive you crazy and you and many others are ready, so long as you can see your beloveds and be together with them always, if it were ever possible, neither to eat nor drink, but just look at them and be together with them. What indeed," she said, [e] "do we think it would be if someone were to see beauty itself, unalloyed, pure, un-mixed, and not full up with human flesh and colours and a lot of the rest of mortal hot air, but were able to come within sight of the divine beauty itself of single form? Do you think," she said, [212] "it is an inferior life if a human being looks there and contemplates that by means of the power he should employ and is to-gether with it? Or do you not understand," she said, "that here alone for him, as he sees the beautiful with that by which it is visible, will there be the possibility of giving birth not to images of excellence, since he is not touching upon an image, but true excellence, because he is touching upon the true; and that when he has given birth to and reared true excellence, it belongs to him to be god-beloved and, if to any human being, to be immortal belongs to him.

2. Plato, Phaedrus: *Selections from 246 a 6–248 c 2*

We shall liken the soul to the natural power of a pair of winged horses and a charioteer. Now the horses and charioteers of the gods are all of them good and of good stock, [246 b] but those of other kinds are mixed; and, first, the one who rules us drives a pair of horses and, second, one of the horses is fine and good and from similar stock, while the other is the opposite in stock and nature. So in our case chariot-driving is necessarily difficult and troublesome. We must try then to say in what way a living creature is called mortal or immortal. All soul cares for everything that is without soul, and she traverses the whole heaven, at different times coming to be in different forms; when, she is perfect then, [c] and furnished with wings she soars on high and governs the whole world; but the soul which has lost her wings is borne along until she takes hold of something solid where she settles down, taking on an earthly body which seems to move itself because of the power of soul, and the whole, soul and body fused, is called a living creature and holds the name mortal; and not even is it immortal by any reasoned account, but we fashion an immortal living creature, though we have never seen or sufficiently conceived [d] a god, a creature which has a soul and has a body, for all time united by nature. But let this be as is pleasing to the god and let us speak about it in that way; let us take up the cause of the soul losing her wings. It is something like this.

The natural power of a wing is to soar on high and lead up what is heavy to where the race of the gods dwells. It, above all of things related to body, shares in the divine. But the divine [e] is beautiful, wise, good and everything of this kind; by these divine things, in fact, the wings of the soul are certainly nourished and grow, and by the opposites, ugliness and evil, they are diminished and destroyed. Now the great leader in heaven, Zeus, driving a winged chariot, goes forth first setting everything in order and caring for all things. And armies of gods and spirits follow him. [247] . . . There are many blessed sights and passageways within heaven, along which the blessed gods pass to and fro, each of them performing his own task, and the person who always wants to, and is able to, follows in their train, for jealousy has no place in the divine chorus. And so when they go to a feast and a banquet, they proceed steeply up [b] to the highest point of the vault under heaven, where the chariots of the gods, since they are well balanced and obey the reins, proceed easily, but the others with difficulty, for the horse which partakes of the evil nature weighs the chariot down . . . [c]. No earthly poet has ever sung nor ever will sing worthily of the place beyond the heaven, but it is like this. For I must dare to speak the truth, especially when I am speaking about truth. For the colourless, shapeless, and untouchable substance, really existing, visible to the intellect alone which steers the soul, with which all true knowledge is concerned, occupies this [d] place. Since then the intelligence of god, nourished by intellect and science, and the intelligence of every soul which is to receive all that will be fitting for her to receive, delights in seeing being for a time and in contemplating the truth is nourished and prospers until the revolution of the heaven brings her round in a circle to the same point again; and in the revolution she sees justice itself, and she sees self-control, and she sees science, not that to which coming-to-be is attached nor that which is in some degree one thing [e] in something different of the things we now call beings, but the science which is really existing in that which it is; and in the same way she sees and feasts upon all the other really existent beings, and then dipping again into the interior of the heaven, she goes homeward and having arrived there the charioteer puts the horses to the manger, throws ambrosia beside them and gives them nectar to drink [248]. And this is the life of the gods. But of the other souls, the best soul, in following a god and becoming like him, lifts up into the outer place the charioteer's head and is carried around with the god in the revolution, but thrown into confusion by the horses, she sees real beings with difficulty; and another sometimes rises and sometimes dips, and because of the compulsion of the horses she sees some things, but others she does not; and the rest of the souls follow after, all eager for the upper place, but being unable to reach it they are carried around beneath it, trampling upon and falling against each other, each one [b] trying to get in front of the other. So there is confusion and rivalry and deep sweat in which, because of the charioteers' lack of control, many are lamed and many have their wings broken; but all after their great toil go off without achieving the vision of being, and when they have gone off they feed upon the food of opinion. But the cause of their great eagerness to see where the plain of truth is lies in this, that the pasturage appropriate to the best of soul [c] happens to be out of that meadow there, and the nature of the wing by which a soul is lifted up is nourished by this.

3. Plato, Timaeus: Selections from 28 c 3–37 d 7

[28 c 3] The maker and father of this universe is difficult to find and, even if we found him, impossible to tell to everybody. But we must examine this question about him again: to which paradigm did the architect look [29] in making the world, to that which is identical and unchanging or to that which has come into being? If indeed this world is beautiful and the craftsman good, it is clear that he looked to the eternal. [29 d 7] Let us now explain the reason why he who constructed coming-to-be and this universe constructed them. He was good and the good can never have any grudging jealousy about anything; and since he was without jealousy, he willed that everything should come to be as like himself as possible [30 a 2] for the god wanted everything to be good and nothing to be evil as far as possible; so now when he took over all that was visible, since it was not in a restful state but full of disorderly motion, he brought it into order out of disorder, thinking that order would be altogether better than this. And it neither was nor is lawful for the best one to do anything other than the finest . . . [30 b 6]. In this way, therefore, in accordance with the likely account, we must say that this cosmos has come to be a living creature, with soul and intelligence within it, be-

cause of the providence of the god . . . [30 c 2]. In the likeness of what living creature did the constructor of the world construct it? . . . [30 c 5] Let us suppose that the world is most of all like that living creature of which all other living creatures are individually and generically parts. For that living creature possesses and embraces all the intelligible living creatures, just as this world contains us and all other visible creatures. For since the god wanted to make it most like the fairest and most perfect of all intelligible creatures, he made it as one visible living creature containing within itself all living creatures naturally akin to it. . . . [34 a 8] This then was all the reasoning of a god who exists for ever about the god who was one day to exist and so he made it smooth and even and equal all round from the centre, a whole and complete body composed of complete bodies. And placing soul into the middle of it he stretched her throughout the whole of it and, furthermore, covered the body completely from the outside with soul; and as a circle revolving in a circle he established a single heaven on its own able of itself because of its excellence to be together with itself, needing none other, intimate and friend sufficiently for itself. Because of all this he certainly generated it as a blessed god.

Now the god did not make the soul to be younger than the body, although we are now trying to describe her as later than body. For in putting them together he would not have allowed the older to be ruled by the younger. But just as we participate largely in what is accidental and by chance, so too do we speak. But he constructed soul to be earlier and older in birth and excellence since she was to be mistress and ruler of the body and the body to be ruled, and [35 a 1] he made her out of the following elements and in this way.

From the being which is indivisible and remains always the same and the being again which becomes divisible about bodies he blended a third, intermediate form of being from both; and from the nature of the same and of the other, and in the same way he put together an intermediate form of that one of them which is partless and that which is divisible about bodies. And taking the three of them he blended them all into one form fitting the nature of the other, which is hard to mix, forcibly together into union with the same.

[36 d 8] And when the entire construction of the soul had been completed to the satisfaction of the one who constructed it, after this he then formed all the corporeal inside her and drawing them together he fitted them together centre to centre. And the soul, having been interwoven everywhere from the middle to the farthest heaven and covering body all round in a circle from outside, made a divine beginning of unceasing and intelligent life for all time. And while the body of the heaven is visible, the soul herself is invisible, and partakes of reasoning and [37 a 1] harmony, having come into being by the agency of the best of intelligible beings which exist forever as the best of things that have been generated. And because she has been blended of the natures of the same and of the other and of being, these three portions, and has been divided proportionally and bound together, and circles back upon herself, whenever she touches upon anything which has a

dispersed being or anything which has indivisible being, she is moved throughout the whole of herself and says what the thing is the same as and from what it is different, and in what relation, where, how, and when it comes about that each thing exists and is acted upon in accordance both with things that come to be and things that remain forever the same. . . . [37 c 6] And when the father who had generated it saw it moving and living, a created likeness of the eternal gods, he rejoiced and in his delight he took thought to make it even more like its paradigm (cf. 28 a 6–b 2). Since the paradigm, therefore, happened to be an eternal living creature, he tried to make this universe as far as he could of the same kind. But the nature of the living creature happened to be eternal and thus it was certainly not possible to attach completely to what is generated; and so he took thought to make a moving image of eternity, and as he set the heaven in order, so at the same time he made of that eternity which stays in unity an eternal image moving in accordance with number, and this is in fact what we have called time.

4. Aristotle, Metaphysics XII

a) 7, 1072 b 13–30

On such an originative principle, then, the heaven and nature depend. And its way of life is like the best we enjoy but for a little time. For that is always [15] like this, but it is impossible for us, since its activity is also pleasure, and for this reason waking up, perception, thought are most pleasurable, and hopes and memories because of these. And thinking in itself belongs to that which is best in itself, and thinking in the most perfect way belongs to that which is best in the most perfect way. And intellect thinks itself [20] by participation in the intelligible object; for it becomes intelligible by touching and thinking it, so that intellect and intelligible object are the same. For what is receptive of the intelligible object and of substance is intellect and it is active in having them, so that this [i.e., having them] rather than that [i.e., what is receptive] is the divine element which intellect seems to have, and contemplation is what is most pleasurable and best. If god then is always in that state of excellence [25] which we enjoy sometimes, this is a cause of wonder; but if more perfect, then it is a cause of even greater wonder. And god is in a more perfect state. And life too must belong to god, for the activity of intellect is life, and god is activity; and god's activity in itself is a best and eternal life. We certainly say that god is a living creature, eternal, best, so that life and eternity, continuous [30] and everlasting, belong to god, for this is god.

b) 9, 1074 b 15–1075 a 10

The nature of the divine intellect involves certain problems. For it seems to be the most divine thing we observe, but how it would have to be situated to be like this involves some difficulties. For if it thinks nothing, what is there to be revered in this? It is just like one who is sleeping. And if it thinks, and something else is in charge of this, for this which is its [20] substance is not thinking, but a potency, it would not be the best substance; for it is because of thinking that what is to be honoured belongs to it. And further, whether its substance is intellect (as subject of thought) or the act of thinking, what does it think? For either it thinks itself or something else, and if something else, either the same always or something different. Does it then make any difference whether it thinks what is noble or what it chances to think? [25] Or are there some things it would indeed be absurd for it to think about? So it is clear that it thinks what is most divine and honourable, and it does not change; for change is into a worse state, and this would already be a movement. First, therefore, if it is not an act of thinking, but a potency, it would be reasonable to suppose that the continuity of its thinking would be laborious for it; then it is clear [30] that there would be something else more honourable than intellect, namely, the object of its thought. For both thought and the act of thinking will belong even to one who thinks of the worst thing, so that if this consequence is to be avoided (and indeed it must be, for it is better not to see some things than to see them), the act of thinking cannot be the best thing. It therefore thinks itself since it is the most powerful, and its act of thinking is a thinking of thinking. [35] But science, perception, opinion, and discursive thought are always of something else as their object, and of themselves only as a side effect. Further, if thinking and being thought are different, in respect of which does the good belong to it? For to be an act of thinking and to be an object thought are not even the same. Or is it that in some [1075 a 1] cases science is (identical with) the thing, in the productive sciences, in the first case, the substance and the essential being without being are the thing, and in the theoretical sciences, in the second case, the definition and the act of thinking are the thing? Since the object thought and intellect are not different, then, in the case of things that have no matter, they will be the same, and the [5] act of thinking will be one with the object being thought. Further, there does remain a difficulty, whether the object thought is composite; for if so, it would change in thinking the parts of the whole. Or is it that everything which has no matter is indivisible—just as the human intellect or the intellect at any rate of composite things is in a certain time (for it does not have the good in this instant or in that, but the best, which is something other than it, it has in a whole period of time)—and so the act of thinking itself has itself for object of thought for all eternity?

Appendix B

Suggestions for Further Reading

1. On the history of philosophy in relation to Plotinus, see A. H. Armstrong, 1947 (repr. 1983); 1967 (ed.); J. Dillon, 1977; E. K. Emilsson (in D. Furley, ed.), 1999, 356–87 (and 147 ff.); W. Theiler, 1964; 1966; M. L. Gatti, 1996; R. T. Wallis, 1972.

2. On Plotinus and Plato see K.-H. Volkmann-Schluck, 1941; J.-M. Charrue, 1978; T. A. Szlezák, 1979.

3. On Plotinus and Aristotle see M. de Gandillac, 1979, 247–59; T. A. Szlezák, 1979; A. C. Lloyd, 1987, 155–86; 1990; K. Corrigan, 1996a.

4. On Plotinus and the Stoics see A. Graeser, 1972; M. van Straaten, 1975, 164–70.

5. On the Aristotelian commentators generally see R. W. Sharples, 1978, 1176–243; 1987; 1992; P. Moraux, 1984; R. Sorabji, 1990.

6. On Plotinus and the Gnostics see V. Cilento, 1963; 1971; C. Elsas, 1975; D. T. Runia, 1984; R. T. Wallis and J. Bregman, eds., 1992; J. D. Turner and R. Majercik, eds., 2000.

7. On Plotinus and Christianity see A. H. Armstrong, 1947 (repr. 1983); 1967 (ed.); 1972; 1979; 1984a; 1990; H. J. Blumenthal and R.A. Markus (eds.) 1981; K. Corrigan, 1996c; J. Daniélou, 1944 (repr. 1953) (on Gregory of Nyssa); E. R. Dodds, 1965; K. Kremer, 1987; D. J. O'Meara (ed.), 1982; J. M. Rist, 1985.

8. For introductions to Plotinus and Plotinian scholarship see A. H. Armstrong, 1947; 1967; J. M. Rist, 1967; H. J. Blumenthal, 1987, 528–70; K. Corrigan and P. O'Cleirigh, 1987, 528–623; E. K. Emilsson, 1999, 356–87; P. Hadot, 1993; D. J. O'Meara, 1993; L. P. Gerson, 1996; F. M. Schroeder, 1990.

9. On substance and the categories of being: *Enneads* VI, 1–3; II, 6; G. Nebel, 1929; C. Rutten, 1961; K. Wurm, 1973; S. Strange, 1981; C. Evangeliou, 1988; A. C. Lloyd, 1990; K. Corrigan, 1996a.

10. On omnipresence: *Enneads* VI, 4–5; D. J. O'Meara, 1975; 1980; K. Corrigan, 1985a; F. M. Schroeder, 1992.

11. On act, activity, and related terms: see generally *Enneads* II, 5 (25); II, 6 (17); C. Rutten, 1956; A. C. Lloyd, 1987; K. Corrigan, 1996a, 102 ff.

12. On numbers: *Enneads* VI, 6; V, 5, 5; J. Bertier, 1980; A. Charles-Saget, 1982.

13. On problems concerned with the soul, descent and return, unity of souls, etc., *Enneads* IV, 3–5; IV, 8; IV, 1; IV, 2; IV, 6 (memory); IV, 9; see especially H. J. Blumenthal, 1971, 1996; W. Helleman-Elgersma, 1980; D. O'Brien, 1977, 1993; J. M. Rist, 1967; 1964; 1971; 1989.

14. On matter and evil: *Enneads* II, 4; II, 5; III, 6; I, 8; B. A. G. Fuller, 1912; E. B. Costello, 1967; J. M. Rist, 1961; 1971; 1974; E. Schröder, 1916; D. O'Brien, 1971; 1981; 1991; 1993; 1996; H. Benz, 1990; K. Corrigan, 1986a and b; 1992; 1993b; 1996a; J. M. Narbonne, 1993.

15. On the problem of the generation of matter: III, 4, 1; V, 1, 7, 47–8; V, 2, 1, 18–27; IV, 3, 9, 20–6; II, 3, 18, 10–13; III, 9, 3; I, 8, 14; IV, 8, 6, 18–23; III, 5, 6 ff.; II, 5, 5, 17–22; I, 8, 14; see also H.-R. Schwyzer, 1973; D. O'Brien, 1971; 1981; 1991; 1993; K. Corrigan, 1986a; 1996a.

16. On perception, sight, and the sensible object: II, 8; V, 5, 7; IV, 3–5; K. Corrigan, 1981; 1996a; E. K. Emilsson, 1988; 1996; W. Beierwaltes, 1991.

17. On nature and related issues: *Enneads* I–III; on contemplative production see J. N. Deck, 1967; P. Hadot, 1988; M. Santa Cruz de Prunes, 1979.

18. On eternity and time: III, 7; W. Beierwaltes, 1967; A. H. Armstrong, 1971; A. Smith, 1996.

19. On the relation among destiny, providence, and free will: III, 1; III, 2–3; VI, 8; II, 3; see A. H. Armstrong, 1982b; G. Leroux, 1990; J. M. Rist, 1967; B. Salmona, 1967; V. Schubert, 1968; 1996; F. M. Schroeder, 2000.

20. On beauty, art, and light: I, 6; V, 8; I, 3; II, 9, 17; VI, 7, 20–34; III, 5, 1; A. H. Armstrong, 1975; 1984; W. Beierwaltes, 1961; K. Corrigan, 1993a; R. Ferwerda, 1965; E. de Keyser, 1955; M. R. Miles, 1999;; F. M. Schoeder, 1984; 1990; S. Stern-Gillet, 2000.

21. On intellect and intelligible being, the forms, etc.: *Ennead* V *passim;* VI, 4–5; VI, 7; III, 8, 8, etc.; see generally A. H. Armstrong, 1967; W. Beierwaltes, 1967; K. Corrigan, 1987b; E. K. Emilsson, 1996; J. M. Rist, 1967, T. A. Szlezák, 1979; .

22. On the relation of intellect to the One: V, 4, 2; V, 1, 7, 1–26; V, 6, 5, 1–6, 11; III, 8, 8, 26–29, 40; 10, 1–11, 26; V, 5, 7, 31–8; VI, 7, 16–17; 35, 19–36, 27; VI, 8, 16; V, 3, 11, 1–18; J. Bussanich, 1988; 1996; K. Corrigan, 1987a; P. Hadot, 1960; J. Trouillard, 1954; 1955a and b.

23. On the question of forms of individuals: V, 7; IV, 3, 5; IV, 3, 12; V, 9, 12; VI, 5, 8; A. H. Armstrong, 1977, 49–68; H. J. Blumenthal, 1971, 112–33; J. Igal, 1973, 92–8.

24. On self-knowledge and the self: V, 3; V, 6; I, 1; W. Beierwaltes, 1991; K. Corrigan, 2000a; P. Hadot, 1993, 23–34; G. J. P. O'Daly, 1973; S. Rappe, 1996; F. M. Schroeder, 1986b.

25. On the One, presence of and language about, mysticism, spirituality, etc.: III, 8; V, 5; VI, 7; VI, 8; VI, 9; A. H. Armstrong, (ed.) 1986; R. Arnou, 1967; W. Beierwaltes, 1985; J. Bussanich, 1988; 1994; I. Hadot, 1986; P. Hadot, 1986; 1993; R. Mortley, 1975; 1986; G. J. P. O'Daly, 1974; D. J. O'Meara, 1990; J. M. Rist, 1962; 1965; 1967; 1973; F. M. Schroeder, 1985; 1990; 1996.

26. On negative theology, see especially A. H. Armstrong, 1977b; 1982a; 1990, 31–7; 129–45; P. Cox Miller, 1986; J. P. Kenney, 2000; H.-R. Schwyzer, 1960; R. T. Wallis, 1986; 1987; M. A. Williams, 2000.

27. On the status of discursive reason and the problem of propositional versus nonpropositional language see generally A. H. Armstrong and R. Ravindra, 1982; J. Bussanich, 1988; A. C. Lloyd, 1969–70; R. Sorabji, 1983, 152–63; A. Smith, 1981.

28. On cognition and consciousness: very generally IV, 3–6; V, 6; I, 4, 10; V, 3; H. J. Blumenthal, 1971; E. K. Emilsson, 1988; 1996; F. M. Schroeder, 1986; 1987b; 1992.

29. On human nature, happiness, the self, etc.: *Ennead* I *passim;* J. Dillon, 1996; J. Igal, 1979, 315–46; G. J. P. O'Daly, 1973; W. Beierwaltes, 1991.

30. On the body-soul relation (and critique of Stoics and Aristotle): IV, 7; IV, 3–4; VI, 7, 1–13; VI, 8, 14; VI, 1–3; and see H. J. Blumenthal, 1971; 1976; S. R. L. Clark, 1996, K. Corrigan, 1985b (and Aquinas and Medieval thought); 1986c; 1996a; E. K. Emilsson, 1988; 1991; L. P. Gerson, 1996; D. J. O'Meara, 1985; 1993; A. N. Rich, 1963.

31. On Plotinus and later thought (including Neoplatonism), see generally A. H. Armstrong, 1967; H. J. Blumenthal, 1981; 1989; 1993; G. W. Bowerstock, P. Brown, O. Grabar, 1999 (repr. 2000); E. K. Emilsson, 1999; S. Gersh, 1978; 1986; 1992; D. J. O'Meara, 1993; H. D. Saffrey, 1986; R. Sorabji, 1990; R. T. Wallis, 1972 (new ed. 1995); and in relation to Augustine R. J. O'Connell, 1968; 1987; J. J. O'Meara, 1992; G. J. P. O'Daly, 1987.

32. On Plotinus and ethics, see generally I, 1–5 and A. Schniewind, *L'Éthique du Sage chez Plotin. Le Paradigme du* Spoudaios, Paris, 2003.

Bibliography

A. Plotinus: Texts and Translations

Plotini Opera. Ediderunt P. Henry et H.-R. Schwyzer, 3 vols., Paris, Brussels, and Leiden, 1951–73 (*Editio maior*) (H-S¹).

Plotini Opera. Ediderunt P. Henry et H.-R. Schwyzer, 3 vols., Oxford, 1964–82 (*Editio Minor*) (H-S²).

Plotini Opera Omnia. Apparatum criticum disposuit, indices concinnavit G. H. Moser; emendavit, indices explevit, prolegomena, introductiones, annotationes adiecit F. Creuzer, 3 vols., Oxford, 1835, *Ennéades*, iterum ed. F. Creuzer et G. H. Moser, Paris, 1855.

Plotinus. Text with an English translation by A. H. Armstrong, vols. 1–7, Loeb Classical Library, Cambridge, Mass., and London, 1966–1988.

Plotinus. English translation of the *Enneads* by S. MacKenna, 3rd ed., rev. by B. S. Page, London, 1962.

Plotins Schriften. Übersetzt von R. Harder. Neubearbeitung mit griechischem Lesetext und Anmerkungen, Hamburg, 1956. (This includes the first twenty-one treatises in chronological order.)

Plotins Schriften. Übersetzt von R. Harder. Neubearbeitung mit griechischem Lesetext und Anmerkungen von R. Beutler und W. Theiler, Hamburg, 1960–7. (This contains treatises twenty-two through fifty-four. The indices were compiled with the help of G. J. P. O'Daly.)

Ennéades. Texte établi et traduit par É. Bréhier, 7 vols., Paris, 1924–38.

Les Ennéades de Plotin. Traduction française, notes et eclaircissements, M. Bouillet, 3 vols. Paris, 1857–1861, rep. Frankfurt, 1968.

Enneadi. Prima versione integra e commentario critico di Vincenzo Cilento, Bari, 1947–49.

Plotino. Enéadas 1–11. Introducciones, traducciones y notas de Jésus Igal, Madrid, 1982.

For an excellent word index consult J. Sleeman and G. Pollet, *Lexicon Plotinianum,* Leiden, 1980.

B. Plotinus

i. Bibliography

Bibliography up to 1987 is contained in two parts in *ANRW* (1987), 36.1, by H. J. Blumenthal for 1951–71, 528–70, and by K. Corrigan and P. O'Cleirigh for 1971–86, 571–623.

ii. Selected Commentaries and Translations

Atkinson, M. (1983) *Ennead V. 1: On the Three Principal Hypostases,* Oxford.

Beierwaltes, W. (1967) *Plotin über Ewigkeit and Zeit* (III.7), Frankfurt.

———. (1991) *Selbsterkenntnis und Erfahrung der Einheit* (V.3), Frankfurt.

Bertier J., et al., (1980) *Traité sur les nombres* (VI.6), Paris.

Boot, P. (1984) *Plotinus, Over Voorzienigheid* (III. 2–3), Amsterdam.

Cilento, V. (1971) *Paideia antignostica: Riconstruzione d'un unico scritto da Enneadi III.8, V.8, V.5, II.9,* Florence.

Corrigan, K. (1996) *Plotinus' Theory of Matter-Evil: Plato, Aristotle, and Alexander of Aphrodisias* (II, 4; II, 5; III, 6; I, 8), Leiden.

Hadot, P. (1988) *Plotin, Traité 38* (VI.7), Paris.

———. (1990) *Traité 50* (III.5) Paris.

Helleman-Elgersma, W. (1980) *Soul-Sisters* (IV.3), Amsterdam.

Leroux, G. (1990) *Plotin. Traité sur la liberté et la volonté de L'Un* (VI.8), Paris.

Meijer, P. A. (1992) *Plotinus on the Good or the One* (VI.9), Amsterdam.

Narbonne, J. M. (1993) *Plotin. Les deux matières, Ennéade II. 4,* Paris.

Oosthout, H. (1991) *Modes of Knowledge and the Transcendental: An Introduction to Plotinus Ennead V.3,* Amsterdam.

Roloff, D. (1970) *Plotin: Die Grossschrift* (III.8-V.8-V.5-II.9), Berlin.

Wolters, A. M. (1972) *Plotinus on Eros* (III.5), Amsterdam.

C. Ancient Sources: Selected Texts and Translations

Albinus, *Didaskalikos, Platonis Dialogi,* VI. 147–89, ed. C. F. Hermann.

Alcinous: The Handbook of Platonism, J. Dillon, Oxford, 1993.

Alexander of Aphrodisias, *De Anima Liber cum Mantissa,* ed. I. Bruns, Berlin, 1887.

———. *The De Anima of Alexander of Aphrodisias,* A. P. Fotinis, Washington, 1979.

———. *In Aristotelis Metaphysica Commentaria,* ed. M. Hayduck, CAG I, Berlin, 1891.

———. *Scripta Minora Reliqua (Quaestiones, De Fato, De Mixtione),* Berlin, 1892.

———. *Alexander of Aphrodisias, On Fate,* R. W. Sharples, London, 1983.

———. *Alexander of Aphrodisias, Quaestiones* 1.1–2.15, London, 1992.

Aristotle, *Categoriae,* ed. L. Minio-Paluello, Oxford, 1949, rep. with corr. 1956.

———. *De Anima,* ed. and comm. W. D. Ross, Oxford, 1961.

———. *De Caelo,* ed. D. J. Allan, Oxford. 1936; rep. with corr., 1950.

———. *De Generatione Animalium,* ed. H. J. Lulofs, Oxford, 1965.

———. *De Memoria, in Parva Naturalia,* ed. W. D. Ross, Oxford, 1955.

———. *Ethica Eudemia,* ed. F. Susemihl, Leipzig, 1884.

———. *Ethica Nicomachea,* ed. I. Bywater, Oxford, 1894.

————. *L'Éthique à Nicomaque,* 4 vols., R. A. Gauthier and J. A. Jolif, Louvain-Paris, 1970.

————. *The Nicomachean Ethics,* H. H. Joachim, ed. D. A. Rees, Oxford, 1951.

————. *Fragmenta,* ed. V. Rose, Leipzig, 1886.

————. *Historia Animalium,* ed. and tr. A. L. Peck, 3 vols., London, 1965.

————. *Metaphysics,* ed. W. D. Ross, 2 vols., Oxford, 1924; rep. with corr., 1953.

————. *Aristote, La Métaphysique,* 2 vols, J. Tricot, Paris, 1986.

————. *Physics,* ed. and comm. W. D. Ross, Oxford, 1936.

————. *Topics,* ed. J. Brunschwig, Paris, 1967.

————. *Aristotle's De Motu Animalium,* Martha Nussbaum, Princeton, 1978.

————. *The Basic Works of Aristotle,* R. Mckeon, New York, 1966.

————. *The Complete Works of Aristotle,* J. Barnes, 2 vols., Princeton, 1984.

Augustine, *Saint Augustine, Confessions,* trans., intro., and notes by H. Chad–wick, Oxford, 1981. (For a list of Augustine's extensive writings with references and dates, see G. J. P. O'Daly, 1987 [section D below]).

Chaldaean Oracles (Oracles chaldaïques), ed. E. Des Places, Paris, 1971.

The Chaldean Oracles: Text, Translation and Commentary, R. Majercik, Leiden, 1989.

Corpus Hermeticum, ed. A. D. Nock-A. J. Festugière, Paris, 1945–1954.

Damascius, *Dubitationes et Solutiones in Platonis Parmenidem,* ed. C. A. Ruelle, 2 vols., Paris, 1901; rpt. Hildesheim, 1971.

————. *De Principiis,* L. G. Westerink and J. Combès, 3 vols., Paris, 1986–1991.

————. *Des premiers principes: Apories et résolutions: Texte intégral,* M. C. Galpérine, Paris, 1987.

————. *Lectures on the Philebus,* ed. L. G. Westerink, Amsterdam, 1959; rpt. 1983.

Diogenes Laertius, *Vitae Philosophorum,* ed. H. S. Long, 2 vols., Oxford, 1964.

Die Fragmente der Vorsokratiker (=DK), ed. H. Diels and W. Kranz, 6th ed., 3 vols., Berlin, 1951–1952.

Gregory of Nyssa, *Works, Patrologia Graeca* 44-6, ed. Migne.

The Hellenistic Philosophers, ed., tr., and comm. A. A. Long and D. Sedley, 2 vols., Cambridge, 1987.

Iamblichus, *De Communi Mathematica Scientia Liber,* ed. N. Festa, Leipzig, 1891.

————. *In Platonis Dialogos Commentariorum Fragmenta,* ed. J. Dillon, Leiden, 1973.

————. *Theologoumena Arithmeticae,* ed. V. De Falco, Leipzig, 1922.

————. *De Mysteriis,* E. Des Places, Paris, 1966.

————. *On the Mysteries,* ed. S. Ronan, Hastings, 1989.

————. *De Vita Pythagorica Liber,* ed. L. Deubner (corrected by U. Klein), Leipzig, 1957; rpt. 1975.

Iamblichus, *On the Pythagorean Life*, G. Clark, Liverpool, 1989.

———. *Vie de Pythagore*, L. Brisson and A. Ph. Segonds, Paris, 1996.

———. *Iamblichus. De Anima*, J. Finamore and J. Dillon, Leiden-Boston-Cologne, 2002.

The Nag Hammadi Library, ed. J. M. Robinson, San Francisco, 1978.

Niomachus of Gerasa, *Introductio Arithmeticae*, ed. R. Hoche, Leipzig, 1866.

Numenius, *Fragments*, ed. E. Des Places, Paris, 1973.

Plato, *Opera*, 6 vols., ed. J. Burnet, Oxford, 1900–1907.

———. *Plato: Symposium*, ed, K. Dover, Cambridge, 1980.

———. *The Collected Dialogues of Plato,* E. Hamilton and H. Cairns (eds.), New York, 1961.

Porphyry, *Ad Marcellam*, ed. A. Nauck, Leipzig, 1886; ed. E. Des Places, Paris, 1982; German text and translation, W. Potscher, Leiden, 1968; English, A. Zimmern and D. R. Fideler, Grand Rapids, 1986; K. O'Brien Wicker, Atlanta, 1987.

———. *De Philosophia ex oraculis haurienda*, ed. G. Wolff, Berlin, 1856.

———. *Sententiae ad intelligibilia ducentes*, ed. B. Mommert, Leipzig, 1907; ed. E. Lamberz, Leipzig, 1974.

———. *Vita Pythagorae*, ed. A. Nauck, in *Porphyrii Philosophi Platonici Opuscula Selecta*, Leipzig, 1886; E. Des Places, Paris, 1982.

———. *Porphyrii Philosophi Fragmenta*, A. Smith, Stuttgart-Leipzig, 1993.

———. *On Abstinence from Killing Animals*, G. Clark, London, 2000; with French translation, J. Bouffartigue and M. Patillon, Paris, 1979.

———. *On Aristotle: Categories*, S. Strange, London, 1992.

———. *The Homeric Questions*, R. R. Schlunk, New York, 1993.

———. *Isagoge*, E. W. Warren, Toronto, 1975; French by J. Tricot, Paris, 1947; and A. Libera and A. Ph. Segonds, Paris, 1998.

———. *The Cave of the Nymphs*, Seminar Classics 609, Buffalo, 1969; in French, Y. Le Lay, Lagrasse (Verdier), 1989.

———. *Porphyry's Against the Christians: The Literary Remains*, R. J. Hoffmann, Amherst, New York, 1994.

Posidonius, *Fragmenta*, vol. I. ed. L. Edelstein and I. G. Kidd, Cambridge, 1972.

Proclus, *Elements of Theology*, ed. E. R. Dodds, 2nd ed., Oxford, 1963.

———. *In Primum Euclidis elementorum librum Commentarii*, ed. G. Friedlein, Leipzig, 1873.

———. *In Platonis Parmenidem Commentarii*. In Proclus *Opera Inedita*, ed. V. Cousin, Paris, 1864; rpt. 1961.

———. *In Platonis Parmenidem Commentarii Pars Ultima*, ed. R. Klibansky and C. Labowsky, London, 1953.

———. *In Platonis Rempublicam Commentarii*, ed. W. Kroll, 3 vols., Leipzig, 1899–1901.

―――. *In Platonis Timaeum Commentarii*, ed. E. Diehl, 3 vols., Leipzig, 1903–1906.

―――. *In Platonis Theologiam*, ed. H. D. Saffrey and L. G. Westerink, 4 vols., Paris, 1968–1981.

―――. *Théologie Platonicienne,* ed. H. D. Saffrey and L. G. Westerink, 5 vols., Paris, 1968–1987.

―――. *Proclus, Alcibiades I*, W. O'Neil, The Hague, 1965; text, L. G. Westerink, Amsterdam, 1954.

―――. *Commentaire sur le Timée*, A. J. Festugière, 5 vols., Paris, 1966–1968.

―――. *Commentaire sur La République*, A. J. Festugière, 3 vols., Paris, 1970.

―――. *Proclus' Commentary on Plato's Parmenides*, G. R. Morrow and J. Dillon, Princeton, 1989; in French, A. E. Chaignet, 3 vols., Paris, 1900.

―――. *Decem Dubitationes circa Providentiam, De Providentia et Fato, De Malorum Subsistentia*, H. Boese, Berlin, 1960; text and French translation, D. Isaac, 3 vols., Paris, 1977–1982.

―――. *Commentary on Euclid's Elements*, G. Morrow, Princeton, 1970.

Pseudo-Aristotle, *De Mundo*, ed. Foster and Furley, London, 1955.

Pseudo-Dionysius, *Works, Patrologia Graeca* 3, ed. Migne.

―――. *De caelesti hierarchia*, ed. and trans. R. Roques, G. Heil, M. de Gandillac, *Sources chrétiennes*, Paris, 1958.

―――. *Divine Names, Mystical Theology*, trans. J. Jones, Milwaukee, 1980.

Simplicius, *In Phys.* CAG 9–10, ed. H. Diels, Berlin, 1892–1895.

Stobaeus, *Anthologium*, ed. C. Wachsmuth and O. Hense, 5 vols., Berlin, 1884–1923.

Stoicorum Veterum Fragmenta (= SVF), ed. J. von Arnim, 4 vols., Leipzig, 1903–1924.

Syrianus, *In Aristotelis Metaphysica Commentaria*, CAG VI. 1. ed. W. Kroll, Berlin, 1902.

D. Select Modern Sources

Alfino, M. (1988) "Plotinus and the Possibility of Non-Propositional Thought," *Ancient Philosophy* 8, 273–84.

André, J. M. (1987) "Les écoles philosophiques aux deux premiers siècles de l'empire," *ANRW* 36.1, 5–77.

Annas, J. (1985) "Self-Knowledge in Early Plato," in D. J. O'Meara, ed., *Platonic Investigations*, 111–38.

Anton, J. (1964–5) "Plotinus' Refutation of Beauty as Symmetry," *Journal of Aesthetics and Art Criticism* 23, 233–7.

―――. (1967–8) "Plotinus' Conception of the Functions of the Artist," *Journal of Aesthetics and Art Criticism* 26, 91–101.

Armstrong, A. H. (1940) *The Architecture of the Intelligible Universe in the Philosophy of Plotinus,* Cambridge.

Armstrong, A. H. (1947, repr. 1983) *An Introduction to Ancient Philosophy*, London.

———. (1955) "Spiritual or Intelligible Matter in Plotinus and St. Augustine," in *Augustinus Magister* I, Paris, 277–83.

———. (1960) "The Background of the Doctrine that the Intelligibles Are Not Outside the Intellect," in *Les Sources de Plotin* (section C above), Geneva, 391–413.

———. (1962) "The Theory of the Non-Existence of Matter in Plotinus and the Cappadocians," *Studia Patristica* 5, 427–29.

———. (1967) (ed.) *The Cambridge History of Later Greek and Early Medieval Philosophy*, Cambridge.

———. (1971) "Eternity, Life, and Movement in Plotinus' Accounts of Nous," in *Le Néoplatonisme*, Paris, 67–76.

———. (1975) "Beauty and the Discovery of Divinity in the Thought of Plotinus," in *Kephalaion: Studies in Greek Philosophy and Its Continuation Offered to Professor C. J. de Vogel*, J. Mansfeld and L. M. de Rijk, eds., Assen, 155–63.

———. (1977a) "Form, Individual, and Person in Plotinus," *Dionysius* I, 49–68.

———. (1977b) "Negative Theology," *Downside Review* 95, 176–89.

———. (1979) *Plotinian and Christian Studies*, London.

———. (1982a) "Negative Theology, Myth, and Incarnation," in D. J. O'Meara, ed., *Neoplatonism and Christian Thought*, 213–22.

———. (1982b) "Two Views of Freedom: A Christian Objection in Plotinus, *Enneads* VI, 8 (39), 7, 11–15," *Studia Patristica* 18, 397–406.

———. (1984a) "Dualism Platonic, Gnostic, and Christian," in D. T. Runia, ed., *Plotinus Amid Gnostics and Christians*, Amsterdam, 29–52.

———. (1984b) "Tradition, Reason, and Experience in the Thought of Plotinus," *Plotino,* 171–94.

———. (1984c) "The Divine Enhancement of Earthly Beauties: The Hellenic and Platonic Tradition," *Eranos Jahrbuch,* 53, 49–81.

———. (1986) (ed.) *Classical Mediterranean Spirituality*, New York.

———. (1987) "Platonic Mirrors," *Eranos Jahrbuch,* 147–81.

———. (1990) *Hellenic and Christian Studies*, Variorum, Great Yarmouth, Norfolk.

———. (1992) "Dualism: Platonic, Gnostic, and Christian," in R. T. Wallis and J. Bregman, eds., *Neoplatonism and Gnosticism*, 33–54.

———. (and R. Ravindra) (1982) "Dimensions of the Self: Buddhi in the Bhagavadgita and Psyche in Plotinus," in R. B. Harris, ed., *Neoplatonism and Indian Thought,* New York, 63–86.

Arnou, R. (1950) "La contemplation chez Plotin," in *Dictionnaire de spiritualité,* ii, 1729–38.

———. (1967) *Le désir de Dieu dans la philosophie de Plotin,* Rome.

Atkinson, M. (1983) *Ennead V.1: On the Three Principal Hypostases: A Commentary with Translation,* Oxford.

Aubenque, P. (1971) "Plotin et le dépassement de l'ontologie grecque classique," in P. M. Schuhl and P. Hadot, eds., *Le Néoplatonisme,* Paris, 101–9.

———. (1975) "Plotin et Dexippe, exégètes des catégories d'Aristote" in *Aristotelica. Mélanges offerts à Marcel de Corte,* Cahiers de philosophie ancienne, Bruxelles-Liège, 7–40.

Baladi, N. (1970) *La pensée de Plotin,* Paris.

———. (1971) "Origine et signification de l'audauce chez Plotin," in P. M. Schuhl and P. Hadot, eds., *Le Néoplatonisme,* Paris.

Bastid, P. (1969) *Proclus et le crépuscule de la pensée grecque,* Paris.

Baümker, C. (1890) *Das Problem der Materie,* Münster.

Beare, J. I. (1906) *Greek Theories of Elementary Cognition from Alcmaeon to Aristotle,* Oxford.

Beierwaltes, W. (1961). "Die Metaphysik des Lichtes in der Philosophie Plotins," *Zeitschrift für Philosophische Forschung* 15, 334–62.

———. (1965) *Proklos: Grundzüge seiner Metaphysik,* Frankfurt.

———. (1967) *Plotin über Ewigkeit und Zeit,* Frankfurt.

———. (1972a) *Platonismus und Idealismus,* Frankfurt, 83–153.

———. (1972b) "Reflexion und Einung: Zur Mystik Plotins," in W. Beierwaltes, H. von Balthasar, and A. Haas (eds.), *Grundfragen der Mystik,* Einsiedeln, 9–36.

———. (1980a) *Identität und Differenz,* Frankfurt am Main.

———. (1980b) *Marsilio Ficinos Theorie des Schönen im Kontext des Platonismus,* Heidelberg.

———. (1981) *Regio Beatitudinis: Augustine's Concept of Happiness,* Villanova.

———. (1985) *Denken des Einen,* Frankfurt.

———. (1987) "Plotins philosophische Mystik," in M. Schmidt and D. Bauer (eds.), *Grundfragen christlicher Mystik,* Stuttgart, 39–49.

———. (1988) "Plotins Erbe," *Museum Helveticum,* 45, 75–97.

———. (1991) *Selbsterkenntnis und Erfahrung der Einheit: Plotins Enneade V. 3. Text, Übersetzung, Interpretation, Erläuterungen,* Frankfurt am Main.

———. (2002) "The Legacy of Neoplatonism in F. W. J. Schelling's Thought," *International Journal of Philosophical Studies* 10, 393–428.

Benz, H. (1990) *'Materie' und Wahrnehmung in der Philosophie Plotins, Epistemata.* Würzburger Wissenschaftliche Schriften, Bd. 85, Würzburg.

Bertier, J. (et al.) (1980) *Plotin. Traité 'Sur les Nombres' (Ennéads VI, 6 [34]),* Paris.

Blumenthal, H. J. (1968). "Plotinus, *Ennead* IV, 3, 20-1 and Its Sources: Alexander, Aristotle, and Others," *Archiv für Geschichte der Philosophie* 50, 254–61.

———. (1970) "Nous and Soul in Plotinus: Some Problems of Demarcation," *Plotino e il Neoplatonismo,* 203–19.

Blumenthal, H. J. (1971) *Plotinus' Psychology.* The Hague: Nijhoff.

———. (1971) "Soul, World-Soul, and Individual Soul in Plotinus," in P. M. Schuhl and P. Hadot, eds., *Le Néoplatonisme*, Paris, 55–66.

———. (1972) "Aristotle in the Service of Platonism," *IPQ* 12, 340–64.

———. (1976) "Plotinus' Adaptation of Aristotle's Psychology," in *The Significance of Neoplatonism*, ed. R. B. Harris.

———. (1981) "Plotinus in Later Platonism," in H. J. Blumenthal and R. A. Markus, eds., *Neoplatonism and Early Christian Thought*, London, 212–22.

———. (1982) and A. C. Lloyd, eds., *Soul and the Structure of Being in Late Neoplatonism*, Liverpool.

———. (1987) "Plotinus in the Light of Twenty Years' Scholarship, 1951–1971," *ANRW* 36.1, 528–70.

———. (1989) "Plotinus and Proclus on the Criterion of Truth," in P. Huby and G. Neal, eds., *The Criterion of Truth,* Liverpool, 257–80.

———. (1993) *Soul and Intellect: Studies in Plotinus and Later Neoplatonism,* Aldershot.

———. (1993) and Clark, E. G., eds., *The Divine Iamblichus: Philosopher and Man of Gods,* Bristol, 1993.

———. (1996) "On soul and Intellect," in L. P. Gerson, ed., *The Cambridge Companion to Plotinus*, 82–104.

———. (1997) and Finamore, J., *Iamblichus: The Philosopher,* Syllecta Classica 8.

Bonitz, H. (1955) *Index Aristotelicum*, 2nd ed, Graz.

Bos, A. P. (1984) "World-Views in Collision: Plotinus, Gnostics, and Christians," in D. T. Runia, ed., *Plotinus and Gnostics and Christians*, Amsterdam, 11–28.

———. (1989) *Cosmic and Meta-Cosmic Theology in Aristotle's Last Dialogues,* Leiden.

Bouillet, M. N. (1857–1861) *Les Ennéades de Plotin,* Paris.

Bowersock, G. W. (1999, rpr. 2000) and P. Brown, O. Grabar, eds., *Late Antiquity: A Guide to the Postclassical World*, Cambridge, Mass.

Bregman, J. (1982) *Synesius of Cyrene, Philosopher-Bishop*, Berkeley.

———. (1992) and R. T. Wallis, eds., *Neoplatonism and Gnosticism*, Albany, N.Y.

Bréhier, E. (1928) *La Philosophie de Plotin*, Paris.

———. (1958) *The Philosophy of Plotinus*, trans. J. Thomas, Chicago.

Brisson, L. (1982–92), et al., *Porphyre: La Vie de Plotin,* 1–2, Paris.

Brown, P. (1971) *The World of Late Antiquity*, AD 150–750, London/New York.

———. (1978) *The Making of Late Antiquity*, Cambridge, Mass.

———. (1988) *The Body and Society*, New York.

Brun, J. (1988) *Le Néoplatonisme*, Paris.

Bussanich, J. (1988) *The One and its Relation to Intellect in Plotinus*, Philosophia Antiqua 49, Leiden.

————. (1994) "Mystical Elements in the Thought of Plotinus,"*ANRW* 36.7, 5300–5500.

————. (1996) "Plotinus' Metaphysics of the One," in L. P. Gerson, ed., *The Cambridge Companion to Plotinus*, 38–65.

Charles-Saget, A. (1982) *L'architecture du divin: Mathématique et philosophie chez Plotin et Proclus*, Paris.

Charrue, J.-M. (1978) *Plotin: Lecteur de Platon*, Paris.

Cherniss, H. (1954) "The Sources of Evil According to Plato," *Proceedings of the American Philosophical Society* 98, 23–30.

Chiaradonna, R. (2002) *Sostanza, movimento, analogia: Plotino critico di Aristotele*, Naples.

Cilento, V. (1963) "La radice metafisica della libertà nell' antignosi plotiniana," *Parola dell Passato*, 18, 94–123.

————. (1967) "Stile e linguaggio nella filosofia di Plotino," *Vichiana* 4, 29–41.

————. (1971) *Plotino. Paideia antignostica.* Firenza.

Clark, E. G.(1993) and Blumenthal, H. J., *The Divine Iamblichus: Philosopher and Man of Gods,* Bristol.

Clark, S. R. L. (1996) "Plotinus: Body and Soul," in L. P. Gerson, ed., *The Cambridge Companion to Plotinus*, 275–91.

Cooper, J. M. (1975) *Reason and Human Good in Aristotle,* Cambridge, Mass.

Corrigan, K. (1981) "The Internal Dimensions of the Sensible Object in the Thought of Plotinus and Aristotle," *Dionysius* 5, 98–126.

————. (1984) "A Philosophical Precursor to the Theory of Essence and Existence in St. Thomas Aquinas," *The Thomist* 48, 2, 219–40.

————. (1985a) "Body's Approach to Soul: An Examination of a Recurrent Theme in the Enneads," *Dionysius* 9, 37–52.

————. (1985b) "The Irreducible Opposition Between the Platonic and Aristotelian Conceptions of Soul and Body in Some Ancient and Medieval Thinkers," *LThPh* 41, 391–402.

————. (1986a) "Is There More than One Generation of Matter in the *Enneads?*" *Phronesis* 31, 167–81.

————. (1986b) "Ivan's Devil in *The Brothers Karamazov* in the Light of a Traditional Platonic View of Evil," *Forum for Modern Language Studies* 22, 1–9.

————. (1986c) "Body and Soul in Ancient Religious Experience," in A. H. Armstong, ed., *Classical Mediterranean Spirituality*, 360–83.

————. and O'Cleirigh, P. (1987a) "The Course of Plotinian Scholarship from 1971 to 1986," *ANRW* 36.1, 571–623.

————. (1987b) "Amelius, Plotinus, and Porphyry on Being, Intellect, and the One," *ANRW* 36.2, 975–93.

————. (1990). "A New Source for the Distinction Between *id quod est* and *esse* in Boethius' *De Hebdomadibus*," *Studia Patristica* 18, 4, 133–8.

Corrigan, K. (1993a). "Light and Metaphor in Plotinus and St. Thomas Aquinas," *The Thomist* 57, 2, 187–99.

———. (1993b) "Plotinus and St. Gregory of Nyssa: Can Matter Really Have a Positive Function?" *Studia Patristica,* vol. 27, Leuven.

———. (1994) "Berkeley and Plotinus on the Non-Existence of Matter," *Hermathena,* 157, 67–86.

———. (1996a) *Plotinus' Theory of Matter-Evil and the Question of Substance: Plato, Aristotle, and Alexander of Aphrodisias,* Leuven.

———. (1996b) "Essence and Existence in the *Enneads,"* in L. P. Gerson, ed., *The Cambridge Companion to Plotinus,* 105–29.

———. (1996c) "'Solitary' Mysticism in Plotinus, Gregory of Nyssa, Proclus, and Pseudo-Dionysius," *Journal of Religion,* 28–42.

———. (2000a) "L'auto-réflexivité et l'expérience humaine dans l'*Ennéade* V, 3 (49) et autres traités: de Plotin à Thomas d'Aquin," *Études sur Plotin,* ed. M. Fattal, Paris, 149–172.

———. (2000b) "Platonism and Gnosticism: The Anonymous Commentary on the Parmenides," in J. D. Turner and R. Majercik, eds., *Gnosticism and Later Platonism,* 141–78.

———. (2003) "Love of God, Love of Self, and Love of Neighbour: Augustine's Critical Dialogue with Platonism," *Augustinian Studies* 34, 1–29.

———. (2003) "La discursivité et le temps futur du langage," in M. Fattal, ed., *Logos et Langage chez Plotin et avant Plotin,* Paris.

Corte, M. de., (1935) *Aristote et Plotin,* Paris.

Costello, E. B. (1967) "Is Plotinus Inconsistent on the Nature Of Evil?" *IPQ* 7, 483–97.

Courcelle, P. (1948) *Les lettres grecques en accident de Macrobe à Cassiodore,* 2nd ed., Paris.

Cox Miller, P. (1986) "In Praise of Nonsense," in A. H. Armstrong, ed., *Classical Mediterranean Spirituality,* 481–505.

Crouzel, H. (1991) *Origène et Plotin: Comparaisons doctrinales,* Paris.

Dalsgaard Larsen, J. (1972) *Jamblique de Chalcis, exégète et philosophie,* Aarhus.

D'Ancona Costa, C. (1996) "Plotinus and Later Platonic Philosophers on the Causality of the First Principle," in L. P. Gerson, ed., *The Cambridge Companion to Plotinus,* 356–85.

Daniélou, J. (1944, repr. 1953), *Platonisme et Théologie Mystique,* Paris.

———. (1974) "Plotin et Grégoire de Nysse sur le mal," in *Plotino e il Neoplatonismo,* 485–94.

Deck, J. N. (1967) *Nature, Contemplation, and the One: A Study in the Philosophy of Plotinus,* Toronto.

De Keyser, E. (1955) *La Signification de l'Art dans les Ennéades de Plotin,* Louvain.

Delbrück, M. (1971) "Aristotle-totle-totle," in J. Monod and E. Borek (eds.) *Of Microbes and Life*, New York.

Des Places, E. (1971) *Oracles chaldaïques*, Paris.

———. (1973) *Fragments (Numenius)*, Paris.

———. (1981) *Études platoniciennes 1929–1979*, Leiden.

Dillon, J. (1969) *"Enneads* III, 5: Plotinus' Exegesis of the *Symposium* Myth," *Agon* 3, 24–44.

———. (1977) *The Middle Platonists*, London.

———. (1980) "The Descent of the Soul in Middle Platonic and Gnostic Theory," in B. Layton, ed., *The Rediscovery of Gnosticism*, Leiden, 357–64.

———. (1987) "Iamblichus of Chalcis (c. 240–325 a.d.)," *ANRW* 36.2, 862–909.

———. (1992) "Plotinus and the Chaldean Oracles," in *Platonism in Late Antiquity,* ed. S. Gersh and C. Kannengiesser, South Bend, Indiana, 131–40.

———. (1992) "Pleroma and Noetic Cosmos: A Comparative Study," in R. T. Wallis and J. Bregman, eds., *Neoplatonism and Gnosticism*, New York, 99–110.

———. (2002) (and J. Finamore) *Iamblichus. De Anima*, Leiden.

Dodds, E. R. (1928) "The *Parmenides* of Plato and the Origin of the Neoplatonic 'One,'" *CQ* 22, 129–42.

———. (1963) *Proclus: The Elements of Theology,* Oxford.

———. (1965) *Pagan and Christian in an Age of Anxiety*, Cambridge.

———. (1973) "Tradition and Personal Achievement in the Philosophy of Plotinus," *Journal of Roman Studies,* 50, 1–7

———. *The Ancient Concept of Progress and Other Essays,* Oxford, 1973.

Donini, P. (1982) *Le scuole, l'anima, l'impero: La filosofia antica da Antioco a Plotino*, Turin.

Dörrie, H. (1955) "Zum Ursprung der neuplatonischen Hypostasenlehre," *Hermes* 82, 331–42.

———. (1976) *Platonica minora,* Munich.

———. (1987–1993) with M. Baltes, *Der Platonismus in der Antike*, 3 vols., Stuttgart.

Dover, K. (1980) *Plato: Symposium*, Cambridge.

Edelstein, L. (1972–1988) and Kidd, I. *Posidonius: The Fragments*, 3 vols., Cambridge.

Elsas, C. (1975) *Neuplatonische und gnostische Weltablehnung in der Schule Plotins,* in *Religionschichtl. Versuche und Vorarbeiten.* Berlin-New York.

Emilsson, E. K. (1988) *Plotinus on Sense-Perception: A Philosophical Study,* Cambridge.

———. (1991) "Plotinus and Soul-Body Dualism," in *Psychology,* ed. S. Everson, Cambridge, 148–65.

———. (1996) "Cognition and Its Object," in L. P. Gerson, ed., *The Cambridge Companion to Plotinus*, 217–49.

Emilsson, E. K. (1999) "Neoplatonism," chapter 11 of the *Routledge History of Philosophy*, vol. 2, *From Aristotle to Augustine*, ed. D. Furley, London, 356–87.

Evangeliou, C. (1988) *Aristotle's Categories and Porphyry*, Leiden.

Everson, S. (1991), ed., *Psychology: Companions to Ancient Thought*, Cambridge and New York.

Fattal, M. (1998) *Logos et image chez Plotin*, Paris-Montréal.

———. (2000) (ed.) *Études sur Plotin*, Paris.

———. (2003) (ed.) *Logos et langage chez Plotin et avant Plotin*, Paris.

Ferwerda, R. (1965) *La Signification des Images et des Métaphores dans la Pensée de Plotin*. Groningen: J. B. Wolters.

———. (1982) "Plotinus on Sounds: An Interpretation of Plotinus' *Enneads* V, 5, 5, 19–27," *Dionysius* 6, 43–57.

———. (1984) "Pity in the Life and Thought of Plotinus," in D. T. Runia, ed., *Plotinus Amid Gnostics and Christians*, Amsterdam, 53–72.

Festugière, A. J. (1944–54) *La Révélation d'Hermes Trismégiste*, vols. 1–4, Paris (rpt.: 1972–1983).

Finamore, J. F. (1985) *Iamblichus and the Theory of the Vehicle of the Soul*, Chico, Calif.

———. (1997) and Blumenthal, H. J., *Iamblichus: The Philosopher*, Syllecta Classica, 8.

———. (2000) "Iamblichus, the Sethians, and *Marsanes*," in J. D. Turner and R. Majercik, eds., *Gnosticism and Later Platonism*, 225–58.

———. (2002) (and Dillon, J.) *Iamblichus. De Anima*, Leiden.

Fleet, D. B. (1995) *Plotinus: Ennead III, 6. Translation and Commentary*, Oxford.

Frede, M. (1987) "Numenius," *ANRW* 36.2, 1034–75.

Früchtel, E. (1970) *Weltentwurf und Logos. Zur Metaphysik Plotins*. Philosophische Abhandlungen 33, Frankfurt/Main.

Fuller, B. A. G. (1912) *The Problem of Evil in Plotinus*, Cambridge.

Gandillac, M. De. (1979) "Plotin et la 'Métaphysique' d'Aristote," in *Actes du VIe Symposium Aristotelicum: Études sur la Métaphysique d'Aristote*, ed. P. Aubenque, Paris, 247–59.

Gatti, M. L. (1996) "Plotinus: The Platonic Tradition and the Foundation of Neoplatonism," in L. P. Gerson, ed., *The Cambridge Companion to Plotinus*, 10–37.

Gersh, W. (1973) *Kinēsis Akinētos: A Study of Spiritual Motion in the Philosophy of Proclus*, Leiden.

———. (1975) *Entretiens Hardt XXI. De Jamblique à Proclus*, Vandoeuvres-Geneva.

———. (1978) *From Iamblichus to Eriugena: An Investigation of the Prehistory and Evolution of the Pseudo-Dionysian Tradition*, Leiden.

————. (1986) *Middle Platonism and Neoplatonism: The Latin Tradition*, South Bend, Ind.

————. and C. Kannengeisser (eds.) (1992) *Platonism in Late Antiquity*, South Bend, Ind.

Gerson, L. P. (1983) (ed.) *Graceful Reason: Essays in Ancient and Medieval Philosophy Presented to Joseph Owens, CSSR*, Toronto.

————. (1990) *God and Greek Philosophy: Studies in the Early History of Natural Theology*, London.

————. (1994) *Plotinus*, Oxford.

————. (1996) *The Cambridge Companion to Plotinus*, Cambridge.

Gill, C. (1990) *The Person and the Human Mind*, Oxford.

————. (1991) "Is There a Concept of Person in Greek Philosophy?" in S. Everson, *Psychology: Companions to Ancient Thought*, Cambridge, 166–93.

————. (1996) *Personality in Greek Epic, Tragedy, and Philosophy*, Oxford.

Graeser, A. (1972) *Plotinus and the Stoics: A Preliminary Study*, Leiden.

Guitton, J. (1959) *Le Temps et l'éternité chez Plotin et Augustin*, 3rd ed., Paris.

Gurtler, G. M. (1988) *Plotinus: The Experience of Unity*, New York.

Haase, W. (1987) and H. Temporini, eds. *Aufstieg and Niedergang der römischen Welt*, 2, 36.1 and 36.2, Berlin.

Hadot, I. (1986) "The Spiritual Guide," in A. H. Armstong, ed., *Classical Mediterranean Spirituality*, 436–59.

Hadot, P. (1960) "Etre, vie, pensée chez Plotin et avant Plotin," *Les Sources de Plotin*, Entretiens Hardt V, Vandoeuvres-Geneva, 107–41.

————. (1968a) "L'Apport du néoplatonisme à la philosophie de la nature en Occident," *Eranos Jahrbuch* 37, 91–132.

————. (1968b) *Porphyre et Victorinus*, 1 and 2, Etudes augustiniennes, Paris.

————. (1973) "L'être et l'étant dans le Néoplatonisme," *Revue de Théologie et Philosophie*, 101–13.

————. (1974) "L'harmonie des philosophies de Plotin et d'Aristote selon Porphyre," in *Plotino e il Neoplatonismo*, Rome.

————. (1981a) "Ouranos, Kronos, and Zeus in Plotinus' Treatise Against the Gnostics," in H. J. Blumenthal and R. A. Markus, eds., *Neoplatonism and Early Christian Thought*, London, 124–37.

————. (1981b) *Exercices spirituels et philosophie antique*, Paris.

————. (1986) "Neoplatonist Spirituality: Plotinus and Porphyry," in A. H. Armstong, ed., *Classical Mediterranean Spirituality*, 230–49.

————. (1988) *Plotin. Traité 38. VI, 7*. Paris.

————. (1993) *Plotinus, or The Simplicity of Vision*, trans. M. Chase, intro. A. I. Davidson (originally *Plotin ou la simplicité du regard*, Paris, 1963), Chicago.

Hager, F.-P. (1962) "Die Materie und das Böse im antiken Platonismus," *Museum Helveticum* 19, 73–103.

Hager, F.-P. (1987) *Gott und das Böse im antiken Platonismus*, Würzburg-Amsterdam.

Happ, H. (1971) *Hylê: Studien zum Aristotelischen Materie-Begriff*, Berlin-New York.

Harris, R. B. (1976) ed., *The Significance of Neoplatonism*, Albany.

———. (1982) ed., *The Structure of Being: A Neoplatonic Approach*, Albany.

———. (1982) ed., *Neoplatonism and Indian Thought*, Albany.

Heinemann, F. (1921) *Plotin*, Leipzig.

Helleman-Elgersma, W. (1980) *Soul-Sisters : A Commentary on Enneads IV, 3 (27) 1–8 of Plotinus*, Amsterdam.

Henry, P. (1934) *Plotin et l'occident*, Louvain.

———. (1956) "The Place of Plotinus in the History of Thought," introduction to S. MacKenna's translation of the *Enneads*, 38–51, London.

———. (1960) "Une Comparaison chez Aristote, Alexandre, et Plotin," in *Les Sources de Plotin*, Geneva, 429–49.

———. (1982) "The Oral Teaching of Plotinus," *Dionysius* 6, 4–12.

Igal, J. (1971) "Commentaria in Plotini 'De Bono sive de Uno' librum," *Helmantica* 22, 273–304.

———. (1971) "La genesis de la inteligencia en un pasaye de las Enéadas de Plotino (V, 1, 7, 4–35)," *Emerita* 39, 129–59.

———. (1972) *La Cronología de la Vida de Plotino de Porfirio*, Deusto.

———. (1973) "Observaciones al texto de Plotino," *Emerita* 41, 75–98.

———. (1979) "Aristoteles y la evolucion de la antropología de Plotino," *Pensiamento* 35, 315–46.

———. (1981) "The Gnostics and 'The Ancient Philosophy' in Plotinus," in H. J. Blumenthal and R. A. Markus, eds., *Neoplatonism and Early Christian Thought*, London, 138–49.

———. (1982) *Porfirio. Vida de Plotino. Plotino. Ennéadas I–II*, Madrid.

Inge, W. R. (1929) *The Philosophy of Plotinus*, 2 vols., London.

Irwin, T. H. (1988) *Aristotle's First Principles*, Oxford.

Jankélévitch, V. (1998) *Plotin "Ennéades I, 3," Sur la dialectique*, Préface par Lucien Jerphagnon, edition établie par Jacqueline Lagrée et Françoise Shwab, Paris.

Jerphagnon, L. (1981) "Platonopolis, ou Plotin entre le siècle et le réve," in *Néoplatonisme: Mélanges offerts à Jean Trouillard*, Cahiers de Fontenay, Fontenay, 215–47.

Joachim, H. H. (1951) *Aristotle: Nicomachean Ethics*, Oxford.

Jonas, H. (1958) *The Gnostic Religion* (repr. 1970), Boston.

———. (1974) "The Soul in Gnosticism and Plotinus," *Le Néoplatonisme*, 45–53 (repr. H. Jonas, *Philosophical Essays*, Englewood Cliffs, NJ).

Katz, J. (1950) "Plotinus and the Gnostics," *JHI* 15, 289–98.

———. (1950) *Plotinus' Search for the Good*, New York.

Kenney, J. P. (1986) "Monotheistic and Polytheistic Elements in Classical Mediterranean Spirituality," in A. H. Armstrong, ed., *Classical Mediterranean Spirituality*, 269–92.

———. (1991) *Mystical Monotheism: A Study in Ancient Platonic Theology*, Providence.

———. (2000) "Ancient Apophatic Theology," in R. Majercik and J. D. Turner, eds., *Gnosticism and Later Platonism*, 259–76.

Krämer, H. J. (1964) *Der Ursprung der Geistmetaphysik*, Amsterdam.

Kremer, K. (1987) *"Bonum est diffusivum sui:* Ein Beitrag zum Verhältnis von Neuplatonismus und Christentum," *ANRW* II, 36. 2: 944–1032.

Kristeva, J. (1983) *Histoires d'amour,* Paris.

Layton, B. (1980) *The Rediscovery of Gnosticism: Proceedings of the International Conference on Gnosticism at Yale, New Haven*, March 28–31, 1978, 2 vols., Leiden.

Lear, J. (1988) *Aristotle: The Desire to Understand,* Cambridge.

Leroux, G. (1990) *Plotin. Traité sur la liberté et la volonté de l'Un (Ennéade VI. 8 [39]),* Paris.

———. (1996) "Human Freedom in the Thought of Plotinus," in L. P. Gerson, ed., *The Cambridge Companion to Plotinus*, 282–314.

Lilla, S. (1992) *Introduzione al media platonismo*, Rome.

Lloyd, A. C. (1955–6) "Neoplatonic Logic and Aristotelian Logic," *Phronesis* 1, 58–72, 146–60.

———. (1969–70) "Non-Discursive Thought: An Enigma of Greek Philosophy," *PAS* 70, 261–74.

———. (1981) *Form and Universal in Aristotle,* Liverpool.

———. (1987). "Plotinus on the Genesis of Thought and Existence," in Julia Annas, ed., *Oxford Studies in Ancient Philosophy*. Oxford, 155–86.

———. (1990) *The Anatomy of Neoplatonism*. Oxford.

Long, A. (1974a) *Hellenistic Philosophy,* London.

———. (1982) "Soul and Body in Stoicism," *Phronesis* 27, 34–57.

Majercik, R. (1989) *The Chaldean Oracles: Text, Translation, and Commentary*, Leiden.

Majercik, R., and Turner, J. D. (2000) *Gnosticism and Later Platonism: Themes, Figures, and Texts,* Atlanta.

Marcel, G. (1971) *Coleridge et Schelling*, Paris.

Markus, R. A. (1981) and H. J. Blumenthal, eds., *Neoplatonism and Early Christian Thought: Essays in Honour of A. H. Armstong*, London.

McGinn, B. (1991) *The Foundations of Mysticism: Origins to the Fifth Century,* New York.

Merlan, P. (1969) *Monopsychism, Mysticism, Metaconsciousness: Problems of the Soul in the Neoaristotelian and Neoplatonic Tradition,* The Hague.

Merlan, P. (1970) "Greek Philosophy from Plato to Plotinus," Part 1 of A. H. Armstrong, ed., *Cambridge History of Later Greek and Early Medieval Philosophy*, Cambridge.

―――. (1975) *From Platonism to Neoplatonism*, 3rd ed., The Hague.

Miles, M. R. (1999) *Plotinus on Body and Beauty*, Oxford.

Moraux, P. (1942) Alexandre d'Aphrodise, exégète de la noetique d'Aristote, Paris.

―――. (1981) "Origine et expressions du beau suivant Plotin," in *Néoplatonisme: Mélanges offerts à Jean Trouillard*, Cahiers de Fontenay, Fontenay, 249–63.

―――. (1984) *Der Aristotelismus bei den Griechen*, 2, Berlin.

Mortley, R. (1975) "Negative Theology and Abstraction in Plotinus," *American Journal of Philology* 96, 363–77.

―――. (1986) *From Word to Silence*, Bonn.

Mosse-Bastide, R. M. (1959) *Bergson et Plotin*, Paris.

Müller, H. F. (1916) "Die Lehre vom Logos bei Plotinos," *AGPh* 23, 38–65.

Narbonne, J.-M. (1993) *Les deux matières (Ennéade II, 4 [12])*. Introduction, texte grec, traduction et commentaire, précédé d'un *Essai sur la problématique plotinienne*. Histoire des Doctrines de l'Antiquité classique, vol. 17, Paris.

Nebel, G. (1929) *Plotins Kategorien des Intelligibilen Welt*, Tübingen.

Neoplatonisme. Mélanges offerts à Jean Trouillard (1981) Cahiers de Fontenay.

Nussbaum, M. C. (1978) *Aristotle's De Motu Animalium: Text with Translation, Commentary, and Interpretive Essays,* Princeton.

―――. (1982) and N. Schofield, *Language and Logos: Studies in Ancient Greek Philosophy*, Cambridge.

―――. (1986) *The Fragility of Goodness*, Cambridge.

Nussbaum, M., and Rorty, A., (eds.) (1992) *Essays on Aristotle's De Anima*, Oxford.

Nuyens, F. (1973) *L'évolution de la psychologie d'Aristotle*, Louvain.

O'Brien, D. (1971) "Plotinus on Evil: A Study of Matter and the Soul in Plotinus' Conception of Human Evil," in P. M. Schuhl and P. Hodot, eds., *Le Néoplatonisme*, Paris, 113–46.

―――. (1977) "Le volontaire et la necessité: Réflexions sur la descente de l'âme dans la philosophie de Plotin," *RPhilos* 167, 401–22.

―――. (1981) "Plotinus and the Gnostics on the Generation of Matter," in H. J. Blumenthal and R. A. Markus, eds., *Neoplatonism and Christian Thought*, 108–23.

―――. (1991) *Plotinus on the Origin of Matter: An Exercise in the Interpretation of the Enneads,* Naples.

―――. (1993) *Théodicée plotinienne, théodicée gnostique*, Leiden.

―――. (1996) "Plotinus on Matter and Evil," in L. P. Gerson, ed., *The Cambridge Companion to Plotinus*, 171–95.

O'Connell, R. J. (1968) *Augustine's Early Theory of Man A. D. 386–391*, Cambridge, Mass.

———. (1987) *The Origin of the Soul in Augustine's Later Works*, New York.

O'Daly, G. J. P. (1973) *Plotinus' Philosophy of the Self.* Shannon.

———. (1974) "The Presence of the One in Plotinus," in *Plotino e il Neoplatonismo*, 159–69.

———. (1987) *Augustine's Philosophy of Mind*, London.

O'Meara, D. J. (1974) "A propos d'un témoignage sur l'expérience mystique de Plotin (Enn. IV. 8 [6], 1. 1–11)," *Mnemosyne,* 27, 238–44.

———. (1975) *Structures Hiérarchiques dans la Pensée de Plotin,* Leiden.

———. (1980a) "Gnosticism and the Making of the World in Plotinus," in B. Layton, ed., *The Rediscovery of Gnosticism*, Leiden, 365–78.

———. (1980b) "The Problem of Omnipresence in Plotinus, *Ennead* VI, 4–5: A Reply," *Dionysius,* 4, 62–74.

———. (1981) (ed.) *Studies in Aristotle,* Studies in Philosophy and the History of Philosophy, vol. 9, ed. D. J. O'Meara, Washington, 1981.

———. (1982) (ed.) *Neoplatonism and Christian Thought*, Albany, N.Y.

———. (1985) (ed.) *Platonic Investigations,* Washington.

———. (1985) "Plotinus on How Soul Acts on Body," in *Platonic Investigations*, Washington, 247–62.

———. (1989) *Pythagoras Revived,* Oxford.

———. (1990) "Le Problème du discours sur l'indicible chez Plotin," *Revue de théologie et de philosophie,* 122, 145–56.

———. (1993) *Plotinus: An Introduction to the Enneads,* Oxford.

———. (1996) "The Hierarchical Ordering of Reality in Plotinus," in L. P. Gerson, ed., *The Cambridge Companion to Plotinus*, 66–81.

O'Meara, J. J. (1992), *Studies in Augustine and Eriugena*, ed. T. Halton, Washington.

Panofsky, E. (1968) *Idea: A Concept in Art Theory,* Eng. trans., New York.

Parente, I. (1984) *Introduzione a Plotino,* Rome.

Pecorino, P. (1981) "Evil as Direction in Plotinus," *PhilResArch* 8, 1450.

Peperzak, A. (1993) *To the Other: An Introduction to the Philosophy of Emmanuel Levinas*, West Lafayette, Indiana.

Pépin, J. (1964) *Théologie cosmique et théologie chrétienne*, Paris.

———. (1971) *Idées grecques sur l'homme et sur Dieu*, Paris.

———. (1982) "Linguistique et théologie dans la tradition platonicienne," *Langages* 65, 91–116.

———. (1986) "Éléments pour une histoire de la relation entre l'intelligence et l'intelligible chez Platon et dans le néoplatonisme," *Revue philosophique,* 146, 39–55.

Plotino e il Neoplatonismo in Oriente e in Occidente (1974) (Atti del Convegno Internazionale), Rome.

Puech, H.-C. (1960) "Plotin et les Gnostiques," in *Les Sources de Plotin*, 161–90.

Rappe, S. (1996) "Self-Knowledge and Subjectivity in the *Enneads*," in L. P. Gerson, ed., *The Cambridge Companion to Plotinus*.

———. (2000) *Reading Neoplatonism: Non-Discursive Thinking in the Texts of Plotinus, Proclus, and Damascius*, Cambridge.

Reale, G. (1983) "I fondamenti della metafisica di Plotino e la struttura della processione," in L. P. Gerson, ed., *Graceful Reason*, Toronto, 153–76.

———. (1989) *Introduzione a Proclo*, Bari.

———. (1997) *Towards a New Interpretation of Plato*, trans. and ed. John R. Caton and Richard Davies, Washington (*Per una nuova interpretazione di Platone*, Milan, 1991).

Rich, A. N. M. (1957) "Reincarnation in Plotinus," *Mnemosyne* 10, 232–8.

———. (1960) "Plotinus and the Theory of Artistic Imitation," *Mnemosyne* 13, 233–9.

———. (1963) "Body and Soul in the Philosophy of Plotinus," *JHP* 1, 2–15.

Richard, M. (1986) *L'Enseignement oral de Plotin*, Paris.

Rist, J. M. (1961) "Plotinus on Matter and Evil," *Phronesis* 6, 154–66.

———. (1962a) "The Indefinite Dyad and Intelligible Matter in Plotinus," *CQ* 12, 99–107.

———. (1962b) "The Neoplatonic One and Plato's *Parmenides*," *TAPA* 100, 63–70.

———. (1962c) "Theos and the One in Some Texts of Plotinus," *Medieval Studies* 24, 169–80.

———. (1963a) "Forms of Individuals in Plotinus," *CQ* 13, 223–31.

———. (1964) *Eros and Psyche: Studies in Plato, Plotinus, and Origen*, Toronto.

———. (1965) "Monism: Plotinus and Some Predecessors," *Harvard Studies in Classical Philology* 69, 339–44.

———. (1966) "On Tracking Alexander of Aphrodisias," *AGPh* 48, 82–90.

———. (1967) *Plotinus: The Road to Reality*, Cambridge.

———. (1969) *Stoic Philosophy*, Cambridge.

———. (1971) "The Problem of 'Otherness' in the *Enneads*," in P. M. Schuhl and P. Hadot, eds., *Le Néoplatonisme*, Paris, 71–87.

———. (1973) "The One of Plotinus and the God of Aristotle," *RMeta* 27, 75–87.

———. (1974) "Plotinus and Augustine: On Evil," in *Plotino e il Neoplatonismo*," 495–508.

———. (1983) "Metaphysics and Psychology in Plotinus' Treatment of the Soul," in L. P. Gerson, ed., *Graceful Reason*, Toronto, 135–52.

———. (1985) *Platonism and Its Christian Heritage*, London.

———. (1989) *The Mind of Aristotle*, Toronto.

———. (1994) *Augustine: Ancient Thought Baptized*, Cambridge.

————. (1996) "Plotinus and Christian Philosophy," in L. P. Gerson, ed., *The Cambridge Companion to Plotinus*, 386–414.

Robinson, J. (ed.) (1977) *The Nag Hammadi Library in English*, New York.

Roloff, D. (1971) *Plotin: Die Großschrift III. 8–V. 8–V.5–II.9.5.* Berlin-New York.

Rosán, L. J. (1949) *The Philosophy of Proclus*, New York.

Rudolph, K. (1984) *Gnosis: The Nature and History of Gnosticism*, Edinburgh, 1984; New York, 1987.

Runia, D. T. (1984) ed., *Plotinus amid Gnostics and Christians*, Amsterdam.

Rutten, C. (1956) "La Doctrine des Deux Actes dans la Philosophie de Plotin," *Revue Philosophique* 146, 100–6.

————. (1961) *Les Catégories de monde sensible dans les Ennéads de Plotin*, Paris.

Ryle, G. (1973) *The Concept of Mind*, 3rd ed., Harmondsworth.

Saffrey, H. D. (1986) "Neoplatonist Spirituality: From Iamblichus to Proclus and Damascus," in A. H. Armstrong, ed., *Classical Mediterranean Spirituality*, 250–68.

Salmona, B. (1967) *La libertà in Plotino*, Milan.

Sambursky, S. (1971) *The Concept of Time in Late Neoplatonism*, Jerusalem.

Santa Cruz de Prunes, M. I. (1981) *La genèse du monde sensible dans la philosophie de Plotin*, Bibliothèques de l'École des Hautes Études, vol. 81, Paris.

Schenke, H.-M. (1980) "The Phenomenon of Gnostic Sethianism," in B. Layton, ed., *The Rediscovery of Gnosticism*, Leiden, 588–616.

Schniewind, A. (2003) *L'Éthique du Sage chez Plotin. Le Paradigme du Spoudaios*, Paris.

Schröder, E. (1916) *Plotins Abhandlung. Pothen Ta Kaka* (Text, Übers, und Interpretation der Enn. I.8), Diss. Rostock, 1916.

Schroeder, F. M. (1980) "Representation and Reflection in Plotinus," *Dionysius* 4, 37–59.

————. (1981) "The Analogy of the Active Intellect to Light in the *De Anima* of Alexander of Aphrodisias," *Hermes*, 109, 215–25.

————. (1984) "Light and the Active Intellect in Alexander and Plotinus," *Hermes* 112, 239–48.

————. (1985) "Saying and Having in Plotinus," *Dionysius* 9, 75–82.

————. (1986a) "Conversion and Consciousness in Plotinus," *Hermes* 114, 186–95.

————. (1986b) "The Self in Ancient Religious Experience," in A. H. Armstrong, ed., *Classical Mediterranean Spirituality*, 337–59.

————. (1987a) "Ammonius Saccas" *ANRW* 36.1, 493–526.

————. (1987b) "Synousia, Synaesthesis, Synesis: Presence and Dependence in the Plotinian Philosophy of Consciousness," *ANRW* 36.1, 677–99.

Schroeder, F. M. (1990) (with R. B. Todd) *Two Greek Aristotelian Commentators on the Intellect*, Toronto.

———. (1992) *Form and Transformation: A Study in the Philosophy of Plotinus,* Montreal.

———. (1996) "Plotinus and Language,"in L. P. Gerson, ed., *The Cambridge Companion to Plotinus*, 336–55.

———. (2000) "Aseity and Connectedness in the Plotinian Philosophy of Providence," in J. D. Turner and R. Majercik, eds., *Gnosticism and Later Platonism*, 303–18.

Schubert, V. (1968). *Pronoia und Logos. Die Rechtfertigung der Weltordung bei Plotin. Epimeleia* II. Munich-Salzburg.

Schuhl, P. M. (1971) and P. Hadot, eds., *Le Néoplatonisme*, Colloques internationaux du Centre National de la Recherche Scientifique (Royaumont 1969), Paris.

Schwyzer, H.-R. (1960) "'Bewusst' und 'unbewusst' bei Plotin," *Les Sources de Plotin*, Geneva, 343–78.

———. (1973) "Zu Plotins Deutung der sogenannten Plationischen Materie," in *Zetesis*, Antwerp-Utrecht, 266–80.

———. (1978) *Plotinos, Paulys Realencyclopädie der classischen Altertumswissenschaft,* ed. G. Wissowa, 21, 1, Stuttgart, 1951, 471–592, 1276, suppl. vol. 15, Munich, 311–28.

———. (1983) *Ammonios Sakkas der Lehrer Plotins*, Opladen, 1983.

Sharples, R. W. (1978) "Alexander of Aphrodisias *De fato*: Some Parallels," *CQ* 28, 243–66.

———. (1983) *Alexander of Aphrodisias on Fate,* London.

———. (1987) "Alexander of Aphrodisias: Scholasticism and Innovation," *ANRW* 36.2, 1176–1243.

———. (1992) *Alexander of Aphrodisias. Quaestiones 1.1-2.15*, London.

Shaw, G. (1995) *Theurgy and the Soul: The Neoplatonism of Iamblichus,* College Park, Pa.

———. (2000) "After Aporia: Theurgy in Later Platonism," in J. D. Turner and R. Majercik, eds., *Gnosticism and Later Platonism*, 57–82.

Sinnige, T. G. (1984) "Gnostic Influences in the Early Works of Plotinus and in Augustine," in D. T. Rujnia, ed., *Plotinus Amid Gnostics and Christians*, Amsterdam, 73–97.

Sleeman, J. H., and Pollet, G. (1980) *Lexicon Plotinianum,* London.

Smith, A. (1974) *Porphyry's Place in the Neoplatonic Tradition,* The Hague.

———. (1978) "Unconsciousness and Quasiconsciousness in Plotinus," *Phronesis* 23, 292–301.

———. (1981) "Potentiality and the Problem of Plurality in the Intelligible World," in H. J. Blumenthal and R. A. Markus, eds., *Neoplatonism and Early Christian Thought: Essays in Honour of A. H. Armstrong*, 99–107.

——. (1987) "Porphyrian Studies Since 1913," *ANRW* 36.2, 717–73.

——. (1993) *Porphyrii Philosophi Fragmenta,* Stuttgart/Leipzig.

——. (1996) "Eternity and Time," in L. P. Gerson, ed., *The Cambridge Companion to Plotinus,* 196–216.

Sorabji, R. (1980) *Necessity, Cause, and Blame: Perspectives on Aristotle's Theory,* Ithaca.

——. (1982) "Myths About Non-Propositional Thought," in M. C. Nussbaum and M. Schofield, eds., *Language and Logos.*

——. (1983) *Time, Creation, and the Continuum: Theories in Antiquity and the Early Middle Ages,* London and Ithaca.

——. (1990) *Aristotle Transformed: The Ancient Commentators and Their Influence,* Ithaca.

Sources de Plotin (1961) *Entretiens sur l'Antiquité Classique,* vol. V, Vandoeuvres-Geneva.

Sprague, R. K. (1984) "Plato and Children's Games," in Gerber, D. E. (ed.), *Greek Poetry and Philosophy: Studies in Honour of Leonard Woodbury,* Chico, Calif., 275–84.

Steel, C. (1978) *The Changing Self, A Study of the Soul in Later Neoplatonism: Iamblichus, Damascius, and Priscianus,* Brussels.

Stern-Gillet, S. (2000) "Le Principe du Beau chez Plotin: Réflexions sur Enneas VI, 7, 32 et 33, *Phronesis,* 38–63.

Straaten, M. van. (1975) "On Plotinus IV, 7 (2), 8," in J. Mansfeld and L. de Rijk (eds.) *Kephalaion: Studies . . . Offered to C. J. de Vogel,* Assen, 164–70.

Strange, S. K. (1981) Plotinus' Treatise *On the Genera of Being: An Historical and Philosophical Study,* Diss. Univ. of Texas at Austin.

——. (1987) "Plotinus, Porphyry, and the Neoplatonic Interpretation of the 'Categories,'" *ANRW* 36, 2, 955–74.

——. (1992) *On Aristotle: Categories,* London.

Sweeney, L. (1983) "Are Plotinus and Albertus Magnus Neoplatonists?" in L. P. Gerson, ed., *Graceful Reason,* Toronto, 177–202.

——. (1992a). *Divine Infinity in Greek and Medieval Thought,* New York.

——. (1992b) "Mani's Twin and Plotinus: Questions on Self," in R. T. Wallis and J. Bregman, eds., *Neoplatonism and Gnosticism,* New York, 381–424.

Szlezák, T. A. (1979) *Platon und Aristoteles in der Nuslehre Plotins,* Basel/Stuttgart.

Thedinga, F. (1919) "Plotin oder Numenius," *Hermes* 54, 249–78.

Theiler, W. (1964) "Einheit und unbegrenzte Zweiheit von Platon bis Plotin," *Isonomia,* ed. G. Mau and E. G. Schmidt, 89–109.

——. (1966) *Forschungen zum Neuplatonismus,* Berlin.

——. (1970) "Das Unbestimmte, Unbegrenzte bei Plotin," *Revue internationale de Philosophie* 92, 290–7.

Trouillard, J. (1953) "L'impeccabilité de l'esprit selon Plotin" *RHR* 143, 19–29.

Trouillard, J. (1954) "Vie et pensée selon Plotin: la vie, la pensée," *Actes du VIIe Congrès des Sociétés de Philosophie de langue française* (Grenoble), Paris.

———. (1955a) *La procession plotinienne,* Paris.

———. (1955b) *La purification plotinienne,* Paris.

———. (1961) "The Logic of Attribution," *IPQ* 1, 125–38.

———. (1982) *La mystagogie de Proclos,* Paris.

Turner, J. D. (1992) "Gnosticism and Platonism: The Platonizing Sethian Texts from Nag Hammadi in Their Relation to Later Platonic Literature," in R. T. Wallis and J. Bregman, eds., *Neoplatonism and Gnosticism,* New York, 425–60.

———. (2000) "The Setting of the Platonizing Sethian Treatises in Middle Platonism," in J. D. Turner and R. Majercik, eds., *Gnosticism and Later Platonism,* Atlanta, 179–224.

———. (2000) (with C. Barry, W.-P. Funk, and P.-H. Poirier) *Zostrien (NH VIII.1),* Bibliothèque Copte de Nag Hammadi, Quebec/Louvain.

———. (2001) *Sethian Gnosticism and the Platonic Tradition,* Bibliothèque Copte de Nag Hammadi 6, Quebec/Louvain/Paris.

Vlastos, G. (1973) *Platonic Studies,* Princeton (2nd ed. 1981).

Volkmann-Schluck, K.-H. (1941) *Plotin als Interpret der Ontologie Platos,* Frankfurt.

Wagner, M. F. (1982a) "Plotinus' World," *Dionysius* 6, 13–42.

———. (1982b) "Vertical Causation in Plotinus," in *The Structure of Being: A Neoplatonic Approach,* ed. R. Baine Harris, Albany.

———. (1996) "Plotinus on the Nature of Physical Reality," in L. P. Gerson, ed. *The Cambridge Companion to Plotinus,* 130–70.

———. (2002) ed., *Neoplatonism and Nature,* Albany, N. Y.

Wallis, R. T. (1972) *Neoplatonism,* London.

———. (1981) "Divine Omniscience in Plotinus, Proclus, and Aquinas," in *Neoplatonism and Early Christian Thought: Essays in Honour of A. H. Armstrong,* eds. H. J. Blumenthal and R. A. Markus, London, 233–35.

———. (1986) "The Spiritual Importance of Not Knowing," in A. H. Armstrong, ed., *Classical Mediterranean Spirituality* , 460–80.

———. (1987) "Scepticism and Neoplatonism," *ANRW* II, 36. 2: 911–54.

Whittaker, J. (1987) "Platonic Philosophy in the Early Centuries of the Empire", *ANRW* 36.1, 81–123.

Whittaker, T. (1928) *The Neoplatonists,* Hildesheim, rpt. 1968.

Williams, M. A. (2000) "Negative Theologies and Demiurgical Myths in Late Antiquity," in J. D. Turner and R. Majercik, eds.,*Gnosticism and Later Platonism,* 277–302.

Witt, R. E. (1931) "The Plotinian Logos and its Stoic Basis," *CQ* 25, 103–111.

Wurm, K. (1973) *Substanz und Qualität: Ein Beitrag zur Interpretation der plotinischen Traktate VI 1, 2 und 3,* Berlin-New York.

Zandee, J. (1961) *The Terminology of Plotinus and of Some Gnostic Writings, Mainly the Fourth Treatise of the Jung Codex,* Istanbul.

Zetesis. Album Amicorum (1973), in honour of E. de Strycker, Antwerp-Utrecht.

Zintzen, C. (1977), ed. *Die Philosophie des Neoplatonismus*, Darmstadt.

Index of Names

Index of Subjects

act/activity/actuality (*energeia*), 16–17, 18, 21, 37–38, 51ff., 56, 57, 80ff., 83–84, 88ff., 93–94, 108–10, 111–12, 113, 118, 121–22, 130ff., 150, 156–57

action, 43–45, 47–48, 51ff., 75–77, 79, 86ff., 89, 90–91, 104–8, 134, 136–37, 140, 155

  compulsory vs. voluntary, 107–8

  external contemplation, 89–90

  and *logos*, 120–22

aesthetics, 203, 248, 219–22

aesthesis. See perception

affections, 51ff., 58, 60 n1, 61ff., 65, 70–71, 74

affirmation (and negation), 27, 164–66, 224

agency, 43, 51ff., 57–59, 72–78, 79–80

allegory (*hyponoia*), 154

Allogenes, 99, 137, 147 and n61, 206n3

animal/living creature, 35, 51–59, 77–78, 82, 84, 104–5, 147, 229–30, 243–46

anthropology. *See* man

apprehension, 8–9, 33, 51ff., 55, 106, 175–77

Arabic thought, 3, 107, 228–39 *passim*

arche (and *telos*), 27, 91, 109, 174, 179–80, 216, 218

archetype, 95, 143, 191–95, 200

Aristotle/Aristotelianism *passim*

  active/passive intellect, 34, 105, 148

  art/nature, 97, 105–6, 125, 142

  biology, 179–80, 206, 219

  causality, 77, 105–6, 121–2, 135, 142–3, 162, 206–7

  cave-image, 204

  commentators, 49

  definition, 115

  entelechy, 38–9, 76, 105

  essence (*ti ên einai*), 19, 63, 115, 135

  eudaimonia (happiness), 107 and n7

  friendship, 140

  genus/specific difference, 115

  holistic soul-body relation, 40–41, 61, 54ff., 72ff., 73ff. (axe analogy)

  intellect, 24, 34, 72, 135, 143, 147, 246–48

  matter/form, 116–18

  moral action, 120, 140

  (primary) substance, 34–36, 63, 116–18, 135, 157–58, 161–62

  privation, 109, 116–18

sciences, 79, 84, 104–8, 143

self-understanding, 104ff.

sophia (wisdom), 81–82, 105, 141

spoudaios (serious person/sage), 120, 140

two-act theory, 121–22, 139

unmoved mover(s), 24, 34–35, 104, 148–49, 162–63

art, 9, 25, 48, 61, 74, 88, 89, 107, 108–9, 110, 125–26, 127, 142, 189ff., 203–27, 232–33

  and intelligible being, 210–13

  mimetic, 125–6

  nondiscursive forms of, 217–29

  Plato and Aristotle on, 125–26, 210

atomism, 40, 154, 158, 208

audacity (*tolma*), 46, 151, 152

awareness

  preintelligible, 124

  simple instantaneous, 93, 175–77

  See also apprehension; consciousness

"beast" (and man), 55, 57, 77, 83, 84, 229

beauty, 9, 13, 25, 30, 36, 42, 81, 95–96, 114, 120, 126, 128, 141, 189–201, 202–27, 232–33, 241–44

  and art, 209–10

  artistic/natural, 189–92

  ascent to, 120 128–29, 202–27

  beautiful (*to kalon*), 205–7

  causality, 81

  eye of the beholder/subjectivism, 208–9

  form of the beautiful, 214, 216–17

  and (the) good, 30, 136, 225–27

  and imagination, 220

  inner, 213–14

  and intellect, 191ff., 202–27

  intelligible, 3, 189–201, 202–27

  and light, 218

  limitations of, 225–27

  and perception, 189–92, 202ff., 211–13

  science/wisdom, 214–19

  and self/ego, 212–13

  shapelessness, 202ff., 225–27

  symmetry, proportion, 207ff.

being(s), 9, 23, 30, 34, 35, 37–38, 88, 95, 99, 122, 143–51, 157–63, 164, 169–74, 221–22, 225–27, 232

  by-product of contemplation, 92

  degrees of, 9–10, 127–29

  expansion of, 225–27